George Thomas

CAMPAIGNS & COMMANDERS

GREGORY J. W. URWIN, SERIES EDITOR

Campaigns and Commanders

GENERAL EDITOR
Gregory J. W. Urwin, *Temple University, Philadelphia, Pennsylvania*

ADVISORY BOARD

George Thomas

Virginian for the Union

Christopher J. Einolf

University of Oklahoma Press : Norman

ALSO BY CHRISTOPHER J. EINOLF

The Mercy Factory: Refugees and the American Asylum System (Chicago, 2001)

This book is published with generous assistance of The Kerr Foundation, Inc.

Library of Congress Cataloging-in-Publication Data

Einolf, Christopher J., 1969–
    George Thomas, Virginian for the Union / by Christopher J. Einolf.
        p. cm.—(Campaigns and commanders ; v. 13)
    Includes bibliographical references and index.
    ISBN 978-0-8061-4121-3 (paper)
    1. Thomas, George Henry, 1816–1870.   2. Thomas, George Henry, 1816–1870—Military leadership.   3. Thomas, George Henry, 1816–1870—Political and social views.   4. Generals—United States—Biography.   5. United States. Army—Biography.   6. Unionists (United States Civil War)—Virginia—Biography.   7. United States—History—Civil War, 1861–1865—Campaigns.   8. Slaveholders—Virginia—Southampton County—Biography.   I. Title.
    E467.1.T4E38 2007
    973.7092—dc22
    [B]

                                                                    2007011375

George Thomas: Virginian for the Union is Volume 13 in the Campaigns and Commanders series.

[A] portion of the people of the States lately in Rebellion do not and have not accepted . . . that the late Civil War was a rebellion, and history will so record it. Those engaged in it are and will be pronounced rebels; rebellion implies treason, and treason is a crime, and a heinous one, too, and deserving of punishment, and that traitors have not been punished is owing to the magnanimity of the conquerors. With too many of the people of the South, the late Civil War is called a Revolution, rebels are called "Confederates," loyalists to the whole country are called d——d Yankees and traitors, and over the whole great crime with its accursed record of slaughtered heroes, patriots murdered because of their true-hearted love of country, widowed wives and orphaned children, and prisoners of war slain amid such horrors as find no parallel in the history of the world, they are trying to throw the gloss of respectability, and are thrusting with contumely and derision from their society the men and women who would not join hands with them in their work of ruining their country. Everywhere in the states lately in rebellion, treason is respectable and loyalty odious. This the people of the United States who ended the Rebellion and saved the country will not permit, and all attempts to maintain this unnatural order of things will be met by decided disapproval.

George Thomas, February 9, 1867

Contents

List of Illustrations   ix

Acknowledgments   xi

Introduction   3

Chapter 1   Childhood and Early Years   11

Chapter 2   West Point and Florida   24

Chapter 3   Mexico   39

Chapter 4   West Point, Fort Yuma, and Texas   58

Chapter 5   Decision   80

Chapter 6   Mill Springs   103

Chapter 7   Shiloh and Perryville   124

Chapter 8   Stones River   140

Chapter 9   From Stones River to Chickamauga Creek   154

Chapter 10   The Rock of Chickamauga   169

Chapter 11   Chattanooga   197

Chapter 12   The Army of the Cumberland   222

Chapter 13   The Atlanta Campaign   239

Chapter 14   Nashville   256

Chapter 15   Victory and Frustration   281

Chapter 16   Occupation   295

Chapter 17   Reconstruction   310

Chapter 18   Late Career and Death   326

Chapter 19   Thomas in Historical Memory   340

Notes   357

Bibliography   387

Index   405

Illustrations

Figures

Thomaston	189
Thomas daguerreotype, ca. 1853	189
Thomas's ceremonial sword	189
Reconnaissance map of the approaches to Martinsburg, Virginia	190
Thomas wearing a civilian hat	191
Thomas in uniform	191
Thomas's map wagon	192
Thomas and officers in the field	192
Thomas Nast cartoon of George Thomas	193
Thomas Nast cartoon of President Andrew Johnson	193
George Thomas, late 1860s	194
Harper's cartoon	194
Funeral	195
Equestrian monument	195
Grant, Sherman, Sheridan, and Thomas	196

Maps

Mexico	40
Monterrey	45
Battle of Buena Vista	51

Kentucky and Tennessee Campaigns   104
Mill Springs   117
Stones River   141
Chickamauga   170
Chattanooga   198
Atlanta Campaign   240
Peachtree Creek   251
Nashville, Day One   269
Nashville, Day Two   275

Acknowledgments

I owe a large debt to a number of historians, archivists, and others who have assisted me in the work on this book. Among the most helpful have been John Cimprich, who assisted on interpreting Thomas's racial attitudes and Reconstruction career, and Daniel Crofts, who reviewed the chapter on Thomas's childhood and made corrections and suggestions. Edward Ayers and Charles Ryan were kind enough to meet with me and discuss my treatment of Thomas, and Albert Castel wrote me with his perspective on Thomas. Lynda Updike and the other members of the Southampton County Historical Society assisted me with my research. Michael Hightower, Louise Einolf, and Ashley Spell read drafts of the manuscript and made suggestions on style and content. Gregory Urwin and the two anonymous reviewers made many helpful comments, and Charles Rankin provided excellent assistance in putting this book in final form.

I would also like to thank a number of archivists and librarians who assisted me with my work: Jill Abraham, Charles Johnson, Rebecca Livingston, and Michael Musick at the National Archives; Suzanne Christoff, Susan Lintelmann, Alicia Mauldin, Deborah Pogue, and Elaine McConnell at the U.S. Military Academy at West Point; and the staff of the Library of Virginia and the Virginia Historical Society.

Finally, my most heartfelt thanks go to my wife, Ashley Spell, who has spent the last five years listening to me talk about George Henry Thomas, and who has put up with my spending hours of time on this project.

George Thomas

Introduction

Southampton County, Virginia, August 22, 1831: George H. Thomas, fifteen years old, hurried to flee his family's plantation. The Thomas family had just received word that local slaves, under the leadership of a slave preacher named Nat Turner, had risen up against their masters. The insurrection had only begun that morning, but the slaves had already massacred dozens of men, women, and children in their own homes. The slayings were brutal; the angry slaves beat some of their victims to death with clubs, and cut others to pieces with knives and axes. That afternoon, one of George's neighbors rode up to warn the family that the Turner band was approaching their home. The neighbor told the Thomases to hurry to Jerusalem, the county seat, where the local whites were gathering to organize a defense.

George rushed into the family carriage with his mother, brothers, and sisters, and they rode quickly off along the main road to Jerusalem. On the way there, George's mother suddenly ordered all of the children to get out of the carriage. She had learned there were several different groups of slaves involved in the uprising—wouldn't Turner have posted a group of slaves to watch the roads and wait in ambush for whites who were going to Jerusalem? Rather than risk the open road, George and his family left the carriage behind and set off across country, hiking through fields, swamps, and forests. By the time they reached the town, they were hot, dirty, and exhausted.

George and his family spent the next several nights hiding in town while the local militia put down the rebellion. Some of the Thomas slaves arrived in Jerusalem, and informed the Thomas family that Turner's band did come to their plantation. The slaves claimed they refused to join the uprising, but said that some of them were captured by Turner and forced to go with him. The white authorities put the Thomas slaves under armed guard, along with most of the other slaves in Jerusalem.

Nat Turner's Rebellion was crushed soon after it began, and all of the rebels were killed or captured. The white authorities captured Turner, tried and convicted him, and executed him along with twenty-one others. Many other slaves were sold out of the country to owners of sugar plantations in the Caribbean. The authorities credited the Thomas slaves' story that they did not willingly go along with Turner and allowed all of them to return to the Thomas plantation without punishment.

While Turner's insurrection was put down quickly, the slave owners of Southampton never felt safe again. The local plantation owners, the Thomases included, had considered themselves to be kind masters, and they thought their slaves were happy and well treated. They never considered it likely that the slaves would rebel. After Turner's rebellion, however, all of these assumptions were placed in doubt. Many of the slaves who joined Turner's rebellion were beloved house servants, who had been given special privileges not allowed to field hands. If these slaves could rebel, then no slave could be trusted, the whites thought.

In the months after the rebellion, whites in Southampton County and the rest of the South debated how best to keep themselves safe. Perhaps we were foolish ever to trust them, people said. No matter how kindly we treat them, they remain savages, ready to commit murders and atrocities as soon as we relax our control. Some whites considered sending all blacks, free or slave, back to Africa, but this idea was soon abandoned as impracticable. Blacks were in Virginia to stay, and so long as they were there, slavery seemed essential as the only way to keep whites safe.

Nashville, Tennessee, December 17, 1864: George H. Thomas, now forty-eight years old and a major general in the United States Army, rode over the battlefield where he had just won the most decisive victory of his career. Unlike most Virginians, Thomas had stayed loyal to the Union when his state seceded. He did not side with the Union out of any feeling of opposition to slavery, but because he felt that his oath as an army officer, to uphold and defend the Constitution, bound him to fight to preserve the Union. After the issuance of the Emancipation Proclamation, Thomas complied with the War Department's policy of recruiting blacks to serve in the army, but he believed that black racial inferiority made them second-rate soldiers. He assigned black soldiers to labor and garrison duties but avoided using them in battle.

What Thomas saw on December 17, however, challenged a lifetime of assumptions about black inferiority. During the Battle of Nashville, which had been fought over the previous two days, a shortage of white troops forced Thomas to put black regiments in the front lines of battle. Thomas assigned them a secondary role, telling them to launch a diversionary attack on one end of the Confederate line. He did not expect the black regiments to succeed, but hoped that their attack would serve to distract the Confederate commander from the main Union assault, which would take place on the opposite side of his line.

The white officers in command of the black regiments exceeded Thomas's orders and launched a major attack against the Confederate fortifications. They were beaten back with heavy losses on the first day of the battle but attacked again on the second day. The black soldiers fought with incredible bravery, continuing to press forward despite heavy losses. Some regiments lost up to 30 percent of their men in casualties. Their bravery contributed to the Union victory, as their attacks did prevent the Confederate commander from taking troops away from the front to reinforce the other part of his line, where the major Union attack succeeded. Thomas knew that his decisive victory was won in part through the bravery of his black troops.

On December 17, the day after the victory, Thomas rode over the battlefield and listened as his subordinate commanders recounted the events of the previous two days. Thomas saw hundreds of bodies on the ground before the Confederate fortifications, still lying in heaps where they had fallen. The black soldiers had attacked in conjunction with several white regiments, and while the regiments had been segregated in life, the black and white men lay mixed together in death. Thomas was greatly moved by the sight, and for a long time he said nothing. Finally, he spoke. "It is settled," he said. "Black troops will fight." Later, he reflected, "This proves the manhood of the Negro."

The performance of black soldiers at the Battle of Nashville forced Thomas to reconsider the beliefs he had held about African Americans throughout his life. As a soldier, Thomas placed great value on discipline, courage, and honor. The Battle of Nashville had shown blacks to be the equals or superiors of whites in all these respects. Did this not make blacks the equal of white men in other respects—and equally deserving of political and civil rights as well?

After the Civil War ended, Thomas was assigned to command the Union forces posted in Mississippi, Alabama, Kentucky, West Virginia, and Tennessee. During his four years of postwar service in the South, Thomas made extraordinary efforts to protect blacks from white violence and mistreatment. Thomas sent his soldiers to the polls to safeguard blacks' right to vote, and ordered them to accompany agents of the Freedmen's Bureau when they went to protect blacks from unfair labor contracts with white plantation owners, and to pursue the white vigilantes and members of the Ku Klux Klan. Thomas performed these duties with energy and courage, often arguing with his military and civilian superiors in favor of a more aggressive policy against white lawbreakers. His actions during Reconstruction demonstrated that he was motivated not only by his duty to obey orders but also by a true personal commitment to protecting the rights of freedmen.

Thomas is known today primarily for his military achievements, and his military career forms the largest part of this biography. Thomas learned the basics of military tactics and strategy at West Point and continued to develop as an officer throughout the two decades he served in the pre–Civil War army. He first fought against the Seminole Indians in Florida, where he earned a brevet promotion for exemplary service and learned the mundane but essential skills of logistics, supply, and administration. He then trained as an officer of the light or "flying" artillery, the army's most advanced modern weapon.

Thomas served as an artillery officer in the war against Mexico, displaying the coolness under fire and tactical skill that remained a hallmark of his leadership throughout his career. Thomas received two more brevet promotions for his Mexico service, making him one of the most decorated junior officers in the army. He advanced steadily in the scope of his responsibilities in the years after the war, first as the senior commander at army posts in Florida and California, and then as acting second-in-command and acting commander of the Second Cavalry Regiment in Texas.

Thomas's pre–Civil War career taught him that battles were won not only by tactical leadership, but by attention to training, discipline, morale, logistics, and supply. He put his experience to good use in the first year of the Civil War, when he shaped a mob of raw recruits into a well-disciplined, organized fighting force, and made sure his men were well supplied with food, shelter, and weapons. These careful preparations paid off in his first major battle, the Battle of Mill Springs, Kentucky, on January 17, 1862. While he made some tactical errors, his overall leadership was sound, and he maintained his calm and sense throughout the fighting. He gave the Union its first major victory since the First Battle of Bull Run (Manassas), gaining national fame for himself in the process.

Thomas continued to learn and grow as a tactical commander in the years 1862–64, serving as a subordinate to Buell, Rosecrans, Grant, and Sherman. Thomas's peak as a tactical commander came on the second day of the Battle of Chickamauga, where Rosecrans' retreat from the front left Thomas as the senior commander on the field. Outnumbered and nearly outflanked by the advancing Confederate army, Thomas mounted a heroic defense that saved the Army of the Cumberland from destruction.

While Thomas excelled as a tactical leader, he did not obtain the opportunity to exercise strategic leadership through independent command until the very end of the war. His sense of honor and his distaste for what he saw as political interference with army affairs led him to refuse one high command during the Corinth campaign, and another during the Perryville campaign. After these refusals Thomas was passed over repeatedly for higher posts, in favor of Rosecrans and then Sherman.

Thomas was finally granted an independent command in late 1864, when he was given the task of defending Tennessee from Confederate invasion while Sherman made his March to the Sea. Thomas retreated before a superior Confederate force to Nashville, where he prepared carefully before making his counterattack. At the Battle of Nashville on December 16–17, 1864, Thomas achieved a tactical and strategic triumph, nearly destroying the Confederate Army of Tennessee and pursuing the remnants of the army into Georgia. Despite his victory, Thomas's handling of the campaign caused his superiors to conclude that he was too slow and unaggressive to lead an offensive campaign, and they never again entrusted him with a major command. They divided his force into detachments and sent it on other campaigns, and Thomas ended the war as an administrator of conquered territory, not a front-line commander.

While Thomas's military career is the greatest source of his fame, his Unionism and change of views on race and slavery are an equally important aspect of his life story. Thomas was a slave owner, and before the Civil War he was similar to other Southerners in his beliefs about race and slavery. He adhered to Southern moral codes of duty, honor, and obedience to the law, but he was also raised to think for himself and make independent moral judgments. His West Point education and military service reinforced these values of duty, honor, obedience, and loyalty.

Thomas's sense of morality was severely tested by secession. Previously, his sense of duty, honor, and obedience had made his moral choices clear, but now he was forced to choose between competing moral demands. Loyalty to his country and obedience to his oath as a military officer to uphold the Constitution would lead him to side with the Union, but loyalty to his family and native state would lead him to fight for the Confederacy. Unlike most Southerners, Thomas decided his first loyalty was to his country. This decision was a hard one for Thomas, as it permanently estranged him from his Southampton County neighbors and from some members of his family.

As he rose in rank and responsibility throughout the war, Thomas was forced to interact with politicians and implement political decisions, a role that he did not enjoy. Thomas had long viewed politics as a matter of "personal intrigue and faction." He valued his career as an officer because it allowed him to live a life of honesty and integrity, separate from what he saw as the expediency, self-interest, and dishonesty of the world of politics. Thomas thought that the prosecution of the Civil War should be left to military professionals, and thought it improper for the political authorities to tell commanders how to conduct military campaigns.

Thomas's dislike of politics led him to refuse promotion on several occasions, as a senior army command would force him to interact frequently with politicians and respond to their requests. He also refused promotion due to his sense of honor, as he did not want to be perceived as having conspired to replace another officer. Thomas's refusal to accept promotion was detrimental to both his own career and the Union cause. For years, the Army of the Cumberland struggled under commanders like Buell and Rosecrans while Thomas served in a subordinate capacity. Thomas should have instead been in command, where he could have led the army to victory.

Despite his own efforts to refuse promotion, Thomas was made commander of the Army of the Cumberland in 1863, and with this position came the responsibility to implement and interpret federal policy on race, slavery, and the recruitment of African American soldiers. Like most Unionists, in both the North and the South, Thomas viewed the Civil War as a struggle to preserve the Union, not a crusade to abolish slavery. He came to accept the Emancipation Proclamation and the arming of black troops as necessary measures to win the war, but he did not initially support emancipation and political rights for African Americans as independent goals. This all changed with his command of African American troops at the Battle of Nashville. Their courage, discipline, and sacrifice under fire convinced Thomas him to reevaluate his attitude toward African Americans. Stating that the soldiers' performance "proved the manhood of the Negro," Thomas decided that African Americans deserved full citizenship and full political rights, and he never swerved from his conviction on this issue during the tumultuous years to come.

When the Civil War ended, Thomas expected Southerners to accept their defeat and return to obeying the laws of the nation. He was dismayed and confused when this did not occur. Southerners refused to acknowledge federal authority, while attempting to keep blacks in a status little better than slavery. Thomas's own role was unclear, as the President and Congress disagreed on Reconstruction policy and gave Thomas conflicting instructions. Thomas favored using force to protect blacks from white violence, but Johnson ordered him not to do so, and Thomas at first felt that he had to obey the president. As time went on, however, Thomas became more willing to take action on his own, particularly as Congress established its own Reconstruction policy and Thomas's superiors in the War Department began to follow the directions of Congress over the orders of President Johnson.

While Thomas was a typical Southern Unionist in some ways, his strong support for civil rights was unusual. Some Northern whites changed their views on race and slavery as a result of the Civil War, but few Southern white Unionists did. Many felt betrayed by the Emancipation Proclamation and by black suffrage, and they opposed granting any civil rights to blacks. Other Southern white Unionists adopted a pragmatic attitude toward these measures, cooperating with blacks during Reconstruction for reasons of political expediency, but abandoning their African American allies later on, when political conditions changed.

Thomas, by contrast, experienced a true change of heart in regards to African Americans, and he continued to defend them throughout Reconstruction even when doing so brought him political difficulties.

Thomas could understand why many white Southerners remained personally opposed to political rights for blacks, but he could not accept white Southerners' continued violent opposition in defiance of the law. After years of fighting white vigilantes and the Ku Klux Klan, who refused to obey the law and accord African Americans the rights to which they were legally entitled, Thomas gave up in despair, unable to comprehend why Southern whites consistently chose the path of violence and lawlessness over the path of obedience to the government.

In making race, slavery, and Southern Unionism a central theme of this biography, I am trying to correct a long-standing imbalance in Civil War historical writing, which has emphasized purely military history at the expense of the political and social issues that surrounded the fighting. These issues are morally charged and difficult to navigate, and historians must strike a balance between two extremes of perspective and interpretation. We must be careful not to judge historical figures by the moral standards of the present, but we must also not take the position that the moral beliefs of individuals are completely determined by their culture and upbringing. Biography offers the challenge of examining the relationship between individual choice and agency on the one hand, and the broader social structure on the other, in the course of a single person's life.

George H. Thomas's story allows us to see how choice, social context, and contingency interact in the life of an individual. If the Civil War had never occurred, or if Thomas had never commanded African American troops, he probably would have continued to hold throughout his life the racial prejudices he acquired in childhood. If Thomas had had a different set of moral beliefs and predispositions, he may have chosen to ignore the evidence of African American soldiers' discipline and courage, and continued to view them as less than fully human. Many whites, in both the North and the South, did so. But when circumstances gave Thomas the opportunity to rethink his racial views, he took that opportunity, and made the right decision. That he did so demonstrates that people do have the freedom to make moral choices, despite the prejudices they acquire from their culture. That so few Southern whites made the same decision demonstrates how difficult this choice can be.

CHAPTER ONE

Childhood and Early Years

Having done what you conscientiously believe to be right, you may
regret, but should never be annoyed by, a want of approbation on the
part of others.

> —*Advice of George Thomas's older brother, John,*
> *upon George's leaving home to attend West Point*

In most respects, George Thomas's childhood was typical of white
Southerners of his class. He was raised to respect traditional Southern
values like duty, honor, integrity, and loyalty and was taught to hold
conservative, paternalistic attitudes toward African Americans, attitudes
that justified the institution of slavery. In some respects, however, Thomas's
upbringing differed from that of other Southerners, and these differences
help explain in part the moral decisions Thomas made as an adult. His
parents and older siblings placed special importance on moral independence, telling him to make his own moral decisions and to stick by them
regardless of the opinion of others. Thomas had both positive and negative
experiences with African Americans, and growing up in Southampton
County exposed him to a wide range of views on the morality of slavery.
Overall, the political and social environment offered Thomas a number
of contradictory moral lessons, which he had to interpret in his own way.
His childhood experiences did not preordain his future decisions, but the
range of views and experiences gained from his community, and the
emphasis on moral independence taught him by his family, set the stage
for the moral choices he made later in life.

Some biographers have looked to Thomas's childhood for signs of
unusual sympathy for African Americans, or feelings of opposition to
slavery, that might explain his later decisions to fight for the Union and

to support civil rights for blacks. The only piece of evidence that might support this explanation is of dubious authenticity, as it comes from an anecdote recounted seventy years after the events it describes. The story appears in an address and published lecture given by Oliver O. Howard, who served with Thomas as a general during the Civil War, and who worked closely with Thomas during Reconstruction when Howard was head of the Freedmen's Bureau. Howard, a devout Christian with abolitionist sympathies, helped found Howard University in Washington, D.C., and undertook other activities to assist blacks.

Howard wanted to explain Thomas's Unionism in terms of an antipathy toward slavery and so looked for early indications of sympathy toward African Americans in Thomas's childhood. In 1890 Howard wrote to George's sisters, Judith and Frances Thomas, and asked them for any stories they had about his childhood. Their response was a single sentence: "In answer to your inquiry respecting the character of the late General Thomas, I can only inform you that he was as all other boys are who are well born and well reared." After failing to get information from Thomas's sisters, Howard tried to learn something from other sources in Southampton County, but none of the white residents of the county were willing to speak about Thomas, whom they considered a traitor to his native state.

Finally, Howard asked a former Howard University student, who taught at a black school in Southampton, to ask local African Americans about Thomas's early life. The student found an eighty-year-old black man named Artise, who claimed to have been a childhood companion of Thomas, and interviewed him. Artise stated that George was "as playful as a kitten when he was a boy, and seemed to love the Negro quarters more than he did the great house. Many times he would obtain things out of the great house for the Negro boys, his playmates, as he would call them." Thomas took sugar from the house kitchen and traded it with black children for raccoons that they had caught in the woods. When George became old enough to go to school, he tried to teach the slave children what he had learned there, against his parents' orders. As an adult, Thomas brought the slaves new suits of Sunday clothes when he returned home from his service in the war with Mexico, and also taught them "the word of God."[1]

While parts of Artise's story are implausible, some aspects at least of his story are probably true. Census records show that several black people with the last name of "Artis" lived on or near the Thomas plantation before the

Civil War, and some of them no doubt would have remembered Thomas. Some aspects of Artise's story describe fairly typical and well-documented aspects of pre–Civil War plantation life. It was common for white and black children to play together in the antebellum South, and it was common for white children to trade items with their black friends. Masters sometimes gave special presents to slaves, so it is quite possible that Thomas did give his slaves a present of new clothing when he returned home from Mexico. It is even possible that Thomas spoke to the slaves about "the word of God," as planters often encouraged their slaves to practice Christianity.

It is unlikely, however, that Thomas taught his family's slaves how to read, or that he was any more sympathetic to slaves' desire for education and independence than other slave owners. While Thomas did eventually come to support education and freedom for blacks, he did not do so until much later in life, when the events of the Civil War had changed his views on race. Throughout most of his life, Thomas's views on slavery seem to have been similar to those of other white Virginians. He owned slaves throughout his adulthood, and he bought a slave on one occasion. While he stated that he "could never sell a human being," his family once did sell a slave "down the river" to Vicksburg, Mississippi, separating the unfortunate man from his family.[2] The key to Thomas's decision to fight for the Union does not seem to lie in any opposition he had to slavery.

It seems instead that Artise was telling Howard's colleague what he thought the teacher wanted to hear. It is unfortunate that this story is one of only two anecdotes in the historical record about Thomas's earliest years. Although we know that Thomas was fifteen years old and living with his mother during Nat Turner's insurrection, we know nothing about George's personal experience of the events. The story of the Thomas family fleeing Turner's men to safety in Jerusalem comes from a local historian, William Sidney Drewry, who interviewed survivors of the insurrection in the 1890s. Thomas's sisters spoke to Drewry about the family's experiences during the rebellion, but Drewry's book makes no mention of George Thomas.[3]

The only other known story of Thomas's childhood is almost certainly true, as it comes from Thomas himself. It was written down by Thomas Van Horne, who had served closely with Thomas in the Civil War as an army chaplain, and who wrote an early biography of Thomas. Thomas once told Van Horne that, as a teenager, he "visited daily the shop of a saddler, observed closely his use of tools, the shaping of each part of a saddle and their final combination. With knowledge and skill acquired by observation alone, he succeeded in his first effort in making a good saddle. In the same way he learned to make boots and furniture." Thomas retained this intellectual curiosity for the rest of his life, but at West Point he replaced his curiosity about human-made objects with an interest in the scientific study of minerals, animals, and plants.[4]

Thomas was an intensely private man, who rarely talked about his family or childhood, even with his close friends. He ordered his personal papers destroyed after his death, leaving no record of his relationship with his siblings or with his wife. According to a journalist who knew him, Thomas once stated, "All that I did for my government are matters of history, but my private life is my own and I will not have it hawked about in print for the amusement of the curious."[5] Thomas's own reticence about his personal life, combined with the refusal of his family and former neighbors to talk about him to biographers, means that there is little information on record about the events of Thomas's youth. Fortunately, there is ample evidence still available in Southampton County records that makes it possible to construct a reasonably accurate picture of Thomas's family and early life. Unlike many Virginia courthouses, the Southampton County courthouse was never burned by Union troops in the Civil War, so extensive census, property, and court records survive. Many of these records mention the Thomas family.[6]

George Henry Thomas was born at his family's home in Southampton County on July 31, 1816, a middle child in a family of three boys and six girls. Both of George's brothers were older than he—John William by six years, and Benjamin by one year. George's oldest sister, Judith Elvira, was born five years before him, and he had two younger sisters, Ann, born in 1824, and Frances, or "Fannie," born in 1827. We know that Thomas had two other sisters, Elizabeth and Juliette, from their tombstones in the family graveyard. There are no records of their births and deaths on their tombstones or in the Southampton County courthouse, and they are not mentioned in family letters, so it seems that they died in infancy.

Thomas had one other sister, Lucy, whose dates of birth and death are also unknown. She seems to have been close to Thomas in age, and some evidence from letters indicates that George and Lucy were particularly close. Lucy married in 1838, but there is no record of her having any children. A county document from 1856 indicates that she was no longer alive at that time, but there is no record of her exact date of death. Thomas's brother John never married, nor did his sisters Judith, Ann, and Fannie, but his brother Benjamin married and moved to Vicksburg, Mississippi, where he started a family. Benjamin was the only one of George's siblings to have children.[7]

Both of George's parents came from respected families. John Thomas, George's father, traced his roots to Wales, while the family of George's mother, Elizabeth Rochelle Thomas, came from France. The Rochelles were descendants of the Huguenots, Protestant refugees from religious persecution in France who had come to Virginia in the late seventeenth century. The Thomases were a respected middle-class family, and the Rochelles were a wealthy and prominent family of planters, whose members included public officeholders in North Carolina and Virginia. During George's teen years, his uncle John Rochelle held the office of county clerk, the highest executive office in Southampton County. One of John Rochelle's daughters later married a son of John Tyler, who later became the tenth president of the United States.

At the time of George's birth the Thomas family was well-to-do, but not considered part of the wealthiest class of Virginia society. County tax records indicate that their farm was a relatively large one, 438 acres, and that the family owned nine slaves and six draft animals. The family's wealth increased through the years, such that by the time George was thirteen years old the family owned 685 acres and twenty-four slaves, placing them among the wealthiest 10 percent of white families in the county.[8]

Evidence from county records and other documents indicate that George's father, John Thomas, was a respected and active member of his community. He served as a volunteer in the Virginia militia for four months during the War of 1812, but he apparently did not participate in any fighting. He served in several voluntary offices during the period from 1810 to 1829, including overseer of elections and highway commissioner, and also assisted the local court as an appraiser or executor in a number of inheritance proceedings. He once represented a friend in court in a civil case and on another occasion was selected as an arbitrator in a lawsuit between two of his neighbors.[9]

George's father died in a farm accident in April 1829, when he was forty-five years old and George was thirteen. There is no record of how his father's death affected George personally, but we do know that his death caused a financial crisis for the family. George's mother sold some of the family land, and she also turned to her own relatives for help. Her brother, John Rochelle, the Southampton County clerk, soon hired her oldest son, John William Thomas, to be his deputy.[10]

Elizabeth Thomas's efforts to keep the family finances together succeeded. She did not have to sell any more property after the initial sale of land in 1830, and county tax records indicate that the family's possessions in land and slaves were roughly equal in 1855 to what they had been when George was born. As Elizabeth Thomas grew older, her children took a more active role in management of the plantation. George's brother Benjamin moved to Vicksburg in 1845, and John moved to Norfolk to pursue a career in accounting, so throughout most of George's adult life his sister Judith managed the family plantation.[11]

The economic and social life in the Southampton County of George's boyhood centered around agriculture. Life was regulated by the passage of the seasons. Hard work was required throughout the growing season, from March through early August, but then there was a slow season of several weeks before harvest time began in September. Another break was imposed by the cold weather that came in December and lasted until February. Religious tradition prohibited working on the Sabbath, so both blacks and whites got one day of rest each week, during which they could go to church, visit neighbors, and relax with their families. Christmas and New Year's Day brought several days of festivities, and religious revivals were often scheduled during the slow season in August. Each harvest season, farmers invited their neighbors to corn-shucking parties, where the work was followed by a feast, singing, and dancing. Other holidays centered around George Washington's birthday in February, the local militia parade in May, and Independence Day in July.[12]

Another regular break in the work schedule was "court day," the third Monday of each month, when the local court held session in the county seat, Jerusalem (present-day Courtland). Residents came to town to watch the court proceedings, conduct other business, and visit one another. The Thomas plantation was only about eight miles from Jerusalem, so George had ample opportunities to visit the town on court day. As the nephew of the county clerk, George had the opportunity to meet all the prominent citizens of the county.

Southampton farmers and plantation owners typically divided their production between subsistence crops and products for sale to outside markets. The local cash crops included cotton, wheat, and sweet potatoes, but the county was most famous for its apple and peach brandy and its hams. Southampton's "apple jack" was especially famous, called by one enthusiast "the best apple brandy to be found in the world," and Southampton hams were equally prized. One observer compared the hams of Southampton, "where the hog grows to the pink of perfection," to the famous English Westphalia hams, while another once claimed that Southampton ham was "so delicate that an invalid is tempted by it when nothing else is palatable." The Thomas family's plantation was typical of the region. The family account book shows that they raised clover as animal feed and potatoes for their own consumption, while producing cotton, hams, and brandy for cash sale. Their brandy business was the most profitable, followed by hams and other pork products, and they sold only a small amount of cotton.[13]

The Nottoway River, which flows southeast into North Carolina's Albemarle Sound, was the main avenue of transport of produce to market, but farmers also shipped goods by wagon to nearby towns. In the mid-1830s the Portsmouth and Roanoke Railroad was built, connecting Southampton County with Richmond and Norfolk. The railroad, along with an improved wagon road to Petersburg and Richmond, made it easier for farmers to find markets for their products and increased the economic opportunities available to George's family. Later, the railroad also made it possible for George to visit home more often during his furloughs from the military.

Like many Southern counties, Southampton had a very limited public school system, and many families educated their children at home. Wealthy planters sometimes operated small private schools on their plantations and invited the children of other families to attend. George attended one or more of these schools and received an education good enough to get him through the entrance exams for the United States Military Academy at West Point.

Little is known about Thomas's religious background or training. The Episcopal chaplain of the Army of the Cumberland, Thomas Van Horne, stated that Thomas planned to become an official member of the Episcopal Church, but his early and unexpected death prevented him from realizing this intention. It may be that Thomas was brought up as an Episcopalian, or he may have only became affiliated with the church after his marriage, as his wife was an Episcopalian. Van Horne described

Thomas as a man who took his religious beliefs very seriously, but kept them to himself. Thomas's religious tendencies are indicated by the fact that he donated one hundred dollars toward the construction of a church in Southampton; unfortunately, the denomination of the church is not known.[14] One of Thomas's staff officers described Thomas as sincerely but privately devout and stated that Thomas often retired to his tent on Sunday mornings, with orders not to be disturbed, to spend an hour in prayer.[15]

In addition to his formal academic and religious instruction, George Thomas received an education just by growing up in the diverse religious, political, and demographic environment of Southampton County. Southampton had an unusually large population of free blacks, 12 percent of the total county population in 1840. Slaves made up another 45 percent of the population, with whites thus being in the minority, only 43 percent. The majority of free blacks lived in poverty, working as farm laborers or artisans, since discriminatory laws and practices made it difficult for them to advance economically. Despite these barriers, a few free blacks managed to buy land and achieve prosperity as independent farmers, disproving the commonly held belief among whites that blacks were incapable of living independently of white supervision.[16]

Religious diversity, and a diversity of religious ideas about the morality of slavery, was also present in Southampton County to a degree unusual in the South. Most residents belonged to either the Methodist or the Baptist church, but there was also a sizable minority of Quakers. All three churches were concerned with the issue of the morality of slavery, and this issue was a topic of active debate in Southampton County during George's youth. The Quakers had opposed slavery for decades, and their views were respected and tolerated by other Southampton County residents. The Methodist and Baptist churches of Southampton County were generally supportive of slavery, but some Southampton County congregations and religious leaders opposed the institution as immoral. An antislavery offshoot of the Methodist Church, called the Republican Methodist Church or the Christian Church, also had a following in Southampton County.

In 1825, when George Thomas was nine years old, a Baptist minister named Jonathan Lankford shocked his Southampton County congregation by announcing that he could no longer perform the holy sacraments in his church. Slavery was a violation of God's law, Lankford stated, so he could no longer in good conscience administer communion to slave owners. After a few months the church voted to remove Lankford from the pulpit. The church members did not try to justify their decision with a defense of slavery's morality but stated only that the issue of slavery was one better left to each person's individual conscience. By trying to force his opinions on others, Lankford threatened to "split the Church asunder." After his removal from the pulpit, Lankford stayed in Southampton County, where he made a living by farming and remained a respected member of the community.[17]

Thomas left no written record of his opinion on slavery, but the fact that he owned slaves during much of his life indicates that he was not opposed to it. Many whites in Thomas's social class had a paternalistic attitude toward slavery, grounded in a worldview that considered inequality both natural and beneficial. Paternalists compared different social classes to different parts of the body, stating that each class had its own function and role in society. It was impossible for all men to be equal, and attempts to make them so, such as the French Revolution, only resulted in anarchy. For paternalists, the subordinate position occupied by slaves was appropriate given blacks' supposed natural inferiority.

Paternalists believed that the upper classes had a set of responsibilities that came with their wealth and privileges, which included taking the lead in public affairs and governing for the good of all. Likewise, white slave owners had a responsibility to care for and look after their slaves. Some paternalists sincerely believed that slavery was the most beneficial arrangement not only for whites but also for blacks. Others believed that slavery was an evil, but a necessary one, given that no other type of social order would make it safe for whites to live with blacks among them.[18]

For George Thomas, the view that slavery was needed as a way of controlling blacks was supported by his personal experience of Nat Turner's Rebellion.[19] Turner was a literate slave who read the Bible regularly and acted as a preacher, delivering sermons to fellow slaves in the gatherings they held in the woods on Sundays after the white services ended. For years whites had used the Christian religion to teach slaves to accept their bondage, reading to them New Testament passages that encouraged slaves to obey their masters.[20] Turner's own reading of the Bible led him to a different conclusion. He told his fellow slaves the story of the Israelites, enslaved in Egypt, who revolted against their masters and fought their way to freedom. He also read passages from Mosaic law that proscribed death for any who made slaves out of their brethren.[21]

Turner was deeply influenced by these verses, and he decided to rise up against the whites who had enslaved him. He convinced six other slaves to join him, and began his revolt during the night of August 21– 22, 1831. Turner took literally God's injunction in Ezekiel 9:5–6 to "let not your eye spare, neither have ye pity" on his enemies, and to "slay utterly old and young, both maids, and little children, and women." Turner's band moved from plantation to plantation killing all the whites they found and recruiting slaves to their cause. During the night and morning of August 21–22, Turner and his followers met little resistance, as the whites were completely surprised by the attack.

Turner's followers reached the Thomas plantation on the afternoon of August 22. By this time news of the insurrection had spread through the white community, and one man rode on horseback ahead of Turner's band, keeping watch on their movements and warning white families of the rebels' approach. The neighbor warned George's mother that Turner's band was heading toward them, and the Thomas family escaped in time. The plantation's slave overseer remained behind and watched the insurrectionists from a hiding place near the farm. The rebels did not loot or destroy the farm but only took some of the Thomases' slaves with them and continued on. After Turner's band had passed, the overseer came out of hiding and went with the remaining slaves to Jerusalem. The slaves who went with Turner later claimed they did not join Turner willingly but were taken prisoner by the rebels. George's family and the other whites apparently believed them, for none of the Thomas slaves were charged with having joined the rebellion freely, and all of them returned to the Thomas plantation after a brief period of imprisonment.[22]

Elizabeth Thomas and her family reached Jerusalem in safety late on August 22, while the white men of the community organized and counterattacked Turner's men. By the evening of August 23, the white militia had defeated and scattered Turner's followers, all of whom were arrested or killed in the days that followed. Turner remained in hiding until October 30, but he finally was captured and was later tried and executed along with twenty-one of his followers. While the rebellion failed, the South was changed forever. Most of Turner's victims were women and children, and some of them were decapitated and dismembered by Turner's men. The brutal nature of the killings and the eagerness with which slaves had joined the rebellion overturned white Southerners' complacency about their slaves. Many whites said they would never feel safe again.

Most whites blamed the rebellion not on slavery but on the supposedly innate savagery of blacks. In the immediate aftermath of the rebellion, white vigilantes and militia killed more than a hundred innocent blacks, and for a long time afterward whites persecuted and intimidated blacks in Southampton County, causing many free blacks to leave the area. The rebellion also spurred an extensive public debate on the institution of slavery and the safety of a white society based on slavery. The Virginia legislature even debated abolishing slavery and sending slaves out of the state, but nothing ever came of the proposal. White Virginians continued to hold blacks in servitude, clinging to the vague hope that time would bring about a solution to the problem.[23]

Of course, slavery was not the only issue debated by politicians in the 1830s. The decade of George Thomas's adolescence was a politically contentious one, particularly in Southampton County, where the newly created Whig Party and the more established Democratic Party fought for dominance. The Whig Party had formed as a successor to the now-defunct Federalist Party, a conservative party whose support base had been primarily in New England. The Whigs had gained strength in the South after the nullification crisis of 1832–33, in which President Andrew Jackson, a Democrat, had threatened to use force against South Carolina when that state claimed the power to nullify federal tariff laws. Many Southerners, angered at Jackson's heavy-handed tactics, supported the Whig Party in opposition to him. Support for the Whigs was particularly high among conservative, wealthy Southerners, like the Thomases.

In most Virginia counties, either the Whig Party or the Democratic Party achieved a clear majority during the 1830s, and elections were not strongly contested. Southampton was unusual in that the Whigs and Democrats were almost evenly matched. Throughout the 1830s and 1840s, elections in Southampton County were marked by active campaigning and high voter turnout, and Whig and Democratic candidates alternated in winning local, state, and national offices.

While George's brother John supported the Democratic Party, George did not, and his letters to John contain occasional criticisms of the Democrats. There is no record of George supporting the Whigs either, and it seems that even as a young man Thomas disliked politics, a dislike that grew stronger as the years went by. Perhaps the partisan squabbling and contentious electioneering that took place throughout his youth turned Thomas against politics at an early age. In any case, there is no record that Thomas ever belonged to any political party, or even voted.[24]

As George reached the age of adulthood, he began to look about for a career. His older brother was already helping his mother manage the family plantation, and as a younger son George was expected to find a profession. At the age of seventeen, Thomas applied for the position of deputy county clerk, a typical first step in pursuing a legal career. As deputy clerk, Thomas would be able to observe and assist with county court proceedings, law enforcement, and tax collection; he would learn about law through practice, and in his free time he could study for the bar. Although his uncle, John Rochelle, had died in August 1835, and a nonrelative now held the office of Southampton County clerk, Thomas's family connections were still influential, as John Rochelle's successor appointed George Thomas to the position of deputy county clerk on November 18, 1835.[25]

A few months later, Thomas changed career plans, as his family asked the United States congressman for their district, John Y. Mason, to recommend George for an appointment to the United States Military Academy at West Point. It is not clear what led to Thomas's change of plans. With his analytical mind, assiduous work habits, and attention to detail, Thomas probably would have made a good lawyer, and he later became something of an expert on military law. Perhaps the tedious nature of the daily business of the county court had already discouraged Thomas from continuing to study law. By contrast, a military career, with its prospects for travel and adventure, must have seemed very exciting. Thomas may also have seen a West Point education as a stepping-stone to a career in civil engineering. The academy was considered the best engineering school in the country, and it was common for its graduates to leave the army for careers in private industry. With his interest in the physical world and in making things, Thomas may have found the prospect of a career as an engineer appealing.[26]

The Rochelle family connections once again worked for Thomas, and he received an appointment to West Point on March 1. Congressman Mason's appointment letter described Thomas as a youth of "fine size, excellent talents, and a good preparatory education." Thomas visited

Mason in Washington to thank him for the appointment, but Mason's reception was chilly. "No cadet appointed from our district has ever graduated from the Military Academy," Mason warned him, "and if you do not, I never want to see you again."[27]

George left for West Point in May 1836, knowing it would be at least two years before he saw his family again. As he was leaving, his brother John gave him some advice that made a lasting impression on him. "Having done what you conscientiously believe to be right," John told him, "you may regret, but should never be annoyed, by, a want of approbation on the part of others." This statement may indicate the key to Thomas's decision to fight for the Union. His family had taught him to follow his own moral compass and make his own choices, and then to stick to them regardless of the approval or disapproval of others. Ironically, in the most important moral decision of his life, the "want of approbation" was to come from Thomas's own brothers and sisters.[28]

CHAPTER TWO

West Point and Florida

This ill be the only opportunity I shall have of distinguishing myself, and not to be able to avail myself of it is too bad.

Thomas's West Point years were crucial ones for his moral and professional development. The moral culture of West Point stressed honor, duty, integrity, and obedience to the rule of law, values that fit well with the values Thomas had been raised with. At the same time, his interaction with cadets from all over the United States exposed him to a wide range of opinions on democracy, slavery, and the legal relationship between the states and the Union. Thomas received a formal education in engineering and strategy at West Point and learned leadership skills there as a cadet officer. He continued to develop as a leader in his first post after West Point, at Fort Lauderdale in Florida Territory, and earned a brevet promotion for his participation in a successful campaign against the Seminole Indians. After completing his tour of duty in Florida, Thomas transferred into an elite unit, the light or "flying" artillery, where he received training on one of the army's most advanced new weapons. In all, the first decade of Thomas's military career was a successful one and set the stage for further successes in the future.

George Thomas arrived at West Point in June 1836, joining the other new cadets in the summer "encampment," a period of field exercises and training.[1] Since each Congressman had the right to recommend one cadet candidate each year, West Point cadets came from all over the country and from a range of socioeconomic backgrounds. Thomas's first-year roommates, Stewart Van Vliet from New York and William Tecumseh Sherman from Ohio, reflected that diversity. They were assigned to the

24

same room by chance, simply because they arrived at the school on the same day. Despite their diverse backgrounds, Van Vliet later recalled, "a warm friendship commenced in that room, which continued, without a single break, during our lives."[2]

The friendship between Sherman and Thomas was particularly important, as they later served together in the Civil War. The two young men were opposite in temperament—Sherman was energetic, impulsive, and talkative, while Thomas was stolid, calm, and deliberate. Both were good students, and they shared an interest in drawing. They were also leaders, but each exercised leadership qualities in different ways. Thomas was appointed a cadet officer in his second year at the academy, and he continued in cadet officer roles throughout his time at the school. Sherman did well academically but gained many demerits and was never made a cadet officer. Sherman exercised his leadership qualities primarily by leading fellow cadets in rule breaking and pranks.[3]

The entrance examinations came at the end of June, a few weeks after Thomas's arrival. Both the physical and the academic exams were rudimentary, and Thomas passed them easily. After the entrance exam was over, the new cadets returned to participate in the summer encampment. They woke up each morning at 5:30 and began practicing military drill and learning other martial skills, working until 5:00 in the afternoon. Their evening and weekend hours were free, however, so the students had opportunities to enjoy themselves. They read books, went for swims in the Hudson, and enjoyed walks in the surrounding countryside. The academy celebrated the Fourth of July with speeches, an artillery salute, and a formal dinner, and at the end of the summer the school held a grand ball, where some of the cadets got to dance with the local girls.[4]

During their first summer, and continuing into the school year, the new cadets had to endure "devilment," a mild form of hazing. This "devilment" was not as severe as the hazing practiced in some modern military schools, consisting mainly of mild practical jokes and orders from upperclassmen to perform personal services, like cleaning muskets and hauling water. The school commanders punished upperclassmen if caught in the act, but the "devilment" continued anyway. George was a target, like other cadets, but he was tall and strong, and at nineteen he was older than many of the other cadets. Van Vliet remembered one attempt at hazing that did not go according to plan. "One evening a cadet came into our room and commenced to give us orders," Van Vliet recalled. "He had said but a few words when Old Tom, as we always called him, stepped up to him and said, 'Leave this room immediately, or I will throw you through the window.' It is needless to say that the cadet lost no time in getting out of the room. There were no more attempts to haze us."[5]

Thomas's nickname "Old Tom" reflects both that he was older than most of the cadets and that his quiet, reserved demeanor made him seem even older than he actually was. William Rosecrans, who attended West Point at the same time, stated that Thomas was so dignified and serious that the other cadets nicknamed him "General Washington." While Thomas was reserved, he was also friendly, in his own quiet way. Of the relatively small number of demerits he was given for disobeying rules during his four years at West Point, a large proportion were for paying social visits to other cadets during hours when socializing was forbidden.[6]

The academic year began in late August. Students followed a rigid schedule that allocated nine to ten hours each day to class time or studying, three hours to military drills, and two hours for meals. This left only two hours a day for recreation and seven or eight hours for sleep, but the curriculum was so difficult that many students did schoolwork during their free periods and at night, studying by the light of the coal fires in their rooms.

Life at West Point had few comforts. The cadets' uniforms were made of stiff woolen cloth, and cadets had to keep their clothing clean, orderly, and tightly buttoned at all times. The food was bland and monotonous, consisting mainly of meat, bread, and potatoes. Alcohol was strictly forbidden, and tobacco was also contraband, although the possession of tobacco was less severely punished. Cadets often stole food from the kitchen and made their own food, or "hash," in the barracks at night, bribing the cadet on guard duty to silence by giving him a share of the hash. Many students gathered together during these hash parties to share the contraband food and an equally illicit smoke. Sherman gained a reputation as an expert hash maker, and his room was the site of many after-hours parties.[7]

Academics at West Point were highly structured and notoriously difficult. West Point students learned through the "recitation" method, whereby students were given an assignment each day and then tested on their knowledge of it the next day in class. Their progress was evaluated through oral exams, held each January and June. Grades on these exams determined a student's class ranking, and class ranking determined which branch of the army the student would join upon graduation.

The curriculum during Thomas's first two years of study was composed almost entirely of mathematics, with some instruction in French and drawing. The French class emphasized reading, writing, and translation, with little attention paid to listening and speaking, as the goal of the class was to understand military and engineering texts written in French.[8] Thomas did reasonably well in French, but he had some initial difficulty with drawing, placing fiftieth in a class of sixty in the January exam. With hard work, he improved his standing to twenty-second, and by the time the course ended he was sixth in his class.[9]

Thomas placed twenty-sixth overall out of a class of seventy-six students during his first year, and he improved to fifteenth out of fifty-eight in his second year. Thomas's low rank in his first year may reflect the difficulty Southern students often had in competing with cadets from the North, where the education systems were more developed. By his second year, Thomas had apparently caught up, and he stayed near the top of his class throughout his career at the academy. Thomas's math professor, Albert Church, praised his ability and work habits, noting that George "never allowed anything to escape a thorough examination and left nothing behind that he did not fully comprehend."[10] While George gradually improved his class rank, many of his classmates failed or dropped out of school. George's class shrank from seventy-six students in his first year to fifty-eight in the second, and only forty-two managed to graduate.

George was honored in his second year with an appointment to the position of cadet officer, a position that carried the responsibility of leading and supervising his fellow students. Second-year students were given the rank of corporal, third-year students were made sergeants, and seniors served as lieutenants and captains. Only sixteen cadets out of his class of fifty-eight were selected to serve as corporals, so the appointment was a significant honor. According to one younger cadet, George was also respected because he refused to engage in "devilment" and instead offered new cadets his protection and advice.[11]

George wrote home frequently during his first two years at West Point, and his letters are filled with questions and comments about local news and gossip. In the summer between his second and third year, George was given a furlough to visit home, during which he was allowed to leave his gray cadet uniform behind and wear a blue officer's uniform that bore no insignia of rank. George must have been proud to display this sign of his new status and happy to rest and catch up with friends and family after two years of hard work far from home.

When George returned, he found a new superintendent at West Point, Maj. Richard Delafield. Delafield was a strict disciplinarian with a cold, haughty personality and a habit of making sarcastic jokes. He was soon widely disliked by both students and faculty, and he infuriated Thomas by refusing his request for a furlough to visit his brother Benjamin, on the grounds that Thomas lacked adequate funds to pay his expenses during the furlough. Thomas wrote John comparing Delafield with a Southampton County resident, "old Red," who was notorious for his cheapness. "I tried to get a leave to visit Ben while he was in New York," Thomas wrote, "but Old Dick the democrat (our Superintendent) would not consent to let me go. I used to think that old *Red*, poor old fellow, was rather close with money, but Dick rather overreaches him, for I believe he would not only skin a flea for his hide and tallow, but would eat the meat."[12]

Despite these problems with the superintendent, George's third year was probably more enjoyable than the first two, as he had better teachers and a more interesting course of studies. His third year was taken up almost entirely with science classes, and he got to work with a noted scientist, Jacob Bailey, who taught the chemistry and geology courses at West Point but whose research interests lay in biology. Bailey, a pioneer in the study of microscopic organisms, was internationally known for his studies of freshwater algae. Many West Point graduates later sent him specimens from their posts on the frontier, and Bailey's personal collection of plant specimens became one of the largest in the United States.[13] Years later, George collected animal specimens from frontier posts and sent them to the Smithsonian Institution, a practice that can be ascribed to Bailey's influence.

The final year was the most interesting and important for West Point students, as they finally got to study engineering and military strategy. The engineering course was taught by West Point's most respected professor, Dennis Hart Mahan, and the course contained a section on military strategy and tactics. The first semester of Mahan's engineering course focused on civil engineering, with sections on technical drawing and architecture. The second semester focused on military engineering, or the construction of permanent and field fortifications. Knowledge of the construction of permanent fortifications was important only to the small number of students who would be serving the army as professional engineers, but the section of the course on field fortifications was useful to all army officers. This part of the course also taught the best methods for the placement of field artillery and the use of terrain in battle.

West Point cadets who spent four years looking forward to the instruction on military strategy were always disappointed with the brevity of the course, as only six lessons, nine hours in all, were devoted to strategy during their entire four years of study. Mahan taught strategy through an analysis of Napoléon's generalship, borrowing largely from the writings of a Swiss military theorist, Henri Jomini. Jomini advised a strategy of limited warfare that focused on maneuvers against strategic points, rather than attempts to defeat an enemy's army in battle. Historians disagree about the influence of Mahan's teaching on those cadets who later became Civil War generals, but it seems possible that Mahan's teaching contributed to the tendency of some Union generals to avoid large battles in favor of campaigns of occupation and maneuver.[14] Mahan's most useful contribution may have been his insistence that students not follow theories too rigidly, but use their own common sense in deciding what to do. His most successful students, such as Thomas, learned tactics and strategy by applying common sense to experience, and adapting their methods to meet the realities of the battlefield.

While only a short period of classroom time was devoted to the study of strategy and tactics, students did receive extensive field practice in military skills. In their first year, students practiced infantry drills only, and added artillery practice in their second and third years. They also practiced fencing. George's letters home mention little about the tactical training they received, but he did send his family a humorous sketch of a demonstration of cavalry tactics. "We had quite an interesting exhibition here, a few days since, of the method of using the Polish lance," George wrote. "[T]he performance was [by] a Monsieur *Booby*, I think— at least that was as near as anybody could come to pronouncing his name—which I think was very well done, for he was certainly the most frightful object I ever saw."[15]

George had continued to serve as a cadet officer in his junior year, with the rank of sergeant, and was promoted in his senior year to cadet lieutenant. His class ranking improved, and he graduated twelfth in his class of forty-two students. A cadet's rank upon graduation was important, as it determined the branch of the army in which he would be placed. The very best students were granted commissions as engineers, traditionally honored as the elite branch of the army. The next-highest-ranking graduates were assigned to the artillery, also a desirable post. Engineers spent most of their time constructing coastal fortifications, and artillery officers were often stationed in coastal forts to man the heavy artillery there. Cadets assigned to one of these branches could expect to serve in the East, near large cities, where living conditions were comfortable and where the families of most would be close by. Officers in the infantry and cavalry were typically sent to fight Indians and could expect to spend much of their time in isolated posts in the West or in Florida Territory. Thomas's ranking was not high enough to get him into the engineers, who only accepted one or two students each year, but he did get an assignment in the artillery.

Thomas graduated from West Point on July 1, 1840, and went to New York to accept his commission as a second lieutenant. He returned a few months later "to see the old place, the *fellows*, as we call each other, and to strut before the officers." He was pleased to see that every one of the officers offered his hand when they met, and "all seemed glad to see as an officer one whom they never spoke to as a cadet." In addition, he was "very much flattered with the reception the cadets gave me—not a man among them but what seemed happy to see me, and I had a crowd around me from the time I arrived there to the time I came away."[16]

Thomas had a right to be proud. In a school where nearly half of the entering class had failed to graduate, he had graduated near the top. He had earned a degree from the United States' most respected engineering school, and a commission in a distinguished branch of the U.S. Army. He had earned the respect of his classmates and teachers and had made friendships that would last for the rest of his life. He now looked forward to active service in the war against the Seminole Indians in Florida. Service there was difficult and dangerous, but it offered the ambitious young second lieutenant what he most desired—the opportunity to earn a name for himself.

Thomas's first assignment was Company D of the Third Artillery Regiment, which was then stationed at Fort Columbus in New York Harbor. The regiment was scheduled to go south to fight the Seminoles, and it would leave its artillery behind and fight as infantry, since heavy guns were of little use in the Florida swamps. At the time of Thomas's arrival, the regiment was recruiting and training new soldiers, and Thomas assisted in training the new recruits.

Thomas wrote several letters to his family during his service there, a period of relative inactivity. He enjoyed his time in New York, particularly as seventeen other recent West Point graduates were posted in the city, and Thomas went with them to plays and other social events.[17] Some of his fellow officers passed the time by reading the newspaper, as presidential and congressional elections were scheduled for November of that year, but Thomas was not interested. He complained to his older brother that "we can learn nothing from the papers now but election news, which to me is like no news at all, for I care nothing about them any further than that they are beneficial to our country."[18]

Thomas's letters home were filled with speculation about his future. Service in the Florida war was difficult, and many officers had resigned their commissions after serving there. For his part, Thomas looked forward to active service, as it held the promise of rapid promotion. He wrote home that the resignation of other officers left him not "so much displeased, as I shall be a little higher in the army list, and as I shall have to depend on my sword for a living for some time, at least, if not always, I shall not grumble a great deal."[19] With his officer's salary, Thomas was eager to begin sharing the burden of providing for his family's welfare. He wrote John that he planned to save his salary and help pay off some of the family's debts, "as I have been told that in the part of the territory I am going to an officer cannot spend more than ten dollars a month, let him live as extravagantly as he pleases." "Now I am able," Thomas concluded, "you must allow me to assist you in supporting the family."[20]

Thomas had also begun thinking about getting married. Thomas had tried to visit a certain Miss Parker during a trip through Philadelphia but had been unable to find her house. While disappointed, he admitted that "if she has to wait until I feel justified in getting married, that there will not be much romance in the courtship," as he did not yet have enough money to start a family. Nor did he expect to be ready to start a family anytime soon, "unless I win a name and a grant of land in Florida, of which I have no likelihood at present. . . . I leave it for time to show." Thomas's later letters never mention Miss Parker, and it was more than a decade before Thomas finally did marry.[21]

In December 1840 Thomas's regiment was finally sent to Florida. By this date the war against the Seminole Indians had gone on for five years, and nearly five thousand U.S. troops were involved in the fighting. The history of the Seminoles, and of their war with the U.S. government, is a complex one. "Seminole" was the name given by whites to Indians from a number of different tribes who had come from the north, fleeing white expansion, and settled in Florida. The Seminole War had started in 1835, over a dispute about the terms of an 1833 treaty that the Seminoles had made with the United States. In the treaty, the Seminoles had agreed to leave Florida, but the terms of the treaty were ambiguous, and each side interpreted it differently. The Seminoles claimed the treaty gave them ten more years before they had to move, but the United States claimed they had agreed to move within two years. In 1835 the U.S. government tried to enforce its interpretation of the treaty, telling the Seminoles that if they did not go west voluntarily, they would be removed by force.

A few Seminoles accepted removal, but most decided to stay and fight for their land. As the U.S. government sent more and more troops to Florida, the Seminoles adopted guerrilla tactics, hiding in the swamps and attacking vulnerable outposts and farms. The war turned into a war of attrition, which the United States was slowly winning, but at a great cost. By the time Thomas arrived in Florida in 1838, only about one thousand of the original five thousand Seminole Indians still remained. Many of them had surrendered voluntarily, having grown weary of the war and the difficulties of surviving in the wilderness. The government offered liberal terms to those Indians willing to surrender, including amnesty for any past acts of violence, a cash bounty at the time they turned themselves in, and supplies, cattle, and land when they resettled in the West. But the government also had a history of violating promises, so the Indians did not trust the federal authorities. This mistrust made Thomas's job much more difficult, as the Seminoles who remained in Florida refused to negotiate or surrender voluntarily.

Thomas arrived in Florida during a discouraging period of the war. Soldiers searched the swamps in long patrols, trying to locate the Indians and capture them or bring them to battle, but most patrols failed. Soldiers often found crops and signs of habitation, but the Indians themselves would leave before the soldiers ever came near them. While few soldiers were killed in combat, tropical diseases made service in Florida deadly. Of the 1,466 soldiers who died in the war, only 328 died in battle, and most of the rest died from malaria, dysentery, and other illnesses.[22]

Thomas's company was posted at Fort Lauderdale, on the eastern edge of the Everglades, an area where the Seminoles were active. Fort Lauderdale was not yet a city, and was not even much of a fort, as it consisted of only a few rough huts surrounded by a wooden fence and some guard towers.[23] The food was poor, and the living conditions rudimentary, but what bothered Thomas more than anything was the fort's isolation. He wrote home often, but rarely received a reply, as the supply boat that carried the mail came to the fort only once a month.[24]

Despite the isolation, Thomas felt "very much pleased" with his situation, at least at first. He wrote home with long descriptions of the Everglades, "one of the greatest natural curiosities in existence," and speculations on what crops might grow well in the area.[25] By the summer, however, Thomas's mood had soured. He complained to a classmate that his duties "are so many that my whole time is taken up. I have to do the duty of commissary, quartermaster, ordnance officer, and adjutant; and if I have time to eat my meals, I think myself most infernal fortunate." What was worse, he was unable to join in the combat patrols, as he was always "left behind to take care of this infernal place in consequence of being commissary, etc. This will be the only opportunity I shall have of distinguishing myself, and not to be able to avail myself of it is too bad."[26]

In August a new post commander arrived, Captain R. D. A. Wade, and Thomas's situation improved, as Wade allowed him to participate in patrols. On Thomas's second patrol, undertaken in November 1841, he finally had the opportunity to distinguish himself. Wade set out from Fort Lauderdale on November 5 with sixty men and two other officers, Thomas and the company surgeon. The company soon surprised and captured a lone Indian. "By operating on his hopes and fears," Wade's report states, the soldiers "induced" the Indian to lead them to his village, fifteen miles away. The men reached the village early the following morning and took the Indians by surprise, capturing twenty of them and killing eight who tried to escape. They took the Indians' rifles and destroyed their provisions and canoes.

One of the Indians that they captured at the village, an old man named Chia-chee, now led them to another village, thirty miles to the north. Wade's men again surprised the Indians at this village, capturing all twenty-seven of them. On the way home, they destroyed another Indian canoe, an old hut, and a field of pumpkins, and captured a lone Indian man. After their return to Fort Lauderdale, Chia-chee asked permission to leave the fort to bring in other Indians, which Wade allowed him to do. He returned four days later with four men and two boys, who also surrendered themselves to the soldiers.[27] Wade's report does not state why the six men and boys turned themselves in, but it seems likely that they were relatives of the Indians already captured, and surrendered so that they could go west with the rest of their tribe.

Later in Thomas's career, when he served in Arizona and Texas, Thomas was greatly sympathetic to the Indians he encountered, often protecting them from the depredations of white militias. At this point in his life, however, Thomas's views on the Indian question do not seem to be different from those of most other whites. Like many other officers, he was critical of the government's handling of the conflict and hoped it would end quickly. But he did not question the basic premise of the war, that the Seminoles and other Indians had to relocate to the West to open up territory for white settlement. While Thomas eventually developed liberal attitudes toward nonwhites, he had not developed these attitudes at the time he served in Florida.

Thomas's main reaction to Wade's patrol was delight at the chance it offered him for promotion. At first glance, Wade's achievement may seem unimpressive, as he captured or killed only sixty-three Indians who did not attempt to fight back. Given that the majority of patrols did not even encounter any Indians, however, Wade's patrol was unusually successful by comparison. There were only about one thousand Indians left in Florida at the time, so the death or capture of sixty-three Indians represented a significant reduction in their overall numbers. In his report, Wade commended Thomas for his "valuable and efficient aid in carrying out my orders," and Colonel Worth, the overall commander in Florida, recommended Thomas for a brevet promotion to first lieutenant.[28] Brevet promotions were temporary promotions made during an active campaign, which were sometimes made permanent at a later date. The army did not yet have decorations or medals for bravery or excellent service in battle, so officers who distinguished themselves were granted brevet promotions instead. While brevet promotions did not automatically lead to a permanent increase in rank, they were a significant form of recognition and were important for an officer who hoped to advance his career.[29]

In December 1841 a new commander, Captain Erasmus D. Keyes, was assigned to Thomas's company, and Thomas spent the next two years in service under Keyes. Keyes described Thomas as six feet tall, "his form perfectly symmetrical, inclining to plumpness; his complexion was blonde, eyes deep blue and large. The shape and carriage of his head corresponded with my idea of a patrician of ancient Rome." Even as a young man,

Thomas "possessed an even temperament." "I never knew him to be late," Keyes recalled, "or to appear impatient or in a hurry. All his movements were deliberate, and his self-possession was supreme, without being arrogant."[30]

While Thomas was "dignified" and "reserved," Keyes wrote, he was nevertheless "social," and "possessed a subtle humor always ready to show itself in similes and illustrations of character." As an example of Thomas's sense of humor, Keyes told of Thomas's response to his inquiry about how to find a particular officer, named "B—."

> [B—] chewed tobacco and spat incessantly. We were at a Southern post in summer. The officer in question would sit reading and spitting; by turning his head to the right he could spit in the fireplace, and to the left out of the window—each being several yards from his chair. "Now," said Thomas, "you may come in at the window and follow up the line of tobacco juice on the floor, or you may descend the chimney and trace from that, and at the intersection of the two lines you will discover B—."[31]

Keyes had been in the military eight years and was a captain in rank, but he had spent his entire service as a staff officer and had never served in the field. Thomas, by this time an experienced field officer, helped Keyes acclimate to his new command. "From the first," Keyes recalled, "we were companions, and my confidence in him was at once complete."[32] Shortly after Keyes's arrival, Thomas's artillery regiment was ordered to New Orleans, and the two men continued to serve together in this more comfortable setting.

Thomas complained of the tedium and administrative workload of his Florida service, but the experience was a useful one for him. His exposure to the mundane aspects of military leadership, including record-keeping, supply, logistics, and the enforcement of discipline, was excellent training. Later, during the Civil War, Thomas had to train volunteer officers how to do all these things, and his mastery of the details of military adminis-tration helped him do so. Also, Thomas's participation in Wade's patrol had earned him a brevet promotion and the attention of his superior officers, putting him in a position to achieve greater things.

Now that he had succeeded in making a name for himself, Thomas was happy to leave Florida, particularly as his next assignment was in the much more comfortable environs of New Orleans. He spent three months there, training new recruits, and was then transferred with his company to Fort Moultrie in Charleston Harbor. The fort had a fairly large detachment of artillery officers, and Thomas was reunited there with his old West Point roommates, Stewart Van Vliet and William Tecumseh Sherman.[33] Thomas also enjoyed mingling with the residents of Charleston, many of whom had summer residences on the islands near the fort.[34]

In December 1843 Thomas's career received a boost when he was assigned to the light artillery, an elite branch of the artillery service, and transferred to Fort McHenry in Baltimore Harbor. Fort McHenry was considered one of the best posts in the army, as it was close enough to the city of Baltimore to allow the officers to share in the city's social life.[35] It was also close enough to Southampton for Thomas to make regular visits home. Thomas's career received further good news in July 1844, when he learned that his brevet rank of first lieutenant had been made permanent.[36]

At Fort McHenry Thomas was assigned to a battery of "flying" artillery, one of the army's most technologically advanced and important new weapons. In the past artillery had been limited in its utility on the battle-field by the amount and weight of the metal used to make the pieces. Large artillery pieces could be used as siege batteries or in fortifications, but they were too heavy to be moved easily on the battlefield. Those artillery pieces that were light and mobile enough to use in the field were too small to be very effective. In recent decades, however, advances in metallurgy had made it possible to make large, lightweight cannons, which could be maneuvered quickly on the field of battle. Napoléon had pioneered the use of mobile artillery in the front lines during battle, and the innovation had spread to other European armies, but not to the Americas. During the War of 1812 both British and American forces continued to make little use of artillery in the field, and after the war the U.S. Army limited its use of artillery primarily to heavy guns placed in coastal fortifications. Artillery regiments fighting in the field usually left their cannons behind and fought as infantry, as Thomas's unit had done in Florida.

In 1838 the U.S. government finally authorized the formation of an experimental battery of mobile, or "flying," artillery. The battery was commanded by Captain Samuel Ringgold, an innovative young officer who had studied the new artillery tactics in France and England. By 1843

Congress had appropriated money for three more batteries of light artillery, and Thomas was transferred to a company that had been assigned the new guns. Thomas was the junior lieutenant in his company, serving under a senior first lieutenant named Braxton Bragg. While they did not become close friends, they did seem to get along well, as Bragg helped Thomas in his career throughout the next decade. Bragg may have later regretted the assistance he gave to Thomas when, as a Confederate army commander, he fought against Thomas in Tennessee.[37]

Thomas served at Baltimore from December 1843 to September 1844. As the junior officer in an elite regiment commanded by experienced artillery officers, his service there was an excellent learning experience. There were four light artillery batteries under Ringgold's command, each battery having four guns, and Thomas personally commanded one of the guns in his battery. An eight-man crew loaded and maneuvered the gun under Thomas's orders, and Thomas himself aimed and fired it.

The flying artillery used "six-pounder" guns, so named for the weight of solid shot they fired. The gun itself was about five and one-half feet long, was made of bronze, and weighed about 880 pounds. It was mounted on a two-wheeled wooden carriage, pulled by a team of six horses, and the carriage had a small ammunition chest called a "limber." When the cannon was set up to be fired, it was "unlimbered," or unhitched from the horses, and arranged to face the enemy. When it was to be moved, the gun "limbered up" and was hitched to the horses again. The relatively light weight of the gun made it possible to tow it to the front lines of a battle, unlimber it and fire at the enemy, and then move it again to advance or retreat with the infantry. The gun's maximum range was about fifteen hundred yards, but it was usually used at shorter ranges.

Thomas's cannon could fire several different kinds of ammunition: solid shot, shells, and spherical case shot for long-range bombardment, and grapeshot and canister for short-range firing at enemy infantry. If enemy infantry was very close, gunners could "double-shot" the guns by putting in two canisters at the same time, which would result in a spray of balls that had only a very short range but that caused a lot of damage. It took a team of nine men, including the commanding officer, to load, aim, and fire a cannon, in a series of complex, coordinated movements that took extensive training and practice to master. In addition to the firing team, Thomas's company had men who drove the horses pulling the gun carriage and who held and managed them while the gun was being fired. Other men were responsible for managing the ammunition, which was transported on a separate wagon.[38]

Thomas trained with the light artillery regiment for eight months. In October 1844 he was sent to Charleston, South Carolina, where he again served at Fort Moultrie and also worked for the recruiting service. On the way there, he was able to schedule a short visit home, and he and his brother John enjoyed a few days of hunting.[39] Upon arriving at Fort Moultrie, Thomas was disappointed to find that many of his old friends were no longer posted at the fort, but he soon made friends with the officers who had taken their place.

Thomas thought often about marriage at this point in his life, and he was frustrated that his lack of financial means prevented him from starting a family. In November 1844 he wrote, "My desire for female society is fast leaving me so much so that I have not paid a single visit," and "I begin to have all the whims and notions of an old bachelor." Although he wanted to get married soon, he admonished himself to "cease thinking of the charms of matrimony at once, for the sooner I do so, so much the sooner shall I be contented with the state of single blessedness." He concluded with an apology for "writing all this nonsense about matrimony," but stated that he could hardly help himself, he found the subject "the most animatory topic of all others."[40]

In January George wrote to his brother again about this "most animatory topic." He had apparently overcome his misgivings about his financial situation and had called on a few of the local ladies, but without much success. "I fear my prospects in this quarter are rather gloomy," he wrote. "The South Carolina girls flirt very charmingly, but when matters become serious they give a very decided practical illustration of the domestic policy of their state, by nullifying instantly."[41]

Thomas's career to this point had gone about as well as a junior officer's career could go in the "peacetime" army. After graduating high in his class at West Point and receiving a commission in the artillery, and had earned a brevet promotion for gallantry and assignment to an elite artillery unit. He had yet to see true military action, however, in a pitched battle. The next few years, and war with Mexico, would expand Thomas's experience and knowledge of war-making beyond anything he had previously known.

CHAPTER THREE

Mexico

I hope they will not enact the absurd ceremony of presenting me
with the sword.... If I could get off with a dinner only I should have
great cause to congratulate myself.

In June 1845 Thomas received the news that his regiment was going to
Texas. Texas had recently been admitted to the Union, and it seemed
likely that the United States and Mexico would go to war over the
admission of Texas and the state's disputed boundary with Mexico.
Thomas arrived in Corpus Christi, Texas, in August 1845, where his unit
joined a large force commanded by Gen. Zachary Taylor.

Texas had been independent from Mexico for nearly a decade, but
political concerns about upsetting the balance between free and slave
states in Congress had delayed its annexation. By 1844 a compromise had
been reached, and Congress voted to admit Texas to the Union as a slave
state. The United States and Mexico disputed the location of the state's
southern border, with the Mexicans placing it at the Nueces River, and
the United States placing the border at the Rio Grande, about 100 to
150 miles farther south. President James Polk also wanted to acquire the
Mexican lands between Texas and the Pacific Ocean, consisting of the
present-day states of California, New Mexico, Arizona, Colorado, Utah,
and Nevada. Polk hoped to purchase this land from Mexico through
negotiations, but he was willing to go to war to acquire it, and American
public opinion generally supported his aggressive policy.[1]

The politics of the Mexican-American border dispute determined
Taylor's choice of where to station his army. Corpus Christi lay just south

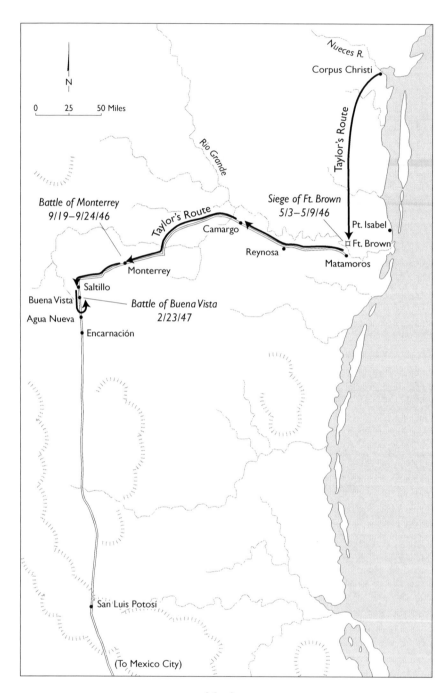

Mexico

of the Nueces River, inside the disputed border region, and by station-
ing his army there Taylor supported the American claim to the disputed
area. Taylor's army numbered about thirty-five hundred men, and
included all of the army's light artillery, twenty guns in five batteries. As
the commander of one of these artillery pieces, Thomas was personally
responsible for one of the army's most advanced and valuable weapons.[2]

Thomas remained at Corpus Christi for another six months, while
negotiations between the United States and Mexico continued. Nearly
the entire U.S. Army had gathered at Corpus Christi, and at first the
encampment took on the character of a West Point reunion. Thomas saw
many old friends and classmates, some of whom he had not seen since
graduation. As the months wore on, however, conditions in the camp
deteriorated, and the men suffered greatly. Supplies were inadequate to
the men's needs, but more volunteers kept arriving, putting additional
strain on the already overburdened supply system. Poor food, clothing,
shelter, and sanitation all took their toll on the soldiers' health, and many
men died of illness. The soldiers became restless with months of inactivity, and despite Taylor's efforts to keep them busy through training and
drill, discipline and morale suffered and fights broke out among the men.[3]

The problems at Corpus Christi were the first in a series of problems
of supply, discipline, and morale that plagued the U.S. Army throughout
Taylor's campaign. Poorly disciplined volunteer troops violated orders,
preyed on the Mexican citizenry, and performed badly in combat. The
inadequate supply system caused much suffering and death among the
men and repeatedly delayed Taylor's progress. Thomas remembered his
experiences in Mexico when he served in the Civil War, and he was
careful not to make the same mistakes as Taylor when he commanded
volunteers.

The months went by as Taylor's men waited for the results of the U.S.-
Mexico negotiations. By January 1846 it was clear that negotiations had
failed, and Polk ordered Taylor to advance his army to the Rio Grande.
Polk hoped that Taylor's advance would provoke Mexico to attack, giving
Polk the war he wanted while allowing him to claim that Mexico was the
aggressor.[4]

Thomas's battery marched out of Corpus Christi on March 8, 1846, as
part of Taylor's vanguard. On March 19 the army encountered its first
opposition, a band of irregular Mexican cavalry blocking the road at a stream
called the Arroyo Colorado. Taylor stopped for the night to consolidate his

troops and to prepare to force the crossing. The next morning, Thomas unlimbered his gun on the north side of the stream and covered the infantry as it approached the crossing. He loaded his gun and prepared for battle, but when the infantry reached the stream the Mexican cavalry retreated without firing a shot. Thomas limbered up his gun again, and the march proceeded.

On March 24 Taylor's army drew close to its destination on the north bank of the Rio Grande, opposite the Mexican town of Matamoros, and about twenty-five miles inland from the Gulf of Mexico. Taylor set up a supply base at Point Isabel on the Gulf and began fortifying a position north of Matamoros. Mexican and American cavalry patrols skirmished in the countryside around the city, and on April 23 a large force of Mexican cavalry attacked an American patrol, killing or wounding sixteen men and capturing the remaining forty-seven members of the unit. As Polk had desired, Taylor's advance had provoked the Mexican army into attacking.[5]

Taylor's position opposite Matamoros was a good one for provoking a war, but a difficult one now that hostilities had actually begun. Twenty-five miles separated his force from its supply base, and the Mexican army could cross the Rio Grande at any point within those twenty-five miles and cut the army off from its supplies. At the end of April Taylor had received intelligence that a large Mexican force had crossed the Rio Grande and was moving toward Point Isabel, with exactly this goal in mind. Taylor decided to go after the Mexican army with nearly his entire force, leaving only a small garrison, including Thomas's battery, to hold the fort.

Taylor left on May 1, and the Mexican attack on the fort began two days later. The defenders worried that the Mexicans would assault the fort, but they seemed content merely to bombard the fort with long-range artillery. At first Thomas returned fire, but it soon became clear that the light artillery did not have a long enough range to be effective against the Mexican guns. Thomas and his men took cover while the American heavy artillery responded to the bombardment. When one of the American guns disabled a Mexican cannon, the Mexican artillery pulled even farther back, no longer firing directly at the fort but launching indirect mortar fire over the walls. The Americans constructed "bomb-proofs" by digging holes in the ground, setting up barrels of pork as walls, and covering the barrels with sticks and earth. Thomas and the other men stayed in these shelters throughout most of the siege, leaving only a few sentinels posted on the walls to watch for an infantry attack.[6]

The siege continued until May 9. Thomas's battery only left their bomb-proof once, to fire at a Mexican battery that had crossed the Rio Grande and taken a position on the north bank, but they once again found that the target was too far, and they ceased firing and returned to shelter. The constant Mexican artillery fire was unnerving but not very dangerous, as it consisted entirely of solid shot and was fired at random into the fort. Since the fort was nearly empty of men, most of the shots bounced harmlessly into the interior, or were halted by the bomb-proofs. Only ten American soldiers were killed or wounded during the entire siege.[7] On May 8 and May 9 Thomas heard the sounds of battle off to the east, and on the evening of May 9 Taylor's army regained contact with the fort. Taylor had defeated the Mexicans in two consecutive engagements: the Battle of Palo Alto on May 8, and the Battle of Resaca de la Palma the following day. In both of these victories, the light artillery had been a key factor in the American victory, and Thomas may have felt upset at having missed the action. On the other hand, he may have felt fortunate, as the light artillery units suffered casualties, including Major Ringgold, their commander, who was mortally wounded during the Battle of Palo Alto.[8]

On May 18 the Mexican army abandoned Matamoros and retreated into the interior.[9] Taylor wanted to follow, but supply problems slowed his progress, and it took him two months before he was ready to advance into Mexico. Polk wanted Taylor to advance west along the Rio Grande and then into the interior, where he could capture Monterrey and Saltillo, the capitals of the Mexican provinces of Nuevo Leon and Coahuila. At the same time, other forces would capture California and the territory between California and Texas. Polk did not want to keep Monterrey and Saltillo, but he planned to use them as a bargaining chip, offering to return them to Mexican control in exchange for recognition of U.S. sovereignty over Texas, California, and the other northern territories.[10]

As Taylor prepared for his advance, he sent Thomas in command of two guns and a detachment of infantry to Reynosa, a small town about sixty miles west of Matamoros. The town's population was entirely Mexican, but they had asked for Taylor's protection from the bands of Mexican and American bandits that had moved into the area after the Mexican army had withdrawn.[11] In August Taylor moved his main base past Reynosa and began his advance on Monterrey. The army moved into the Mexican highlands, a fertile, well-watered, and cool region of the country, and a welcome break from the hot, dusty plains around the Rio Grande. They encountered little resistance along the route, and it soon became clear that the Mexican army had decided to make its stand in the strong fortifications in and around Monterrey.[12]

Taylor's advance units arrived at Monterrey on September 19, approaching the town from the northeast. The Mexican force at Monterrey, which outnumbered the Americans, was stationed in a ring of fortifications surrounding the town. This ring included several strong forts on the eastern edge of the city, a nearly impregnable fort called the Black Fort, or the Citadel, which stood on a hill to the north of the town, and two forts on hills to the west. The southern side of the town was protected by the Río Santa Catarina. The key to controlling the town were the two western forts, named the Bishop's Palace and Fort Soldado. If Taylor could take these forts, he could put artillery in position to bombard both the town and the road over which the Mexican army drew its supplies.[13]

On September 20 Taylor sent a large force, commanded by Gen. William J. Worth, on a march around the Black Fort to attack the Bishop's Palace and Fort Soldado. While Worth's men marched around the city, Taylor ordered a "demonstration," or a minor attack, against the city's eastern defenses, as a way of distracting the Mexican commander from his true intentions. Thomas participated in this demonstration, which was not pressed very hard and stopped short of the main Mexican line. The Mexican commander, Gen. Pedro de Ampudia, was not fooled by this half-hearted diversion and shifted forces westward to meet the threat posed by Worth.

On September 21 Worth's forces attacked the southern of the two forts, El Soldado. As a diversionary measure Taylor ordered two of his subordinates, Col. John Garland and Maj. Joseph K. Mansfield, to attack the outermost fort on the eastern edge of the city, called the Tenería. Behind the Tenería lay another fort, named El Diablo or El Rincón, and behind these main forts lay other fortifications, constructed around the heavy stone buildings of the town itself. Taylor encouraged Garland and Mansfield to assault the Tenería if they thought it could be taken, but he did not explicitly order an attack. Taylor then rode off to check on the

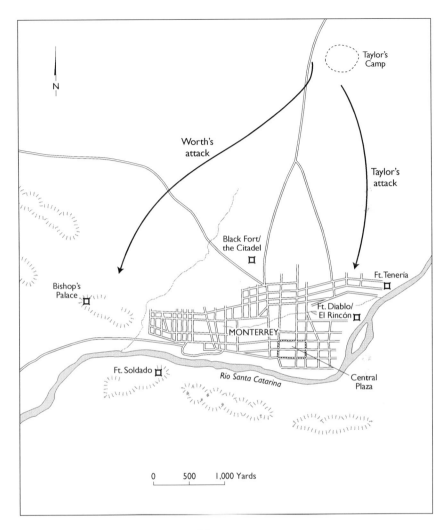

Monterrey

progress his heavy artillery was making against the guns of the Black Fort, north of the city.

After Taylor departed Garland and Mansfield led their men toward the Tenería. Their reconnaissance discovered that the fort was a difficult target, as it had strong, thick walls, was garrisoned by a large force of infantry and artillery, and was difficult to approach through the streets and buildings of the city. Garland and Mansfield decided to attack the position anyway, a decision they soon regretted. The Mexican defenders killed and wounded a large number of American soldiers before they even got close to the fort, the guns of the Black Fort opened up a long-distance fire on the attackers, and snipers fired from the streets and buildings around the Tenería, exposing the Americans to a terrible crossfire.

Mansfield and Garland tried to support the infantry assault by ordering Bragg's battery to the front. Thomas rushed forward, but Bragg soon found that his guns were ineffective against the well-constructed fort, while his own men suffered heavy casualties from the return fire. The streets were so narrow that Bragg could get only one cannon into position, and it fired ineffectually down the length of a single street, its shots easily avoided by the Mexican soldiers. Bragg requested permission to retire, and it was granted. With great difficulty, and under heavy fire, Thomas and the other artillerymen turned their guns around in the narrow street and retreated.[14]

An infantryman who saw Thomas's company shortly after its retreat described it as

> a perfect wreck. A few of [Bragg's] artillerymen, and more than a dozen of his horses, were down in the same spot, making the ground about the guns slippery with their gasped foam and blood. The intrepid Captain and his men, though exposed the while to a galling fire, were deliberately engaged in re-fitting the teams and in stripping the harness from the dead and disabled animals, determined that not a buckle or strap should be lost upon the field.[15]

Thomas was again ordered into action a few hours later, as Bragg's battery rushed northeast to fend off a threatened cavalry attack on the American base camp. Bragg and Thomas galloped into position and unlimbered their guns, and after a few shots from the artillery, the Mexican cavalry retreated.[16] Meanwhile, Taylor returned from the Black Fort and personally supervised the attack on the Tenería. He succeeded in capturing the position on this second attempt, and followed up with an assault on the other main fortification on the eastern edge of the town, El Diablo. Bragg and Thomas were called in again to support the attack, but they found that their artillery could do little to help and therefore retreated. Taylor's army suffered 394 casualties during the fighting in the eastern part of the city, far more than the Mexicans, and gained little of strategic importance.[17]

While Taylor's assault had cost the United States greatly and gained little, Worth had managed to capture one of the western forts, El Soldado. The next day, Taylor's men rested while Worth's men attacked the Bishop's Palace. Thomas was called to arms that afternoon to defend Taylor's base camp against another threat from the Mexican cavalry, but the cavalry retreated as soon as the artillery unlimbered their guns. Worth captured the Bishop's Palace that day, then posted artillery pieces on the heights of the two hills, where they could bombard the city with impunity. During the night, Ampudia withdrew the bulk of his army to the center of the city.[18]

On September 23 Taylor ordered a second attack on the eastern part of the city. The Americans advanced cautiously through the suburbs toward the city's central plaza, at first meeting little resistance. As they proceeded the Mexican resistance became more stubborn, and Thomas was sent in again to support them. To get to the city, the gunners had to cross a wide plain within easy range of the guns of the Black Fort, and Thomas and the other men pulled their guns across the field as fast as they could, pushing their horses to a gallop. The guns of the Black Fort fired at them, but they moved quickly enough to escape injury and reached the cover of the buildings of the city in safety. An officer who saw Thomas that day later noted that "even then he wore the impassive, unmoved countenance in dangerous places which became during the Civil War so marked a characteristic."[19]

Once in the city, Thomas and his men faced the same problem they had encountered before: their guns were of little use in the house-to-house fighting, while they themselves made easy targets for the Mexican infantry. Thomas and the other officers devised a way to use their guns to support the advance while minimizing the risk to their men. Each gunnery team loaded its cannon while sheltered behind the wall of a house, pulled it out into the street with ropes, fired it in the general direction of the enemy, and then pulled it back to load it again. This unaimed fire did little damage, but it created cover for the infantry's advance. An infantry officer later recounted how the artillery helped his unit cross a heavily defended street. "One of Bragg's pieces played up this street with very little effect, as the weight of metal was entirely too light. . . . The Mexicans, whenever the piece was pointed at them, would fall behind their barricade, and at that time we could cross without a certainty of being shot." They had to hurry, for as soon as the defenders could get up again, "their balls (as if bushels of hickory nuts were hurled at us) swept the street."[20]

With the help of Thomas and the rest of the light artillery, the American infantry slowly advanced into the city. By September 24 the American soldiers had penetrated far into the town from both the east and the west and were only a few blocks away from the central plaza. Ampudia had stored his ammunition near the plaza in the town's main cathedral, and the American army was now firing mortar shells into the area. If a shell hit the cathedral, the ammunition depot would explode, killing Ampudia and all his men. Ampudia asked Taylor to hold his fire and offered to negotiate terms for the surrender of the town. By the night of September 25 a surrender agreement had been reached, in which Ampudia's men were allowed to march away but had to leave most of their arms and ammunition behind them. Taylor also agreed to an eight-week truce, during which he would not advance beyond a certain point on the road between Monterrey and his next objective, Saltillo.[21]

Thomas had fought bravely throughout the battle, and several officers praised his courage in their reports. General Twiggs, the overall commander of the forces that attacked the Tenería on the 21st, praised Thomas and the other artillery officers "for their skill and good conduct under the heaviest of fire of the enemy, which, when an opportunity offered, was concentrated on them." Gen. J. Pinkney Henderson, who commanded an infantry regiment in the advance through eastern Monterrey on September 23, commended Thomas in his report "for the bold advance and efficient management of the gun under his charge. When ordered to retire, he reloaded his piece, fired a farewell shot at the foe, and returned (we hope without loss) under a shower of bullets."[22] Thomas received a brevet promotion for his role in the battle.[23]

Now that the battle was over, Thomas and Bragg faced the task of restoring the battery to effectiveness. Their men had suffered many casualties in the fighting, and they needed time before they would be ready to fight again. In November and December Thomas took command of the entire company while Bragg was assigned to temporary service elsewhere.[24] During this period Taylor resumed his advance, marching to Saltillo, seventy miles southwest of Monterrey. He captured the city without a fight, only to discover that the Mexican army had retreated far southward, destroying all the wells and water tanks on the road behind them. Apparently, the Mexican government's biggest concern was that Taylor's army would continue southward on this road to the Mexican capital and thus the Mexicans decided to concede Saltillo without a fight so they could concentrate their defense closer to the capital.[25]

After occupying Saltillo, Taylor concluded that the lack of water made a further advance impossible. At the same time, an attack by Mexican forces seemed out of the question, as they would have to march over the same waterless road to reach him. It seemed that active fighting was now over in the north. Fighting was also over in New Mexico and California, where the American army had defeated the small Mexican garrisons and now controlled the entire territory. Taylor divided and restructured his force, sending contingents to occupy a number of northern towns, while the navy captured the port of Tampico, on the Gulf of Mexico south of Matamoros. Bragg was promoted to Captain and moved to command a different company of artillery, and Captain Thomas W. Sherman was appointed to command Thomas's company.

Despite its defeats, the Mexican government refused to cede its northern territories to the United States. Polk concluded that the only way to force Mexico to surrender these territories would be to capture Mexico City, and he appointed Winfield Scott, the general in chief of the army, to lead an invasion of central Mexico. Scott assembled an army of regulars and volunteers in the United States and set up a base at Tampico, with the goal of assaulting the Gulf port city of Veracruz and then marching westward to the Mexican capital. To strengthen his force for the campaign, he took thousands of soldiers from Taylor, including nearly all of Taylor's regular infantry and most of the regular cavalry. Scott also took two of the batteries of flying artillery, leaving three, including Thomas's, with Taylor. It appears that Thomas was originally selected to go with Scott's expedition, but this decision was later changed and Thomas was left behind.[26] Thomas must have been disappointed to find out that he would have to stay with Taylor in northern Mexico, where little fighting was expected, rather than continue with Scott in the risky but potentially glorious campaign to capture Mexico City.[27]

Scott considered it safe to leave only a small volunteer force with Taylor, because neither he nor Taylor considered it likely that General Santa Anna would attack Taylor once the invasion of central Mexico had begun. Santa Anna did the unexpected, however, and moved his main army northward, leaving local troops to defend Mexico City while his men attacked Taylor's reduced force. He then led his twenty thousand men on a three-day forced march across the waterless stretch of road between San Luis Potosí and Saltillo, reaching the town of Encarnación, just south of Taylor's army, on February 17, 1847. More than four thousand Mexican soldiers died of thirst and exhaustion on the march, but the force that reached Encarnación still outnumbered Taylor's five-thousand-man army by more than three to one.[28]

American scouts detected the approach of Santa Anna's army soon after its arrival at Encarnación, and Taylor worked quickly to gather and concentrate his forces for a defensive battle. He retreated to a point where the road from Encarnación to Saltillo passed through a narrow pass, called La Angostura, or "The Narrows," just south of the town of Buena Vista. The forward elements of the Mexican army reached La Angostura on February 22, and there was some light skirmishing that afternoon while the rest of the Mexican army moved into position. The Battle of Buena Vista began the next morning.[29]

The position that Taylor had chosen at La Angostura was a strong one. The Encarnación–Saltillo road ran through a deep ravine there, only twenty feet wide at its narrowest point. Taylor posted a small infantry force and a battery of guns at the Narrows and had them construct field fortifications, which made the position nearly impregnable. To the east of the road rose a mountain ridge, too steep to climb. To the west of the road rose a plateau, about 150 feet wide, and this plateau was where Taylor expected the main Mexican attack to come. The bank between the plateau and the road was too steep to climb at most points, but there was a series of gullies leading down from the plateau to the road that infantry could climb up. Taylor posted most of his troops and artillery, including Thomas's gun, in a line across this plateau. East of the plateau lay another steep ridge, but far to the east there was a mountain path leading around the main American position to the rear. Taylor did not defend this path at the outset of the battle because he did not think it likely that the Mexican commander would use such a roundabout route.[30]

Thomas's gun was detached from the rest of Sherman's battery and placed near the center of the American line, along with a 12 lb. howitzer under the command of Lt. Samuel G. French. To the west of Thomas, and slightly ahead of him, was the Second Illinois Volunteer Infantry. To the

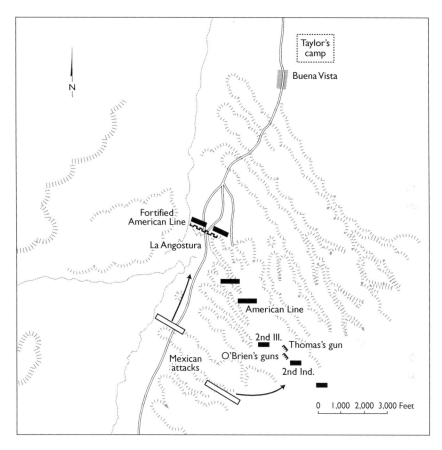

Battle of Buena Vista

east, and slightly ahead, was the Second Indiana Volunteer Infantry and three guns under the command of Lt. John P. O'Brien.

The Second Indiana and O'Brien's guns were posted just north of where one of the gullies ascended from the road to the plateau. In the first action of the battle, Mexican infantry advanced through the gully to the plateau and began forming into line of battle directly in front of the Second Indiana. Thomas, French, and O'Brien fired their guns at the infantry, inflicting heavy casualties, but the Mexicans' numbers were great, and they soon began to advance on the American position. The Second Indiana held its ground for a while, but when its commander ordered it to fall back the unit lost cohesion, and the men soon began to flee in a panic. This left O'Brien without infantry protection, and although he retreated as quickly as he could, he had to abandon one of his guns.[31]

The Mexican infantry now surged past Thomas's position into the gap left by the rout of the Second Indiana. Two small units of American cavalry, fighting dismounted as infantry, were ordered forward to fill the gap, but they broke and ran as well. The Mexicans continued forward, leaving Thomas, French, and the Second Illinois behind them as they sought to exploit the break in the American lines. Thomas kept firing, doing terrible damage to the Mexican troops running past him, but his own position was dangerous. If the Mexicans succeeded in exploiting their breakthrough, Thomas would surely be captured or killed.

Thomas kept firing, holding the attackers off, and after a few minutes he heard additional American artillery opening up upon the Mexican force from the rear. These guns belonged to Thomas W. Sherman and Braxton Bragg, who had originally been posted elsewhere on the battle-field but had moved quickly to the danger point. As Sherman and Bragg's fire slowed the Mexican advance, a regiment of volunteer infantry, commanded by Jefferson Davis, the future president of the Confederacy, moved forward and counterattacked. Davis's men were fewer in number than the Mexicans, but they were a fresh, organized force, and the Mexicans were tired and disorganized from their advance and had suffered heavy casualties. Davis's men pushed the Mexicans back, and other American infantry soon joined them, reestablishing a secure American line. Thomas, now out of danger, continued to fire at the now-retreating Mexicans, inflicting even more casualties.[32] Once they moved out of range, Thomas's men rested for a few minutes and then began a long-range fire against the enemy on other areas of the battlefield.[33]

While the battle on the plateau was taking place, the Mexicans had also attacked the American force blocking the road, and this attack had been driven back with heavy losses. Now Santa Anna tried sending cavalry over the mountain path to the east. Taylor sent a force to meet this new threat, leaving Thomas and O'Brien where they were. The cavalry attack failed as well, and soon Thomas saw the survivors retreating past his position. Thomas and O'Brien began to fire on them, as American infantry and cavalry pursued them, and the Mexican retreat soon turned into a confused rout.[34]

As the American infantry prepared to cut off and destroy the Mexican force, three Mexican officers appeared carrying a white flag. The Americans ceased firing, and the officers came forward with a message that General Santa Anna wanted to discuss with Taylor "what he wanted." General Wool rode to the front to speak with Santa Anna, but as he went forward the Mexican artillery continued to fire on the American troops. Wool concluded that the request for negotiations was a trick, and he ordered his men to resume firing. By this time, Mexican cavalry had managed to reorganize and retreat out of range. The officers' trick saved hundreds of soldiers from death or capture.

Taylor now sought to take advantage of the disorganized state of the Mexican army by ordering an advance. He sent three infantry regiments forward, but they soon ran into a fresh Mexican force moving through a gully from the road to the plateau. The American forces, finding themselves outnumbered, fell back and took cover in another gully, leaving the plateau undefended. Some of the Mexican troops fired at the Americans trapped in the gully, while others moved forward, advancing toward the gap in the American lines.

The Mexicans' advance was opposed only by Thomas's cannon and O'Brien's two guns; all of the infantry had taken shelter in the gully in Thomas's front, leaving the artillery completely exposed to capture. Thomas's position was extremely dangerous. He fired canister after canister into the masses of Mexican soldiers, killing and wounding dozens, but they kept coming at him. His men loaded and fired as fast as they could, but at their fastest they could fire only three rounds per minute, and the Mexicans were moving toward them quickly. Soon Taylor himself rode up to Thomas and O'Brien and encouraged them to hold on, as he had ordered infantry supports forward. These troops had not yet arrived, however, and it looked as if Thomas's gun would be overrun before the reinforcements arrived.

Thomas and O'Brien gained some time by allowing their guns to "retreat on recoil." Normally, cannons were anchored to the ground so the recoil from the gun's firing would not drive them out of position. Thomas and O'Brien now pulled up the anchors, so the cannon rolled a few yards backward with every shot. This made the guns difficult to aim, but the Mexican soldiers were so close and packed together so tightly that careful aiming was unnecessary.

As Thomas slowly retreated, he heard the welcome sound of other artillery being fired from the rear. Once more, Bragg's company had galloped forward to support him, followed closely by Sherman. They were too late to save O'Brien, whose position was overrun by Mexican infantry; O'Brien was wounded in the fighting, and nearly all of his men were wounded or killed. The Mexican soldiers now turned on Thomas, but the infantry arrived just in time to save him, driving back the Mexican attackers and establishing a secure line. This was the last crisis of the battle, and the Mexicans launched no more attacks that day.[35]

Taylor's army had held off the Mexican assault, but at a heavy cost: 673 Americans were killed or wounded, hundreds more ran away during the fighting, and all of Taylor's men were exhausted. During the night, Taylor moved additional units forward from Saltillo, bringing his army almost back up to full strength. The Mexicans had suffered about two thousand casualties, many more than the Americans, but they still outnumbered Taylor's army three to one. The Americans expected Santa Anna to continue the attack the next day, and they were not sure they could hold out.

When the sun rose, however, the American troops were relieved to see that Santa Anna had retreated during the night. The Mexican general decided the American position was too strong to attack and had withdrawn, hoping that Taylor would follow him so he could attack the Americans in the open. Taylor, content to have escaped with his army intact, stayed where he was. Santa Anna never attacked Taylor again, and the war was essentially over in the north.

Thomas's company suffered severe losses during the Battle of Buena Vista. Of the 117 officers and men present for duty when the battle began, 5 were killed and 21 were wounded, some of them mortally.[36] Thomas's commanding officers again commended him for his bravery. Taylor reported that "the services of the light artillery, always conspicuous, were more than usually distinguished" at Buena Vista.[37] General Wool singled out Thomas and O'Brien for special mention, stating that "without our artillery we would not have maintained our position a single hour."[38] Captain Thomas W. Sherman, Thomas's immediate superior, reported that Thomas "behaved nobly throughout the action," and that his "coolness and firmness contributed not a little to the success of the day. Lieutenant Thomas more than sustained the reputation he has long enjoyed in his regiment as an accurate and scientific artillerist."[39]

After the Battle of Buena Vista, the scene of active fighting switched to central Mexico. The men of Taylor's army settled down to garrison duty in the cities they occupied, as Scott fought his way across central Mexico toward the capital. In May orders came from Washington transferring Thomas out of the artillery service and into the commissary department, but his immediate superiors, recognizing Thomas's value as a combat officer, opposed the transfer.[40] Bragg arranged for Thomas to be temporarily assigned to his company, and he later arranged for this transfer to be made permanent.

The rest of the year passed uneventfully. On December 23 Thomas received word that his brevet commission to captain, which had been requested after the Battle of Monterrey, had been approved.[41] On January 9, 1848, Taylor asked that all of his light artillery officers, including Thomas, be given brevet promotions for their performance at Buena Vista.[42] Thomas received a third brevet promotion later that year, making him one of the most highly decorated junior officers in the army.

Meanwhile, Winfield Scott had fought a brilliant campaign in central Mexico, capturing Veracruz on March 29, 1847, advancing steadily on Mexico City in the months that followed, and capturing the Mexican capital on September 14. The Mexican government signed the treaty of Guadalupe Hidalgo in February 1848, officially ending the war. The treaty gave the United States all Mexican territory north of the Rio Grande in return for an American payment of $15 million. Thomas stayed in Mexico until August 20, 1848, when the last American occupation troops left northern Mexico and returned to Texas.[43] On August 25 Thomas's regiment arrived at the American base at Brazos Island, Texas, just north of Matamoros.

Thomas's artillery unit left Texas in October, but he was assigned to temporary commissary duty at Brazos Island and had to stay several months longer. During this period a young second lieutenant, John C. Tidball, met with Thomas and recorded his impressions. Thomas was thirty-one years old at the time, just eight years older than Tidball, but Tidball described Thomas as a kind man who took a "fatherly interest" in him. Just as at West Point, Thomas's serious, reserved demeanor made him seem older than he really was.[44]

In October 1848 Thomas wrote his brothers, John and Ben, asking them if they would go in with him to buy a farm in Southampton or a house in Norfolk. He did not specify in the letter whether the farm was meant for him or for one of his siblings, but he may have been thinking about retiring from the army and settling down. In an earlier letter Thomas had asked John to search for a wife for him, but John had not found anyone that he considered suitable. George replied, "I am sorry you are not successful in your selection of a fair lady to share her fortunes with me, as I should prefer one from the Old State to any other, and as I am now so much of a stranger there I am afraid I should not know where to look for one."[45]

Thomas left Mexico in January 1849 and passed through Vicksburg on the way home to visit his brother Benjamin. When he returned to Southampton in February, he received the hero's welcome that his neighbors had been planning for some time.[46] After news of the Battle of Buena Vista had reached Southampton, the county leaders had called to discuss how they should honor Thomas's achievements. They decided to present him with a ceremonial sword when he returned home, and they took up a voluntary subscription to pay for it. The committee passed a resolution commending Thomas for his "military skill, bravery, and noble deportment," as exhibited in his service in Florida and Mexico, "in which he has given ample proof of the best requisites of a soldier: patience, fortitude, firmness and daring intrepidity."

Thomas's siblings wrote him with the news about the sword, and he also received a letter from the committee, to which he sent a polite and formal thank-you letter.[47] Thomas was both pleased and embarrassed by the attention. From Texas he wrote his brother that he did not want to be honored with any special ceremony, as this "will be a great source of annoyance to me, and will take away a great deal of the pleasure I antici-pated on having in visiting the country again." Thomas had initially planned to cancel his visit home, just to avoid the attention, but decided in the end to return home "and have the thing off my mind" as soon as possible. "I hope they will not enact the absurd ceremony of presenting me with the sword," he wrote. "If I could get off with a dinner only I should have great cause to congratulate myself."[48]

Thomas did not "get off with a dinner only," but had to endure a ceremony in which the sword was formally presented.[49] At the least, Thomas must have been pleased with the sword itself, which was well made and beautifully decorated. The grip and hilt were of engraved silver, and the pommel of the sword held an amethyst, set in gold. The silver scabbard was engraved and decorated with scrollwork, military trophies, the words "Florida," "Fort Brown," "Monterey," and "Buena Vista," and a small picture of the Battle of Buena Vista. The sword was not designed to be used as a weapon, and Thomas left it in the care of his sisters when he returned to active duty.[50]

Many historians have described the Mexican–American War as a training ground for Civil War generals, and this was certainly true in Thomas's case. He learned the importance of drill, discipline, supply, and morale in making good soldiers, and he learned that an army that took care of these concerns could consistently defeat a poorly disciplined force, even when the enemy was more numerous and fighting on its own terrain. He learned that supply, logistics, and discipline were as important as battlefield leadership in winning victories. From Taylor he learned that daring tactics could work, but that attention to supply and logistics were as important as battlefield leadership when it came to winning campaigns. Thomas gained confidence and skill from his experience under fire, and he gained favorable attention within the army for his own excellent performance.

CHAPTER FOUR

West Point, Fort Yuma, and Texas

I am afraid that this speculation in town lots will attempt to locate a city on the banks of the Colorado, which I sincerely wish the first flood of river will wash away with its inhabitants. I cannot comprehend how a decent white man could desire to live in this country.

Thomas continued to grow as a military leader as he served in a variety of posts during the years after the Mexican-American War. He served as a fort commander in Florida and the Arizona Territory, an instructor at West Point, and a cavalry leader and acting regimental commander in Texas. In each of these command settings Thomas learned different lessons, so that by the time the Civil War broke out he had commanded artillery, infantry, and cavalry units, had fought in both Indian and conventional wars, and had extensive experience as an independent commander.

Thomas's interaction with Indians as a post commander in Arizona and Texas helped broaden his thinking on issues of race. When Thomas stated that he could not understand how "a decent white man" could want to live in Arizona, he was not implying that "decent" and "white" meant the same thing. During his frontier service, he had as much or more difficulty with unscrupulous white settlers than with Indians, and he as often protected Indians from white attacks as the other way around. During his service with the Yumas in Arizona, Thomas developed an interest in Indian culture, compiled a glossary of Yuma words, and helped broker a peace treaty between the Yumas and their traditional enemy, the Cocopas. He also came into frequent contact with Comanche and Kiowa

Indians while serving in Texas, and while he pursued renegade bands of Comanche raiders, he also helped to protect the Comanches and Kiowas who agreed to settle on reservations. Thomas's experience with the Yumas, Comanches, and Kiowas may have led him to question long-held assumptions about white superiority, and may have made him more open minded about racial differences in general, contributing to his later change of views on African Americans.

Thomas spent six months in Southampton after his return from Mexico, then rejoined his artillery company at Fort Adams, Rhode Island, in August 1849. He only served there a little over a month at this easy post before being sent once more to Florida.[1] Little had changed in Florida since he last served there seven years ago. The U.S. government had made peace with the Seminoles in 1842, but tensions between the Indians and white settlers continued, and the government had begun once more to pressure the Seminoles to relocate to the West. In July 1849 a small band of Seminoles attacked two white outposts, killing two men and wounding two others. The state government immediately called out the militia, and the Federal government sent more than one thousand troops to Florida and prepared for another protracted war.[2]

Thomas spent the next year commanding at a series of forts in the state's interior. His service was uneventful, however, as the Seminoles did not want another war with the United States. They made no further attacks, and their chief apprehended most of the individuals responsible for the earlier attacks and turned them over to U.S. authorities for punishment.[3] Thomas was unhappy with his Florida assignment, and he sought a position in the commissary department in Washington, D.C.[4] He was also critical of the government's handling of the crisis, and he sympathized with the Indians' desire to stay in Florida. He wrote his brother John that the Indians had consistently acted and negotiated "in good faith" and had agreed to relocate to southern Florida, far from white settlements. "As they have agreed to take more territory out of land which would never be settled by the whites," Thomas wrote, "it would be by far the best policy to make this treaty with them and get rid of this business."[5]

As frustrated as Thomas was, he made no move to resign from military service. Not only was his time in Florida difficult, but the prospects for future advancement seemed slim, as the size of the regular army had been reduced after the end of the war with Mexico and its funding had been reduced as well. Thomas could have found lucrative employment as an engineer in the private sector, a path that many of his fellow officers had already taken. Thomas's decision to remain in the army seems to have been a moral one, as he viewed the worlds of business and politics as corrupt ones, where honor was not respected, and where a man with a high sense of integrity would have a difficult time. By contrast, he wrote, "a man can be true to his own highest ideal" as a military officer, "better than in business pursuits." Thomas's sense of honor and distaste for the business world led him to stay in the military regardless of the difficulties of his assignments and the difference between what he earned as an officer and what he could have earned as a commercial engineer.[6]

The federal government eventually made peace with the Seminoles, and Thomas left Florida in December 1850 for an appointment as instructor of artillery and cavalry tactics at West Point. Two years before, Braxton Bragg had recommended Thomas for this position by writing to John Mason, the congressman from Thomas's district, and Mason had recommended Thomas to the War Department.[7] At that time the War Department appointed another officer to the position, but this officer died in September 1850, and Thomas was then named to replace him. Thomas had to wait in Rhode Island for several months before his commanding officer gave him permission to leave the regiment, but he was finally able to report for duty at West Point on April 1.[8]

Despite the extensive travel that Thomas's career required, he remained in close contact with his family in Southampton. In April 1850 George wrote his brother John about his sister Lucy, with his concern that she and her husband "lead a most lonely life" on their rural plantation. "It is true they appear to be contented," George wrote, "but they really have no associations which are more than barely tolerable." He proposed to give the couple $3,000 to allow them to buy a home in Norfolk, where they would have more company and a more interesting life.[9] Since Thomas's salary at the time was only $1,668 per year, his offer was extremely generous.[10]

One advantage of Thomas's transfer to West Point was that he would be able to visit home from time to time. The Richmond-to-Norfolk railroad was nearing completion, and the new railroad would make it possible for him to reach Southampton fairly quickly. Thomas wrote his brother John that he hoped to be able to make visits of two or three weeks' duration but expected that his duties at West Point would make it impossible for him to leave for more than a month at a time.[11]

The good news of Thomas's transfer to West Point was tempered with continuing bad news from Lucy, who was not getting along well with her husband. In the spring of 1851 Thomas wrote John that he hoped "some of the gloom has disappeared from our sister's brow," as "domestic differences are to me the most horrible of which I can conceive." He counseled John on his own personal troubles, repeating the advice that his brother had given him years earlier: "Having done what you conscientiously believe to be right, you may regret, but should never be annoyed by, a want of approbation on the part of others." His letters were not all about serious matters, however. George proudly told his brother about a gun he had recently acquired, one that he had arranged to be crafted according to his own specifications. This "perfect jewel of a gun" delighted George and inspired "the admiration of all beholders."[12]

Upon arrival at West Point, Thomas assessed the equipment, buildings, and horses available to him as instructor of artillery and cavalry tactics. He was not pleased with what he found. The artillery course now taught the kind of light artillery tactics that Thomas had used in the Mexican-American War, but the students had only old, heavy guns to use for practice. The horses used for cavalry practice were old and sick, and the same horses were used for riding and for pulling artillery pieces, which was bad for both the riders and the horses. Of the forty horses that the school possessed when Thomas arrived, thirty had been condemned as unfit for service by the Board of Visitors. The stone building used as a stable was literally falling down, and one of its walls had to be held up with scaffolding. The saddles the school owned were obsolete heavy cavalry saddles, which were so large, stiff, and awkward that the cadets often developed bleeding sores from riding.[13]

The worst aspect of cavalry instruction was the indoor riding hall that the cadets used when it was too cold to ride outside. The riding hall was located in the basement of the academic building, in a room that had originally been designed as a storage room for artillery pieces. The room was almost two hundred feet long and sixty-five feet wide but had a double row of iron columns down its length. When the cadets practiced formation riding, they constantly had to break formation or alter direction to avoid the columns, and students were frequently injured in collisions. The Board of Visitors, who observed cavalry exercises in this hall each January, reported that the exhibition of "rapid riding and wheeling by a corps of some thirty cadets," which should have been "most interesting to the spectator," was "rendered almost painful from the constant apprehension that some serious accident will happen to the riders and horses from the narrow limits within which they perform their evolutions."[14]

While Thomas had to deal with poor equipment, buildings, and horses, he was fortunate in that his predecessor, Lieutenant Hawes, had been an effective and innovative teacher. When Hawes began teaching, West Point taught only riding skills, so Hawes instituted the practice of teaching cavalry tactics as well, both in the field and in the classroom. Thomas expanded the scope of tactical instruction by substituting classroom instruction for riding practice during the months of December to February. Dennis Hart Mahan and some other members of the Academic Board initially objected to this move to classroom instruction, as they thought it would distract the cadets from their academic studies. Thomas convinced the Academic Board to form a special committee to research the issue, and when this committee found that tactical instruction would not distract the students from their other classes, Mahan approved the change.[15]

Hawes had also initiated the practice of selecting cadets with exceptional riding skill and leadership qualities for leadership positions in the cadet cavalry troop, and recommending them for assignment to cavalry regiments after graduation. Hawes's recommendations were not formally binding, but the leadership of the army took them seriously and often followed them. During Thomas's tenure, the academy formalized this practice by recording official grade rankings for riding, cavalry tactics, and artillery tactics. Among the students who Thomas recommended for assignment to the cavalry were J.E.B. Stuart and Fitzhugh Lee, both of whom went on to become successful cavalry commanders in the Confederate army.[16] Thomas's other students included William D. Whipple, Thomas's future chief of staff, and a number of other men who served with Thomas during the Civil War: William S. "Baldy" Smith, Philip Sheridan, Alexander McCook, David S. Stanley, James McPherson, John Schofield, and Oliver Otis Howard. Thomas also taught John Bell Hood, who later opposed Thomas as commander of the Confederate Army of Tennessee during the Nashville campaign.[17]

During a student's four years at West Point, he received a total of 204 hours of artillery drill and 268 hours of cavalry drill and riding practice, as compared with 540 hours of infantry drill and 54 hours of fencing instruction.[18] Much of this practical instruction occurred during the summer encampments. Cadets practiced firing a wide variety of cannons, including mortars, heavy siege and coastal guns, and light, mobile artillery pieces. They first learned how to work as a team to fire a single gun and then learned how to maneuver and operate artillery in groups. They learned the characteristics of different guns and types of ammunition and received practical instruction in how to operate and test cannons and how to make artillery ammunition and flares. In the classroom, they studied the physics and chemistry of artillery pieces and ammunition, and the strategy of siege batteries, counter-artillery fire, and coastal artillery placement. Thomas expanded the hours devoted to instruction in artillery tactics and also allowed second- and third-year cadets to practice using artillery, not just fourth-years as had been the case in the past.[19]

Cavalry drill began with basic instruction in riding and progressed to jumping over low obstacles and hitting targets with the cavalry saber while riding at a gallop. The students then progressed to cavalry tactics, first learning how to maneuver in small groups and then learning how to ride in companies and squadrons, and how to maneuver in lines and columns.[20] From the way Thomas managed riding instruction, the cadets gave him a nickname that was to follow him throughout his career. The horses at West Point were too tired, old, and sick to handle hard riding, and Thomas tried to preserve their precarious health by preventing the cadets from riding too fast. In a normal practice session, a student would start moving at a walk, increase to a trot, then a canter, and then a gallop. During Thomas's sessions the students moved from a walk to a trot, and then eagerly awaited the order to speed up. Thomas almost always disappointed them by ordering "slow trot," and then "walk." Amused and annoyed by their cavalry instructor's refusal to let them ride fast, the cadets started to call him "Old Slow Trot," and the name stuck.[21]

As a professor Thomas was reserved, aloof, and somewhat strict, but the students respected him for his expertise and heroic war record, and they came to like him for the care and concern he showed for their welfare.[22] Henry Coppee, who served with Thomas at West Point, recalled that Thomas had a "cool and equable temper," was respected for his "impartial justice," and was appreciated for his "courteous bearing and kindly spirit toward the cadets," as "he treated them as gentlemen of honor as well as soldiers."[23]

While Thomas had a reputation for strictness, in formal disciplinary proceedings he actually tended toward leniency. For example, Thomas presided over the court-martial of Oliver Otis Howard and another cadet, named L. R. Browne. Browne and Howard had gotten into an argument in the mess hall, in which Browne had insulted Howard and hit him over the head with a glass and Howard had retaliated by throwing the glass back at him. While physical fighting was a severe breach of discipline, Thomas punished them only with extra guard duty. In another court-martial, Thomas gave such a light punishment to the offenders that the superintendent reprimanded Thomas for leniency.[24]

In at least one case, however, Thomas was quite strict, and his strictness may have made him a lifetime enemy. A cadet named John Schofield, who worked as a teaching assistant in a mathematics section, was accused of allowing other cadets to enter the classroom during his teaching period and make inappropriate sexual and scatological jokes and drawings on the blackboard. Schofield was expelled for the incident, but he appealed the decision to the secretary of war, who remanded the matter to West Point for reconsideration by a Board of Inquiry. The majority of the board members recommended that the sentence be revoked, but Thomas and one other member voted to sustain the expulsion. Years later, Schofield served under Thomas as a corps commander, and the two men did not get along well; after Thomas's death, Schofield wrote a number of articles that criticized Thomas's generalship. While Schofield always claimed that this incident had nothing to do with his criticisms of Thomas, it seems plausible that Schofield did indeed hold a grudge, given how extensively and persistently he criticized Thomas.[25]

Despite the problems with horses and equipment, Thomas did an effective job of training the cadets in riding, cavalry tactics, and artillery skills, and the Board of Visitors always gave high praise to his students' performance.[26] Thomas's job became easier in September 1852, when Robert E. Lee succeeded Henry Brewerton as Superintendent. Lee was a more effective superintendent than Brewerton, and while Thomas and Lee had never served together before, the two men had similar person-alities and social backgrounds, and they worked together well. Matters improved further in March 1853, when the newly elected President, Franklin Pierce, appointed Jefferson Davis to be secretary of war. Davis was an active and competent secretary, and he and Pierce convinced Congress to allocate more funds for West Point. Some of this money went toward the construction of a new stable and riding hall, and Thomas also procured new saddles and equipment.[27] Lee managed to purchase horses for low prices by acquiring some of the horses left behind when the main cavalry recruiting barracks moved from Carlisle, Pennsylvania, to St. Louis, Missouri.[28]

Outside of his classroom duties, Thomas expanded his knowledge of military science by attending the meetings of the "Napoleon Club," a society for the study of military strategy founded by Dennis Hart Mahan. Thomas presented a paper to the society that reviewed the battles of Frederick the Great. He also checked out a number of technical books in military strategy from the library.[29]

In the summer of 1852 an unusual item appeared on Thomas's library record—a book of poetry. Thomas had begun spending more and more time with Frances Lucretia Kellogg, a thirty-one-year-old single woman who lived in Troy, New York. The Kelloggs were an old and respectable New York family, and Frances was the daughter of a prosperous hardware merchant, who had died when Frances was fourteen. Frances had attended the Troy Female Seminary and had an advanced education by the standards of the day. One of Frances's cousins, Lyman Kellogg, was a cadet at West Point, and Frances often went with her mother and sister to West Point to visit him.[30]

Frances was a tall, big-boned woman, but she was attractive, and her large stature was no problem for the tall, heavily built George Thomas. One of Thomas's officers recalled Frances as well educated, fond of reading, "pleasing in her manner," and "handsome in her appearance." She was quiet and reserved, like Thomas, but once engaged in conversation she was articulate and charming. Another acquaintance of the couple described Frances as "large and of stately presence," like her husband, and recalled that she excelled in "appearance, culture, and an exceeding charm of conversation."[31]

George Thomas and Frances Kellogg were married on November 17, 1852, at St. Paul's Episcopal Church in Troy. George wore his full dress uniform and had his ceremonial sword shipped to him from Southampton. Thomas's family did not attend the wedding, but he took a one-month leave of absence after the wedding so he could bring his new wife home to meet his family.[32]

Thomas was an intensely private man, and he left little record of his relationship with Frances. Three of Thomas's biographers—Richard Johnson, Henry Coppee, and Thomas Van Horne—knew the Thomases well but respected their privacy and said little about the marriage in their biographies, other than that it was a close and happy one.33 Frances supported George in his career and patiently endured the difficulties of life as an army spouse. She was separated from him for over a year while he served at Fort Yuma, and for three years during the Civil War, but she accompanied him to the Texas frontier in 1855–1860, and to all of his post–Civil War assignments. After George's death, Frances remained devoted to George's memory, following closely the books and articles that were written about his military career. Thomas wrote in 1865 that he and Frances "have been very happy in one another," and while his military career often kept them apart, "our mutual love and confidence has sustained us from desponding."[34]

The couple's first such separation came very early in their marriage. In the spring of 1854, just a year and a half after their wedding, Thomas learned that he was to be reassigned to California. In September 1853 two hundred officers and men in Thomas's Third Artillery regiment died when the ship that was transporting them to California hit a storm. The Third Artillery recruited new men throughout the winter, and another attempt was made to reach California in April, but the transport ship was also hit by a storm and disabled. No soldiers were killed, but the ship had to go to Hampton Roads, Virginia, for repairs.[35]

The War Department needed Thomas's help in this crisis and ordered him to meet his regiment in Virginia and accompany the men in their third attempt. After arriving in San Francisco, Thomas was to take two companies and march overland to Fort Yuma, and the rest of the regiment would be assigned to other posts. Fort Yuma was located on the Colorado River, near its junction with the Gila River, on what is now the border between California and Arizona. One of the major overland trails to California crossed the Colorado at this point, and Fort Yuma was the only U.S. military presence on the trail for hundreds of miles around. Fort Yuma was infamous for its remote location and hot climate and was thus considered one of the worst posts in the army.

Thomas's main task would be maintaining order and preventing violence between white settlers and the Yuma Indians.[36] The Yuma tribe, now known as the Quechan, numbered about three thousand people at the time. The Yumas had lived along the lower Colorado River for centuries, and they raised about half of their food by farming and the rest from hunting, fishing, and gathering wild plants. Farming was made easy for them by the Colorado, which overflowed its banks each year, leaving the land near the river inundated with fertile soil. During the spring and summer, when the Yumas farmed, they lived in large settlements of hundreds of people; in the winter they dispersed into smaller bands. One of their largest farming settlements was located near where the immigrant trail crossed the river, and several others were located nearby.

For decades the Yumas had little contact with white people, but after gold was discovered in California in 1849, the Yumas found their way of life disrupted. They lived near the only viable crossing of the Colorado River, and all of the travelers who took the southern overland route to California went across Yuma land. An estimated twelve thousand to twenty-four thousand settlers crossed through Yuma territory in 1849 alone, and thousands more passed through in the years that followed.[37] The Yumas welcomed the travelers initially, as they were able to acquire money and trade goods by charging the travelers a fee to ferry them across the river, but the Yumas soon began to have problems with the settlers.

In 1850 the U.S. government sent a force of infantry to establish a fort at the crossing and maintain order. The post's first commander, Samuel P. Heintzelman, launched a military campaign against the Yumas. They retreated without a fight, so he destroyed their crops and homes along the river. A famine in 1851 further weakened the tribe, and they then suffered a defeat in battle with the neighboring Cocopa tribe, so the Yumas sued for peace with the U.S. government. When Thomas arrived the government had been at peace with the Yumas for several years, and he had only to maintain the peace and preserve order.

Thomas learned of his assignment to Fort Yuma through private channels before his official orders came, and he wrote the War Department in April asking for permission to leave West Point so that he could take charge of his new command. In late April or early May, Thomas left West Point for Fort Monroe, Virginia, where his men were waiting to be transported by ship to California. His command consisted of four companies of the Third Artillery Regiment, the regiment's staff officers, and the regimental band.[38] They left Fort Monroe on May 6 and went by sea to Panama, crossed the isthmus over land, then sailed again for California. Thomas arrived at San Francisco on June 1, 1854, and spent two weeks there before setting out for Fort Yuma.[39]

In San Francisco Thomas met up with his old friend William T. Sherman, who had recently left the army and was managing a bank. The economy in California was booming, and Sherman's bank was doing well, so Thomas gave $2,000 to Sherman to invest for him.[40] Thomas and Sherman renewed their old friendship and frequently exchanged letters throughout the following year. Thomas's trust in Sherman's management of his money seems to have been complete, and he solicited and followed Sherman's investment advice. The two men traded information about local events, discussed political affairs in Europe, and shared news about mutual acquaintances in the army.[41]

After pausing in San Francisco to rest, Thomas set out with two companies of the Third Artillery on the 650-mile march to Fort Yuma. The march took place in the middle of the summer, and the last segment of the march, through the Arizona desert, was terribly difficult. The temperature during the day rose above 115 degrees, so Thomas had his men take shelter during the day, and marched only during the night.[42] Thomas's two companies arrived at Fort Yuma on July 14, 1854, where they joined a third company already stationed there, making for a garrison of about seventy men.[43] They found no solace from the heat at their new post. One officer recalled that "the hills around the garrison seemed to concentrate the rays of the sun upon the parade ground," and that the thermometer sometimes read as high as 116 degrees. The nights were so hot that the soldiers had to sleep on the roofs of their barracks, and even then the heat kept them up past midnight.[44] In later years, Thomas liked to describe the heat at Fort Yuma by telling a joke that had been common among the soldiers at the fort. A notoriously bad man, the story went, died at the fort and was buried. One night, shortly after his funeral, his ghost reappeared at the fort. When his comrades asked the spirit what he wanted, the ghost replied that it was too cold for him in Hell, and he had come back to the fort to get his blankets.[45]

Thomas commanded Fort Yuma for nearly a year, his main task being to manage relations between the white travelers and the Indians. Thomas's duties were similar to those of other commanders of military posts along immigrant trails westward. In areas where whites planned to settle, the army's task was difficult, as violent conflict between whites and Indians was common. At Fort Yuma, as at other posts along immigrant trails, whites passed through Indian territory without trying to settle there, so Thomas only had to make sure the whites and Indians maintained peaceful relations as the whites passed through. Thomas's predecessor, Capt. Samuel Heintzelman, had followed a punitive policy against the Yumas, but

Thomas favored more peaceful methods. He also undertook to learn the Yumas' language and customs, tried to negotiate a peace treaty between them and a neighboring tribe, and learned from them about the wildlife of the area. While this type of interest in Indian culture was not unheard of among army officers, Thomas was more friendly with Indians and more interested in Indian culture than the majority of his colleagues. He was already showing signs of kindness and open-mindedness toward nonwhites that would later characterize his treatment of African Americans.[46]

While Thomas advocated using peaceful methods to treat with the Yumas, he recognized that force and compulsion might also be necessary. Thomas asked his commanding officer to send him farming implements, which he could give to the Indians as presents. Thomas pointed out that this supply of farming implements could be cut off if the Yumas engaged in "improper conduct" toward whites or toward neighboring tribes.[47] Thomas also recommended that the government station a steamboat on the Colorado River to bring supplies to the garrison, instead of continuing to rely on privately owned steamboats. In addition to providing supplies, this steamboat would be a useful tool if war broke out with the Yumas. Since the Yumas' farmland was all located near the river, Thomas argued, a military detachment traveling by steamboat could quickly destroy the Yumas' crops, and thus "bring them to terms in a month."[48]

Thomas tried to establish peace and order in the area under his command by brokering a peace treaty between the Yumas and their traditional enemy, the Cocopa tribe. His efforts met with little initial success, as the Yuma chief considered the Cocopas completely untrustworthy.[49] By February, however, Thomas had succeeded in getting the two tribes to sign a peace treaty, in which they agreed to forget past differences, respect each other's claims to the land each tribe currently occupied, and settle future differences through negotiation, not war.[50] The treaty did not hold after Thomas left Fort Yuma, and in 1855 the tribes resumed hostilities. This fighting culminated in a major battle in 1857, in which the Yumas were badly defeated by the Cocopas and their allies, the Maricopa tribe.[51] Still, Thomas's efforts at peacemaking were praiseworthy, and a demonstration that his attitudes toward Indians were relatively tolerant and friendly in the context of his time.

While Thomas succeeded in maintaining good relations with the local Indians, he had a much more difficult time with the whites. Having found some potentially productive sources of mineral wealth in the mountains around the post, prospectors had begun to establish mines. These mines, and the continued flow of settlers across the Colorado, had led many white settlers and speculators to consider building a town near the river. The best land for a town was located on Indian land near the fort, and white settlers had already begun staking off plots. Thomas resented these squatters, who undermined discipline and encouraged desertion among the soldiers in his command. Also, the settlers had angered the Yumas by settling on Indian land, and the tensions between the groups threatened to flare up into violence.[52]

Thomas wanted to evict the white squatters from Indian and U.S. government lands, and he repeatedly asked his commanding officer whether he had the authority to do so.[53] When his commander did not give a definite response, Thomas decided on his own authority to evict the squatters, citing as his justification U.S. law and army regulations that forbade whites from settling within one mile of an army post, or on land recognized to belong to an Indian tribe.[54] The settlers protested his action, and Thomas's commanding officer in San Francisco ruled in favor of the settlers. Thomas complied with the decision, but registered his protest with headquarters. "I have done all in my power to prevent collision between citizens and the Indians and up to this time have succeeded," he wrote, "but if squatters are allowed to occupy their lands, trouble with the Indians will be the inevitable consequence."[55]

Thomas found his situation extremely frustrating, and he expressed his anger in his letters to Sherman. In March he wrote Sherman that gold, copper, and silver had been discovered in the region, which had created "quite an excitement" among the whites. "If it results in freeing me of their presence, I shall be duly glad," he wrote, "but I am afraid that this speculation in town lots will attempt to locate a city on the banks of the Colorado, which I sincerely wish the first flood of river will wash away with its inhabitants. I cannot comprehend how a decent white man could desire to live in this country."[56] The white settlement did not wash away, and is now the city of Yuma, Arizona.

While Thomas's command responsibilities could be frustrating, he did have the opportunity to engage in scientific studies of the Yuma people and the geology and animal life of the area. Thomas compiled a list of Yuma words and their English equivalents, which he later sent to the Smithsonian Institution. There are only seventy-one words on the list, and most of them are the names of people, animals, and things, indicating that Thomas's ability to communicate with the Indians in their own language was limited.[57] Thomas also spoke with the Yumas about the identity of other Indian tribes living nearby, the geography of the area, and the navigability of the upper reaches of the Colorado River.[58]

Thomas also studied the geography and biology of the area around the fort, with the help of two of his lieutenants and the post's medical officer.[59] He asked for permission to explore the upper Colorado, but this permission was not granted.[60] In 1855 Thomas sent samples of the sediment of the Colorado River to the Smithsonian,[61] and in 1856 he sent twelve samples of mammals and reptiles preserved in alcohol. The 1856 Smithsonian *Annual Report* described his contribution as "an important addition to our knowledge of the Mexican boundary line" that included "several new species, the most important of which was a *Phyllostome* bat, the first member of that family ever found within the limits of the United States."[62] The bat was a specimen of the California leaf-nosed bat, *Macrotis californicus*.

In addition to the California leaf-nosed bat, Thomas sent in five other specimens that were either newly discovered species or species that had not been studied in detail by scientists. These specimens, many of which are still in the Smithsonian's collection, are considered the "type," or defining specimen of the species. These were the California round-tailed ground squirrel (*Spermophilus tereticaudus*), the cactus mouse (*Peromyscus eremicus*), the California myotis bat (*Myotis californicus*), the Yuma myotis bat (*Myotis yumanensis*), and the western pipistrelle bat (*Pipistrellus hesperus*).[63] Thomas's geological and botanical findings were also published in the *Pacific Railroad Survey Reports*, which described the discoveries of the surveying and scientific expeditions that had been conducted while the government was searching for a suitable route for a transcontinental railroad.[64] Listed in the *Pacific Railroad Survey Reports*, but not present in the Smithsonian catalog, is a specimen that Thomas collected of *Dipodomys agilis* (Pacific kangaroo rat).[65]

Thomas's interest in science was not unusual for an army officer. All cadets at West Point studied geology, chemistry, and botany, and many of them maintained a lifelong interest in the natural sciences. Many collected specimens from their posts on the western frontier and sent them to the Smithsonian, or to Jacob Bailey, West Point's professor of chemistry and biology.[66] In 1853, for example, Thomas's friend and former classmate Stewart Van Vliet sent the Smithsonian samples of birds, mammals, fish, reptiles, and crustaceans that he had collected from the lower Rio Grande region.[67] In 1856, when Thomas sent in most of his Fort Yuma specimens, there were seventeen other military officers listed among the 150 individual contributors to the Smithsonian's collections.[68]

While Thomas was trying to make the best of his time at Fort Yuma, he had no desire to stay there. He began searching for another assignment only a few months after arriving there, applying for a position in the paymaster's department in Washington.

In November 1854 Braxton Bragg wrote Thomas that he was planning to resign from the army and offered to recommend that Thomas fill his place when he left. Thomas wrote Sherman that he was interested in the position, but that he did not want to accept Bragg's offer until he heard back from the paymaster. This application was denied, but Thomas was granted an even better post, that of major in the newly formed Second Cavalry. The Second Cavalry was to serve along the Texas frontier, which was still a remote post, but one where his wife could join him. Thomas was far down in the seniority list of captains, so Bragg's influence may have been an important factor in Thomas's appointment. Bragg wrote privately to Sherman, a mutual friend, to express his approval. Bragg described Thomas as "not brilliant," but "a solid, sound man," "an honest, high-toned gentleman, above all deception and guile," and "an excellent soldier."[69] Thomas left Fort Yuma on July 23, looking forward to his new assignment and a reunion with Frances.

Thomas arrived at Jefferson Barracks, St. Louis, in September. He was the last senior officer to join the regiment, which by that time had nearly finished its training. The Second Cavalry was a completely new regiment, authorized by an 1855 act of Congress that designated two new cavalry regiments to serve in the West. In the past the army had relied almost exclusively on infantry in its combat with Indians, a system that had worked in the East but was of little use on the western plains. Jefferson Davis, the secretary of war, had repeatedly asked Congress to authorize more cavalry, but mounted troops were much more expensive than infantry to equip and supply and Congress did not want to incur the expense. Eventually, Indian attacks on settlers became so frequent that Congress could no longer ignore the public outcry, and Congress approved Davis's request.

The army already had three cavalry regiments, named the First Mounted Rifles and the First and Second Dragoons, so the two new regiments were named the First and Second Cavalry. The different names were a borrowing from European practice, where different types of cavalry performed different functions. In the American army, the different types of cavalry had different uniforms and weapons, following the European models, but in practice all three types performed essentially the same job of frontier defense.

Of the two new cavalry regiments, Jefferson Davis favored the Second Cavalry, giving it the best weapons, equipment, and horses. The men received new, state-of-the-art rifles and were equipped with Colt revolvers in addition to cavalry sabers. The rifles and revolvers proved to be excellent weapons, but the sabers turned out to be nearly useless in Indian fighting, and the men generally left their sabers in the barracks when going out on patrol. The horses, which were also of high quality, were assigned to the regiment's companies on the basis of color: grays to Company A; sorrels to Companies B and E; bays to Companies C, D, F, and I; browns to Companies G and H; and roans to Company K.

While the Second Cavalry got the best arms and equipment available, what truly marked the regiment's elite status was the quality of its officers. Davis chose some of the army's best officers for the Second Cavalry, including many who had served with distinction in the Mexican-American War. Most of these officers were from the South. Col. Albert Sidney Johnston was chosen to command the regiment, and the second-in-command was Lt. Col. Robert E. Lee. The senior major was William J. Hardee, and the captains included Earl Van Dorn, Edmund Kirby Smith, and George Stoneman. All of these officers, except for Thomas and Stoneman, later rose to high command in the Confederate army, leading to speculation that Jefferson Davis had organized the Second Cavalry as a training ground for a future army of secession. According to Van Horne, Thomas believed this to be true, and he also believed that Davis had assigned him to the Second Cavalry in the expectation that he would later fight for the South.[70]

On October 27 the regiment left Jefferson Barracks on a long march to its new headquarters at Fort Mason, Texas. Thomas rode with them for the first two weeks of the journey, but on November 11 he parted from the rest of the group and went to report for duty as a juror on a court-martial. He remained absent on court-martial duty until January 1856, at which point he arranged to travel to New York before returning to Texas. While in New York, he was reunited with Frances, and she later traveled to Texas with him. Thomas also visited Southampton during this trip.[71] He joined the regiment at Fort Mason, Texas, on May 7, 1856.[72]

On their way to Texas, the Thomases traveled through New Orleans, where Frances hired an Irish immigrant woman to come to Texas with her to work as a domestic servant. In March 1858 the woman married one of the soldiers at Fort Mason and resigned her position with Frances. Unable to find a white woman to hire as domestic help, Frances bought a slave, named Ellen, instead.[73] The purchase of Ellen represents the only time that George Thomas ever bought or sold a slave. Thomas spent nearly his entire adult life away from his family's plantation. One of the family slaves did act as his personal valet during at least part of his military service, but other than this George had little to do with the management of the family's slaves. On the other hand, there is nothing in the historical record to indicate that Thomas opposed slavery. He seems to have shared the attitude of many Upper South slave owners that their form of slavery was a paternalistic and relatively benevolent institution.[74] According to Van Horne, Thomas stated that he "could never sell a human being," and he provided for Ellen even after the Civil War ended and she was free.[75]

On May 21, 1857, Thomas took command of Fort Mason, as the previous commander, Maj. William J. Hardee, had left the post for West Point, where he had been appointed commandant of cadets.[76] Thomas remained in command of Fort Mason for only three months before being assigned to jury duty on another court-martial. He left Fort Mason on September 8 and traveled to Ringgold Barracks, on the lower Rio Grande, with Col. Robert E. Lee. The court-martial stayed in session for five months, and in November it moved to Fort Brown, across the Rio Grande from Matamoros, where Thomas had been stationed in 1848. Thomas and Lee shared quarters during the trip, at one point gallantly giving up their hotel room to a woman visitor and sleeping in their tents instead.[77] Lee and Thomas resumed the friendship they had begun at West Point, and when they returned home from the court-martial, Lee frequently dined with Frances and George Thomas at their residence.[78]

Duty at another court-martial took up Thomas's time until April 1857, but after this he was finally able to return to field command.[79] Thomas was next stationed at Camp Cooper, one of a number of forts that had been constructed in Texas along the northern frontier of settlement to protect settlers from Comanche and Kiowa raiders. These tribes lived primarily on the Great Plains north of Texas, but they frequently raided southward through Texas and into Mexico. At first the government had tried to protect settlers with infantry, but these soldiers could do little against the mounted Indians. The Second Cavalry's main job in Texas was to intercept and pursue Indian raiders, and the regiment had been broken up into companies, with one or two companies stationed at different frontier camps and forts.

In addition to sending cavalry to fight the Indians, the federal government sent civilian officials to try to convince the Indians to cease raiding and to settle on reservations. The government had established two reservations in 1855, the "upper" reservation, near Camp Cooper, for the Comanches, and the "lower" reservation, downstream of Camp Cooper on the Brazos River, for several less aggressive tribes.[80] While the lower reservation was fairly successful, the Comanche reservation was not. Only a small number of Comanches ever settled there, and the majority of the tribe continued to live on the plains and raid into Texas. The numbers of Comanches on the reservation fluctuated between about 200 and 500 in the first few years of its existence, becoming a steady population of about 350 by 1858. Some white settlers, angered by the continuing Comanche raids, blamed the reservation Indians for the attacks and made violent reprisals. Other whites raided the reservations and stole the Indians' livestock, and the nomadic Indians sometimes raided the reservations as well. Thomas thus had two jobs: protecting whites from Indian raiders, and protecting reservation Indians from Indian raiders and predatory whites.[81]

In October 1857 Colonel Johnston left Texas to command U.S. forces in Utah, where war with the Mormons seemed imminent. Major Hardee was still posted at West Point and Colonel Lee was on leave, so Thomas became acting commander of the regiment, a post he held for the next two and a half years. He coordinated the regiment's actions from Fort Mason, sending out subordinates to lead patrols against Indian raiders. He sent out dozens of such patrols in 1857–58, fourteen of which managed to locate hostile Indians and engage them in combat.[82]

In the spring of 1858 the different companies of the Second Cavalry were pulled back from their frontier stations and brought together at Fort Belknap. The government expected war with the Mormons, and Thomas prepared to lead his regiment on a march to Utah. The war did not materialize, however, and General Twiggs, commander of the Department of Texas, decided to send the Second Cavalry on a raid northward to strike the Comanches in their home base on the plains. As commander of the regiment, Thomas would have been a logical choice to lead the expedition, but instead Twiggs selected Earl Van Dorn, the senior captain in the regiment and a brevet major.

Richard W. Johnson, who served in the Second Cavalry at this time, asserted in his biography of Thomas that Twiggs passed over Thomas because of a disagreement that had occurred between them during the war with Mexico. According to Johnson, Twiggs had once requested one of the mule teams assigned to Thomas's artillery company for his headquarters' wagons, but Thomas had refused to send them. After "much discussion and the use of quantities of red tape," Thomas prevailed and got to keep his mule team. According to Johnson, Twiggs remembered the disagreement years later and never passed up the opportunity "to heap an indignity upon or do an underhanded injustice to Thomas."[83] While Van Dorn went out to win glory in the field, Thomas returned to his administrative duties at regimental headquarters. He wrote his family that "this place continues as wretchedly dull as ever" and he tried to obtain a leave of absence. Unfortunately for him, with Lee on leave and Hardee on assignment at West Point, Thomas was the regiment's senior officer and could not be spared.[84]

In 1859 Thomas found himself spending more and more energy defending the reservation Indians from whites' attacks. Local settlers, angered by the repeated raids from nonreservation Comanches, tried to take their revenge on any Indians they could find. Others took advantage of the anti-Indian sentiment to prey upon the reservation Indians and steal their possessions and livestock. Thomas consistently took the Indians' side, sending troops to defend them from these attacks, and asking headquarters for reinforcements. Thomas tried to assuage white settlers who complained that reservation Indians were raiding their farms and abducting white children. He personally investigated complaints of abductions and reassured whites that the reservation Indians were not responsible for the attacks.[85]

Thomas's attempts to protect the reservation Indians and negotiate with the settlers did not succeed. In July a band of 250 whites attacked the reservation, and six whites and three Indians were killed in the battle.[86] The governor of Texas, who knew that anti–Indian policies would help him gain re-election, supported the whites' aggression.[87] By the end of July Thomas and the local Indian agent concluded that the Indians would have to leave Texas to be safe from attacks by whites. They decided to help the tribes move north to Indian Territory (present-day Oklahoma). As Thomas helped the Indians prepare for the trip, a band of whites attacked the reservation again, wounding one Indian so severely that he had to be taken to Camp Cooper for medical treatment.[88]

On August 1, 1859, nearly 1,100 Indians began their trek from the Brazos Reservation, escorted by one company of the First Infantry Regiment and two companies of the Second Cavalry, under Thomas's command. Before setting out on their journey, Thomas arranged for the Indians' animals to be penned in the corral of a local judge, to give local citizens the opportunity to examine them and determine whether the Indians had stolen any of their animals. No animals were claimed, and the Indians, with all their cattle and horses, continued on their journey. With federal troops acting as escort, the white settlers did not dare attack the Indians, and they traveled unmolested to the northern border of the state.[89] As they continued northward, a large party of Kiowas attacked a group of Indians, stealing their horses but inflicting no casualties. Thomas followed the Kiowas for a while but turned back after concluding that they were out of reach of pursuit. The rest of the journey proceeded without incident, and Thomas returned to camp on August 21.[90]

With the reservation Indians safely relocated, Thomas could turn his attention to tracking down the nonreservation Comanches who continued to raid white settlements. Thomas planned an expedition into northwestern Texas, the goal of which was to put an end to Indian raids by attacking the raiders in their base camps. Thomas gathered men from different forts and left Camp Cooper on May 2, 1860, and spent the rest of the month exploring the area near the headwaters of the Red and Canadian Rivers in northwestern Texas. Thomas learned much about the geography of the area, but found he no Indians and little evidence of an Indian presence. He concluded that the Indians did not have any long-term camps in the area, but only passed through it briefly at times on their way to raid farther into Texas. The location of the raiders' base camps was still unclear.[91]

Thomas immediately began planning his next expedition, this time to the headwaters of the Concho and Brazos Rivers where they approached the Colorado. While the expedition was being planned, another band of Indians raided near Camp Cooper. A party of local citizens attacked the raiders, killing a few of the Indians and taking back some of the stolen horses. Thomas sent a detachment to pursue the Indians, but it was unable to catch them. Frustrated, Thomas complained to departmental headquarters that he needed reinforcements if he were to have any chance of intercepting and defeating the Indian raiding parties.[92]

Thomas's second expedition left Camp Cooper on July 23, 1860, met up with several companies from other posts, and continued northward. When the force, numbering about one hundred men, reached the headwaters of the Concho and the Brazos, Thomas divided it into smaller groups and spent about a month exploring the area. Once again they found no Indians and little sign of an Indian presence. On August 25, as the patrol began to head home, Thomas's Indian guide came across a fresh horse trail, and Thomas followed it. Early the following morning, they discovered the camp of eleven Comanches, who had about forty horses with them, apparently captured in raids. The Indians spotted Thomas's guide at the same time the guide spotted them, and they quickly gathered the horses together and rode away, with Thomas's troops in pursuit.

The Indians were camped on the opposite side of a deep ravine, which Thomas's horses could not cross. As his men rushed to find a crossing point, the Indians galloped off, putting about a half mile between themselves and their pursuers by the time Thomas's men made it across. Pushing their horses hard, Thomas and his men began to catch up with the Indian band. To increase their speed, the Indians released their captured horses, but Thomas's men still continued to gain on them. Finally, the Indian at the rear of the party turned around, dismounted, and began shooting arrows at the pursuing troopers. Thomas called on the Indian to surrender, but he shot at Thomas instead. The arrow glanced off Thomas's chin and embedded in his chest.

The Indian hit three of Thomas's men with arrows and inflicted a minor wound on a fourth man with his spear. The soldiers fired back and repeatedly wounded the Indian, but he kept fighting. One of Thomas's men dismounted to get a better shot, but his horse kicked him and he fell down. The Indian staggered over and tried to kill the fallen man, but he was so weak from his wounds that his blows did little damage. Thomas's men fired again, and the Indian finally fell, dead from more than twenty bullets. He had sacrificed himself to buy time for his comrades, and his tactic worked. Thomas was himself wounded, his horses were exhausted, and the Indians were at least two miles away, so Thomas reluctantly gave up the pursuit.[93]

Thomas's wound was apparently not severe, as he remained in command of the expedition and barely mentioned his own wound in his report. Van Horne stated that Thomas pulled the arrow out himself, and it seems that the arrow had lost much of its force when it glanced off Thomas's chin, making only a shallow chest wound, or perhaps only embedding in his uniform. This wound was the only wound that Thomas ever suffered in combat.[94]

In November 1860, about a month after returning from this expedition, Thomas left Texas for a one-year leave of absence. The year 1860 marked his twentieth year in military service, during which time he had advanced in rank from second lieutenant to major, and gone from serving in a remote Florida fort to an instructorship at West Point to the acting command of a regiment. Thomas had learned the mundane details of administration, supply, and logistics, and in Mexico he had seen the negative results of neglecting these aspects of military command. He had learned how to train regular enlisted men and cadet officers and had seen the results of poor training and discipline among the volunteer forces in the war with Mexico. Thomas had commanded in all three branches of the army in combat conditions: infantry in Florida, artillery in Mexico, and cavalry in Texas. Throughout his career, Thomas had served with distinction, and his Mexican-American War record, his three brevet promotions, and his assignment to the elite light artillery and Second Cavalry marked him as one of the best officers in the army.

From Texas Thomas first traveled to Vicksburg to visit his brother Ben. He then traveled by rail to Southampton, with plans to continue to New York for a visit to his wife's family. Thomas expected to return to active service in Texas after a year, but he never did. A personal accident and the national crisis would drastically change the course of his life and career.

CHAPTER FIVE

Decision

Turn it every way he would, one thing was uppermost, his duty to the government of the United States.

—*Frances Thomas to Alfred Hough, 1876*

As Thomas headed to Southampton in November 1860, he had little idea of the tumultuous year that was in store for him. After Abraham Lincoln's election to the presidency, South Carolina stated its intention to secede from the Union, but most observers did not expect a war. South Carolina had defied the federal government before, during the nullification crisis of the early 1830s, and there had been other crises in previous decades over the extension of slavery to new states and territories. All of these crises had been solved through negotiation and compromise, and while this crisis was the worst to date, it seemed possible that it would be resolved peacefully as well.[1] Thomas was concerned with a more immediate matter, an accident he suffered that he thought might cripple him and disqualify him from military service.

On the way from Vicksburg to Southampton, Thomas stepped off the train for a moment during a nighttime stop in Lynchburg, Virginia. Misjudging the distance from the train to the platform in the darkness, he fell off the platform and down an embankment, severely injuring his back.[2] Thomas continued by train to Norfolk, but he was so badly injured that he could not travel by coach from Norfolk to Southampton. Frances, who had left Texas before him to visit her family in New York, came down to Norfolk to care for him, and after a few weeks George recovered enough to travel to Southampton. He stayed there from December 15 to January 8 and then left for New York.[3]

Years later, George's sister Judith recalled that George promised to return to Southampton in March. His sister Fannie stated, "he had much of his army baggage sent here and left it, wishing it to be stored in the house, implying that he would return for it, and it would be ready for his use; he also brought his servants [slaves] and left them in my sister's care until such time as he and his wife might require the services of the cook, whom Mrs. Thomas wished to retain."[4] Fannie spoke of "servants" in the plural, meaning that George and Frances Thomas brought at least one other slave with them besides Ellen, the woman they had bought in Texas. Some memoirs of officers who served with Thomas mention that he had a "colored attendant," so it seems likely that Thomas also owned a slave who acted as his personal valet, possibly a slave from the Thomas plantation.[5]

On his way to New York, Thomas spent some time in Washington, where he conferred with Gen. Winfield Scott about the brewing secession crisis. According to Van Horne, Thomas warned Scott that General Twiggs, commanding the Department of Texas, was prosecession and not trustworthy.[6] After Thomas arrived in New York, he began to consider leaving the army. On January 18 he sent a letter to Col. Francis H. Smith, the superintendent of the Virginia Military Institute (VMI), responding to an employment advertisement for the post of commandant of cadets and instructor of tactics that had appeared in the *National Intelligencer* newspaper. In his letter of inquiry, Thomas asked the superintendent to inform him "what salary and allowances pertain to the situation, as from present appearances I feel it will soon be necessary for me to be looking up some means of support."[7] Thomas sent the letter to his former West Point comrade William Gilham, who currently held the position of commandant of cadets, and asked him to pass it along to Smith. Smith's answer to Thomas is no longer extant, but evidently Thomas was not offered the position.

There is some dispute as to what the "present appearances" were that had made it necessary for Thomas to seek other employment. When Thomas's letter was published shortly after his death, Southerners claimed that the letter referred to the secession crisis, meaning that Thomas sought an appointment at VMI as a way of remaining neutral in the coming conflict. This is possible but not likely. At the time Thomas wrote the letter, only South Carolina, Mississippi, Florida, and Alabama had left the Union, and war did not seem imminent. Unionist sentiment was still strong in Virginia, and it did not seem likely that Thomas's home state would join the seceding states of the Deep South.[8] Frances Thomas later wrote that "no person (in the North at least), thought, or had any idea of war" at that time, and George was "very unwilling to believe" that the South would be "so crazy and unjust to herself" to go to war over secession.[9] It seems more likely that the "present appearances" Thomas was referring to related to his back injury. The injury was serious and slow to heal, and even as late as April, Thomas considered himself unfit for field duty. In January he may have thought he would never be able to return to active service.

After Thomas sent the letter to VMI, the secession crisis intensified. By early February Texas, Louisiana, and Georgia had seceded from the Union, and the seven seceded states joined to form the Confederate States of America. None of the Upper South states had yet joined the Confederacy, and many people still hoped that the secession crisis could be resolved through compromise. A vocal minority of Virginians now favored secession, but the majority of the state's residents and leaders wanted to wait and hope for a compromise.[10] The Virginia legislature called for a special election on February 4, 1861, to nominate delegates to a February 13 convention to consider secession. Voters also decided whether the convention could institute secession by itself, or if the decision of the convention would have to be submitted to a popular referendum before taking effect.

The state legislature also called for a "Peace Conference" of delegates from every state to meet in Washington, D.C., and scheduled the conference to begin February 4. The timing of the conference was no coincidence, as the majority of Virginia legislators wanted to encourage voters to support antisecession candidates by holding out the hope that compromise could still be reached. Their strategy worked, as two-thirds of the convention delegates elected were procompromise, and the provision that any decision of the convention would have to be ratified by a referendum also passed by a two-thirds majority. The prosecession vote in Southampton County was higher than the state average but was still less than 50 percent.[11]

On February 18 the commander of the Department of Texas, Gen. David E. Twiggs, surrendered the Second Cavalry regiment to the authorities of the state of Texas. The state government took the arms, horses, equipment, and forts occupied by the Second Cavalry but allowed the individual soldiers to leave the state, if they so chose.[12] One of Thomas's officers, Richard Johnson, wrote in 1884 that Thomas expressed anger at Twiggs and regretted that he had not been present in Texas at the time. "I would have taken command of the men," he reportedly said, "[and] marched them north until they reached the loyal states, and the rebels should not have taken a prisoner or captured a cannon or a flag." Both this statement and Van Horne's claim that Thomas warned Winfield Scott of Twiggs's disloyalty should be treated with some skepticism, as they were written decades after the events in question and were motivated by a desire to defend Thomas against Southern accusations that he was not a sincere Unionist.[13]

On March 1 Thomas wrote the adjutant general of the army and asked for the position of superintendent of the mounted recruiting service. He explained that he requested this position because "I am still quite lame from the injury which I received last November in Lynchburg, Virginia, and although I could attend to all my ordinary duties I fear that I shall not have sufficient strength to perform every duty which might be required of me if with my regiment." Thomas asked to be detailed to the position for two years, perhaps in expectation that it would take that long for his back to heal completely.[14]

On March 9, five days after Lincoln's inauguration, Thomas received a letter from William Gilham, of the Virginia Military Institute. Gilham told Thomas that he had spoken with John Letcher, the governor of Virginia, about Thomas's wish to leave the army, and the governor had asked Gilham to approach Thomas and offer him the position of chief of ordnance for the Virginia state militia. William Mahone, a state legislator from Southampton County, had also recommended Thomas for the position, acting without Thomas's knowledge.[15] Gilham told Thomas to write directly to the governor with his answer, and Thomas responded to Letcher on March 12. Thomas stated that "it is not my wish to leave the service of the United States as long as it is honorable for me to remain in it, and, therefore, as long as my native state remains in the union, it is my purpose to remain in the army, unless required to perform duties alike repulsive to honor and humanity."[16]

Thomas's letter seems to indicate that he was still undecided about whether he would side with the Union. He implied that he would leave the army if Virginia seceded, and his reference to "duties alike repulsive to honor and humanity" seems to indicate that he was reluctant to fight against the South, even if Virginia did not secede. Only a month later, however, Thomas decided to stay in active service even after Virginia seceded and war broke out. It is possible that he replied in this manner out of politeness or evasiveness, but it seems more likely that the letter reflects real ambivalence and conflict in Thomas's thoughts and feelings.

On April 6, 1861, Winfield Scott asked Thomas to return to active duty in command of the Second Cavalry. The men of the regiment who had stayed loyal to the Union were traveling by boat from Texas to New York City and were scheduled to arrive soon. Scott wanted Thomas to take command of the men there, move them to the cavalry training barracks at Carlisle, Pennsylvania, and get them reequipped and ready to return to active duty. Thomas received Scott's orders on April 10 and considered his reply. Frances advised him to stay home, as he had not recovered from his injury. Thomas decided to accept the assignment, but he advised Scott that he was still too injured to command in the field. Frances recalled later that "not one in a dozen injured as he was would have reported to duty." Thomas could not ride but felt capable of supervising the reorganization of the Second Cavalry in camp. While his health soon improved enough for him to command in the field, his back never healed completely, and he continued to suffer from severe back pain throughout the war.[17]

Thomas was reunited with his old command in New York City on April 12, and he immediately began the trip to Carlisle Barracks. He arrived on April 14, and three days later, Virginia seceded from the Union.[18] Earlier, he had written that he would serve in the U.S. Army as long as his native state remained in the Union. Now, with Virginia seceded, if war broke out he would have to fight against his home state, a duty he might consider "repulsive alike to honor and humanity."

Before the attack on Fort Sumter and Lincoln's call for volunteers to suppress the rebellion, most Virginians favored remaining in the Union and hoped for a compromise solution to the crisis. After war broke out, however, many of these conditional Unionists changed their minds and favored secession. On April 17 the same Virginia convention that had voted against secession in February now voted 88–55 in favor of secession. Prosecession forces captured the federal arsenal at Harpers Ferry on April 18. In the May referendum on secession, Virginians voted

132,000 to 37,000 to leave the Union. In eastern Virginia, the margin was even higher, with voters supporting secession by a margin of nearly twenty to one.[19]

According to Van Horne, Thomas did not consider secession to be legally valid. Thomas did think that the people of a country had a natural right to rebellion, as Americans had exercised in the Revolutionary War, but they could only do so justly in response to tyrannical rule. In the present case, Thomas reportedly said, Southerners did not have the right to rebel, as "the tyranny did not exist, and they well knew it." Thomas dismissed the idea of a peaceful secession as "a fantasy." He criticized officers who supported secession because they had broken their oath of service to the Constitution. "The government cannot dissolve itself," he stated. "It is the creature of the people, and until they had agreed by their votes to dissolve it, and it was accomplished in accordance therewith, the government to which they had sworn allegiance remained, and as long as it did exist, I should have adhered to it."[20]

In an 1866 speech before the Tennessee legislature, Thomas emphasized that his decision to remain loyal to the Union was dictated by the oath he had taken on entering the army, by which he had promised "to sustain the Constitution of the United States, and the Government, and to obey all officers of the Government placed over me." "I did not regard it so much as an oath," he stated, "as a solemn pledge on my part to return the Government some little service for the great benefit I had received in obtaining my education at the Academy."[21]

Thomas blamed extremist politicians in both the North and the South for rejecting compromise, undermining the balanced approach toward slavery enshrined in the Constitution, and goading the nation toward war. A fellow officer, George L. Hartsuff, who spoke with Thomas in New York in early 1861, later recalled that Thomas "was strong and bitter in his denunciations against all parties North and South that seemed to him responsible for the condition of affairs." Thomas "reprobated, some-times very strongly, certain men and parties North, in that respect going as far as any of those who afterward joined the rebels," but he never supported secession, and he "denounced" others' plans of "going with their States."[22]

During the war and afterward, Southern critics of Thomas claimed that his Northern-born wife had influenced his decision, but Frances Thomas always insisted that George never discussed the matter with her.

In 1884 she wrote that "there was never a word passed between myself or any one of our family upon the subject of his remaining loyal to the United States government. We felt that whatever his course, it would be from a conscientious sense of duty, [and] that no one could persuade him to do what he felt was not right." While claiming that she never discussed the matter with him, Frances Thomas asserted that she knew her husband well enough to know in advance what he was going to do. While Frances may not have influenced him directly, the mere fact that Thomas's wife was a Northerner made his decision to fight for the Union easier. Even when his siblings cut all ties with him, he still had one close family member he could confide in and rely on.[23]

Despite his disagreement with the legality and wisdom of secession, it would not have been surprising if, like Robert E. Lee, Thomas had decided to side with his native state. Lee wrote in January 1861 that it was "idle" to talk of secession, and that "the framers of our Constitution never exhausted so much labor, wisdom, and forbearance in its formation, if it was intended to be broken up by every member of the [Union] at will." However, when Winfield Scott offered Lee command of the Union army on April 18, Lee refused the appointment and resigned from the army. "Save in defense of my native State," he told Scott, "I never desire again to draw my sword." Privately he wrote, "I cannot raise my hand against my birthplace, my home, my children." In contrast with Thomas, Lee was married to a Southern woman who was ardently prosecession, and Emory Thomas, one of Lee's biographers, speculates that this may have influenced Lee's decision to support the Confederacy.[24]

Both Lee and Thomas thought of themselves as Southerners, and both based their decisions on the particularly Southern moral values of honor and duty. For Lee, honor and duty required him to side with his family and community. As Emory Thomas writes, loyalty to "blood and bonds" came first for Lee, and the Union, in comparison, "was a mere abstraction." George Thomas, by contrast, thought that his oath as an army officer and the debt that he owed his country were more important than his feelings of affection for his family and native state. For Thomas, duty and honor meant following ethical principles based on moral rules, as opposed to making decisions according to one's sentimental attachments.[25]

Thomas pondered his decision throughout March and early April, but the secession of Virginia forced him to make up his mind. From Carlisle Thomas wired Frances to tell her that he was planning to continue in active service, and he asked her to come and join him there. As Frances later recalled, Thomas stated that, "turn it every way he would, the one thing was uppermost, his duty to the government of the United States."[26] Thomas also sent word of his decision to his family in Southampton. While his entire family was angry with him, his sisters were the angriest of all. Judith stated later that she wrote him "in plain but courteous language" that he "had been false to his state, his family, and to his friends." When George asked Judith to send his possessions to him in Carlisle, including the ceremonial sword he had been awarded after his service in the war against Mexico, she refused. If the people who had given George the sword told her to surrender it to him, Judith wrote, she would do so, but not before.[27]

George's brothers were more forgiving of his decision to fight with the Union than his sisters. John continued to care for Ellen, the slave whom his wife had bought in Texas, and Ellen remained at the Thomas plantation throughout the war. John's account books indicate that he purchased clothing and shoes for her and recorded the expenses as money owed him by George. George's other brother, Ben, was living away from the family plantation in Vicksburg, Mississippi, and there is no record of how he reacted to George's decision. It is known, however, that they reconciled after the war.[28]

While George's brothers eventually accepted his decision and reconciled with him, George's sisters never spoke to him again. According to a family friend, the Thomas sisters' "love and admiration for their soldier brother, prior to the decision he made in 1861, was unbounded. They were proud of him as a type of a vigorous manhood, as a courteous Virginia gentleman and of his career as a distinguished officer in the war with Mexico." George's sisters had never married, and their father had passed away years ago. Of the three Thomas brothers, George was the most successful, and the sisters seem to have been extremely proud of their brother, the war hero. In the one letter of Fanny to John that survives, she refers to George not by name, but as "the Major," indicating how important his military career was in her perception of him.[29]

Judith and Fanny attributed George's decision to his wife's influence and claimed that he had assured them in December and January that he would side with the South if war broke out. Since George apparently changed his mind after he left Southampton, Judith and Fanny concluded that Frances Thomas was to blame for the change. Where John and Benjamin Thomas saw George's decision in impersonal terms of politics and ethics, George's sisters considered his decision a matter of siding with his wife instead of his birth family, and thus a betrayal of those who loved him the most. Because they took George's decision so personally, they were unable to forgive George during his lifetime.[30]

His siblings' rejection was a personal tragedy for George, perhaps even more so for him than it would have been for other men. Thomas had few close friends, and he relied on his wife and siblings for company and emotional support. When his family disowned him, he lost almost every person who was important to him. His wife went with him to Carlisle, but once he entered active service she no longer lived with him, and he went for three years without seeing her at all. The separation from his family made the Civil War years extremely difficult and lonely ones for Thomas. Less important, but still a loss, were Thomas's estrangement from his friends and former neighbors in Southampton County, and the loss of thousands of dollars he had on deposit in Virginia banks.[31]

Thomas's decision to remain loyal to the Union was unusual, as most Virginians sided with their state, not their country, in the Civil War. Only in northwestern Virginia, in what is now the state of West Virginia, did the majority of people remain loyal to the Union. Several hundred recruits from the northern part of the Shenandoah Valley did join the Union army, and about 120 men from Loudoun County, on the Maryland border, formed two companies of light cavalry. Many of these recruits were of German or Quaker ancestry, who had moved south to Virginia from Pennsylvania.[32] Almost no whites from Thomas's part of the state fought with the Union. When Union troops captured Norfolk in 1862, the federal government tried to recruit Unionists from the area. Federal recruiting agents circulated notices calling on all "loyal Virginians" to enlist, offering a bounty of $100 to those who did so. The government set up recruiting stations on the Eastern Shore and around Norfolk; one of these recruiting stations, in Suffolk, was only about thirty miles east of Southampton. Despite years of effort, fewer than one hundred whites from southeastern Virginia were recruited.[33] In all, only about one thousand whites from the present-day state of Virginia joined the Union ranks. Only Georgia, South Carolina, and Mississippi provided fewer white recruits to the Union army.[34]

Most Southern whites who did serve in the Union army had little in common with Thomas. While white Southerners did make up a sizable minority of the recruits to the Union army, few of them were similar to

Thomas. Over three-quarters of the white Southern volunteers came from highland and mountain areas like northwestern Virginia, eastern Tennessee, western North Carolina, northern Alabama, and the Ozark region of Arkansas. These highland areas were populated by small, independent farmers, few of whom owned slaves, and the economies of these areas were not dependent on cotton, rice, or tobacco cultivation, as in the rest of the South. Both during the war and after, Southern Confederates characterized Southern Unionist volunteers as foreign-born recent immigrants and "poor white trash," who were outside the boundaries of "good" Southern society. As Catherine Edmondston, a strongly pro-Confederate resident of North Carolina, stated in her diary:

> This company of Union men which they boast so of raising in Chowan and Gates [counties in North Carolina] is composed of the offscouring of the people and foreigners, people who can neither read or write and who never had a decent suit of clothes until they [the Northerners] gave it to them, poor ignorant wretches who cannot resist a fine uniform and the choice of the horses in the country and liberty to help themselves without check to their rich neighbors' belongings. We should judge them leniently, but justice to ourselves demands that we shoot them down like wolves on sight.[35]

Edmondston's description of Southern Unionists was typical of Southern attitudes at the time, but inaccurate. Foreign-born Southerners fought for both the Union and the Confederacy, and pro-Union Southerners were not taken only from the lowest classes. Unionists were found among all social classes, but Unionist volunteers most often came from the middle class, particularly from the class of yeoman farmers who owned their own land, but did not own slaves.[36]

While most Southern Unionists were not slaveholders, many, perhaps most, believed in white racial supremacy and were supporters of slavery. They differed from other Southerners in that they placed more importance on the preservation of the Union than on the preservation of slavery. Unionists and Confederates alike considered themselves patriots and revered the Constitution, the Declaration of Independence, and America's military heritage. Where pro-Confederate Southerners associated these symbols of patriotism with their state or with the South

as a section, pro-Union Southerners associated these symbols of patriotism with the nation as a whole. Many Southern Unionists identified
strongly with the American flag and reacted strongly against the decision
of Confederates to fire on the U.S. flag in Charleston Harbor. Despite
their support of slavery, most Southern Unionists were willing to accept
the Emancipation Proclamation when it was announced, and they
remained loyal even after it became clear that the abolition of slavery
would be a result of a Union victory.[37]

Many locations contained some individuals who remained loyal to the
Union in sentiment, but few of these individuals took the risk of going
north to join the Union army. In a study of Culpeper County, a
slaveholding area in Virginia's piedmont, historian Donald E. Sutherland
found that a small minority of residents supported the Union but that
none of them left to join the Union army. Only during a brief period in
1862, when the Union army moved through the area, did Unionist
residents step forward to assist the Federal troops by providing food,
supplies, and information. Many of these Unionists had opposed secession
because they knew it would bring a destructive war, and many of them
were older people, with families, who felt they had more to lose from war.
While there were a large number of these Unionists, they were largely
passive supporters. People whose opposition to secession was based on a
fear of war were not likely to leave their homes to fight for the Union.[38]

While the majority of Southern Unionists were yeoman farmers, there
were also a number of wealthy slave owners who were Unionist in
sentiment. Their Unionism stemmed from a general conservative outlook,
and a desire to preserve the institutions that they had inherited from their
forebears. Their Unionism was also a matter of self-interest, in that they
viewed the Union as the best guarantee of the institution of slavery. They
feared, correctly, that secession would lead to war and ultimately the end
of slavery.[39] The largest number of wealthy Unionist slaveholders owned
plantations near the Mississippi River in Louisiana and Mississippi, but
many also lived in Virginia, and others in Tennessee, Alabama, Arkansas,
and Georgia. Only a few of these served in the Union army, but many
provided information and supplies to Union troops. One wealthy
Louisiana slave owner even acted as a Unionist spy.[40]

Other Southern Unionists were people who had emigrated to the
South from Northern states, or whose parents had done so. Atlanta, the
South's second-largest city, contained only about one hundred Unionists,

and most of these people were emigrants to Atlanta from the North.[41]
Elizabeth Van Lew, who secretly directed a Union spy ring in Richmond
throughout the war, was a native of Richmond, but her parents had
moved there from the North and her grandfather was a prominent
Philadelphia abolitionist.[42]

Many Unionists were former members or supporters of the Whig
Party and admirers of Henry Clay, the Whig leader who had brokered
earlier compromises on slavery and other sectional issues. The Whig Party
broke apart in the 1850s and was replaced by the Republican Party, which
had almost no supporters in the South. Still, many former Whigs
remained loyal to the party's ideology of compromise and national unity,
and for a few Whigs these ideas sustained their Unionism even after their
states seceded.[43]

General in Chief Winfield Scott, the 1852 Whig presidential candidate,
was now again famous as Virginia's most prominent Unionist. Scott was
seventy-four years old in 1861, and he had served as the country's general
in chief for twenty years. A hero of the War of 1812, he had led the U.S.
Army to victory in Mexico City in 1849. Scott identified much more
strongly with the nation than with his native state, so he seems not to
have hesitated at all in his support for the Union. Even so, Scott was
apprehensive about the prospect of a civil war, perhaps because he was
one of the few people to realize that such a war would be long and
terrible. While he followed Lincoln's orders once war started, he
advocated compromise while the possibility still existed and even favored
ceding Fort Sumter to the Confederates in the hopes of eventually
achieving a compromise and peace.[44]

Besides Thomas, a large number of regular army officers who had been
born in the South decided to stay in the army, instead of siding with their
native states. Virginia alone contributed eighteen generals to the Union
cause, although this number includes four who were born in the part of
Virginia that became West Virginia, and five who left Virginia at an early
age. The remaining nine included Scott, Thomas, Philip St. George
Cooke, a senior cavalry officer, and Alexander B. Dyer, who served as
assistant chief and later chief of ordnance of the army. Three lesser-known
Union generals from Virginia—John Newton, John D. Stevenson, and
William R. Terrill—served with Thomas in the western theater.[45]

In June 1861 Philip St. George Cooke wrote a public letter explaining
why Southern-born regular officers felt they owed a greater allegiance to

the United States than to their state of origin. When he attended West Point, Cooke explained, "the national government adopted me as its pupil and future defender; it gave me an education and profession; and I then made a solemn oath to bear true allegiance to the United States of America, and to 'serve them honestly and faithfully against all their enemies or opposers whatsoever.' This oath and honor alike forbid me to abandon their standard at the first hour of danger." After arguing at length that secession was illegal and unjustified, Cooke concluded, "I owe Virginia little; my country much . . . and I shall remain under her flag as long as it waves the sign of the National Constitutional Government."[46]

Thomas's decision to side with the Union came with some risk. When captured, Southern Unionists were sometimes treated as traitors, not prisoners of war, and captured Southern Unionist soldiers who had earlier deserted from the Confederate army were sometimes executed. Southern Unionists were certainly detested by pro-Confederate Southerners, and Thomas was no exception. In 1864 Catherine Edmondston wrote in her diary in response to a false rumor that Thomas's body had been found among a number of dead black soldiers in the aftermath of the Battle of the Crater in Petersburg:

> Amongst the Yankee dead within our lines was found the renegade and traitor Gen Thomas, a base son of Virginia. . . . Meet was it that her soil should drink his blood when he turned against her and led to the conquest of his native land a band of Negro assassins which he had organized! He it was who has been most strenuous for the employment of Negro troops, making himself their champion and exponent. The mill of the gods grind slowly, it is true, but none the less surely for its delay.[47]

The most notorious execution of Southern Unionist soldiers occurred at Kingston, North Carolina, in 1864, but other examples are known.[48] At Fort Pillow, Tennessee, in 1864 forces under the Confederate cavalry commander Nathan Bedford Forrest massacred a force of black Union troops and white loyalist soldiers from East Tennessee after these soldiers tried to surrender and be taken prisoner. The massacre is better remembered today for the treatment of the African American troops, but Forrest's men were almost as angry with the white Southerners who were fighting for the Union. One survivor remembers that "the rebels were very bitter against these loyal Tennesseans, terming them 'home-made Yankees,' and declaring they would give them no better treatment than they dealt out to the Negro troops with whom they were fighting."While the majority of soldiers killed at Fort Pillow were African Americans, white Unionists were also murdered by the Confederates.[49]

While Thomas's former student J.E.B. Stuart once wrote his wife that he would like to hang Thomas "as a traitor to his native state," it seems unlikely that Thomas would have been executed if captured. While there are records of Southern Unionists being murdered while attempting to surrender, of the execution or murder of Unionist guerrillas, and of the execution of Unionist soldiers who had formerly deserted the Confederate army, there seems to be no recorded incident of a Southern officer in the Union army being executed for treason after capture.[50]

While few white Virginians served in the Union army, many white Southerners from other slave states did so. Richard Current estimates the total number of white Union soldiers from states that seceded and from West Virginia at 104,000; William W. Freehling estimates the total number of white Union soldiers from the slave states of Kentucky, Missouri, Maryland, and Delaware at 200,000. Freehling has argued that the contribution of these white Southerners, combined with the contribution of Southern free blacks and escaped slaves, made the difference between Union victory and defeat. The Confederate government adopted a policy of universal conscription in 1862, so young male Unionists who did not flee to the north or hide from the conscription agents were forced to serve the Confederacy. Thus, the contribution of white Southerners to Union victory is doubly important, given that each white defection to the Union represented both an increase in the size of the Union army and a decrease in the size of the Confederate force. Freehling makes a convincing argument that the decision of white Southerners to fight for the Union, either with their states or as individuals, was one of the key turning points of the war.[51]

After making his decision, Thomas had little time to reconsider it, as he found himself immersed in work. Thomas's superiors in the Second Cavalry—Col. Albert Sidney Johnston, Lt. Col. Robert E. Lee, and Maj. William J. Hardee—had all resigned to side with the Confederacy, leaving Thomas as the regiment's de facto commander. The soldiers of the regiment were demoralized by the officers' defections, and by Twiggs's surrender of the regiment's arms and equipment to the Texas state government.[52] When the first men arrived in New York City on April 12, the same day as the attack on Fort Sumter, the local citizens welcomed them as heroes. Thomas met the soldiers at the docks and arranged for them to travel by rail to the cavalry training school at Carlisle, Pennsylvania, where they were to reorganize and refit for active service. Thomas arrived at Carlisle on April 14.[53]

When the Virginia militia captured the federal arsenal at Harpers Ferry on April 18, Lincoln feared that the militia might be able to successfully attack Washington, which was lightly defended at the time. The War Department ordered Thomas to refit the Second Cavalry and to bring its troops to Washington as soon as possible. Because this mission was so important, the regiment's needs were given first priority, and Thomas was able quickly to procure horses, saddles, and rifles for his soldiers. Two of the Second Cavalry's ten companies were ordered to proceed immediately to the capital to guard public buildings, and they arrived there on April 17.[54]

Shortly after this, a group of Maryland secessionists attacked a regiment of Massachusetts volunteers as they passed through Baltimore on their way to Washington. Another group destroyed one of the bridges on the railroad that connected Washington to the North. According to Lucius Chittenden, a member of Lincoln's staff, some of the Union men of Baltimore objected to Thomas's command of a regiment assigned to guard the capital. So many other Southern officers had resigned from the regiment that the Baltimore Unionists feared Thomas would do the same. According to Chittenden, Winfield Scott told Lincoln that Thomas was "incapable of disloyalty," and Lincoln retained Thomas in command of the mission. Chittenden stated that he "never heard the loyalty of General Thomas questioned after this endorsement."[55]

On April 22 Thomas was ordered to take all of the men he had available and rush to Washington. Half of the Second Cavalry's soldiers had still not arrived from Texas, and some of the soldiers in Pennsylvania did not yet have mounts, but four companies of the regiment were ready for active duty. At York, Pennsylvania, near the Maryland border, Thomas was met by a courier carrying orders from the secretary of war, Simon Cameron. The courier told Thomas not to proceed to Baltimore, as that city's mayor feared that the presence of Federal troops would provoke more violence. Instead, Thomas should guard and keep open the railroad connecting Pennsylvania and Baltimore.[56]

Maj. Fitz John Porter, the War Department staff officer in charge of keeping the railroads open, stated in his official report that Thomas's leadership was essential in maintaining the loyalty of the Second Cavalry's junior officers. These officers, many of whom were Southerners, were "all anxious, excited, in doubt as to what should be their immediate action and gloomy as to the future." Unsure whether they were willing to fight against Maryland civilians, they "looked to Major Thomas' action as their present guide." Porter "knew Major Thomas' views" and "had no doubt of his course," but he did fear that some of Thomas's subordinate officers might resign once they got to Maryland, as one of them had recently done in Carlisle. As the men were boarding the train at Carlisle, one officer turned to Thomas and asked, loud enough that the other men could hear him, "What shall we do?" Thomas replied, "We are ordered to Washington, and there we go. There will be time enough after getting there for you to decide what to do." The men got on the train.[57]

Thomas continued to guard the railroad north of Baltimore until other units arrived to relieve him, then returned to Carlisle on April 23. On April 25 Thomas received orders to come to Washington as soon as his men were mounted, armed, and fully equipped for active service. Thomas sent his men to Washington by companies as they became ready. As the rest of the men arrived on a second ship from Texas, he mustered them back into service, and he also recruited new soldiers to replace the ones who had deserted or resigned.[58]

Training the new recruits, both officers and men, was difficult. Richard Johnson, a regular officer who had been with the Second Cavalry in Texas, recalled that the camp was unusually dangerous because of the nervous volunteer sentries. Instead of calling out "Who goes there?" and awaiting a reply, the sentries shot first and called out later. The volunteer officers were little better. One of the new volunteers neglected to mention that he did not know how to ride a horse. He was thrown the first time he got on, and this ended his career in the cavalry.[59]

The volunteer soldiers, as with Civil War volunteers throughout the country, were willing to serve but resistant to discipline, only obeying orders that they saw as fair and reasonable. Officers had to walk a fine line between being too lenient and too strict, and many regular officers, accustomed to army discipline, had difficulty working with the new volunteer troops. Thomas won his troops' affection with his care for their welfare, lack of pretentiousness, and fairness, but he could be a strict disciplinarian when the situation required it. One volunteer officer, Thomas M. Anderson, often asked Thomas for advice on how to deal with discipline problems. Once, a private soldier under his command became mutinous and threatened to shoot anyone who came near him. When Anderson asked Thomas what to do, Thomas told him, "[I]n last resort, death." Anderson did not have to go this far, but he had "no doubt" that Thomas "meant what he said." Later, Anderson discovered that a local shoemaker was violating regulations by selling troops drinks from a barrel of whiskey he kept in his shop. Thomas learned of the whiskey also, and he sent for Anderson and asked him whether he had done anything about it. Anderson replied that he had knocked the head of the barrel in and emptied it out into the street. Thomas approved, adding, "I am glad you did not come to ask this time what you should do."[60]

Later that summer, Thomas was called to put down a mutiny in a regiment of three-month volunteers from New York. The men of the regiment claimed that their term of enlistment had expired and insisted they had the right to return home, while the army authorities stated that they still had time left to serve. The men marched to the railroad at the army's base camp in Maryland, planning to seize a train the next morning to take them back to New York.

At dawn the regiment stopped the train, and then the men stacked their weapons and prepared to get breakfast before boarding the train. Thomas walked into their midst and announced that he had something to say to them, and a large crowd gathered, expecting a speech. When they were all clustered around him, Thomas took off his cap and waved it above his head. At this signal, a battery of artillery moved forward on one side, a loyal infantry regiment moved in on the other, and a cavalry detachment rushed in between the men and their guns. "There is your train," Thomas said. "I will give you five minutes to decide whether you will go back to duty or to [the military prison at] Dry Tortugas!" All but twenty decided to go back to duty, and the rest were placed under arrest.[61]

Thomas also had to deal with political divisions and disagreements among the officers and men of the regiment. Throughout the month of April, the officers and men discussed the coming conflict and debated what they should do. Robert E. Lee's decision to resign from the army was widely discussed, and individuals from the border states of Maryland, Missouri, and Kentucky thought about what they might do if their own states seceded. During two months that the regiment spent in Pennsylvania, one of its officers was arrested for suspicion of disloyalty, and several others resigned to join the Confederate service. The officers and soldiers who remained began to view one another with suspicion. One of Thomas's officers, Richard W. Johnson, later recalled that the paranoia in the regiment grew so great that one officer suspected another of disloyalty because he had inadvertently placed a stamp bearing Washington's portrait upside down on an envelope. The suspicious officer thought that "no loyal man would turn the image of the Father of his Country upside down."[62]

Nineteen of the thirty-six officers in the Second Cavalry eventually resigned to join the Confederate service. In May, in response to the many desertions, the War Department sent out an order requiring each officer to take again the oath he had sworn when he first joined the army. Thomas also had to retake the oath when he was promoted to lieutenant colonel to replace Robert E. Lee on April 25, and when he was promoted to colonel to replace Col. Albert Sidney Johnston on May 3. Richard Johnson considered the War Department's order to be "an uncalled-for insult to every officer in the army," and he asked Thomas what he thought it. "I do not care a snap of my finger about it," Thomas replied. "If they want me to take the oath before each meal I am ready to comply."[63]

As the regiment began moving south to its first campaign in Virginia, news came of the defeat of Gen. Benjamin Butler at the Battle of Big Bethel, in southeastern Virginia. Butler was a well-known Massachusetts politician and abolitionist, and one of the officers remarked during a meal that he was "glad the damned old abolitionist was whipped." Another officer replied, "It seems to me, sir, you are fighting on the wrong side," and an argument ensued. The officers prepared to fight a duel over the issue. At the next meal, Thomas called all the officers to attention and asked the two officers what had happened. The officer who had criticized Butler repeated what he said and defended his right to say what he wanted. Thomas did not agree. He stated, "with great emphasis," that the dispute "was not a mere personal matter but concerned the whole regiment." If the officer did mean what he said, then "he was fighting on the wrong side," and Thomas wanted there to be no more talk about this being a "damned abolition war." The argument stopped, and the duel was canceled.[64]

Thomas's own loyalty was put to the test later that month when he found himself in the front lines of a Federal invasion of Virginia. Six of the Second Cavalry's ten companies had been detached to defend

Washington, but the other four were assigned to scout the advance of an
infantry force, commanded by Maj. Gen. Robert Patterson, that was to
cross the Potomac near Williamsport, Maryland, about seventy miles west
of Washington. Their goal was to recapture the federal arsenal town of
Harpers Ferry and proceed southward to occupy the Shenandoah Valley.
On June 1 Thomas and his four companies of cavalry joined Patterson's
force at Chambersburg, where a detachment of volunteer Pennsylvania
cavalry and a brigade of Pennsylvania volunteer infantry were added to
Thomas's command.[65]

While at Chambersburg, Thomas had time to discuss the coming war
with other officers. One of these men, Alexander McClure, remembered
a conversation at a dinner party at his home, attended by Generals Patterson, Cadwallader, Doubleday, and Keim, Colonel Thomas, Maj. Fitz John
Porter, and Senator John Sherman, William Tecumseh Sherman's brother.
In discussing the impending war, most of the officers agreed that a major
battle would have to be fought but thought that after a single battle the
two sides would make peace on a compromise basis. Doubleday dissented,
arguing that it would be a long and terrible war. McClure recalled that
Thomas said almost nothing but agreed with Doubleday. Later, McClure
tried to talk to Thomas privately regarding his feelings about the coming
war but found that Thomas was still reluctant to say much about it.[66]

As Patterson's force moved southward, Joseph E. Johnston, who
commanded the force occupying Harpers Ferry, decided the town was
indefensible and abandoned it. He moved the arms and manufacturing
equipment out of the arsenal and withdrew southward to Winchester,
Virginia. Patterson crossed the Potomac on June 16 at Williamsport and
moved downstream toward Harpers Ferry.[67]

The night before the crossing, Thomas received a visit from his old
friend William Tecumseh Sherman, now a colonel, who was there visiting
his senator brother John, who was acting briefly as a volunteer officer on
Patterson's staff. William T. Sherman had written John the week before,
criticizing most of the officers in Patterson's command but describing
Thomas and another officer as "A-Number One men." Sherman told his
brother to "mention my name to both, and say to them that I wish them
all the success they aspire to, and if in the varying chances of war I should
ever be so placed I would name such as them for high places." Sherman
added, however, "Thomas is a Virginian from near Norfolk, and say what
he may, he must feel unpleasant at leading an invading army. But if he says

he will do it, I think he will do it well. He was never brilliant, but always cool, reliable, and steady—maybe a little slow."[68]

When Sherman arrived at camp, he asked Thomas how he felt about the war, and Thomas assured him that he was firm in his decision to stay loyal to the Union. The two friends then spread a large map of the United States out on the floor and speculated about the crucial points in the coming war, singling out Richmond, Vicksburg, Nashville, Chattanooga, and Knoxville as the points most likely to be fought over in the war to come. In his memoirs John Sherman stated that it "appeared strange that they were able confidently and correctly to designate the lines of operations and strategic points of a war not yet commenced, and more strange still that they should be leading actors in great battles at the places designated by them at this country tavern."[69]

Thomas crossed into Virginia with his brigade on June 16 but did not stay long. The next day, General in Chief Scott ordered Patterson to send part of his force back to Washington in order to assure the safety of the capital. Patterson, worried that he did not have enough troops to support an advance, ordered Thomas's brigade to return to Maryland, and Thomas retreated across the river on the evening of June 17. Thomas waited in Maryland for two weeks as Patterson built up his forces again, and he then returned to Virginia on July 2, crossing the Potomac near Martinsburg, in what is now the state of West Virginia.[70]

Confederate officers soon learned that Thomas was serving with the invading army. On June 18 Confederate colonel J.E.B. Stuart, Thomas's former student, wrote his wife, "Old George H. Thomas is in command of the cavalry of the enemy. I would like to hang, *hang* him as traitor to his native state." In the original letter, one can see where the ink smudged as Stuart bore down hard on his pen in writing and underlining the word "hang." There is little doubt that he meant it.[71] Stuart got the chance to confront Thomas on July 2, during Thomas's first active fighting of the Civil War, on the soil of his own state. During the first day's march, Thomas's brigade was second in the line of march, and as they passed near Falling Waters, Virginia, on the way to Martinsburg, they heard the sounds of fighting from up ahead. A force of infantry, cavalry, and artillery was posted there to oppose their advance, under the leadership of J.E.B. Stuart and Thomas Jackson, soon to be known as "Stonewall" Jackson.[72]

Thomas put his infantry in line to the left of the brigade already engaged and posted part of a battery of artillery in the front line. The

Union forces now outnumbered and outflanked the Confederate defenders, and the artillery soon began to take effect. The Confederates retreated in haste and the Union forces pursued, passing over the Confederate camp and capturing some of their supplies. The true number of casualties in this skirmish is uncertain. Union reports state that Thomas's brigade suffered no casualties, and that the other Union brigade suffered fifteen casualties and one soldier missing. The Union reports estimate that the Confederates lost sixty to eighty killed and an unknown number of wounded. The Confederate report claims that an unknown number of Union troops were killed and forty-nine were captured, while the Confederates only lost three of their own men. In reality, there were probably few casualties on either side in this brief delaying action. The fighting had little effect on the campaign to come, but Thomas was pleased to see that his troops acted "with the utmost coolness and precision" during this engagement, their first experience under fire. Thomas's troops moved forward and occupied Martinsburg on July 3.[73]

Having crossed the Potomac, Patterson was supposed to move south to prevent Johnston's force, posted to the southwest at Winchester, from joining up with the main rebel force at Manassas, to the southeast. But Patterson found it difficult to move forward. On July 9 he decided to move down the Potomac to Charlestown, seven miles to the southeast, from which point a good road led southward. Using Charlestown as a base, it would be much easier for the army to advance and remain in supply. The army's subordinate commanders, including Thomas, approved of this decision, even though it delayed his advance against Johnston.[74]

While Patterson moved slowly in the Shenandoah Valley, a more successful campaign took place farther west. Union troops led by George B. McClellan and William S. Rosecrans defeated a smaller Confederate force at the Battles of Rich Mountain and Corrick's Ford, returning the northwestern counties of Virginia to Union control. Later that year, Rosecrans solidified his control of the area and fought off a Confederate counteroffensive, securing what later became the state of West Virginia. In addition to the successes of McClellan and Rosecrans, a Union force in Missouri under Nathaniel Lyon defeated the Confederate force there and took control of nearly the entire state.

On July 15 Patterson finally began moving south out of Charlestown, encountering only minor opposition from J.E.B. Stuart's cavalry. Thomas's brigade, which was posted at the front of the army, fought a brief skirmish with Stuart's cavalry at a town called Bunker Hill. As he approached Winchester, Patterson paused again and asked General in Chief Scott for further instructions. Most of his soldiers were three-month volunteers, whose enlistment was about to expire, and the volunteers were not willing to serve past the expiration of their enlistments. Reluctant to attack Johnston with these unreliable troops, Patterson requested permission to retreat again to the Potomac. Stuart kept up cavalry movements in Patterson's front, tricking him into believing that Johnston's main force was still at Winchester. In the meantime, Johnston marched his entire army south to a rail line and then moved the troops by rail to Manassas.

Johnston's force thus escaped Patterson and reinforced P. G. T. Beauregard's men at the Battle of Bull Run (Manassas) on July 20. After a day of intense and inconclusive fighting, the arrival of Johnston's fresh troops during the afternoon tipped the balance in favor of the Confederates. While the Union troops at first fell back slowly, the retreat soon became disorganized and turned into a rout, with panicked officers and men running away from the battlefield as quickly as possible. Thomas's friend William T. Sherman commanded a brigade during the battle, and Sherman played a significant and positive role in keeping his troops in order to form a rearguard for the rest of the army. Patterson was widely condemned for allowing Johnston's force to slip away from him, and on July 27 Winfield Scott relieved Patterson of command and put Gen. Nathaniel Banks in his place.[75]

Shortly after Patterson's removal, Thomas was called to Kentucky to serve under Maj. Gen. Robert Anderson. Anderson, a native of Kentucky, had commanded the U.S. garrison at Fort Sumter during its siege and surrender, and he was considered a hero in the North. He was appointed to command the Union effort in Kentucky in the hopes that his prestige would encourage that state to stay in the Union. He was allowed to select four brigadier generals to serve under him and had already selected three: William T. Sherman, Don Carlos Buell, and Ormsby M. Mitchel. General Anderson's nephew, Thomas A. Anderson, who had served under George Thomas in Virginia, now visited his uncle in Washington. Thomas Anderson recommended Thomas for the fourth appointment, assuring his uncle of Thomas's competence and loyalty. Sherman also recommended Thomas to General Anderson.[76] On August 17, 1861, Thomas was promoted to brigadier general of volunteers on General Anderson's request, and on August 26, 1861, Thomas was transferred out of the

Second Cavalry and ordered to Kentucky. Thomas wrote Anderson on August 26 to state that he would be in Cincinnati on September 1, adding that he was glad to be serving with Sherman, whom he considered an "old and valued friend."[77]

Only seven months had passed since Thomas left Southampton County to visit his wife's family in New York, but tremendous changes had occurred since then. War had seemed a remote possibility but was now a reality, and Thomas had been forced to choose between his nation and his state, between his duty and his family. He then had rushed into a whirlwind of duties and responsibilities, training raw recruits and throwing them into action in Maryland and northern Virginia. He performed well under the pressure, training his men to act as effective cavalry troops their engagements with the Confederate force. Although the campaign had failed, his participation was successful and he received a promotion to brigadier general of volunteers and assignment to an independent command in southeastern Kentucky. There he would face problems of training, discipline, and supply that exceeded all his previous experience and would also have his first test as an independent commander in a major battle.

CHAPTER SIX

Mill Springs

Damn this speech-making! I won't speak! What does a man want to make a speech for, anyhow?

Thomas's service in Kentucky was difficult from both a military and a political standpoint. Kentucky had declared its neutrality in the secession crisis, neither seceding from the Union nor cooperating with the federal effort to suppress the rebellion. Kentucky would not let the troops of either side cross its borders, but the state government did allow the federal government to set up recruiting camps for Unionist volunteers. Thomas's first assignment was to command one of these recruiting camps in southeastern Kentucky. Open war broke out in Kentucky soon after Thomas's arrival, and Thomas had to quickly turn his mob of recruits into an effective fighting force. His goals were to defend Kentucky against Confederate invasion and, if possible, to advance southward and liberate Unionist East Tennessee. Thomas's skill in training, supply, and logistics served him well, and he soon turned his recruits into an effective army and won a significant victory at Mill Springs.

On September 6, when Thomas arrived in Kentucky, the state still claimed to be neutral in the secession crisis, despite the extensive military activities that were being carried out on its soil. Lincoln had handled Kentucky's declaration of neutrality carefully, denying any legal right to neutrality but respecting the state's wishes in practice. His careful approach was working, as Unionist candidates had won large majorities in state and federal elections held over the summer.[1] Meanwhile, both Unionist and secessionist Kentuckians had begun to arm themselves. The

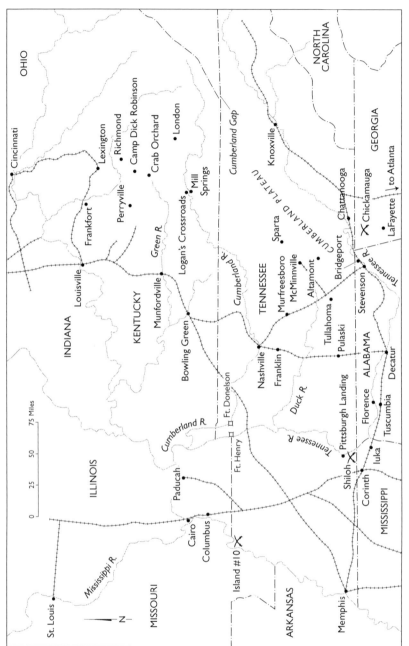

Kentucky and Tennessee Campaigns

secessionist governor of Kentucky had encouraged the formation of a prosecession militia, called the State Guard, and Unionist Kentuckians responded by forming their own militia, the Home Guard, which Lincoln covertly supported with weapons and other supplies.

In August, after the state legislative elections, Lincoln authorized the federal recruitment of Unionists from eastern Kentucky and East Tennessee, and he sent a navy lieutenant, William Nelson, into the state to organize their recruitment and training. Nelson set up a recruiting station and training camp on land owned by a local pro-Union citizen, Richard M. Robinson, in east-central Kentucky, south of the town of Lexington. The camp, called Camp Dick Robinson, soon became one of the largest Union army posts in the state. On September 12 Thomas was assigned to command at Camp Dick Robinson, with the responsibilities of training the force of recruits there to be soldiers, and using the force to keep southeastern Kentucky under Union control.[2]

Meanwhile, the Confederates violated Kentucky's neutrality by crossing into the state's territory and occupying the town of Columbus on September 4. The commander of the occupying force, Gen. Leonidas Polk, justified his action as a defensive measure, as the city commanded a strategic position on the Mississippi River that guarded the approaches to Memphis. The Kentucky legislature demanded that the Confederates leave the city, but Polk refused. On September 6 a Union force under Brig. Gen. Ulysses S. Grant occupied Paducah, Kentucky, a strategic position on the Ohio River northeast of Columbus. In this case, the Kentucky legislature did not protest Grant's move, as they considered the Confederates to be the aggressor.[3] Realizing that their state could no longer remain neutral, the legislature voted on September 18 to side with the Union.

With the truce broken, both sides hurried to advance their armies into the state. A Confederate force under the command of Gen. Simon Bolivar Buckner advanced from Nashville to Bowling Green, then continued north toward Louisville. To meet this threat Maj. Gen. Robert Anderson sent a force of new recruits and Home Guards southward under the command of Brig. Gen. William T. Sherman. Sherman's force took up position on a ridge of hills about thirty miles south of Louisville, and Buckner's force returned to Bowling Green. Neither commander felt that his troops were prepared to fight a battle, so they remained in these positions for several months. Union troops also moved to take control of

Lexington and the state capital, Frankfort, while Confederates moved north from East Tennessee to occupy southeastern Kentucky.[4]

When Thomas arrived at Camp Dick Robinson, he found six regiments of untrained recruits, three infantry regiments and one cavalry regiment from Kentucky, and two infantry regiments from East Tennessee, about six thousand men in all. The previous commander, Lieutenant Nelson, had been strict to the point of being a bully, and the men had resented his overbearing leadership style and arbitrary infliction of punishments. Despite Nelson's strictness, the men had not yet learned proper drill. Thomas wrote Sherman on September 19, a week after assuming command, that the troops were still only "a mob of men," not fit to take the field. While he lacked arms, ammunition, and supplies, Thomas's worst problem was a lack of trained subordinate officers capable of doing administrative and logistical tasks. Until he was assigned such officers, or was able to train the volunteer officers at the camp, Thomas had to do all of these duties himself. He wrote Sherman that though he recognized that he ought to be among the men, administrative duties kept him in his office most of the day. Thomas "almost despaired" of ever getting his command into a fit condition.[5]

Thomas worked day and night to train volunteer officers, secure adequate supplies and weapons, and teach the men the basics of drill and formation fighting. While Thomas was frustrated that he could not spend more time with the men, he made the right choice in concentrating on administration, supply, and the training of officers, as these were the first priorities in getting the soldiers ready to fight. For their part, the volunteers appreciated Thomas's strict but fair discipline and his concern for their welfare. According to one soldier, Thomas "was not as much seen as General Nelson," but "his administration was agreeably felt."[6]

One of the first tests of Thomas's leadership came when an outbreak of measles affected the camp. The camp lacked good medical facilities, and many of the men sent to the camp infirmary died. (This was common during the Civil War; twice as many men died of disease than died in battle.) Many of the soldiers had family or friends nearby, and Thomas gave these men furloughs so they could be cared for in private homes. Most of these sick men recovered and later returned to their units.[7]

Another test of Thomas's leadership came only a week after he arrived, when his position at Camp Dick Robinson was threatened by Confederate movements in both the front and the rear. From East Tennessee, a

Confederate force under Gen. Felix Zollicoffer advanced northward toward Thomas's camp. At the same time, Confederate sympathizers in central Kentucky posted handbills and took out newspaper advertisements calling for "State-Rights" and "Peace-Men" to gather at the fairgrounds at Lexington on September 20 for the purpose of having a "camp drill." Union officials suspected that this call for a "camp drill" was really a call to form a pro-Confederate militia in Lexington, which would then seize the armories in Lexington and Frankfort. Thomas sent a regiment of infantry to the Lexington fairgrounds with orders to observe the gathering. If the gathering remained peaceful, he instructed, the troops were not to interfere, but if the men seemed to be preparing to launch a military campaign, his soldiers were to arrest them. When the Union troops arrived in Lexington, the assembly was called off. Thomas's men arrested some of the secessionist leaders, but most of them managed to flee the state.[8]

At the same time, Thomas sent two regiments of infantry south to a line along the Rockcastle Hills, near the town of London, to prevent Zollicoffer's men from advancing further. Finding his way blocked, Zollicoffer decided not to risk a battle and retreated to Barboursville. The front stabilized along these lines, and Thomas returned to training and equipping his men. His letters and dispatches from this period are full of requests for more food, clothing, tents, ammunition, and transport wagons. He also needed mustering officers to do the record-keeping tasks involved in enrolling the volunteers into regiments, a quartermaster to handle supplies, a medical officer to treat the outbreak of measles in the camp, and an engineer to help with building fortifications. At first he performed all these tasks himself, but by the end of October the army had sent him enough trained officers to form a competent staff.[9]

Thomas maintained a good relationship with his men, but his interaction with them was formal, and he did not joke with them or otherwise socialize with them the way some other commanders did. He also did not make speeches, issue inspirational proclamations, or try to present a charismatic presence through fancy clothing or ostentatious riding. His plain, slow manner of riding and speaking formed such a contrast with the behavior of other officers that his soldiers began calling him by the nickname he had at West Point, "Slow Trot." His solicitude for his men's welfare was even more striking, and the nickname the men most commonly used was "Old Pap Thomas."

Thomas worked hard to get the raw volunteer recruits trained and ready for battle. One officer noticed the difference between Thomas's leadership and that of other commanders soon after his regiment's arrival at Camp Dick Robinson. His regiment had already been trained at another recruiting camp, and he thought they were fairly well prepared. Shortly after their arrival at the camp, the men were awakened in the middle of the night by the sound of the "long roll," the alarm that called men to battle. The men got up and tried to form ranks, only to find that they could not assemble quickly because they had left their clothing, weapons, and accoutrements scattered all over the camp and could not find them in the darkness. Many of their officers performed poorly, failing to form the men into companies or to form the companies into a regimental formation. When they discovered that the alarm was only a drill, the men were relieved, but they were also embarrassed by their poor performance. They worked hard to improve and responded much better in the future. Thomas's preparation and training helps explain the good performance of his troops later on, in meeting a real surprise attack at the Battle of Mill Springs.[10]

On one occasion, Gen. William T. Sherman, Senator Andrew Johnson, and some other politicians and officials visited Camp Dick Robinson, where they reviewed the troops and made speeches. One of Thomas's aides, R. M. Kelly, recalled that Thomas avoided the speechmaking by sitting in his office and working on his correspondence. Absorbed in his work, Thomas did not notice that Kelly was present in the room with him. When the soldiers called on Sherman to make a speech, Thomas realized that they would probably want him to make a speech as well. He paced in agitation as Sherman spoke. Finally, when Sherman finished, the soldiers began calling out for Thomas. "Damn this speech-making!" Thomas shouted. "I won't speak! What does a man want to make a speech for, anyhow?" He then noticed Kelly's presence and strode out of the room in embarrassment, slamming the door behind him. He spent the rest of the evening in his quarters.[11]

Once Thomas had trained and equipped the men under his command, he planned to march southward to invade East Tennessee. Like western Virginia, eastern Kentucky, and the other mountainous regions of the South, East Tennessee had few slaves, and most of the population there supported the Union. East Tennessee was thus important politically, and Lincoln himself strongly favored an early offensive into the region to liberate its loyal citizens from Confederate rule. Though less important from a military standpoint, it had some strategic importance in that the Confederacy's main east–west railroad, which connected Tennessee with Richmond, ran through the region. If an invasion could sever this rail line, it would be more difficult for the Confederacy to ship supplies and troops to the Virginia theater.

Thomas was eager to advance into East Tennessee, and in early October he wrote Anderson that he was nearly ready to advance. His plan was ambitious, unrealistically so, given the problems of movement and supply he would face in the mountainous region. Once he received more men and supplies, Thomas wrote, he would "enter Tennessee by way of Somerset, move on Knoxville, seize the railroad, push toward Nashville and Greenville, and destroy the bridges as near to Nashville and Greenville as we can get, and then turn upon Zollicoffer whilst he is in the passes of the Cumberland. Being between him and his supplies, he could soon be captured or destroyed." The leaders of the East Tennessee Unionists proposed to cooperate with Thomas's advance by ordering local partisans to destroy railroad bridges in the area, thus delaying the movement of Confederate troops and supplies to the front. Sherman initially opposed the plan, but Thomas convinced him to go ahead with it. Lincoln, who took a personal interest in freeing the loyal citizens of East Tennessee from Confederate rule, endorsed the proposal and arranged for Thomas to receive reinforcements.[12]

At this point, only a month after he had taken command at Camp Dick Robinson, Thomas had organized his forces, helped consolidate Union political control of central and eastern Kentucky, and formulated a plan to advance into East Tennessee. He had also successfully opposed a Confederate attempt to advance into eastern Kentucky. Despite this progress, it seemed that Thomas's superiors in Washington were not satisfied with his performance. On October 10 the War Department ordered Brig. Gen. O. M. Mitchel to report to Camp Dick Robinson to take command of an invasion of East Tennessee. The orders did not specify what Thomas's role would be, but they apparently intended that Thomas should remain in the area as second-in-command to Mitchel.[13]

Mitchel was the commander of the Department of the Ohio, which consisted of the states of Ohio and Indiana and a small part of Kentucky. His previous duties had consisted of recruiting troops and acquiring food, supplies, and ammunition to send to the front in Kentucky. Thomas wrote to Mitchel, "I have been doing all in my power to prepare the troops for a move on Cumberland Ford and to seize the Tennessee and Virginia Railroad, and shall continue to do all I can to assist you until your arrival here." He provided Mitchel with some details about recent activity at the camp and recent troop movements, demonstrating that he was willing to assist Mitchel by giving him information that would help him assume command. At the same time, Thomas told Mitchel that "justice to myself requires that I ask to be relieved from duty with these troops, since the Secretary has thought it necessary to supersede me in the command, without, as I conceive, any just cause for so doing."[14]

Thomas's protest was understandable, as he had been doing well in his command and his replacement was not justified by his performance. However, the decision to appoint Mitchel as his superior was also a reasonable one. Mitchel was a native Kentuckian who was well known as a scientist and community leader. While Thomas had more combat experience, Mitchel had performed effectively in his earlier duties and seemed competent to lead in the field. As Kentucky had only recently joined the Union war effort, it was politically wise to appoint a native Kentuckian to a field command.[15]

By this time William T. Sherman was in overall command in Kentucky, having been promoted on October 8 after Robert Anderson stepped down for reasons of poor health. Sherman attempted to support Thomas in retaining his command. On October 11, just before Thomas received word of Mitchel's being sent to Camp Dick Robinson, Sherman wrote Thomas and encouraged him to make some sort of advance southward, even just a "show of force." "Of necessity," Sherman wrote, "I cannot give minute directions, and can only say that if your men simply move, the effect will be good." The meaning of this strange directive soon became clear when Thomas received notice of his replacement by Mitchel. Sherman had been trying to warn Thomas to begin a movement southward, so that he could claim that an invasion of East Tennessee had already begun.[16]

Sherman continued to support Thomas during the days that followed. He replied sympathetically to Thomas's letter of protest stating, "I would start for your camp at once, but am notified by the Secretary of War that he will be here to meet me." He reassured Thomas that "General Mitchel is subject to my orders, and I will, if possible, give you the opportunity of completing what you have begun." However, he warned Thomas that he might not be able to do so, and encouraged him to stay regardless of the result. "[O]f course I would do anything in my power to carry out your wishes," Sherman wrote, "but feel that the affairs of Kentucky call for the united action of all engaged in the cause of preserving our Government."[17]

Over the course of the following week, Sherman met with Secretary of War Simon Cameron and Adj. Gen. Lorenzo Thomas, who had come to Kentucky on a tour of inspection. On October 16 Cameron telegraphed President Lincoln that "matters are in a much worse condition than I expected to find them." Cameron's personal inspection made him finally realize that the army's inability to advance was not the fault of the commanders, but the result of their lack of ammunition, supplies, and trained, reliable soldiers. On October 20 Mitchel was ordered to remain at his post organizing troops and supplies in Cincinnati, meaning that Thomas's command had been preserved. Even better, Thomas received additional troops and an experienced field officer, Brig. Gen. Albin Schoepf, to serve under his orders. By the end of October, Thomas's command had expanded from the six poorly supplied volunteer regiments he had found upon his arrival at Camp Dick Robinson to sixteen regiments and several batteries of artillery. The ten new regiments were made up from one regular infantry regiment and nine volunteer regiments from Ohio, Indiana, Minnesota, Michigan, and Wisconsin. All but one of the new regiments were properly armed and equipped. The regiments were soon organized into three brigades of four regiments each and were designated the First Division of the Army of the Ohio.[18]

When Albin Schoepf reported for duty, Thomas sent him to command his advance position, south of Camp Dick Robinson near the Rockcastle River, while Thomas stayed in camp and continued training and organizing his force. On October 21 Schoepf's force of about five thousand men was attacked by a Confederate force of about equal size. As the Union men occupied a strong, fortified defensive position in a line of hills, they repulsed the attack easily, with losses of about twenty-four men killed or wounded on the Union side and about fifty-three on the side of the Confederates. Thomas was delighted with the results of the battle, and afterward he went to the Rockcastle River position to congratulate his troops and inspect the battlefield.[19]

The Confederates retreated after the battle, and Thomas pushed his own line forward slightly. He moved his base camp to the town of Crab Orchard, about fifteen miles south of Camp Dick Robinson, and Schoepf advanced to the town of London, about thirty-five miles southeast of Crab Orchard. Continuing to prepare for a move into East Tennessee, Thomas began improving the roads and building a forward supply depot. He also organized a company of "pioneers," special troops who could construct and repair roads, bridges, and fortifications. Thomas wrote Sherman to state that all he required to launch an offensive were four armed, trained regiments and some more supply wagons. Unfortunately, commanders in all areas of the country were asking for reinforcements, so there were not four regiments available.[20]

Meanwhile, Unionist partisans continued to mobilize in East Tennessee. On November 8 Unionist guerrillas rose up to destroy bridges and telegraph lines and then assembled in anticipation of meeting the invading Union army to join it as volunteers. The invasion never came. Sherman had become convinced that a large Confederate army had invaded Kentucky and was moving into position to cut off Thomas's force from the Union troops defending Louisville. Sherman wanted to concentrate all his forces to meet the invasion, and he ordered Thomas to move his troops northwest, toward Louisville. While Thomas complied with Sherman's orders, he protested that the intelligence he had received did not indicate that an invasion was in progress.[21]

Sherman's order to retreat filled the Tennessee recruits with fury and despair. Instead of advancing to reclaim their homes, as they had long expected, they were retreating, leaving their friends and relatives back home to face arrest and persecution by the Confederate authorities. When some of the troops mutinied, Thomas allowed Brig. Gen. Samuel Carter, a respected leader from East Tennessee, to handle the situation. Carter spoke with his men at length and finally convinced them to obey orders. At one point, loyalist Tennessee senator Andrew Johnson and Representative Horace Maynard threatened to take control of the Tennessee regiments themselves and march them southward, but Thomas prevented them from doing so.[22]

Sherman's retreat order was a disastrous error. Not only was he mistaken about the Confederate invasion—there was none—but he had also misinterpreted the entire military and political situation in Kentucky. Sherman, who commanded eighteen thousand soldiers, estimated that the Confederates in Kentucky outnumbered him five to one, but in reality, the Union and the Confederacy had equal numbers of men. The Confederates had tricked Sherman by keeping their troops in constant motion, creating the impression of having a greater force than they really had. These movements had also tricked Sherman into believing that a Confederate invasion was in progress. Sherman was also convinced that the population of Kentucky was largely pro-Confederate and was ready at any moment to rise up against his occupying force, whereas in reality, a majority of Kentuckians were pro-Union.[23] The consequences for the East Tennessee Unionists were harsh. In the aftermath of the guerrilla operations in the region, five Unionists were tried and executed for treason, and an unknown number were summarily killed. More than one thousand Unionists were arrested, and over two hundred of them were sent to military prisons in the Deep South.

Sherman's retreat order and its consequences led to widespread criticism against Sherman, Thomas, and everyone else involved in the campaign. In eastern Kentucky Andrew Johnson openly criticized the military leadership within the hearing of the officers and men. One of Thomas's subordinates, General Schoepf, fell into an argument with Johnson, outside Thomas's headquarters in the public square of Crab Orchard, Kentucky. As the two men argued, Schoepf became more and more angry, finally threatening to have Johnson expelled from the camp. Johnson responded that he was a U.S. senator and dared Schoepf to expel him. At this point Thomas intervened, leaving his headquarters near the square and walking through the crowd of onlookers toward Schoepf. Without saying a word, he took Schoepf by the arm and escorted him back into headquarters, ending the argument. Thomas continued to handle Johnson carefully and tactfully and maintained good relations with the difficult and argumentative Unionist politician throughout the war.[24]

The East Tennessee debacle, combined with other errors in his command of the Kentucky theater, almost ended Sherman's career. On October 17 Sherman shocked Secretary of War Cameron by stating that he would need a force of sixty thousand men just to defend Kentucky, and more than two hundred thousand to invade Tennessee. This statement, along with Sherman's orders canceling the invasion of East Tennessee, led Cameron to believe that Sherman was no longer mentally fit for his command. In late October the War Department sent an officer to Kentucky to observe the situation, and the officer concluded that Sherman was on the verge of nervous exhaustion. On November 13 Sherman's superiors approved a request that Sherman had made earlier to be relieved of his command.

The problems in Kentucky were just one of a series of setbacks to the Union cause in late 1861. At the Battle of Wilson's Creek, in Missouri, a Union army under Nathaniel Lyon was soundly defeated, and Lyon was killed during the battle. His men retreated to Springfield, the state capital, leaving a large part of southern Missouri in Confederate hands. Stalemate continued in Virginia, as the new commander of the Army of the Potomac, George B. McClellan, insisted that he needed to train and prepare his men before beginning an offensive against Richmond.

After Sherman left Kentucky, the senior command position fell to Maj. Gen. Don Carlos Buell. Like Thomas, Buell was a West Point graduate with decades of experience in the regular army, and had served with distinction in the Mexican-American War. Buell was calm and aloof in demeanor and was serious and strict with the men. He was effective in organizing, training, and supplying his soldiers, but somehow he never won their affection in the way that Thomas had. The men detected kindness behind Thomas's impassive exterior, but they sensed only more sternness in Buell. By the time Buell took over from Sherman, it had become obvious that the supposed Confederate invasion of central Kentucky was only a figment of Sherman's imagination. Buell canceled Sherman's orders for Thomas to move closer to Louisville and told Thomas to hold an advanced line of defense in eastern Kentucky. Thomas moved his troops forward to occupy a line stretching from London to Somerset and remained there throughout November and December. The Confederates made some minor attacks during this time, but neither side undertook any significant offensive.

Thomas, who still wanted to advance into East Tennessee, was frustrated to discover that Buell did not support his plans. Buell considered Nashville to be the most important goal of the campaign. Not only was it the state capital, but it was also an important strategic point, located at the junction of the Tennessee River and the north–south railroad that the Confederate commander, Albert S. Johnston, was using to supply his forces around Bowling Green. Buell discounted East Tennessee as strategically unimportant and was reluctant to advance directly into the region from Kentucky because of the difficulties inherent in bringing supplies across the mountains. Instead, he planned on spending the rest of his winter preparing his army, then launching an offensive against Johnston's army in Bowling Green, with the goal of eventually capturing Nashville. Only after Nashville was under his control would he try to move eastward, along the line of the Tennessee River and the state's main east–west railroad, to capture Chattanooga, Knoxville, and the rest of the eastern part of the state.[25]

Buell's appointment to command meant that Thomas's plan to invade East Tennessee was postponed indefinitely. Instead, a Confederate force invaded eastern Kentucky. In December 1861 a Confederate army commanded by Gen. Felix Zollicoffer moved north from Tennessee and crossed the Cumberland River near the town of Mill Springs, intending to attack Thomas's forces in central Kentucky. After crossing the river, Zollicoffer stopped and entrenched on the north bank. Soon afterward, heavy rains caused the river's level to rise, making it difficult for Zollicoffer to receive reinforcements and making it impossible for him to retreat. Buell and Thomas realized that Zollicoffer's army was trapped with the river blocking its retreat. They tried to move quickly to concentrate a stronger force and attack Zollicoffer, before he could get away.[26]

Thomas began advancing to Mill Springs in early January, but the same heavy rains that blocked Zollicoffer's retreat slowed Thomas's advance. The men had to stop at every swollen creek and river, and the rain turned the roads into a mass of mud. It took them sixteen days to march the sixty-four miles between Crab Orchard and Mill Springs. The supply wagons had an even more difficult time on the roads, and the men often went hungry. The muddy soil of the region was the same color as the soap issued by the commissary, and the miserable soldiers joked they were making the advance in order to protect the army's source of soap supplies. Thomas had intended to link up with Schoepf's force at Mill Springs, but the bad roads delayed Schoepf's advance even more than Thomas's. On January 17 Thomas set up camp at Logan's Crossroads, ten miles north of Mill Springs, and waited for Schoepf to join him.[27]

During this time, Thomas made the acquaintance of an unusual character, a sixty-four-year-old civilian wagon master named Wilk Beatty. When Beatty's wagon train arrived at Logan's Crossroads, he tried to unload immediately, as his orders were to return the wagons to the supply base as soon as possible. But the commissary officer refused to let him unload, explaining that he had no dry place to store the provisions. In the words of the historian of Beatty's regiment, the wagon master then "broke for Thomas' tent, and entered without ceremony, and in his rattling, garrulous way demanded a place to unload the stores. . . . His frank clattering way of talking, and his entire innocence to what was due persons of rank or station, amused the old general; and strange to say, the two became intimate friends, and often during the war, would engage in friendly chats, planning what they would do when the war was over." Their friendship lasted throughout the war, and the regimental historian reports that "no man in the corps got more favors from General Thomas than did the old wagon master."[28]

Thomas did not now have long to wait for a resolution of the campaign. Zollicoffer's superior officer, Maj. Gen. George B. Crittenden, having joined the Confederate army in the field, realized that their position was dangerous. As the Cumberland River was too high to cross with their supply wagons and heavy equipment, retreat would be difficult. Instead, Zollicoffer and Crittenden decided to attack Thomas's force at Logan's Crossroads before Schoepf's troops could join him. Intending to launch a surprise dawn attack, they set out on a night march on the evening of January 18.

Thomas was prepared for them. His pickets had already skirmished with Zollicoffer's advance forces on the night of January 17, so he knew that the enemy was close. As a precaution against a surprise attack, Thomas put the entire army on alert, and he had several lines of guards posted around the camp. There was no fighting on January 18, but Thomas's troops remained on alert as they waited for Schoepf to join them. When the Confederates attacked at dawn on January 19, Thomas's soldiers were ready.[29]

Thomas awoke at 6:30 to the sound of alarms and scattered firing. He ordered the "long roll" to be beaten, calling all troops to arms, and got dressed for battle.[30] Knowing that soldiers took courage from the presence and appearance of their commander, he put on his new brigadier general's uniform, the first time that he had worn it. After first ordering a battalion of engineers and a company of infantry to remain at camp and guard the supplies, he rode toward the sound of firing. As Thomas moved forward, he met up with Col. Mahlon Manson, the commander of the Tenth Indiana Volunteer Infantry, who had rushed back from the front to inform Thomas that the enemy was attacking. Thomas, nervous before the first major battle in which he would hold independent command, lost his temper. "Damn you, sir," he yelled at Manson, "go back to your command and fight with it." Manson immediately returned to the front. As Thomas continued forward, he found part of Manson's regiment standing in

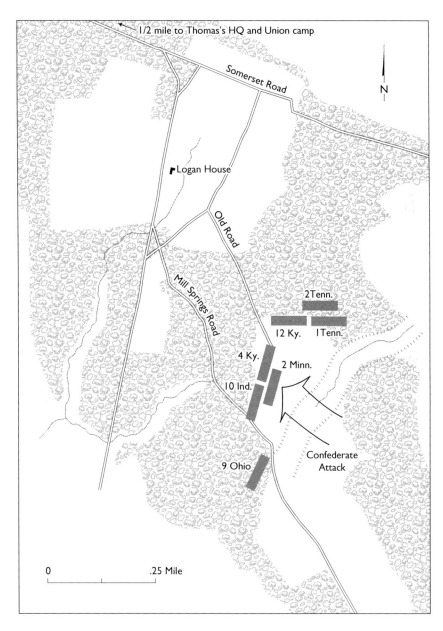

1/2 mile to Thomas's HQ and Union camp

Somerset Road

N

Logan House

Old Road

Mill Springs Road

2 Tenn.

12 Ky.   1 Tenn.

4 Ky.

2 Minn.

10 Ind.

Confederate
Attack

9 Ohio

0   .25 Mile

Mill Springs

formation at their camp, awaiting orders, and he commanded them to march toward the sound of firing.[31]

When Thomas arrived at the front, he found the Fourth Kentucky Infantry, the First Kentucky Cavalry, and part of the Tenth Indiana Infantry formed in line of battle, holding off the attack of a much larger Confederate force. The Tenth Indiana and First Kentucky Cavalry had been the first to meet the Confederates' attack, and Col. Speed S. Fry, the commander of the Fourth Kentucky Infantry, had ordered his men forward to support them. The Union line stretched along a road, and the men had taken positions behind a fence. Woods lay to their rear, and their line faced a cornfield. The Confederates had advanced from the cover of another wood, through the cornfield, and had taken shelter in a ravine near the road. Protected by the ravine, they were sending a deadly fire against the Union defenders, while other troops advanced on the Union right flank. Unless Thomas did something soon, the men, outnumbered in front and outflanked on the right, would certainly break and run.

Thomas sent an aide to call more troops forward. He placed artillery on the left flank of his line, where it could fire on the Confederates who were moving to outflank him. When the Second Minnesota and the Ninth Ohio came up to the front, he ordered the Second Minnesota to reinforce the main line and ordered the Ohio regiment to extend the line to the right. Both regiments soon met the enemy, and this established a stable line. Fierce fighting continued for nearly half an hour; at one point the Confederates got so close to the Union line that the soldiers stabbed at each other through the fence with their bayonets. Despite the fierceness of the attack, the Union line held. Three regiments of Kentucky and Tennessee volunteers came to the front, and Thomas ordered them to extend the left of his line and outflank the Confederates.[32]

By this point, it was clear to the Confederate soldiers that their attempt to surprise the Union army had failed. The Union men felt encouraged by the reinforcements that kept arriving, and the Confederates began to feel that the battle was going against them. The Union men were well rested, but the Confederates were tired, having marched all night on muddy roads just to reach the Union camp. Some of them had useless weapons, old flintlock muskets that failed to fire in the damp weather. The two sides were about equal in numbers, but the Confederate commanders had mismanaged their regiments' alignment, putting them too close together to be effective. They were so close together that Thomas was able to outflank them, even though he did not have more troops on the field. Finally, both of the Confederate generals were out of the action. Early in the battle, Zollicoffer had accidentally ridden into Union lines and had been shot. Crittenden, who was strangely absent from the field, did not direct his troops' movements; later on, Crittenden was accused of being drunk during the battle, and he was relieved of command.

As the three Tennessee and Kentucky regiments moved forward on the left, the commander of the Ninth Ohio Infantry on the right, Robert McCook, ordered a bayonet charge. The Confederates fled before the men of the Ninth Ohio. At the same time, the three fresh regiments moved forward to outflank the other end of the Confederate line, and the Union center, sensing victory, advanced also. Faced with this overwhelming surge forward, the entire Confederate line gave way and fled the field in what Thomas described as "the utmost disorder and confusion."[33]

Thomas paused at this point so his soldiers could reorganize their lines and draw new ammunition. He then advanced in pursuit of the enemy, who offered little resistance, and his men picked up hundreds of discarded muskets, haversacks full of food, and other items during the course of their advance. By the afternoon Thomas's men had reached the enemy camp on the north bank of the Cumberland River. Assuming that the enemy was trapped by the river's high waters, Thomas stopped there for the day. He placed artillery on the hills overlooking the enemy position and ordered them to shell the camp. He also ordered them to remain watchful during the night, and to fire on any boats seen crossing the river. Thomas put his infantry into positions surrounding the Confederate camp, intending to attack it the following morning.

When the next day dawned, Thomas's men moved forward, only to discover that the camp had been abandoned during the night, and that the Confederate army had escaped across the river. The Confederates had found a place where the hills near the bank of the river blocked the ferryboat from Union artillery fire and had thus managed to evacuate their men. They had left everything else behind, however, including all of their artillery, a large quantity of small arms, most of their ammunition, more than 150 wagons, much food and supplies, and over one thousand horses and mules. The Confederates also abandoned some of their regimental flags. While these flags had no military value, they were objects of pride to the units, and it was considered shameful to allow them to be captured. The fact that the soldiers left these flags behind indicates how frightened, demoralized, and hurried they were.[34]

Thomas had no boats of his own, so he could not pursue the Confederate army any further. He stated in his report that "their command was completely demoralized, and retreated with great haste and in all directions, making their capture in any numbers quite doubtful if pursued. There is no doubt but what the moral effect produced by their complete dispersion will have a more decided effect in re-establishing Union sentiments than though they had been captured." While this may have been true, Thomas must have been disappointed at the enemy's escape. The historian of the Army of the Cumberland, Larry Daniel, states that Thomas "stumbled" by not storming the Confederates' base camp on the afternoon of January 19, and Daniel's criticism seems to be justified. Thomas admitted as much in a conversation he had on January 20 with one of his regimental commanders, Col. Speed S. Fry. When Fry asked Thomas why he had not sent in a demand for surrender the night before, Thomas thought for a moment and then replied, "Hang it, Fry! I never once thought of it."[35]

While Thomas erred in allowing Zollicoffer's men to escape, his overall performance in the battle was impressive. He had prepared his force well for battle, ensuring that his troops were well trained, that his officers were competent, and that his men had adequate supplies of food, shelter, and ammunition. He defeated the Confederate attempt at a surprise attack by training his men to respond quickly to the "long roll," announcing battle, and by posting multiple picket lines. While these may seem like obvious measures, many other commanders were careless in this regard, and the Union army was often surprised by Confederate attacks early in the war. Sherman, Grant, and Rosecrans were each caught off guard by Confederate surprise attacks, in the Battles of Shiloh, Fort Donelson, and Stones River, but Thomas was always careful and was never surprised.[36]

Thomas made sure he was present and visible on the front lines, as a way of encouraging his men. Thomas put on a new uniform for the battle, so that his troops would be able to identify him easily. When the soldiers, crouching behind trees and other cover, saw their commander riding on horseback in plain view of the enemy, they were more likely to stand firm and hold their positions. The soldiers admired Thomas's calm demeanor and were reassured by his apparent lack of fear; as one of his officers recalled, "[A]ll through, the General was as 'cool as a cucumber.'" In addition to inspiring them to bravery by example, Thomas's visible presence assured his men that he was aware of the events of the battle and engaged in directing its outcome.[37]

Thomas was skilled in assessing the capabilities of his soldiers and using them accordingly. He had high regard for his volunteer regiments from Ohio, Indiana, and Minnesota, but little confidence in some of the Kentucky and Tennessee volunteers. These soldiers resisted discipline, and their officers were poor leaders; Thomas had complained about them for months, but for political reasons he could not replace their officers or do much to improve their discipline. The two exceptions among the Kentucky troops were the First Kentucky Cavalry and the Fourth Kentucky Infantry, which were well disciplined and effectively led. Thomas relied heavily on these two regiments during the battle, along with the regiments of volunteers from Northern states, and used them to form his main line of defense. He had posted the less reliable Kentucky and Tennessee volunteers at the rear of the army's camp, so these were the last to reach the field during the battle. Thomas used them to extend the Union line far to the left, where they would outflank and frighten the Confederates but would do little actual fighting. Meanwhile, the more reliable regiments on the Union center and right did the more difficult work of breaking the Confederate line.

Thomas was skillful in his placement of troops. The terrain of the battlefield, which was mostly wooded, did not allow for much use of artillery, but he was able to place artillery in one key position, defending the left of his line early in the battle. He was able to calculate how long the defenders in the center were able to hold out against the Confederate attack, sending a regiment to reinforce them when they began to run out of ammunition, and using the rest of his regiments to outflank the attackers. The forces involved in the battle were of roughly equal size, but Thomas's skillful disposition of his troops caused the Confederates to believe they were badly outnumbered, and this led to their eventual panic and retreat.[38]

The strength of the Confederates' perception that they were outnumbered was indicated by a story told by one of the Confederate prisoners, which was repeated often by Thomas's men. A young Confederate prisoner who had been slightly wounded during the battle was allowed to move freely about the Union camp. The Union soldiers often teased him about how the Confederates had run away in such a panic that they had thrown away their guns, packs, and rations. "Well," he answered, "we were doing pretty good fighting, till old man Thomas rose up in his stirrups, and we heard him holler out, 'Attention, Creation! By kingdoms right wheel!' And then we knew you had us, and it was no time to carry weight."[39]

The Battle of Mill Springs, also known as the Battle of Logan's Crossroads or the Battle of Fishing Creek, was a small victory both in terms of the number of troops engaged and the number of casualties. Each side had only about 4,000 soldiers present at the battle, and while the Union lost about 250 men killed and wounded, the Confederates lost about 400. But Mill Springs was one of the first Union victories of the war, and it both renewed Union hopes of victory and brought Thomas's name to national attention. The *Chicago Tribune*'s headline exclaimed, "Victory at last!" The *New York Herald* called the battle a "glorious" and "significant" victory, "of the utmost importance to the Union cause," and the *Boston Daily Advertiser* called the battle "the most brilliant victory of the war." Northern papers frequently portrayed the battle as revenge for the Union defeat at Manassas. The *New York Tribune* referred to the Confederates' rapid flight from the field as "a Bull Run Stampede," and the *New York Herald* described it as "a panic more terrible than the famous one at Bull Run."[40]

The victory at Mill Springs destroyed Zollicoffer's army and left the way open to East Tennessee. However, the difficult march from Crab Orchard to Mill Springs left Thomas less eager to invade East Tennessee. Thomas told Buell that the bad roads, and the lack of a railroad or navigable river in the region, would make it too difficult to move adequate supplies to the front, while the country was too poor and too heavily foraged by the retreating Confederates for the army to live off the land. Thomas asked Buell to let his troops move west, to participate with Buell's projected offensive against the Confederate position north of Bowling Green.[41]

Thomas's first six months of service in Kentucky had started badly but had ended well. Arriving at Camp Dick Robinson in September, he had found a mob of poorly disciplined volunteers, with few arms and supplies and even fewer qualified officers. By setting priorities and working hard, Thomas had transformed his recruits into an effective fighting force, which had then routed a Confederate army at the Battle of Mill Springs.

Thomas had also been successful in the political aspects of his military service, warding off a threat to his command from O. M. Mitchel, and mediating the disputes between the military leadership, who advocated caution, and the politicians from East Tennessee, who demanded an immediate offensive into their home state. Thomas had earned fame for himself and a moral victory for the Union, but problems with supply and transportation made it impossible for him to follow up on his victory by advancing into East Tennessee. As Thomas considered how to advance, news came of a tremendous victory in western Tennessee, one that changed the character of the war in Kentucky and set Thomas's career on an unexpected new course. Thomas would no longer hold an independent command but would act as a subordinate commander in a large army, the first in a series of such positions he would hold during the next three years.

CHAPTER SEVEN

Shiloh and Perryville

> We have never yet had a commander of any expedition who has been allowed to work out his own policy, and it is utterly impossible for the most able General in the world to conduct a campaign with success where his hands are tied, as it were, by the constant apprehension that his plans may be interfered with at any moment.

Thomas had achieved a victory during his first independent command, but some two years would pass before he was granted the opportunity to command his own force again. From early 1862 to late 1864, Thomas served as second-in-command under a succession of generals: Don Carlos Buell, Henry W. Halleck, William S. Rosecrans, Ulysses S. Grant, and William T. Sherman. Thomas performed well in these settings, acting as both an adviser and a corps commander to each of his superiors. Thomas was offered promotion on several occasions, but he refused promotion because he thought it would seem dishonorable to take command at the expense of his superior officer, and because he objected to what he saw as political interference from Washington. Thomas's misguided concerns about honor and politics crippled his career; after refusing to replace Buell in 1862, he was not offered independent command again until the end of 1864. Thomas performed effective service as a subordinate commander, but his refusal to accept a senior command hurt his career and diminished his contribution to Union victory.

At the beginning of 1862, Thomas was not yet under consideration for army command. His victory at Mill Springs was impressive, but the forces involved were small, and he had not yet had experience commanding large bodies of troops. In February 1862, just a month after Mill Springs, Gen. Ulysses S. Grant won an even more impressive victory by capturing Forts Henry and Donelson, on the border of Tennessee and Kentucky west of Nashville. While the Union and Confederate armies lost roughly equal numbers of men during the fighting, Grant took more than twelve thousand prisoners when the garrisons surrendered. More importantly, the capture of the two forts gave the Union navy control of the Tennessee and Cumberland Rivers, which opened up all of western and central Tennessee to the Union and cut the Confederate supply line to Kentucky. The Confederate commander, Albert S. Johnston, had little choice but to retreat out of the state, and Buell pursued him. Buell captured Nashville without a fight in late February and continued southward into central Tennessee.[1]

Grant's success at Forts Henry and Donelson was one of the most important victories of the war, and it brought Grant to the nation's attention as one of the Union's most promising generals. Grant followed up his victory by advancing southward toward Corinth, Mississippi, and Buell and Thomas marched southwest from Nashville to join him. Corinth was a small city that held great strategic importance as it was located on the Tennessee River at the junction of two important railroad lines: the north–south line that connected northern Mississippi with Mobile, Alabama, and the east–west line that ran from Memphis to Richmond. The east–west railroad was the more important of the two, as it was one of only two railroad lines that connected the eastern and western sections of the Confederacy. Thomas had recognized the importance of this railroad in 1861, when he proposed advancing into East Tennessee to cut the railroad near Nashville. The railroad was also the main Confederate supply line to Memphis, meaning that the capture of Corinth would probably force the Confederates to abandon Memphis as well.

Thomas's division, being located on the eastern flank of Buell's army, had the longest way to travel to Corinth, and it thus marched in the rear of Buell's column. As a result, Thomas's division was not present at the Battle of Shiloh, arriving the day after the battle ended. During the battle, which took place on April 6 and 7, the Confederate army launched a surprise attack on Grant's force, which at first succeeded, in part due to Grant and Sherman's carelessness in not guarding against such an attack. While Grant was driven back with heavy losses on the first day, he counterattacked on the second day and regained all the territory he had lost. Grant was assisted in this attack by Buell's army, whose advance units arrived on the battlefield during the night of April 6–7 and continued to arrive throughout the second day of the battle.[2]

Shiloh was by far the bloodiest battle of the war to date, with roughly thirteen thousand casualties on the Union side and more than eleven thousand for the Confederates, including Johnston, the Confederate commander. The Union army was exhausted and demoralized from the fighting and had to rest and refit before continuing south. The command organization of the army was also changed, which resulted in a large increase in the number of troops under Thomas's command. Henry W. Halleck, the overall commander in the West, came to the field to command in person, and he divided the force of more than one hundred thousand men into four armies, commanded by Don Carlos Buell, John Pope, John McClernand, and George Thomas. Thomas's army consisted of his old division plus four divisions from Grant's army.[3]

One of Thomas's divisional commanders was William T. Sherman. After serving for a short period in Missouri, Sherman had taken time away from the army to rest, and this had restored his health and mental stability. While he had erred in not detecting the Confederates' surprise attack, after this Sherman had performed very well at Shiloh, stubbornly resisting the Confederate attack in some of the first day's heaviest fighting. Sherman also did not seem to mind being placed under the command of his former subordinate. In his *Memoirs* Sherman stated, "We were classmates, intimately acquainted, had served together before in the old army, and in Kentucky, and it made to us little difference who commanded the other, provided the good cause prevailed." When their roles were reversed again later in the war, their good relations continued.[4]

Unfortunately, Thomas's new assignment put him at odds with Grant. While Grant had ultimately won at Shiloh, his failure to guard against a surprise attack had almost resulted in defeat. Halleck, and some others, blamed the first day's disaster on Grant, while crediting the eventual Union victory to Buell. Halleck had also been jealous of Grant's popularity after his victory at Forts Henry and Donelson, and Shiloh provided him with a justification for removing Grant from independent command and putting Thomas in his place. Grant still had his defenders, however, so Halleck did not dismiss him from command entirely. Instead, he "promoted" Grant to second-in-command of the western theater, serving directly under Halleck himself. As Grant had no troops of his own to command, and Halleck gave him nothing to do, the "promotion" was essentially a step down in rank. Humiliated, Grant considered resigning, but Sherman convinced him to stay and wait for matters to improve.[5]

Once the Union army had recovered from its losses at Shiloh, Halleck resumed the advance on Corinth. Halleck's army greatly outnumbered the Confederate force, but his fear of another surprise attack led him to move slowly, stopping his men after each advance to dig entrenchments. It took Halleck a month to advance the twenty-two miles to the city. The Confederates contested the Union advance, and Thomas's division fought in a few minor engagements along the way, but no major battle developed. Finally, as the Union troops neared Corinth on May 25, the Confederates abandoned the city and retreated southward. When Thomas's forces moved to occupy the city, they found the sanitary conditions there to be "in miserable condition," and many of Thomas's men became ill. Thomas ordered the camp cleaned up and put in order, which helped reduce the rate of sickness among his men.[6]

With Corinth under Union occupation, the Confederates could not hold Memphis, and after losing a naval battle for control of the river, the Confederates abandoned the city. Thomas then asked Halleck to return him to his former command. Van Horne states that Thomas asked to be relieved out of courtesy to Grant, who had been "deeply hurt" by being replaced with Thomas. Halleck put Grant back in charge of his army, and Thomas returned to command his old division. It is not clear why Thomas waited until after the fall of Corinth to request to be relieved of Grant's command, but it seems that he considered it unsafe to change commanders in the middle of an active campaign, when a battle was expected at any moment.[7]

The capture of Corinth and Memphis were two of a large number of Union triumphs in the spring of 1862. In February 1862 Union troops under Gen. Ambrose Burnside fought a successful campaign on the North Carolina coast, capturing or blocking off several Confederate port cities. In March, at the Battle of Pea Ridge, Union forces turned back a Confederate invasion of Missouri, leaving the entire state firmly in Union control. In April a Union naval expedition captured New Orleans, and in May and June the same force captured Baton Rouge and Natchez. Another Union naval force, working in conjunction with an army detachment commanded by John Pope, captured an important Mississippi River fort at Island Number Ten, near the border of Tennessee and

Kentucky. McClellan had finally moved forward in the eastern theater, and by June McClellan had advanced from his base near Norfolk to a point only ten miles from the Confederate capital.[8]

While these successes were encouraging, the Union high command in the West now faced a difficult decision. In the past the Union armies had been able to use the Tennessee, Cumberland, and Mississippi Rivers as avenues of advance and lines of supply, but at this point the Union was running out of objectives easily reached by river. Port Hudson, Louisiana, and Vicksburg, both on the Mississippi River, were the most obvious Union targets, but these were well-defended fortresses on difficult terrain. There were other points not yet captured along the Tennessee and Cumberland Rivers, but drought conditions had caused the level of these rivers to fall, and they were not navigable through most of their courses. Except for attacks on the two remaining Mississippi River fortresses, any further Union advance would have to rely on the railroads for supply.

Halleck decided to divide his army, sending part of it to work in conjunction with the navy against Port Hudson and Vicksburg, leaving part of it to hold Corinth, and sending the rest, including Thomas's division, under Buell to complete the conquest of Tennessee.[9] Buell began his march in June, moving eastward along the railroad that connected Corinth with Chattanooga and Knoxville, and drawing supplies from other railroads leading north.[10] At this stage of the war the Union forces were badly prepared to guard and repair the railroads, and the Confederates took full advantage of their weakness. Confederate cavalry leaders Nathan Bedford Forrest and John Hunt Morgan launched a series of raids behind Buell's lines, taking thousands of prisoners, and destroying hundreds of thousands of dollars' worth of supplies. Buell had to slow his advance to deal with the threat, and it took him two months to reach Chattanooga. Buell halted at Stevenson, Alabama, in August and waited there for his engineers to build a railroad bridge over the Tennessee River before moving on to attack the city.[11]

Thomas's division spent July 4, 1862, at Tuscumbia, Alabama, near Stevenson. During the Independence Day celebration, Thomas's subordinate officers gave speeches, and Thomas presided over the gathering but did not speak. As one of his soldiers remembered, "'Pap'Thomas listened quietly to the oratorical tournament. But when the tides of bombast rose to a flood, he said it was time to go home." As Thomas left, one of his soldiers heard him mutter, "If the boys can't keep within bounds, they must omit celebrating the Fourth of July hereafter!"[12]

The slow pace of Buell's advance had been widely criticized, and some politicians and officers already favored replacing him. In August Thomas learned that Andrew Johnson, the Union military governor of Tennessee, had requested that Thomas be placed at the head of an expedition to invade East Tennessee. Thomas asked Johnson not to push his name for command of this expedition, for several reasons. "We have never yet had a commander of any expedition who has been allowed to work out his own policy," Thomas wrote, "and it is utterly impossible for the most able General in the world to conduct a campaign with success where his hands are tied, as it were, by the constant apprehension that his plans may be interfered with at any moment." Thomas added, "General Buell's dispositions will eventually free all Tennessee and go very far to crush the rebellion entirely. If our army will not permit itself to degenerate into idleness, the rebels will be crushed out in sixty days, for the Confederacy cannot possibly subsist its troops a great while longer."[13]

Thomas could not have been more wrong. As Buell waited at Stevenson for the bridge to be completed, a Confederate army, under the command of Gen. Edmund Kirby Smith, moved northward from East Tennessee and invaded eastern Kentucky. In August a larger force moved northward from Chattanooga toward Nashville and central Kentucky. This force was commanded by Braxton Bragg, Thomas's former friend and commanding officer, who was now a major general in the Confederate army. While Buell had struggled slowly across Tennessee, Bragg had quickly shifted the larger part of his army by rail from the Corinth area to Chattanooga. It was unclear at this point whether Bragg meant to attack Nashville or central Kentucky, but losing either would be a disaster for the Union cause. Once Buell realized what Bragg was doing, he abandoned his campaign to take Chattanooga and went over to the defense.[14]

Buell's first important decision lay in where to concentrate his army in defense, a task made particularly difficult by the terrain. Two geographic features, the Tennessee River and the Cumberland Plateau, separated Confederate-controlled southern and eastern Tennessee from the Union-controlled northern and western parts of the state. The Tennessee flows from east to west through Chattanooga, and the ridge of the Cumberland Plateau runs parallel to and north of the river. The

Confederates could move their forces along the river undetected, and then cross the plateau ridge at any of four different points, which made it difficult for Buell to block the Confederate advance.[15]

Buell stayed in the rear of his army, supervising its retreat, and put Thomas in command at the front, with orders to concentrate the Union rearguard at Altamont, where it would block the direct route from Chattanooga to Nashville. Although Thomas obeyed, he protested Buell's decision and asked him to reconsider. Altamont was located atop the Cumberland Plateau, where the terrain was rocky and there was no forage for the army's horses. Thomas did not think his army could be provisioned there for any length of time. Worse, by concentrating at Altamont, the force would only defend against Confederate movement along the Chattanooga–Nashville road, leaving undefended another passage through the plateau, about fifty miles east of the main road. If Bragg took that route, he could bypass Nashville and advance, unopposed, into central Kentucky. Thomas favored a concentration at McMinnville, a town halfway between the Nashville road and the eastern route. McMinnville was well stocked with supplies, and a railroad spur connected the town with the main rail line between Nashville and Chattanooga. From McMinnville, Thomas argued, the Union army would be able to defend both roads north, as the army could move east or west quickly and intercept Bragg once his true course of advance was discovered.[16]

Buell ignored Thomas's advice and insisted that he remain at Altamont. As Thomas had feared, the Confederate army bypassed his force and marched unopposed along the eastern road toward Kentucky. Buell retreated to Murfreesboro, about forty miles southeast of Nashville, and ordered Thomas to go to Nashville and organize the city's defenses. Thomas agreed with the concentration at Murfreesboro but urged Buell to cease retreating and to use the town as a base for an attack on the Confederate army. "By convenient roads," he wrote, "our main force can be thrown upon the enemy, . . . overcome him, and drive him toward Sparta, his longest line of retreat. A large force of cavalry and light infantry can be pushed across the mountains, . . . attack him in the rear, and completely rout his whole force." Buell again ignored Thomas's advice and retreated to Nashville to await Bragg's attack.[17]

Bragg bypassed Nashville and marched north into Kentucky. Leaving a small force under Thomas to garrison Nashville, Buell took the rest of his army and followed Bragg, marching north along the rail line that connected Nashville and Louisville. Bragg marched along a road that ran parallel to the railroad, off to the east, and managed to keep slightly ahead of Buell's force. As Louisville was lightly defended, it was vulnerable to Confederate capture, and the Union soldiers perceived the movement as a race to see who could reach the city first. The march was a difficult one, with the fast pace made more difficult by the hot, dry weather and the lack of water. While the men of the army began to take pride in their ability to march under tough conditions, they also began to resent their commander, whom they blamed for the difficulties of the march and the disgrace of the retreat. When the men learned that Thomas had wanted to attack Bragg in Tennessee instead of retreating through Kentucky, their admiration of Thomas increased and their resentment of Buell grew.[18]

On August 30 General Smith's force in eastern Kentucky nearly annihilated a Union army at Richmond, leaving eastern Kentucky nearly empty of Federal troops, and opening the region to Confederate occupation. In early September Smith captured Frankfort, Kentucky's capital, and Lexington, one of its largest cities. As Bragg and Buell continued their dual movement toward Louisville, the Confederates prepared to inaugurate a secessionist governor in Frankfort. More bad news came on August 30 from Virginia. Having already driven McClellan away from Richmond during the Seven Days' Battles, Robert E. Lee had now inflicted a crushing defeat on the Union army at the Second Battle of Manassas. Matters were beginning to look very bleak for the Union cause.[19]

After the fall of Frankfort, Bragg paused at Munfordville, Kentucky, to force the Union garrison there to surrender, and Buell's main army came within striking distance of the Confederate force. Many of Buell's men hoped for a battle, but Buell chose instead to halt at Bowling Green for five days, allowing Bragg's army to move past him once again. A rumor spread through the army that Thomas had accused Buell of incompetence and treason and had nearly challenged him to a duel. This rumor had no foundation, but the fact that many soldiers believed it indicates how hated Buell had become in the army, and that the men had come to see Thomas as their champion.[20]

At the end of September, Buell finally reached Louisville, where he paused to rest and resupply his army and to absorb newly recruited units into his command. Bragg did not attack the city but headed eastward to join up with E. Kirby Smith. From the eastern theater, the Union men heard the good news of the defeat of a Confederate invasion of Maryland on September 17. Perhaps the Union army might achieve a similar victory in Kentucky.[21] But the officers of Buell's army did not have confidence in his ability to win a battle, and a group of them, working without Thomas's knowledge, decided to petition the War Department to replace Buell with Thomas. Before they could put this plan into action, however, Halleck and Secretary of War Edwin M. Stanton decided on their own initiative to relieve Buell of command, and Halleck sent a staff officer to Kentucky to deliver the orders.[22]

The staff officer reached Louisville on September 29, and Buell called Thomas to his headquarters. As Buell later recalled, Thomas refused to accept the command, explaining that "he was not prepared by information and study for the responsibility." Buell tried to convince Thomas to take his place but was not successful. "I thought that he was actuated in his course by a generous confidence in me and a modest distrust of himself with so little warning," Buell wrote, "and I considered that both motives did honor to his sterling character.[23] Thomas wrote Halleck, "General Buell's preparations have been completed to move against the enemy, and I therefore respectfully ask that he may be retained in command. My position is very embarrassing, not being as well informed as I should be as the commander of this army and on the assumption of such a responsibility."[24] In the meantime, Lincoln had decided to give Buell another chance, and Buell received word later that day that the orders relieving him were suspended.[25]

Thomas's refusal to replace Buell was unusual for a Civil War commander, and quite a contrast to the ambitious behavior of so many generals in the war. Thomas knew that many people attributed his refusal to his "extreme modesty and distrust of his own ability as a general," but he always insisted that his refusal had to do with the timing of the change. Years later, Thomas told Van Horne, "I am not as modest as I have been represented to be. I did not request the retention of General Buell in command through modesty, but because his removal and my assignment were alike unjust to him and to me. It was unjust to him to relieve him on the eve of battle, and unjust to myself, to impose upon me the command of the army at such a time."[26] This explanation is unconvincing, however, because the army was not on the eve of battle at the time of Halleck's orders but was safe in its base at Louisville. There was time for Thomas to take over the army and learn its dispositions before taking the field against Bragg.

Thomas's refusal to take command from Buell lay not in his apprehension of changing commanders on the eve of battle, but from Thomas's abhorrence of politics and his extreme concern for his own honor. As he had stated earlier to Andrew Johnson, Thomas did not want command of an army unless he could be assured that the political authorities would not dispute and overrule his decisions. Thomas had never been fond of politics, but his experience in eastern Kentucky had left him particularly opposed to what he saw as political interference in military affairs. Thomas also did not want to be seen as grasping at command at the expense of his superior officer, particularly after he had already been promoted at Grant's expense during the Corinth campaign. Thomas may have felt that the only honorable thing to do was to refuse the command, at least at first. Later in his career, Thomas initially refused to replace another superior officer, William Rosecrans, but then agreed to do so. Perhaps in this case, if Lincoln had not rescinded Halleck's order, Thomas would have eventually agreed to take Buell's place.[27]

While Thomas's refusal to take command helped Buell, Buell did little to repay him, as he reorganized his army at Louisville in such a way that Thomas lacked an independent command. Buell's reorganization absorbed the newly recruited regiments into his command structure and divided his force into three corps—commanded by Maj. Gen. Alexander McCook, Maj. Gen. Thomas L. Crittenden, and a third officer, Charles C. Gilbert. Buell had originally planned to put William "Bull" Nelson in charge of one of the corps, but Nelson was murdered on September 29 after an argument with another Union officer, Gen. Jefferson C. Davis.[28] Instead of promoting Thomas, the most logical choice, to corps command, Buell promoted Gilbert, who had a rank of captain in the regular army, to the rank of major general and gave him command of the third corps. Buell gave Thomas the position of second-in-command of the army, with no independent command of his own. It is possible that Buell resented Thomas's popularity within the army and with the War Department and so placed him where he could not be a threat, but there is no record of ill feeling between Buell and Thomas that would support this speculation. During the retreat from Tennessee, Buell had deployed Thomas as an active field commander, placing Thomas in charge of the army's rearguard, at Altamont, and in command of the garrison he left at Nashville when his main force moved north. Perhaps Buell planned to continue to use Thomas in this manner, sending him to command at key locations when Buell's own attention was directed elsewhere.

Buell's alternate choice for corps commander, Charles C. Gilbert, had a solid record as a regular army officer, but he performed poorly in corps command.[29] He imposed harsh and arbitrary punishments on his men, a tactic that might have worked in the regular army, but that only served to anger and alienate his volunteer soldiers. As Buell prepared to march out of Louisville, Thomas had to intervene to prevent a regiment from mutinying against Gilbert. The men of the regiment had become angry because they had not been paid with the rest of their brigade, and they refused to march or fight. As their officers tried to reason with them, without success, Gilbert rode up and took charge. Trying to assert his authority, he "began a tirade of profanity and abuse" and then ordered one of the artillery batteries to "blow them to hell." When the artillerymen refused, Gilbert became even angrier. Finally, Thomas came over and settled the dispute. Speaking to the men in a quiet, reasonable tone, he said, "Boys, I am sorry marching orders came before you were paid off, [but] we are on a very important march and in all probability will get Bragg before he gets many miles away. Now if you will fall in, I will promise you the next stop we make long enough, I will have the paymaster there, and you shall be paid before you move again." The soldiers cheered Thomas saying, "All right, 'Pap,' we will go."[30]

Buell left Louisville on September 30 and marched southeast toward Bardstown, where Bragg's army was reported to be, while sending a smaller force toward Frankfort as a diversion. Tricked by the diversion, Bragg and concluded that Buell's entire army was advancing on the state capital. Bragg ordered Smith's force to stay at Frankfort and delay Buell's advance, while Bragg attacked the flank of the advancing Union army. The inauguration of a Confederate governor in Frankfort took place on October 4, as scheduled, but as the ceremony ended, the participants heard the booming of distant artillery, signifying the approach of the Union force. Bragg ordered Smith to retreat from Frankfort, and the newly inaugurated Confederate governor went with him, never to return.[31]

Buell captured Bardstown on October 4, then continued southeast toward Perryville, where he suspected the Confederates might stand and fight. To save time on the march, Buell divided his army into three parts, with Gilbert's corps taking the direct road to Perryville, and the other two corps on either flank. Buell ordered Thomas to accompany Crittenden's corps on the march, in effect reducing Thomas to the role of assistant corps commander. Gilbert's corps approached Perryville on October 7, but the other two corps, taking a longer route, lagged behind.[32]

So far, everything had gone well with Buell's campaign. The main problem was a lack of water, as the continuing drought had dried up many of the streams, wells, and springs along the army's route of march. There was water in a creek near Perryville, but Confederates held the high ground on the far side of the creek, making it inaccessible to the Union soldiers. Buell ordered his men to drive the Confederates away from the creek the next morning. Knowing that this attack might develop into a major battle, he ordered McCook and Crittenden to bring their corps to Perryville as quickly as possible, and he told Thomas to come in person once he had made sure that Crittenden's corps was in motion. Meanwhile, Thomas and Crittenden had marched their corps away from Perryville, in search of water. Buell's messenger had a hard time finding them, meaning that Thomas did not receive Buell's orders until 3:00 A.M. on the morning of October 8, the time that Buell had set for the beginning of the march. Thomas sent a message back to Buell explaining their difficulty, and promising that Crittenden's soldiers would set out as soon as they could get water. Thomas then stayed with Crittenden's corps, ignoring Buell's orders to report to him in person.[33]

Thomas's decision to disobey Buell's orders caused him to miss the entire Battle of Perryville. His reasons for disobeying Buell are unclear, but it seems Thomas had lost faith in Buell's ability to lead. When Buell stated that he wanted Thomas to rush Crittenden's corps to Perryville so that Buell could attack Bragg the next day, Thomas may not have believed that Buell would really attack. Buell had passed up a number of good opportunities to attack Bragg's army already, making it seem likely that he would not attack Bragg now. Thomas probably feared that he would exhaust the men with a forced march to Perryville, only to find once he got there that Buell had changed his mind.

While this seems to explain why Thomas did not rush Crittenden's corps to Perryville, it is less clear why Thomas also failed to report to Buell in person. Thomas may also have resented Buell's decision to deprive him of an independent command and have disobeyed Buell because of this feeling of resentment.[34] Finally, Thomas had apparently lost confidence in Buell overall, as had a number of Buell's other officers.

As they had done at Louisville, they met in secret on the night of October 7 to petition the War Department to replace Buell with Thomas, but the battle the next day put an end to their plan.[35]

The Battle of Perryville was a strange one. Buell wanted to attack Bragg on October 8 but was unable to do so because Crittenden's corps remained far from the rest of the army. Meanwhile, Bragg still thought the main Union army was located to the north, near Frankfort. Assuming that the force before him was a small, isolated detachment, Bragg sent three divisions forward in an all-out attempt to annihilate it. These three divisions discovered that the Union troops in their front were more numerous than they expected and were soon locked in fierce fighting with two divisions of McCook's corps. The battle continued until sunset, with the units engaged suffering heavy casualties. Despite the intense nature of the fighting, neither commander committed the rest of his army to the struggle, and the battle ended at sunset with neither side holding the advantage.[36]

Since his own army outnumbered Bragg's and was fairly well concentrated, Buell could have moved the rest of his army forward to outflank and defeat the Confederate attackers. Buell did not do this; in fact, he did not even learn that a battle was occurring in his front until the day was almost over. Not expecting Bragg to attack, Buell had spent the day resting at his headquarters in the rear, recuperating from injuries that he had suffered from being thrown from his horse the day before. Buell should have been able to hear the sounds of fighting from his headquarters, but a strange phenomenon called an "acoustical shadow," caused by weather conditions and the topography of the battlefield, prevented the sound of fighting from reaching him. Buell's staff officers also should have informed him of what was happening, but a series of errors and miscommunications caused the message not to reach Buell until late in the afternoon. Buell immediately ordered part of Gilbert's corps forward to support McCook, but they reached the battlefield too late to take any significant part in the fighting.

Thomas and Crittenden did hear sounds of fighting far to the north on the afternoon of October 8, and they could have marched to Buell's aid. One of Thomas's staff officers wanted to investigate, but Gilbert, who was closer to the front, assured the officer that the fighting was just skirmishing, similar to what they were facing in their own front. Crittenden also thought the noise indicated only a skirmish, but Thomas insisted on sending a staff officer to Buell to find out what was going on. Unfortunately, by the time the staff officer reached Buell and returned to Crittenden, it was too late in the day for Crittenden's corps to participate in the battle. Meanwhile, Thomas spent the day coordinating the movements of Crittenden's troops, riding so near the front lines that at one point he was nearly captured by Confederate cavalry.[37] Thomas would have been able to perform much better service if he had ridden to Buell's headquarters the previous evening as he had been ordered. He was not injured, as Buell was, and he had the authority, rank, and ability to command in the field while Buell was incapacitated. If Thomas had been present at Perryville on October 8, the Battle of Perryville might have been a Union victory instead of a draw.[38]

Buell wanted to resume the battle the next day, but when morning came he found that the Confederates had retreated during the night. Bragg had realized that he was facing Buell's entire army, and with Smith's force separated from his own, Bragg was outnumbered. He was also short on supplies and discouraged by the failure of the population of Kentucky to come out strongly in support of the Confederacy. Bragg retreated to Tennessee, giving up most of the gains of his campaign.[39]

Buell pursued Bragg as far as London, Kentucky, but he followed slowly and cautiously, worried that Bragg might turn to fight and catch his army off guard. Bragg's cavalry, which outnumbered the Federal cavalry, also worked effectively to delay the Union pursuit. Buell never got close to catching Bragg in his retreat, and at London he stopped following Bragg at all. He moved southwest toward Nashville and prepared to go into winter quarters, putting off any further advance into Tennessee until the spring.[40]

Both armies suffered from a lack of supplies during these last stages of the campaign, as they moved over territory that had been repeatedly foraged. Commanders on both sides tried to prevent their soldiers from taking advantage of the civilian population but had limited success in preventing theft by their hungry, poorly supplied men. One such abuse provoked Thomas to intense anger. According to the war correspondent William Shanks, one Kentucky farmer, whom Thomas knew to be a Union loyalist, complained that one of Thomas's officers had stolen his horse. The farmer identified the officer, who served with one of the regiments under Thomas's command. When Thomas confronted him, the officer admitted that he had "impressed" the horse. The officer had no official authority to do this, however, and Thomas was furious. According to Shanks, Thomas was "choking with rage" and "poured on the devoted head of the delinquent a torrent of invective. He drew his sword, and putting the point under the shoulder-straps of the officer, ripped them off, and then compelled him to dismount and lead the animal to the place whence he had stolen him. He also required him to pay the farmer for his trouble and the loss of service of the animal."[41]

Officers who wrote about Thomas often mentioned his severe temper, but they rarely gave examples of angry outbursts. It seems that Thomas worked hard to control his temper, and only rarely lost control. As his staff aide Henry Stone recalled, "[I]t was exhibitions of meanness or cruelty to those who could not defend themselves, rather than any great faults or crimes, which chiefly stirred his passion." On one occasion, Thomas saw a teamster beating his team of mules over the head with the butt of his whip, to compel them to move forward. The mules were stuck in the mud and could not move forward despite their struggles to escape the pain of the whip. Thomas intervened so forcefully that the teamster ran away from Thomas and hid in the woods.[42]

By the end of October, Bragg's invasion of Kentucky had ended, with unsatisfactory results for both sides. About forty-two hundred Union soldiers and thirty-four hundred Confederates were killed or wounded at Perryville, with no decisive outcome. By invading Kentucky, Bragg had succeeded in driving the Union army from middle Tennessee, but he had failed to capture Kentucky for the Confederacy. Buell had turned back Bragg's invasion, but he could not claim a victory either. He had responded too cautiously to Bragg's advance, letting him get much farther north than he should have, had failed to force a decisive battle against Bragg's smaller army, and had failed to pursue effectively when Bragg retreated from Perryville.[43]

While Thomas deserves credit for advising Buell to attack Bragg in Tennessee, instead of retreating to Murfreesboro, his performance during the rest of the Perryville campaign was less effective. His distaste for politics and his concern about others' perceptions of his honor led him to refuse command of the army, despite his no longer having confidence in its commander. As Thomas did not respect Buell's leadership, he did not comply with all Buell's orders, and he thus missed an opportunity to march to the army's assistance at the Battle of Perryville. In later years

Thomas developed a better approach to the politics of generalship, became less concerned about his honor, and became more effective at working as a subordinate to commanders whose decisions he did not agree with. In 1862, however, Thomas's decision neither to replace Buell nor to obey him fully had negative consequences both for his own career and for the Union cause.

CHAPTER EIGHT

Stones River

This army can't retreat.

Thomas's refusal to take command from Buell at Louisville hurt Thomas's prospects for promotion later on. By the time the Perryville campaign had ended, President Lincoln, Secretary of War Edwin M. Stanton, and other members of the political leadership all supported removing Buell from command. They wanted a commander similar to Grant, who was now leading the campaign against Vicksburg, someone who would take the initiative and lead an aggressive campaign. While the political leadership agreed that Buell had to go, they disagreed about whom to choose to replace him. Stanton favored Thomas, but Treasury Secretary Salmon P. Chase advocated giving the appointment to Maj. Gen. William Starke Rosecrans instead. Rosecrans had served well in western Virginia, and had recently played an important role, with Grant, in turning back the attempted Confederate invasion of western Tennessee. Rosecrans was also a political asset, in that he was a Catholic and a native of Ohio. Most Catholics supported the Democratic Party, and antiadministration sentiment and the Democrats were particularly strong in Ohio. Appointing Rosecrans to senior command would help build support among both of these important groups of voters. Thomas was the other logical choice, but his earlier refusal to take command from Buell worked against him. Besides making it seem that he did not really want an independent command, it created the impression that he approved of Buell's leadership during the Perryville campaign and would follow similar tactics if he were promoted.[1]

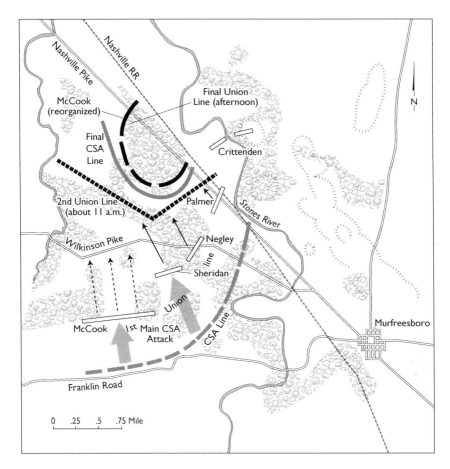

Stones River

After considering all these factors, Lincoln decided to appoint Rosecrans. Only one problem remained: Rosecrans had been promoted to Major General of Volunteers after Thomas, and Thomas's seniority over Rosecrans might cause confusion or resentment when Rosecrans became Thomas's commanding officer. To solve this problem, Lincoln signed an order moving back the date of Rosecrans's commission from August 21, 1862, to March 31, 1862, giving Rosecrans seniority.

Thomas had known Rosecrans at West Point, from which Rosecrans graduated in 1842, two years after Thomas, with a rank of fifth in a class of fifty-six students. After his graduation, Rosecrans served as an officer for nine years and then went into private enterprise, where he made a fortune as an inventor and businessman. He rejoined the military when the Civil War broke out and served with distinction in western Virginia and Mississippi in 1861–62. Rosecrans was a highly intelligent and creative person, whom the historian Peter Cozzens describes as "perhaps . . . the only true genius to command a Union army in the field." Rosecrans was a devoutly religious man, generous and congenial, and well liked by his officers and men. His character had a negative side, however. He was emotional and sensitive, and under stress these traits could make him nervous and indecisive. He was also subject to outbursts of temper, in which he would fly into a rage and scream insults at subordinates. In business and in everyday life, Rosecrans's nervous temperament made him energetic and quick-witted, but in the stress of combat his excitable nature could be a handicap.[2]

Thomas was deeply offended that Rosecrans was selected to command the army over himself, and he sent a letter to Halleck protesting against being replaced by an officer lower in seniority. "Although I do not claim for myself any superior ability," Thomas wrote, "no just cause exists for overslaughing me by placing me under my junior, [and] I feel deeply mortified and aggrieved at the action taken in this matter." Thomas did not ask for command of the army, but he requested either that he be transferred elsewhere or that an officer senior to him in rank be placed in command, so that he would not have to endure the insult of being commanded by a junior officer.[3]

After sending this dispatch, Thomas spoke to Rosecrans. As Rosecrans recalled their conversation, Thomas politely stated that he thought Rosecrans was capable and deserved the command, but that he felt aggrieved by the decision and wanted a transfer. Rosecrans agreed that Thomas had been treated unfairly, adding that Thomas was his superior "in service, and in years, and in merit," but asked him to stay, as he needed Thomas's support and advice. Thomas agreed, on the condition that he would not be assigned the position of second-in-command that he had held under Buell. Instead, he wanted an independent command, preferably the largest of the army's three wings, the center. Thomas got what he asked for.[4]

Two weeks later, Halleck informed Thomas that he was mistaken about Rosecrans being junior to him in rank, because Rosecrans's commission to major general of volunteers predated Thomas's. Thomas apologized, replying that he would not have written Halleck to begin with had he known that Rosecrans had been commissioned before him. Later, when Thomas learned that Rosecrans had been made senior to him only by Lincoln's having backdated Rosecrans's promotion, Thomas was furious. "I have made my last protest while the war lasts," he told Halleck. "You may hereafter put a stick over me if you choose to do so. I will take care, however, to so manage my command, whatever it may be, as not to be involved in the mistakes of the stick."[5]

To his credit, Rosecrans did not view Thomas as a threat to his authority, and he instead welcomed Thomas's presence. The war correspondent William Bickham, who traveled with Rosecrans's headquarters, described Thomas as Rosecrans's "true chief of staff" and stated that Rosecrans always consulted Thomas when making important plans. Rosecrans often praised Thomas to his staff and called him his "chief counselor." According to Bickham, Rosecrans once told him, "Thomas is a man of extraordinary character. Years ago, at the Military Academy, I conceived that there were points of strong resemblance between his character and that of Washington. I was in the habit of calling him General Washington."[6]

Thomas and Rosecrans got along well together and worked together effectively. Thomas generally respected Rosecrans and agreed with his decisions, but when they disagreed, Thomas felt comfortable expressing his disagreement openly with Rosecrans. Thomas supported Rosecrans's leadership style even when the authorities in Washington did not. They had hoped that Rosecrans would break away from Buell's passivity and launch an immediate offensive, but Rosecrans disappointed them. Buell had abandoned much of central Tennessee to the Confederates, and the War Department wanted Rosecrans to recapture the area immediately and move on to take East Tennessee. Rosecrans insisted on waiting until the railroads between Nashville and points north had been repaired, and he sent repeated requests to the War Department for additional weapons, equipment, and supplies. Rosecrans's delays frustrated his superiors, but he was supported in his desire to prepare before advancing by his subordinate commanders, including Thomas.[7]

While Rosecrans delayed action in the western theater, he at least used the time productively. He reorganized the army's cavalry, uniting it under a single commander so that it could better respond to Confederate raids.[8] He expanded and improved his army's engineers, uniting them in a single "pioneer brigade" of about two thousand men. Himself an expert engineer, Rosecrans paid close attention to his engineers' training and operations and personally contributed to the design of an improved and more easily transportable pontoon bridge.[9] Rosecrans also reorganized the hospital corps and ordered his medical director to cooperate fully with the Sanitary Commission, a volunteer organization that provided the Union army with doctors, nurses, and medical supplies. Rosecrans developed a system to transport wounded men by rail to hospitals in rear areas for treatment, making use of special hospital cars designed by the Sanitary Commission.[10]

As a final improvement, Rosecrans completely restructured the army's mapmaking department. He appointed an innovative young engineer officer, William Merrill, as its director, and he made sure that Merrill had the authority and resources he needed to be effective. Merrill set up a lithography press at headquarters for making high-quality, permanent maps and also developed a photographic reproduction process that required only minimal, lightweight equipment. This innovative process allowed Merrill quickly to make simple, functional maps for immediate distribution to field commanders. Rosecrans and Merrill also restructured the staff organization of the topographical department, ensuring that scouts, topographical engineers, and field commanders shared information about field conditions and geography in a timely manner. Rosecrans soon had the best topographical department in the Union army, which was far superior to the mapmaking facilities used by the Confederates.[11]

As Rosecrans got his army ready to move, news came from Virginia of the defeat of the Army of the Potomac, now commanded by Ambrose Burnside, at the Battle of Fredericksburg on December 13. Rosecrans began his own offensive later that month. His objective was Chattanooga, and his line of advance ran southeast, along the railroad line and wagon roads that connected Chattanooga and Nashville. About halfway between the two cities lay the town of Murfreesboro, where the wagon roads and the railroad converged. Rosecrans knew that Bragg's army was located somewhere between Nashville and Murfreesboro, but he did not know its exact dispositions. He set out along the roads surrounding the railroad line, in search of Bragg's army.

Rosecrans's advance, coming so late in the year, at first caught Bragg off guard. Bragg had already put his army into winter quarters, keeping his men widely dispersed in the countryside north of Murfreesboro where they could take food and forage from the countryside. As a result,

Rosecrans's advance met with little opposition at first, until Bragg could concentrate his forces. On December 29 the Union army approached Murfreesboro, and its leading units ran into heavy Confederate troop concentrations near Stones River. Since the Confederates were protected by the river line and by entrenchments, the Union advance troops halted and waited for the rest of their army to catch up. It took the rest of the next day for the Union army to concentrate, by which time it had become clear that the entire Confederate army lay before them. Rosecrans made plans to launch a major attack the next day.[12]

The Union troops were deployed in a northeast–southwest line, perpendicular to the Nashville–Murfreesboro railroad and turnpike, and faced the Confederate army to the southeast. The right wing of the army, commanded by Maj. Gen. Alexander McCook, was on the southwestern part of the line; the center was commanded by Thomas, and the left wing, commanded by Maj. Gen. Thomas L. Crittenden, occupied the northeastern end of the line. The terrain in the area was a patchwork of fields, low hills, and dense cedar forests. Stones River, which meanders in a curving path south to north, crossed the Federal line north of the road. The river was shallow and could be forded easily by infantry and cavalry, but it did form a barrier that slowed the progress of artillery and supply wagons.[13]

On the evening of December 30, 1862, Rosecrans summoned his generals to his tent to describe his plan for the next day's battle. He intended to strengthen Crittenden's command on the left wing and have it lead the attack against Bragg, with support from Thomas in the center. McCook's right wing would only have to hold its portion of the line against an expected Confederate attack. Some of Crittenden's troops had already crossed Stones River, and Rosecrans wanted Crittenden to move the rest of his wing across and occupy Wayne's Hill, a commanding height on the eastern bank. After Crittenden took the hill, he was to move artillery to the top, where it could fire down on Bragg's army and force it to retreat. After approving this plan, Thomas went back to his command and made arrangements to prepare his troops for battle.[14]

Thomas's force, the largest of the three sections of the army, normally consisted of five divisions, but two of these divisions and part of a third had been detached to guard Nashville and the railroad supply line. Thomas thus had on hand only thirteen thousand men: one division of four brigades under Maj. Gen. Lovell H. Rousseau, another division of two brigades under Brig. Gen. James S. Negley, and a single detached brigade commanded by Col. Moses B. Walker. Of these seven brigades, only the two under Negley were currently in the front line. Walker's brigade was still on its way to the front, and the four brigades of Rousseau's division, having arrived late on December 30, were encamped in the army's rear.[15]

Rosecrans's attack began the next morning as planned. Thomas had little to do at first but wait, as Crittenden's troops moved into position. As Crittenden's men began crossing the river, Thomas and Rosecrans heard sounds of heavy firing from the southwest. At first neither general felt concerned, as they had expected the Confederates to launch some sort of attack in that sector. But it soon became evident that the firing was getting closer, and it also seemed to be moving toward the army's rear. One of McCook's staff officers arrived and reported that the right wing of the army had been surprised and defeated. An entire division had been routed, and the Confederates were advancing so rapidly that the rest of the wing was hard pressed to put together a defense. Thomas soon began to see evidence of the rout. As one of his officers recalled, men were "running with hats off" away from the front line, "their arms thrown away and their tongues out of their mouths, panting for breath."[16]

Unless something was done quickly, the entire army might be routed. Rosecrans ordered Thomas to send Rousseau's division into action on the left. As Thomas went off to help direct the placement of Rousseau's troops, Rosecrans told Crittenden to call off his attack and cross his forces back over the river, where they would form a defensive reserve. Rosecrans also posted artillery on a hill near his headquarters, from which they could hold off the Confederates if they broke through Rousseau's line. Thomas sent his provost guard, a regiment of soldiers whose job it was to round up stragglers from the rear, to a position far behind McCook's former line. The men were so panicked that the provost guard had to fix bayonets and charge them to make them stop running, but they slowly began putting a stop to the rout.[17]

Rosecrans reacted quickly to the crisis and spent the day rushing from place to place on the battlefield, improvising a defense. His initial decisions probably saved the army from disaster, but as the day wore on, fatigue began to affect his judgment. Animated by nervous energy, Rosecrans rode up and down the line, attempting to manage the entire battle himself and even ordering the placement of individual regiments. His efforts some-times did more harm than good, as his own orders occasionally contradicted the orders of his division and brigade commanders. While some officers later criticized him for this, his men were reassured by Rosecrans's presence on the front line, and the impression he gave of energy and authority.[18]

After Thomas left Rosecrans's headquarters, an orderly rode up and told Thomas that Confederate cavalry had broken through the lines and was threatening his headquarters. Thomas sent a few members of his cavalry escort to the rear to secure his headquarters camp and then rode forward to coordinate the movement and placement of Rousseau's division.[19] When Thomas arrived at the front, he discovered that most of the left wing had broken, but that the left-center of the line was still holding out, despite repeated Confederate assaults. Gen. Thomas Negley's division, of Thomas's wing, held an exposed position in a salient of the center line, and a division under Gene. Philip H. Sheridan extended this line to the southwest. Both divisions held strong defensive positions in a dense cedar forest, but the collapse of McCook's wing had left Sheridan's right flank unprotected, and the Confederates threatened to advance around this flank and surround him. Thomas and Rousseau moved Rousseau's division into a position where it extended Sheridan's line to the west, and Thomas supervised the placement of artillery where it would best aid the defense. After Rousseau's division moved into line, Rosecrans sent reinforcements from Crittenden's corps to extend the line even farther west.[20]

Thomas's two divisions were thus committed to the battle. His third force, a single brigade under the command of Colonel Walker, arrived on the field at around 10:00 A.M., after spending the previous day and that morning protecting the army's baggage trains from Confederate cavalry. At first Thomas ordered Walker to join Rousseau's line, but then he changed his mind and used the brigade as an additional provost guard. Throughout the morning, Walker's brigade worked with Thomas's regular provost guard, the Ninth Michigan Volunteer Infantry regiment, in rounding up the fugitives from McCook's corps and organizing them to fight again. It was unusual to have an entire brigade act as a provost guard, but the decision was justified by the enormous number of men who had been routed that morning by the Confederate surprise attack. Walker's brigade and the regular provost regiment rounded up hundreds of fugitives, who contributed to the Union defense later that day. In the afternoon, after most of the fugitives had been rallied, Rosecrans ordered

Walker's brigade into line on the western flank. For the rest of the battle, Walker took orders from McCook, who commanded the western sector, not from Thomas.[21]

At around 11:00 A.M., Sheridan sent word to Thomas that he had almost run out of ammunition and had to retreat. Sheridan had held out for hours against a force of attackers that greatly outnumbered him; many of his men had been wounded or killed, and the survivors were exhausted. Sheridan's division could not fight any longer, but their retreat meant that Negley and Rousseau would have to retreat also. To avoid having to abandon the artillery during the withdrawal, Thomas set up a temporary rear defense line of infantry, and then ordered the artillery and some of the infantry to retreat past the temporary line to a main line on strong defensive ground. Only when the artillery made it back to the main line did Thomas allow the rest of the infantry to retreat. As soon as Negley's and Rousseau's divisions began to withdraw, the Confederates pushed forward, attacking the defenders while they were out of their entrenchments and inflicting heavy casualties. Their casualties were increased by Thomas's orders to establish a temporary line, but he was able to save all the artillery except for six guns of Negley's division. The Confederates managed to rout one brigade as it withdrew, opening a hole in the Union line, but Thomas ordered a brigade of Rousseau's division to counterattack, and this brigade managed to close the gap.[22]

By noon, all of Thomas's troops had completed their withdrawal and established a new defensive line. This line was a strong one, set up to take full advantage of the terrain, with artillery effectively placed on high ground behind the front. The Union army held this position for the rest of the day, beating off a number of attacks and causing great loss to the attackers. Thomas remained active on this front for the rest of the day, riding up and down the line to keep an eye on the battle's progress and to inspire the men with his presence. One officer remembered him as "calm [and] inflexible, from whose gaze skulkers shrank abashed." Another remembers Thomas riding along the front lines throughout the day, always "the same steady, earnest, and energetic leader, cool where all were in a blaze of excitement."[23]

Once Thomas had established a strong defensive position and the impetus of the initial Confederate attack had passed, the Confederates probably should have either attempted to outflank the western end of the Union line or attacked its eastern end, which had been weakened when Rosecrans took units from it to strengthen his right flank. Instead, the Confederates launched a series of uncoordinated attacks against the strongly defended Union center. The anchor of the Union center was a wooded area on a slight hill, surrounded by open fields, that came to be named the "Round Forest." The forest was defended by a full brigade, commanded by Col. William B. Hazen. To attack him the Confederates had to cross the open fields to his front, exposed to fire from Hazen's men and from artillery posted behind them, and then stay in the open, firing at Hazen's troops in the forest. Hazen's troops took many casualties in these assaults, but they held their ground, inflicting much more damage than they took. The Confederates kept hammering at the Round Forest position all day but never succeeded in breaking it.[24]

The day ended with the two armies in the same positions they had held since the afternoon. The Confederates had nearly won the day, but the resourceful leadership of Rosecrans, Thomas, Negley, Sheridan, and Hazen, combined with great bravery on the part of their men, had prevented a disaster for the Union army. The blame for the near-defeat lay with McCook, who had failed to keep his men on alert for a Confederate attack. During the night of December 30–31, Bragg had taken units from elsewhere in his line to strengthen his left wing, meaning that he outflanked and outnumbered the surprised men of McCook's command. The units on the far right end of McCook's flank broke first, and then most of the rest of his command broke and ran as well. Some regiments and brigades put up a resistance, but they were soon outflanked and had to retreat to avoid being surrounded. Out of McCook's entire corps, only Sheridan's division offered effective resistance, delaying the rebel advance long enough for Rousseau to form a second defensive line.[25]

Rosecrans called a council of war on the evening of December 31, to discuss the army's options for the next day. His army had taken heavy casualties, its lines had been driven back, and thousands of men had fled the field in panic. While Rosecrans's attention had been taken up by the battle in the front, Confederate cavalry operating far in the army's rear had raided the Union baggage trains and had destroyed much of the army's food and ammunition. An eyewitness to the scene later recalled that the officers were crowded into the tent, seated in chairs and on the floor, their "cheerless and somber" faces illuminated by the yellow light of a tallow candle. Rosecrans, looking "worn and anxious," asked his generals what they thought the army should do on the following day. Some of them counseled retreat, while others wanted to stay and fight. The exhausted officers listened to the discussion with "nodding heads," and Thomas napped in his chair as the discussion went on. Rosecrans, exploring his options, woke Thomas with the question "Will you protect the rear on a retreat to Overall's Creek?" "This army can't retreat," Thomas replied, and went back to sleep.[26]

Thomas's statement can be seen as a bold call to arms, but it can also be interpreted as a simple statement of fact. On the one hand, Confederate cavalry was roaming in the Union army's rear, the Union soldiers were tired and short of supplies, and the army's draft animals were weak from lack of forage. In this condition the army really was incapable of retreating, as it lacked the strength, organization, and supplies for a movement in any direction. On the other hand, the army was dug in to strong positions and had defeated every Confederate attack made on it that afternoon. Under the circumstances, the safest course was to stay and fight.

Rosecrans also favored staying and renewing the fight, and after the council of war ended, he issued orders that rearranged Union lines for the second day of fighting. During the first day, Rosecrans had pulled troops from his left wing to reinforce his threatened right and center, and he was now concerned that the Confederates would take advantage of this weakness and attack the Union left. Rosecrans pulled some of Crittenden's units out of the right and center and sent them to the left. He also told Crittenden to cross Stones River again and occupy a series of hills on the other side. These hills, which lay north of Wayne's Hill, Crittenden's original objective, were high enough to dominate the area around them, so that as long as the Union army maintained control of this ground its left flank would be safe.[27]

After the council of war, Thomas rode along his lines arranging and aligning his units for an effective defense the next day. A staff officer who saw him that night recalled that Thomas "had plenty on his mind" and noticed that "this was the first occasion I had ever observed him trotting his horse. Walking was his pace, his quiet, grand presence always inspiring confidence." Thomas had to move quickly that night, as his entire line had to be adjusted in preparation for the next day's fighting. After reviewing his troops' positions, Thomas got a few hours sleep at his temporary headquarters, a small cabin near the Murfreesboro Pike.[28]

As the morning of January 1, 1863, dawned, the Union soldiers braced for another Confederate assault. Strangely, none came. The morning dragged on, and the Union troops waited, but the Confederates still did nothing. The afternoon passed quietly as well, and the sun set, with no fighting occurring other than some minor skirmishing along the lines. The Confederates did not leave the battlefield but remained in their positions near the Union lines, doing nothing. When night fell, the Union soldiers felt relieved that the day had passed so peacefully, but they were also very hungry. Confederate cavalry raiders had destroyed much of the army's supplies, and there were no rations left for the troops. Soldiers were given meals that consisted only of a handful of beans, or a tiny portion of flour to cook bread with. Others cooked the horses' feed corn, or carved out horse steaks from animals left dead on the battlefield. Thomas could do little to correct the supply problem, but he did visit his soldiers to commiserate, to encourage them, and to assure them that the officers were suffering from the same lack of rations. One officer reported that the soldiers felt "much encouraged" by "the constant presence and solicitous anxiety of General Thomas for their welfare," and their morale remained strong despite their hunger.[29]

When the next day dawned, the Confederates were still in their positions but still seemed unwilling to attack. The morning of January 2 passed without fighting, but the Federals could see enemy troops moving around on the eastern side of Stones River, opposite Crittenden's corps. It looked like the Confederates were finally preparing to launch the attack that Rosecrans had expected the previous day. To make sure that his line would hold, he sent the two brigades of Negley's division and two brigades from Crittenden's corps to a reserve position behind the main line on the hills east of Stones River. From this position the four reserve brigades could either reinforce the front line or launch a counterattack, as the situation demanded.[30]

The day wore on into afternoon, and still the Confederates did not attack. Finally, at 4:00 P.M., a line of Confederates moved forward against Crittenden's line. His men put up a fierce resistance but had to fall back, ceding the hill to the Confederates. Their victory was short-lived, however. Now that their own men were out of the way, the Union artillery batteries posted on the west side of the river were able to open fire on the Confederates. The enemy soldiers, standing exposed on the treeless hilltop, made easy targets, and the Union guns inflicted hundreds of casualties in less than an hour. Thomas then ordered Negley to counterattack with his two brigades, but his orders were unnecessary, as the

Union brigade commanders moved forward on their own initiative and retook the hill. When night fell, the Union soldiers held their original positions, and all Bragg had to show for his attack were hundreds of killed, wounded, and captured soldiers.[31]

The night of January 2 was cold and rainy, but the Union soldiers felt cheerful, as the tide of events was turning in their favor. On the morning of January 3, the Confederates launched a minor attack on Thomas's front but withdrew after brief fighting and did little else that day. Late in the afternoon, Rousseau asked Thomas for permission to launch his own attack, which Thomas granted. The attack was limited in scope but succeeded in capturing a small part of the Confederate main line.[32] Bragg retreated that night, but the Union army was so exhausted and out of supplies that Rosecrans did not attempt a pursuit. On January 5 Rosecrans learned that the Confederates had abandoned Murfreesboro, so he sent infantry to occupy the town and sent cavalry forward to scout out the enemy's positions. They soon met resistance from Confederate cavalry, which indicated that Bragg's main force had not retreated very far. Rosecrans did not want to bring on another battle until his army had recovered, as his men had suffered worse from their narrow victory than the Confederates had by their defeat. The Union army had suffered 12,900 casualties during the three days' fighting, compared to the Confederates' 11,700; these casualty figures were very high, almost as severe as at Shiloh, amounting to 31 percent and 33 percent, respectively, of the men engaged in each force.[33] Rosecrans stopped his advance and settled into winter quarters in and around Murfreesboro.[34]

Thomas was much more effective as a subordinate commander under Rosecrans than he had been under Buell. The two men agreed on most questions of strategy and tactics, and they trusted and relied on one another. Thomas had confidence in Rosecrans's orders and carried them out effectively, and Rosecrans knew he could rely on the commander of his largest corps. Thomas's role was primarily limited to helping his division and brigade commanders set up their lines in fulfillment of Rosecrans's orders. Rosecrans always claimed that the decision to stay and fight after the first day of battle was his own, but Thomas's advice may have influenced Rosecrans's decision.

While Thomas held a subordinate role to Rosecrans at Stones River, some of the decisions he made independently had a positive effect on the battle's result. Thomas placed great importance on having a skilled provost guard, and he selected the Ninth Michigan, one of his best regiments, for this role. During the morning and afternoon of the first day of battle, the Ninth Michigan worked quickly to halt McCook's fleeing soldiers and reform them. Only a half hour after the rout began, the regiment had collected one thousand cavalrymen, nearly two regiments of infantry, and seven artillery pieces. These troops were reorganized into a provisional force, which was later sent to form part of the second line of defense that Rosecrans pieced together behind the original line. Thomas also deserves credit for sending Walker's brigade to assist the Ninth Michigan in provost duties. With the right wing routed, it must have been tempting to rush Walker's brigade directly into the battle when it arrived on the field at 10:00 A.M. Instead, Thomas planned for the long term, using Walker's troops to rally men who would be needed later in the day.[35]

While Stones River was touted in the North as a Union victory, in reality the battle was a stalemate. The two sides suffered roughly equal casualties, and while Rosecrans managed to hold the field and occupy Murfreesboro, Bragg's attack had halted Rosecrans's advance. Furthermore, Rosecrans had no intention of resuming his advance anytime soon. He had given in to political pressure and begun his advance earlier than he had intended, with results that were almost disastrous. He now felt justified in preparing for as long as he thought necessary before he advanced again. Thomas supported him in this decision, and the two men spent months equipping and training their army before moving forward.

CHAPTER NINE

From Stones River to Chickamauga Creek

I have educated myself not to feel.

Rosecrans spent six months after Stones River preparing his army before taking the field again against the Confederates. By taking so long to prepare, Rosecrans incurred the opposition of Lincoln, Stanton, and others in the federal government. Thomas supported Rosecrans's decision to delay, and by doing so Thomas also began to acquire a reputation for slowness and caution. At the same time, Grant and Sherman led an active campaign against Vicksburg, improvising new tactics in the face of difficulties, and ultimately capturing the Confederate fortress on July 4, 1863. As the year progressed, Grant and Sherman came to represent the kind of quick and aggressive leadership that Lincoln and Stanton wanted, while Thomas was increasingly identified with the overly slow and cautious approach of Rosecrans and others.

The War Department had no objection to Rosecrans's decision to go into winter quarters after Stones River, but he was expected to advance again once spring arrived. Spring turned into summer, however, and Rosecrans still failed to move. Halleck and Stanton considered relieving Rosecrans from command, but Rosecrans was still popular after his victory at Stones River, so they were reluctant to remove him. They tried a series of threats and inducements instead, but Rosecrans resisted their efforts to get him to move, and his subordinates, including Thomas, supported his decision to delay.[1]

Rosecrans spent the six months after Stones River stockpiling supplies, building up the capacity of his logistics department and engineers to supply the army during its advance, and strengthening the army's cavalry. The cavalry was a particularly important project for him, and Rosecrans's goals went beyond just building a force that would be larger than the Confederates'. He wanted to develop an entirely new type of cavalry—a massive, mobile strike force that would spearhead the army's advance. It had been decades since cavalry had been used as an offensive weapon, due to the fact that improvements in musket and rifle technology had made it easy for infantry to repel cavalry charges. Civil War commanders rarely used cavalry as an offensive unit in battle, and they instead used cavalry for scouting, guarding supply lines, and protecting the army's rear and flanks.

Rosecrans wanted to use cavalry as mounted infantry, units that would ride to critical points during a battle or campaign and then dismount to attack on foot. They would not attack on horseback, as mounted men presented too easy a target for infantry, but their mounts would allow them to move quickly, so that a commander could use them to place a strong force unexpectedly at a crucial point. While Rosecrans deployed the mounted infantry to good purpose during the campaign to come, it was Thomas who finally completed the development of the army's cavalry, using them to strike a knockout blow two years later at the Battle of Nashville.[2]

While Rosecrans prepared for his advance, Thomas drilled and trained the soldiers in his corps. Benjamin Scribner, an officer who served with Thomas at Murfreesboro, recalled that Thomas was "an undesirable person to approach if you had nothing to say." His office was not a place for socializing, and "if you had no point to make pertinent for his action, he would fix those cold gray eyes of his upon you, and with his immobile countenance, so embarrass and confuse you that you would wish yourself far away." The journalist William Shanks also noted Thomas's "severe and grave" expression, which "forbids trifling." On the one hand, his presence was "no place for loungers. . . . Visitors must have business to transact or retire, and they never require any other hint than the countenance of the general." On the other hand, Scribner noted, if you did have something of relevance to report or inquire, Thomas was patient and attentive.[3]

Thomas's forbidding personality and demeanor may have resulted from his own feelings of sadness and loneliness. While Thomas rarely showed his feelings, wartime was difficult for him. In his earlier career, he had been sustained during difficult assignments by the presence of his wife and his correspondence with his family in Southampton. Now his wife was far away, and his siblings refused to write to him. Time and again, he witnessed the frustration of the Union cause, and he also felt frustration at his own career as other generals were promoted ahead of him.

While Thomas rarely let his guard down, he and Benjamin Scribner became close enough friends that Scribner gained some insight into Thomas's inner feelings. Once, Scribner told Thomas about a difficulty he was having, finishing with the exclamation "Any man with a heart would feel as I do!" Slowly shaking his head, Thomas replied, "I have educated myself not to feel." "He uttered these words with lengthened pauses between each," Scribner remembered, "as if every one of them recalled some bitter recollection."[4] The pressures and frustrations of command, the sorrow he felt at waging war against his fellow Southerners, and the isolation from his wife and family all weighed heavily on him.

Thomas obtained some comfort by accompanying Scribner on visits to Scribner's wife and children, who were spending the winter in Murfreesboro. Scribner wrote that Thomas, "having no children of his own, took much notice and seeming interest in mine, and would take them in his arms and caress them in a manner that won their mother's heart, and made her his friend for life." One day, Thomas took Scribner's little boy on his knee and teased him about his curly hair, asking him, "What do you wear this for?" The boy replied by pulling on Thomas's shoulder-straps, the insignia of his general's rank, and asking, "What do you wear this for?" "The general, with a smile," Scribner recalled, "replied that the child's question was more difficult to answer than his own." On another occasion, Thomas told Scribner's little boy that he could draw, with only three strokes of a pencil, a sketch of a soldier with a musket on his shoulder, followed by his dog, entering a door. Scribner and his children asked Thomas to demonstrate this, and he did—drawing a vertical line, representing the door frame; a diagonal line, representing the bayonet of the musket; and a short curved line below it, representing the dog's tail. "The soldier and the dog are inside," Thomas explained to the child. "With all his gravity," Scribner remembered, "he had a vein of humor in him, and enjoyed a joke hugely."[5]

Thomas also found relief from the pressures of command by attending the amateur theatrical entertainments that the officers put on during the winter encampment. Porter recalled that Thomas "had a great deal more fun in him than is generally supposed," and was "a constant attendant" at the entertainments. Thomas enjoyed the performances immensely and "would nod approval at the efforts of the performers, and beat time to the music, and when anything particularly comical took place, he would roll from side to side and nearly choke with merriment."[6]

Thomas greatly enjoyed good food and drink and made sure his staff provided him with good food. The journalist William Shanks, who frequently ate at Thomas's table, recalled that "better beef and better coffee could not have been found in the country in which the army was campaigning, while the hot rolls and potatoes, baked in the hot ashes of a neighboring fire, would have made many a French cook blush."[7] Thomas also kept a set of silver flasks and decanters of punch and whiskey on hand for guests.[8] While not a heavy drinker himself, he did drink on social occasions. One officer recalls how Thomas enjoyed a glass of wine and some conversation with one of the local ladies at a party held after a military review. Thomas "arose from the table evidently much refreshed, and proceeded to make himself exceedingly agreeable." The officer, who had previously seen only Thomas's official side, remarked that "I never knew the old gentleman to be so affable, cordial, and complimentary before."[9]

Rosecrans finally began his offensive on June 24, 1863. He knew his task would be difficult. Bragg had posted his army along a naturally strong position, a ridge of mountains that could be crossed in only four places. Bragg's men had spent months improving this line by digging in and building defenses. While attacking this line directly would be costly, moving around it would also be difficult. The mountains, woods, and rivers of the region made movement slow, and there were few roads through the region over which an army could travel. Also, Rosecrans could not maneuver his army too far away from the Nashville–Chattanooga railroad, as this was his only line of supply.[10]

To get around Bragg's strong front line, Rosecrans decided to split his army in two. He would leave half of it where it was, keeping Bragg's army in place, and move the other half around Bragg's line and behind it, cutting the Confederates off from their supply base at Chattanooga. If successful, the movement would force the Confederates to retreat. But if Bragg realized what Rosecrans was doing, he could concentrate his whole army against one half of the Union army and defeat it before the other half could come to its assistance. Rosecrans's success depended on his ability to conceal his true intentions and move quickly.[11]

Rosecrans sent one corps of infantry and some cavalry to the western part of Bragg's line, where the terrain was most favorable for an attack, and acted as if he was preparing to launch a major assault there. When Bragg shifted his forces to meet this threat, Rosecrans launched his real attack, against a pass called Hoover's Gap, on the eastern part of Bragg's line. Rosecrans used one of his new mounted infantry brigades to surprise and defeat the Confederates defending the pass, and Thomas's infantry poured through the gap, moving into the rear of Bragg's army.[12] Bragg retreated several times, but the Union army kept outflanking him, and Bragg had to keep retreating. He finally stopped on a strong defensive line behind the Tennessee River, centering on the city of Chattanooga.[13]

On July 3 Rosecrans moved his base of operations forward to Tullahoma, Bragg's former base camp. In nine days he had driven the rebels back more than fifty miles and had cleared middle Tennessee, at the cost of only 84 dead and 476 wounded Union soldiers. While Rosecrans considered this a major accomplishment, his superiors in Washington were not impressed, as his limited achievement was overshadowed by George Meade's defeat of Robert E. Lee at Gettysburg on July 3, and Grant's capture of Vicksburg on July 4.[14]

After pausing at Tullahoma for six weeks, Rosecrans then continued his offensive, trying to maneuver the Confederates out of Chattanooga instead of engaging them in battle.[15] He set a small force in motion to the east of the city, making it seem that he would attack it from that direction.[16] Meanwhile, he sent the main part of his force, under Thomas, across the Tennessee River to the west of Chattanooga, from whence they marched south and east to cut the city's rail lines. Thomas's corps crossed the river unopposed on August 29 and then struggled over the steep mountains and through the dense woods south of the river, finally emerging into the open south of the city. Bragg reacted slowly but eventually had to retreat to protect his supply lines. Bragg evacuated Chattanooga on September 7, and the Union army entered the city two days later.[17]

At this point, Thomas and Rosecrans disagreed strongly about the army's next move. The Union cavalry had not yet located Bragg's position and had learned little about the condition of the Confederate army. In the absence of information, Rosecrans made two incorrect assumptions about Bragg's army. First, he assumed that Bragg's forces had retreated southeast, directly along the Atlanta–Chattanooga rail line. Second, Rosecrans convinced himself that the Confederates were demoralized and were fleeing in disorder. Sensing victory, Rosecrans decided not to wait and concentrate his army, as he had done at Tullahoma, but to pursue Bragg immediately, keeping his three corps widely separated to facilitate their rapid movement.[18]

Thomas was not as optimistic as Rosecrans about the Confederates' retreat, and he advised Rosecrans to consolidate his forces. Thomas's counsel failed to convince Rosecrans, and Rosecrans ordered him to continue his advance. Thomas hurried to join his corps, which Rosecrans had ordered to cross the ridge of Lookout Mountain, southwest of Chattanooga, and then advance southward to the town of LaFayette, Georgia. One division, under General Negley, had already crossed Lookout Mountain at a pass called Steven's Gap, but the rest of the corps was still on the northern side of the ridge. Thomas was concerned that Negley's division had gotten too far ahead of the rest of the corps. Thomas feared that the main Confederate army might lie in Negley's front, and if this were true, Bragg might be able to surround and destroy Negley's division before the rest of the corps made it over the pass to reinforce him. Rosecrans had discounted this possibility, but Thomas wanted to check in with Negley just to make sure.

When Thomas arrived at his corps headquarters, he found evidence to justify his suspicions. Negley's scouts had detected what might be a large Confederate force in his front, and Negley had ordered his division to halt. After riding over the mountain to speak with Negley in person, Thomas endorsed his decision. Rosecrans disagreed and sent Thomas a message that evening ordering him to move Negley forward "with the utmost promptness." He chastised Thomas for his caution, telling him that "your advance ought to have threatened La Fayette yesterday evening."[19]

Thomas did not attempt to carry out Rosecrans's order the next day, September 11. The Confederate force in Negley's front seemed quite strong, and Thomas's cavalry reported that more enemy troops were moving along the roads nearby. This intelligence seemed to confirm Negley's suspicion that the Confederates were trying to cut off his division from the rest of the army. After riding to the front to evaluate the situation in person, Thomas endorsed Negley's decision to retreat to the base of the mountain and wait for reinforcements. At first Thomas wanted to make Negley's retreat preliminary to a counteroffensive, by sending one division to reinforce Negley while sending two other divisions over the mountain by a different route, to attack the Confederate force in flank. Thomas soon realized that the Confederates were too strong in his sector for this plan to work.[20]

The Confederates attacked in force that afternoon, but Thomas and Negley's caution had saved Negley's division from being cut off, and they were able to fall back, under fire, to a safe position at the base of the mountain. One officer remembered that Thomas stayed with them even while the "shot and shell were flying thick and fast" around them, and that his demeanor, "as undisturbed and impassive as the craggy mountains around," inspired them to hold fast. Another officer recalled that shortly after being attacked that afternoon, "General George H. Thomas rode slowly up looking as peaceful and calm as the summer sky, inspiring all with new hope and courage, and causing many to say, 'There's Pap Thomas, boys, it's all right now.'"[21] Under Thomas's leadership the division fought a rearguard action as it retreated, suffering about 150 casualties but reaching safety at the base of the mountain.[22]

Rosecrans was not impressed with Thomas's and Negley's performance. On September 12 he chastised Thomas for his excessive caution and maintained that Negley had withdrawn from his advanced position "more through prudence than compulsion." As the day wore on, however, and more reports came in from his scouts, Rosecrans realized that he had been wrong. Bragg's army had not retreated southeast along the railroad, as Rosecrans had thought, but had gone directly south, meaning that the bulk of Bragg's army was in Thomas's front. As Thomas had suspected, Bragg had indeed tried to surround and destroy Negley's division on September 11, but mistakes by Bragg's subordinate commanders, combined with Thomas and Negley's caution, had caused the plan to fail. If Thomas had not defied Rosecrans's orders to advance, Negley's division might have been destroyed.[23]

Finally realizing the danger he was in, Rosecrans began to concentrate his three scattered corps. The next day, Bragg attempted to trap another isolated division, this time one in Maj. Gen. Thomas L. Crittenden's corps, but the plan misfired when Bragg's subordinates once again failed to carry out his orders. After this failure, Bragg did not attempt another attack, and Rosecrans had the time he needed to pull his scattered army together.[24]

By September 17 Rosecrans had concentrated his army in defensive positions behind West Chickamauga Creek, about ten miles south of Chattanooga. The creek runs south to north, and the army was lined up to the west of it, with McCook's corps holding the southern flank, Thomas's corps holding the center, and Crittenden's corps positioned on the northern end of the line. Behind and parallel to this line lay a road that connected Chattanooga with LaFayette, to the south. The LaFayette road would be an asset to the Union forces if a battle took place, since Rosecrans could use the road to shift forces north and south along his line. Behind the army, to the north and west, ran Missionary Ridge, and behind the ridge lay Chattanooga. Rosecrans posted his Reserve Corps, under the command of Maj. Gen. Gordon Granger, at Rossville, a small town between Missionary Ridge and Chattanooga.[25]

Rosecrans knew that Bragg's army was somewhere to the east of the Union army, on the opposite side of West Chickamauga Creek. Information from his scouts indicated that Bragg may have been reinforced by Lee's army, meaning that the Confederate army might now outnumber his own force. Rosecrans decided to stay in his defensive position and let Bragg attack him. As Rosecrans was soon to learn, his army was in fact outnumbered, as the Confederates had sent an entire corps of the Army of Northern Virginia, under the command of Gen. James Longstreet, to reinforce Bragg. Instead of attacking Rosecrans directly, Bragg had decided to move his own army northward, to get between the Union army and its supply base at Chattanooga.[26]

On September 18, 1863, Bragg's advance units encountered Union cavalry and infantry forces protecting the Union northern flank. The outnumbered Union soldiers fell back slowly, gaining time for Rosecrans to shift his forces to meet the threat. Rosecrans, correctly surmising that Bragg was trying to maneuver around his northern flank, knew he had to move his own army northward. But shifting an army sideways along a front, in the presence of an attacking enemy, was a difficult maneuver, made even more difficult in this case by the hilly, wooded terrain. Rather than shift each unit in his army northward, Rosecrans decided to leave Crittenden's corps where it was and send Thomas's entire corps around it. In the new alignment, Thomas's corps would hold the northern part of the line, Crittenden would hold the center, and McCook would still hold the southern part of the line.[27]

Rosecrans began writing orders to shift his forces around noon, but the terrain was unfamiliar both to him and to his officers, making communication difficult. Rosecrans's orders were not clearly written, and a series of miscommunications among his subordinate generals further confused matters. Couriers got lost, generals rode through the woods trying to find one another, and men stood in the roads for hours, waiting for orders. Thomas received orders to move his corps northward but was not informed that he was supposed to go all the way around Crittenden's corps. By the evening of September 18, Thomas's corps was still south of Crittenden's. Rosecrans and Thomas decided that the only remedy for the problem was for Thomas to make a night march with his corps. The night march was exhausting for the men, but they reached their objective by dawn, in time to block the Confederate flanking movement.[28]

As Thomas's column moved into position in the early morning of September 19, Thomas was greeted by Col. Daniel McCook, the commander of a brigade in Granger's Reserve Corps. McCook's brigade had been detached from the rest of Granger's corps the previous day and had been ordered to guard the area where Thomas's troops were now arriving. Colonel McCook's men had captured some Confederate stragglers the night before, and from this he guessed that there was a single Confederate brigade in his front, separated from the rest of Bragg's army by Chickamauga Creek. McCook had burned the only bridge that the Confederate brigade could use as an escape route and had prepared to attack it, but Rosecrans had sent him orders to retreat instead. Rosecrans was concerned that the forces in McCook's front were more than just a brigade, and that if McCook attacked them he might be overwhelmed.[29]

McCook thought Rosecrans was mistaken, and he urged Thomas to let him attack. Thomas told him to withdraw his brigade and join the rest of the Reserve Corps and then sent one of his own brigades, under the command of Col. John T. Croxton, to investigate. As McCook's brigade withdrew, it was attacked by Confederate cavalry, and Croxton's brigade, moving forward, counterattacked the cavalry. Croxton's men drove back the Confederate cavalry for a while, but the cavalry stopped at strong defensive positions on a wooded ridge, from which Croxton's men could not dislodge them. Croxton's divisional commander, Brig. Gen. John M. Brannan, sent Col. Ferdinand Van Derveer's brigade forward to help him, and together the two brigades began inflicting heavy casualties on the Confederate cavalry.[30]

Thomas undertook something of a risk in sending Croxton's brigade forward, as he did not know how strong the Confederate force ahead of him might be. But his decision to seize the initiative brought positive results. Bragg's original intention had been to launch a large-scale, coordinated advance through Thomas's sector, with the goal of cutting off the Union army's line of retreat to Chattanooga. Bragg thought the sector was empty of troops, and Thomas's sudden attack unnerved the Confederate commander, causing him to abandon his original plan. It was fortunate for the Union cause that Bragg did so, as Thomas's men had just reached the front and were tired from their night march. If Bragg had pressed forward with his original plan, he could have gotten between the Union army and Chattanooga. Instead, he engaged the Union army where it stood, on terms much less favorable to the Confederate forces.[31]

Bragg responded to Thomas's attack by sending in two infantry brigades to reinforce the cavalry and waited to see what the Union army would do next. The Confederates drove back Croxton's men, and Croxton, a friend of Thomas's who had served with him since Mill Springs, sent Thomas a sarcastic dispatch asking which of the four or five enemy brigades in his front Thomas had wanted him to capture. General Brannan, Croxton's divisional commander, sent his third brigade into the battle, while asking Thomas for reinforcements.[32]

Brannan's messenger found Thomas at his headquarters, resting after the long march and "taking his breakfast as calmly and coolly as anyone could be who was seated in a much less dangerous locality." Thomas got up from his meal and rode forward to investigate, soon concluding from the sounds of battle that his men had encountered a large Confederate force. He ordered another division, commanded by Brig. Gen. Absalom Baird, into the fight, telling him to extend Brannan's line northward and attack the Confederates' northern flank.[33]

Thomas also wanted to extend Brannan's line to the south, but he had no more troops available. One of the two remaining divisions in his corps, commanded by Maj. Gen. Joseph Reynolds, had gotten lost on its march the night before, and it was still two hours away from the front. His other division, commanded by General Negley, had been detached the previous day to serve with Alexander McCook's corps at the far southern end of the Union line. Thomas asked for help from Maj. Gen. John M. Palmer, commanding the nearest division in Crittenden's corps, telling him, "If you will advance on [the rebels] in front while I attack them in flank, I think we can use them up."[34] Since Palmer's division was not in his own corps, Thomas had to get Rosecrans's approval for the movement, and Rosecrans refused the request. Rosecrans felt that he did not know enough yet about Bragg's location and intentions to commit so many troops to action, and he also thought it unlikely that the main part of Bragg's army was in Thomas's front.[35]

Without Palmer's division there to help, the Union and Confederate forces in Thomas's front were about evenly matched. The line of battle went back and forth in the dense woods throughout the morning, and both sides took heavy casualties, but neither side gained the advantage. By 11:00 both sides were exhausted, and the fighting died down temporarily as the soldiers rested, resupplied their ammunition, cared for the wounded, and reorganized their units.[36] Meanwhile, Rosecrans received additional intelligence that convinced him that the Confederates' main force was in fact in Thomas's front. Rosecrans sent Palmer's division to Thomas's assistance, along with Richard W. Johnson's division, taken from McCook's corps to the south. At about 11:30 A.M., before these divisions arrived, two fresh Confederate divisions attacked, driving back Thomas's men and taking many prisoners. Thomas's line was barely holding when Palmer's and Johnson's divisions arrived on the field.[37]

Rather than reacting to Bragg's attack by sending these reinforcements directly to the threatened sector, Thomas tried to regain the initiative by extending his line southward and launching a counterattack. He placed Johnson's division south of Brannan's and ordered Palmer's division into line south of Johnson's. By 12:30 P.M. the two divisions had deployed and began marching eastward into the thick woods. They soon ran into a Confederate division that Bragg had sent to extend his own line to the south, and another bloody, inconclusive struggle began. As Johnson later recalled, "[T]he field of battle was a vast forest, whose dense foliage prevented us from seeing fifty yards distant. No one commander could see the flanks of his regiment even, and so division commanders could only learn how the battle progressed through their orderlies, staff officers, and occasional wounded men brought from various parts of the line." After a long struggle, a line stabilized in the woods, and the fighting died down once again.[38]

Meanwhile, Reynolds's division of Thomas's corps finally arrived on the field. Thomas was unsure at first where to send these troops, and he ordered Reynolds's men to march to several different positions as he changed his mind about where to use them. Finally, he divided Reynolds's division into several parts, detaching individual brigades and regiments to reinforce divisions already involved in the fighting. By 1:30 P.M. Reynolds was left with only five regiments and some artillery under his direct command, and he suggested to Thomas that he post these forces as a reserve. Thomas agreed, telling him to "exercise your own judgment and give help where it was needed." Reynolds put the artillery and two infantry regiments on a ridge behind the front line and sent the other three regiments to extend the Union line farther south and link up with Crittenden's corps.[39]

By the afternoon what had begun as a small skirmish between Croxton's brigade and the Confederate cavalry had turned into a general engagement, with troops fighting back and forth all along the northern half of the Union line. Thomas' decision to attack with Croxton's brigade, and his counterattack later that morning with Johnson's and Palmer's divisions, had unnerved Bragg and thrown off his plan of battle. Reacting poorly to Thomas' attacks, Bragg spent the day sending his forces into action piecemeal instead of concentrating them for a coordinated assault. The battle followed a repeated pattern: Each Confederate attack met with initial success, was driven back by a Union counterattack, and was then followed by another Confederate attack. Thomas could not give his divisional commanders detailed instructions, because the terrain made it impossible for him to see what was going on. Instead, he sent divisions to the general area where they seemed needed, leaving tactical decisions to the discretion of the commanders on the spot.

As the fighting continued to spread southward through the afternoon, the Confederates managed to rout a Union division and advanced across the LaFayette road. The Union could not afford to lose control of the road, as it was their only way to shift forces quickly north and south along their front. If the Confederates had been able to follow up their success, they could have made a significant breakthrough, but fortunately for the Federals, the assaulting troops were not reinforced. A small force of Union troops, including Reynolds's reserve infantry and artillery, stopped the attackers just past the LaFayette road. Thomas sent Brannan's division to recapture the road, but by the time Brannan's men got there, the crisis had passed and the Confederates had retreated.[40]

By nightfall the shape of the Union line resembled a question mark, with the southern part of the line running straight along the LaFayette road, and the northern part of the line bulging eastward in a broad arc. Thomas decided to pull back the northern section of his line to better defensive ground, closer to the LaFayette road. As Thomas was getting ready to direct this movement, General Brannan asked him his opinion of the day's fighting. Thomas replied that the battle was "all sixes and sevens, and we were merely holding our ground on the left without any movement ordered, or any known future definite object or purpose." Thomas complained that he had little idea of Rosecrans's intentions, and had heard so little from Rosecrans that day that he was not even sure where Rosecrans's headquarters was now located.[41]

Just as the Union troops prepared to withdraw, they were hit by a surprise night attack. Night attacks were unusual in the Civil War, for a number of reasons. Darkness made troop movements difficult to coordinate and created a danger that soldiers might fire on friendly units. Even if a night attack were successful, the darkness made exploiting an initial success nearly impossible. Gen. Leonidas K. Polk, commanding the north wing of the Confederate army, had decided to make a night attack after being reinforced by a fresh division late in the afternoon. Polk reasoned that the Federal troops were tired from having fought all morning, and that one more attack might cause them to break. His attack succeeded, but at a heavy cost to both sides. Both armies had difficulty identifying the units they encountered in the darkness, and soldiers fired at friendly troops; units of both armies got lost in the darkness and were easily surprised by enemy counterattacks. The Confederates took and gave heavy casualties, as they drove the Union troops back about half a mile. This was not a major setback for Thomas, as it simply pushed his men back to the line he had already selected for his withdrawal.[42]

After a day of extremely intense fighting, the Union army had fought the Confederates to a draw. The Union suffered about seven thousand casualties, and the Confederates from six thousand to nine thousand. This even result represented a victory of sorts for the Union side. The beginning of the campaign had seen the Union army separated into three parts, which were vulnerable to defeat in detail. Even after Rosecrans had successfully drawn his army together, Bragg threatened to get around his northern flank and cut him off from Chattanooga. Rosecrans had avoided both of these dangers and had also avoided being caught by surprise, as he had been at Stones River. Furthermore, the equal number of casualties damaged the Confederacy more than the Union, as the Union could more easily replace its losses.[43]

Because of the difficulty that the terrain created both in ascertaining the enemy's location and in directing the movements of his troops, Thomas was only able to exercise limited tactical leadership, but his actions were still decisive in determining the course of the battle. He employed his divisions effectively, placed his artillery where it had a good field of fire, and maintained an infantry reserve. The artillery and the infantry reserve ended up playing a crucial role in driving back the Confederates' only significant breakthrough, their afternoon advance past the LaFayette road. Most important, Thomas never surrendered the initiative to Bragg but made his own attacks and counterattacks, keeping the enemy uncertain of the strength, location, and intentions of the Union force. This seizure of the initiative caused Bragg to abandon his original plan to move around the northern flank of the Union army, a move that could have been devastating to the Union cause. Instead, Bragg wasted the advantage he held in numbers and position by responding to Thomas's moves with piecemeal, uncoordinated attacks.

Rosecrans's leadership during the first day of fighting was also effective, but the crisis was beginning to take its toll on him. Rosecrans had slept little the night before, had eaten little during the day, and had worked without a break since early in the morning. So far, he had been able to command effectively, but the strain on his nerves was beginning to show. The fighting had also taken its toll on the organization of Rosecrans's army. In sending units to reinforce Thomas as quickly as they became available, Rosecrans had mixed up brigades and divisions from different corps, making it difficult for him and his subordinates to keep track of their commands.

As the Confederate night attack petered out, Thomas began arranging his troops' dispositions for the next day. He suspected that Bragg would once again attack the northern end of the Union line, and he wanted to use the night hours to strengthen his position. He rode down the line and reconnoitered the terrain in person, aligning his troops and using the terrain to maximum effect. The defensive line that Thomas chose formed another arc, bulging eastward, about a half mile behind the front line of the first day. As he arranged his forces, he found that he could not make his defense as strong as he wanted and still have enough troops to cover his far northern flank. At 7:10 P.M. he wired Rosecrans and asked for additional troops. Shortly after Thomas sent this telegram, Rosecrans directed Thomas to come immediately to a council of war.[44]

By the time Thomas reached Rosecrans's headquarters, he was exhausted. He reported on the events of the day, explained that his line did not extend far enough to the north, and asked for reinforcements. While the other generals continued to talk, he dozed in his chair.

Whenever Rosecrans asked him a direct question, he woke up, straightened up in his chair, and answered, "I would strengthen the left," and then fell back to sleep again. Rosecrans agreed with him but kept asking, "Where am I going to take it from?" Thomas recommended pulling the right wing of the army far back to better defensive terrain, a suggestion that Rosecrans partially adopted.[45] The discussion ended at about 10:00 P.M., and Rosecrans's staff began drafting orders for the next day. Thomas was ordered to keep his troops in their current positions, while Rosecrans made detailed plans to detach portions of the other two corps to support him. After midnight, when the business part of the meeting ended, Rosecrans kept the generals a little longer to socialize. He served coffee, bacon, and crackers and even had one of the officers, who had a good singing voice, entertain them with a popular ballad.[46]

Thomas returned to his headquarters around 2:00 A.M. and finished giving his orders to his division commanders. He ordered his soldiers to construct defensive breastworks during the night, which they did, using logs and fence rails. According to Shanks, who was present at the battle, only Thomas's men constructed defensive works during the night, and these works made a significant difference in the results of the battle the next day. Thomas repeated his demand to Rosecrans for reinforcements for the far northern end of his line, this time asking specifically for Negley's division. Finally, he lay down on the ground to get a few hours of sleep before dawn.[47]

Rosecrans could not sleep, and he spent the rest of the night pacing outside his tent. Knowing that Bragg's army had been reinforced with troops from Virginia and Mississippi, he feared that he was badly outnumbered. He had captured soldiers from many different regiments that day, and, not realizing that many of the Confederate regiments were only a fraction of their normal size, he estimated the Confederate army's strength at more than 90,000 men. His army was, in fact, outnumbered, but not as badly as he thought. The Confederates had about 66,000 men in the field, compared to the Union's 58,000. Rosecrans's overestimate of the enemy's strength led him to fear that his army would be overwhelmed. His orders to Thomas that night stated, "You will defend your position with the utmost stubbornness. In case our army should be overwhelmed it will retire on Rossville and Chattanooga. Send your trains back to the latter place." While Thomas prepared a defense, Rosecrans prepared for defeat.[48]

CHAPTER TEN

The Rock of Chickamauga

It is doubtful whether [Thomas's] heroism and skill exhibited last Sunday afternoon, has ever been surpassed in this world.

Abraham Lincoln

Thomas slept for only a couple of hours on the night of September 19–20, and he rose before dawn to prepare for battle. Rosecrans rode over from his headquarters that morning, wanting to examine personally the situation in Thomas's front. Rosecrans was tired, nervous, and apprehensive, while Thomas was confident and energetic. Talking about the success of the counterattacks he had ordered the day before, Thomas exclaimed to Rosecrans, "Whenever I touched their flanks they broke, General, they broke." Thomas then noticed the journalist William Shanks standing by, listening intently. Thomas was embarrassed by his show of enthusiasm, Shanks recalled, "the blood mounted in his cheeks and he blushed like a woman. His eyes were bent immediately to the ground, and the rest of his remarks were confined to a few brief replies to the questions addressed to him."[1]

While Thomas was optimistic, he was also careful. He assumed that the Confederates' main attack would come against his line, and he felt that he did not have enough troops on hand to withstand it. He asked Rosecrans to send him reinforcements and specifically asked that Negley's division, which had previously been detached from his corps, be returned to him. When Rosecrans assured him that Negley's division was on its way, Thomas did little to extend his line northward, being content merely to wait for Negley's arrival.[2] Thomas's inaction was an error, as he had

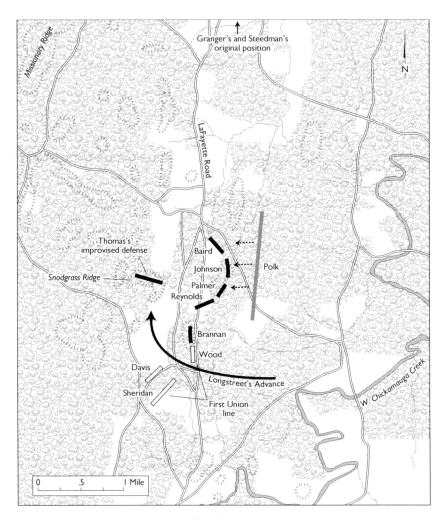

Chickamauga

several other brigades available to him at the time, which he was holding in reserve. He should have sent those brigades north immediately to extend his line and used Negley's division, when it arrived, as his new reserve force. If the Confederates had attacked early enough, they could have taken advantage of Thomas's error and outflanked him. Fortunately for the Union army, the Confederate commanders were having problems of their own, and the Confederate attack, which had been scheduled to begin at dawn, did not start until later in the morning.[3]

The first brigade from Negley's division, commanded by Gen. John Beatty, arrived around 8:00 A.M., and Thomas sent it to extend the northern end of his line. Thomas ordered Beatty to defend a wide front, far too much territory for one brigade to handle. This was another error on Thomas's part, as he should have given the brigade less territory to defend or sent another brigade from his reserve to help Beatty. In attempting to carry out the order, Beatty had to divide his brigade into individual regiments and put them in dispersed positions with wide gaps between.[4]

Bragg's attack began shortly after Beatty got his brigade into position. Bragg had ordered his brigades to attack in echelon, meaning that his northernmost brigade would attack first, followed by the next one down the line, and so on. If the maneuver went as planned, each brigade in the Union line would be outflanked and defeated, and by retreating it would allow the attackers to outflank and defeat the next one. This kind of attack was difficult to coordinate, but if successfully executed, it could lead to a major victory.

Bragg's plan almost succeeded. The Confederates routed Beatty's thinly stretched brigade and then angled southward, trying to get in the flank and rear of Thomas's line. In response, Thomas sent part of his reserve force to counterattack and moved artillery to a position on a ridge where it had a good line of fire on the attackers. As the reserve brigades moved toward the threatened sector, the commanders on the spot quickly improvised a defense, and the artillery began a destructive fire. When the reserves arrived on the scene and counterattacked, they easily threw the weakened Confederates back.[5]

Bragg's entire plan depended on the success of the initial attack. Once it failed, the other attacks had little chance of succeeding. A series of miscommunications and disagreements among the Confederate commanders made matters worse, as their units ended up attacking in a piecemeal, uncoordinated fashion. When they advanced, they met with Union defenders tightly massed behind extremely strong positions, protected by woods, ridges, and breastworks. The Confederates were repulsed all along the line, taking heavy losses while inflicting relatively few casualties on the Union troops. In a few places the attackers broke through, but they were unable to follow up their successes and were soon driven back.[6] Thomas stayed near the front throughout the morning, supervising the defense, and was often exposed to enemy artillery fire. As Shanks recalled, at one point a shell passed through the space between Thomas and one of his staff aides. The two men "looked at each other with a quiet smile," but they did not move and kept talking. A moment later, another shell passed between them. "Major, I think we had better retire a little," Thomas said, and the two moved back a few yards to the cover of a small wood.[7]

Thomas was relieved to see that his lines held, but he remained concerned about the safety of his northern flank. The Confederates could still march around the northern end of Thomas's line, cutting two of the three roads that led to Chattanooga, and separating Thomas's command from the Reserve Corps to the north. Thomas was still fixated on Negley's division, and he continued to send messages to Rosecrans asking him to hurry the rest of Negley's division forward. He also sent his chief topographical engineer to find Negley and escort him to the front. Thomas told the engineer to direct Negley to put his division's artillery, and any other artillery that came northward, on top of Snodgrass Ridge, a hill in the army's rear. Having reconnoitered this terrain personally, Thomas had determined that artillery placed on this hill would have a clear field of fire against any Confederate troops who attempted to outflank his line to the north.[8]

The fighting along Thomas's line had died down for the moment, but he now began to hear heavy firing from the Union center, just south of the area under his command. The fighting seemed to be coming closer, and the reinforcements that Rosecrans had promised to send him hours ago had still not arrived. Thomas rode south to see what was going on. Along the way he met the second brigade of Negley's division, marching north, and he sent them to the far left flank with orders to extend the line northward.[9]

As Thomas rode south, he next met Captain Sanford C. Kellogg, his aide-de-camp and nephew, whom he had sent to Rosecrans's headquarters that morning to ask for reinforcements. Kellogg was returning and had been looking for the division of Maj. Gen. Philip Sheridan, which Rosecrans had ordered north to reinforce Thomas. Kellogg told Thomas that he had not found Sheridan's division where it was supposed to be but instead discovered a large body of troops, which he could not identify. They were within what was supposed to be Union lines but were deployed in battle formation and were advancing northwest, as if they were attacking the Union army. Kellogg had not been able to make out their uniforms or flags, and when he rode closer to see who they were, they fired at him.[10]

Kellogg's news was puzzling and disturbing. If the troops Kellogg had seen were Confederates, their presence behind Union lines indicated that there had been a breach somewhere to the south. Thomas continued riding south to investigate and next met up with a division commander from Crittenden's corps, Thomas J. Wood, who was moving northward with one of his brigades. Wood reported that he had been sent to reinforce Joseph J. Reynolds's division in the southern part of Thomas's line, and that his other two brigades were coming up behind him.[11] Thomas told Wood that Reynolds's division did not need any reinforcements, but that help was desperately needed to the north. Wood pulled papers from his pocket and showed the order to Thomas. Rosecrans had ordered him to move his division to support Reynolds, he said, and he would not take the responsibility of disobeying Rosecrans's orders. But if Thomas was willing to take the responsibility on himself, Wood would go wherever Thomas sent him. Thomas agreed to take responsibility and told Wood to move his division northward as quickly as possible.[12]

Meanwhile, Thomas kept moving south, where he found one brigade of Wood's division, commanded by Col. Charles G. Harker, arrayed in line of battle on a small hill. Harker's brigade had just driven off an attack from a Confederate force that had somehow appeared nearby, despite the fact that they were well behind the Union front line. As Thomas arrived, another force, wearing blue uniforms, began to approach. Because Confederate soldiers wore uniforms of a variety of colors, including blue, Thomas could not be sure the soldiers were Union men. Unsure of the identity of these troops, Harker ordered his troops to hold their fire. The unknown unit was advancing from the same place where the Confederates had earlier attacked, but Harker still hoped that the troops were Union soldiers coming to reinforce them, not Confederates coming to attack. As Harker later recalled, "I could not conceive it possible that our troops had been so suddenly routed. I was therefore in the most painful state of uncertainty that it is possible to conceive a commander to be placed in. The idea of firing upon our own troops was a most horrible one to me, yet if perchance they should be rebels, valuable time was being lost to me, and they would take advantage of it."[13]

Thomas came up with a solution to this dilemma. He ordered Harker's color-bearers to raise their flags and wave them prominently at the advancing force. If the force opened fire after seeing the Union flags, it would be clear that they were Confederates. The force did open fire, the color-bearers ducked for cover, and a battle ensued. Harker's men held out for a while, but they were outnumbered and outflanked and were soon forced to retreat. As they reformed their lines on another hill behind the first one, Thomas assessed the situation and considered what he should do.[14]

The presence of Confederate troops this far behind the Union lines could only mean that the line had been pierced somewhere, and that some kind of disaster had overtaken the other half of the Union army. Thomas could not now count on further communications or reinforcements from Rosecrans, and he would have to make a stand with the troops he had available. Earlier that day, Thomas had placed artillery along a high ridge about a half mile behind the hill that Harker had just been driven from. The ridge ran from the southwest to the northeast and was heavily wooded along its length, except for the northeastern end, where a man named Snodgrass had cleared the woods for his farm. With its wooded terrain, steep incline, and artillery already present, Snodgrass Ridge, also known as Horseshoe Ridge, would be the best place for Thomas to anchor his southern flank.

Thomas rode to Snodgrass Ridge to organize a defense. There were a number of soldiers already present on the ridge, but they were disorganized and discouraged, having just retreated from the rout of the army to the south. The soldiers came from many different units, which indicated to Thomas that the breakthrough in the south had affected a large part of the Union army. Thomas could also tell that the disaster had occurred recently, because the third brigade under Wood's command, which had been right behind his other two brigades on the road, had been caught up in the rout, and only a few of its soldiers had reached the hill. Another unpleasant surprise awaited Thomas when he arrived on the ridge, as most of the artillery that he had posted along the ridge was no longer there. Thomas had counted on using this artillery to form a defensive line, but he would now have to get along without it.[15]

On the positive side, things seemed calm at the northern end of Thomas's line. Snodgrass Ridge was high enough that Thomas could see parts of this line from the top, and he saw little movement there and heard only occasional firing, which indicated that the Confederates had ceased their attack. Since he was not needed at the northern end of his line, Thomas could stay on Snodgrass Ridge and personally supervise its defense. He told his subordinate officers that the hill must be defended at all costs, and they reassured him that it would be.[16]

While Snodgrass Ridge was the best defensive ground available, it was about a half mile southwest of the rest of Thomas's command, and there were no forces available to bridge the gap between the two positions. If the Confederates sent troops into the gap, they could divide, outflank, and defeat Thomas's entire force. However, the terrain between the two halves of Thomas's line was heavily wooded, and the Confederates had apparently not realized that it was undefended. Since he did not have enough men to meet all his needs, Thomas decided to defend Snodgrass Ridge with the troops he had on hand, only later filling the gap between that position and the rest of his army whenever he found enough men to do so. While this was a risky strategy, retreating from the field would be even riskier. The northern portion of his line was still in contact with the enemy, and the day was only half over. If his troops withdrew from their strongly fortified positions, the enemy would just follow them and attack them in the open. Thomas determined to hold his ground until nightfall and then use the cover of darkness to retreat to safety.

Deciding to anchor his defense on Snodgrass Ridge was the first in a series of important decisions Thomas would make that day. The second important decision was to stay on Snodgrass Ridge and direct its defense in person. The soldiers defending the hill were a scratch force, made up of the remnants of brigades that had been routed earlier that morning. Some soldiers had made it to the hill after their commanders had fled the field and were now being commanded by officers who were strangers to them. Thomas was the one officer whom all the soldiers knew and respected.

All of the soldiers who wrote about the fighting on Snodgrass Ridge mentioned how Thomas's presence inspired them. "It is strange what an effect the appearance of Old Pap, as they familiarly called General Thomas, at any point of danger had upon his men," remembered one officer. "It always restored confidence. Indeed his old corps believed they could not be whipped when he commanded them." Thomas took pains to project an image of calmness and control. At one point an aide galloped off with a message, and Thomas called the aide back, instructing him to ride at a normal pace, so as not to frighten the men. One soldier remembered Thomas as always "calm, cool, and impassive," and that the men instinctively turned and watched him as he rode back and forth along the ridge, taking courage from his calm demeanor. An officer recalled seeing Thomas sitting motionless on his horse on the hill behind them, intently watching the progress of the battle, revealing no concern about the sharpshooters' bullets whizzing by him.[17]

At times Thomas led counterattacks in person, when key positions were at stake. As one officer recalled, "When it seemed we could not stand the shot and shell that were hurled at us in such showers and were about to give way, all the officers pitched in promiscuously to cheering and encouraging the men of all regiments alike. Gen. Thomas would jump off his horse, swing his hat, rush among the men and encourage them by his own acts of valor."[18] Another recalled, "[W]here the energy of the attack most endangered our line, he strengthened it with cannon and regiments drawn from points in less peril; and when the soldiers asked for more ammunition, Thomas said, 'Use your bayonets.'"[19]

The Confederates attacked Snodgrass Ridge many times that afternoon, often coming close to breaking the Union line but never quite succeeding. The first attempt on the hill was made by the same troops who had successfully driven back Harker's brigade half an hour earlier. The Confederates tried the same tactic that had worked before, sending a force around the hill to ascend it and attack the defenders in flank. This time, the Union troops were stronger and better organized, and the Confederates had become disorganized from their advance. The Union troops easily pushed the attackers off the hill.[20]

The Confederates paused to reorganize and coordinate their efforts, and in the meantime they sent sharpshooters forward to target the Union officers. The snipers wounded one regimental commander, and their shots forced the other officers to take cover or retreat to the far side of the ridge. Annoyed by this disruption, Thomas rode up to the Third Kentucky Volunteer Infantry and asked the men of the regiment if there were any good squirrel hunters among them. Of course there were, they replied. Thomas ordered the nearest officer to take a detail of good marksmen out in front of the lines and shoot at the enemy snipers. Once the Union marksmen killed one sharpshooter, the rest fled, and Thomas and his officers went back to directing the battle.[21]

As Thomas waited for another Confederate attack to develop from the south, his attention was called by the sight of clouds of dust rising up from the north, indicating that a large body of troops was heading his way. While these troops were coming from behind the Union lines, Thomas had no idea whether they were Union troops or Confederates. Bragg had already made two attempts to get around the northern flank of his army that day, and it had been two and a half hours since Thomas had last visited the northern end of his line. Perhaps Bragg had attempted another flanking maneuver to the north, and perhaps this time it had succeeded. If it had, that meant that Thomas was completely surrounded. Thomas's fate, and that of his army, depended on the identity of the approaching soldiers.

As Thomas watched the column approach, it was clear that the stress of the day was finally getting to him. Thomas tended to pull at his beard when he was anxious, and now he had pulled at it so much that it stood out from his face at all angles. He tried to look at the oncoming force through his field glasses, but his hands shook so much that he could not focus. His horse, sensing the nervousness of its rider, began to jump about. "Take my glass, some of you whose horse stands steady—tell me what you can see," he asked. William Shanks, observing the force through his own field glasses, told Thomas he could see the United States flag. "Do you think so? Do you think so?" asked Thomas. Thomas ordered an aide to ride ahead to verify the column's identity. Confederate sharpshooters fired at the aide, but he made it back safely and reported that the column was a division of infantry from the Reserve Corps. Thomas breathed a sigh of relief, smoothed out his beard, and became calm once again.[22]

Gordon Granger, the commander of the Reserve Corps rode up at the head of his men at about 1:45 P.M. Granger told Thomas that he had seen and heard signs of heavy fighting to the south and had waited all morning for Rosecrans to direct him where he was needed. By 11:30, still not having heard from Rosecrans, Granger decided not to wait any longer and marched to Thomas's aid. Granger had brought two brigades with him, under the command of Brig. Gen. James B. Steedman, and left behind a single brigade to guard the roads in the army's rear. Steedman asked Thomas what the Confederates' strategy was, and Thomas replied, "[T]he damned scoundrels are fighting without any system."[23]

Delighted to have the reinforcements, Thomas thought he could finally fill the gap between the Snodgrass Ridge position and the rest of his line. He ordered Granger and Steedman to station their troops in this gap, but as they began to carry out his orders, the noise of heavy fighting came from nearby. The Confederates had gained a foothold on the western side of Snodgrass Ridge, and if Thomas could not push them off again, his men would be outflanked and would probably have to retreat from the hill.[24]

Thomas now had to choose one of three courses of action. He could send both of Granger's brigades to fight off this attack, leaving the gap between the two halves of his forces still undefended. He could send both brigades to fill the gap and try to repulse the Confederate assault on the ridge with the troops he already had there. Finally, he could compromise by sending one brigade to each sector. This course would run the risk that one brigade would not be enough to defend either sector, meaning that Thomas could lose both. He decided to send both brigades to the western part of Snodgrass Ridge, and this decision turned out to be the correct one. The Confederates, finally coordinating their efforts, had sent an entire division to attack the hill, and they gained the top of the hill before Granger's troops could get into position. Granger ordered his troops into line, gave them a few minutes to rest, and counterattacked. After heavy fighting, Granger's men drove the Confederates off the ridge. The battle was a close one, and if Thomas had used only one brigade, the counterattack would have failed.

When Granger reported back his success, Thomas shook his hand telling him, "Fifteen minutes more, General, might have been too late." A few minutes later, another Union brigade, commanded by Col. Ferdinand Van Derveer, marched up to Snodgrass Ridge. This brigade had been posted in a reserve position on the northern front, and Van Derveer, hearing the sound of heavy fighting to the south, had decided, like Granger, to march toward it. Thomas ordered this brigade to relieve the men defending the eastern part of the ridge, allowing them to withdraw, rest, and replenish their ammunition. One of the regiments in this brigade was the Second Minnesota Volunteer Infantry, which had fought in the Battle of Mill Springs two years earlier. Thomas encouraged the men by complimenting their commander on the regiment's good order, speaking in a loud voice so the men could hear him. Years later, the officer wrote, "We did not know how many troops he had seen in disorder during the day, nor did he know that within an hour's fighting [that morning] we had just lost more than one third of our regiment in killed and wounded, yet we greatly appreciated the compliment at the time."[25]

So far, Thomas had managed to defend against all of the Confederate attacks, but he was growing concerned over the matter of ammunition.

The ammunition wagons belonging to his corps had disappeared during the rout of the rest of the army, and his soldiers were beginning to run out of cartridges. Granger had brought ammunition with him but had expended most of it in his counterattack on the ridge. As Thomas sent two of his aides to look for ammunition, he tried to reassure his men that more was on the way.

Thomas received some good news when a staff officer arrived bearing a message from Philip Sheridan and Jefferson C. Davis, who commanded divisions in McCook's corps. The staff officer reported that although Sheridan's and Davis's divisions had been driven back in the general retreat that morning, the two generals had managed to halt and reorganize their troops and were now moving back to the front. Thomas sent the staff officer back to Sheridan and Davis, to tell them to bring their divisions to Snodgrass Ridge as quickly as they could.[26]

At around 3:30 P.M. the Confederates launched another coordinated assault on Snodgrass Ridge, which nearly succeeded. As one soldier remembered, the attackers gained a foothold on the top of the ridge, but Thomas "drew his sword, rose in his stirrups and rode among his men, shouting to them: 'Go back! Go back! This hill must be held at all hazards!' Riding up to the top with his sword flashing in the light, and his face expressive of determination, his words acted like magic." The men turned around and counterattacked, sweeping down "like an avalanche" on the enemy, and drove them back off the hill.[27]

James Garfield, Rosecrans's chief of staff (and the future twentieth president of the United States), arrived at Thomas's headquarters bringing news of what had happened to the rest of the Union army. Somehow, a Confederate attack had broken through the center of the Union line that morning. The breach had widened, discipline had completely broken down, and the army had disintegrated into a collection of panicked men running away from the point of danger as fast as they could. Rosecrans, thinking that the day was lost, had gone to Chattanooga to organize a last-ditch defense.

Rosecrans had assumed that Thomas's command had also been caught in the general defeat, and he had sent Garfield to the field to find Thomas and report on the condition of his command. Garfield had ridden through the chaos of the army's retreat, had been fired at several times by enemy soldiers, but had arrived at Thomas's headquarters safely. Garfield told Thomas not to expect further ammunition or reinforcements from

Rosecrans; Thomas would have to hold out until nightfall with the troops and ammunition he had on hand. The aides whom Thomas had sent out to look for ammunition returned and reported that they had found little. One private remembered that they went out between assaults and "robbed the dead of ammunition, both ours and the rebel dead, lying by the hundreds on the slope."[28]

At some point after Garfield's arrival, Thomas regained telegraphic communication with Rosecrans in Chattanooga, perhaps via lines running through Rossville Gap. Garfield told Rosecrans that Thomas was managing to hold his own and recommended that Rosecrans stop the army's retreat at Rossville, halfway between Thomas's position and Chattanooga. At the same time, Rosecrans sent a telegram from Chattanooga that ordered Thomas to fall back to Rossville, where he should "take a strong position and assume a threatening attitude" in conjunction with the corps of Crittenden and McCook. Despite these orders, Rosecrans failed to send the two corps to Rossville, and he did not take any effective action to organize a defense at Chattanooga. Instead, he told Crittenden and McCook to lie down and rest, saying, "I am nearly worn out and want someone with me to take command, if necessary to assist me."[29] Even if Rosecrans had sent only ammunition to Thomas, this would have helped him greatly, but Rosecrans did nothing, leaving Thomas unsupported on Snodgrass Ridge.

At 5:00 P.M., an hour before sunset and two hours before total darkness, Thomas decided to retreat. As the commander in the field, Thomas had the authority to disregard Rosecrans's order, and some contemporaries and historians have considered Thomas's decision an error. Years later, Garfield stated that both he and Granger counseled Thomas to hold out until nightfall. Thomas was aware that a retreat during the daylight hours would leave his men vulnerable but decided that it was even more risky to wait. The rebels had begun yet another attack on his Snodgrass Ridge position, this time with fresh troops, and had gained a foothold on the western part of the ridge. Thomas's men were tired and nearly out of ammunition, and Rosecrans's promised reinforcements were nowhere to be seen. If Thomas was driven off Snodgrass Ridge, the Confederates would surround and destroy the northern part of Thomas's line. Thomas decided that the best course of action was to withdraw.[30]

At some point between 5:00 and 5:30 P.M., the brigade of William B. Hazen arrived at Snodgrass Ridge, having marched there from Thomas's main position to the north. The Confederates had been inactive in this sector since the morning, and the commanders there had heard the fighting going on to the south, so they had conferred among themselves and decided to send a brigade southward to assist Thomas. Thomas broke Hazen's brigade into its individual regiments and used them to reinforce different Union positions on the ridge.[31]

As these troops moved into line, Thomas rode toward the northern half of his army to give them instructions on their retreat. On the way, he ran into two Union soldiers who had left their regiments to look for water. They warned Thomas that there was a large Confederate force, supported by artillery, in the woods to the north. For the third time that day, Bragg was trying to get around the northern flank of Thomas's army. Thomas rode to the threatened sector and ordered one of his reserve divisions, under the command of Maj. Gen. Joseph Reynolds, to form in line of battle facing northward. The crisis was so acute that Thomas gave orders directly to some of the regimental and brigade commanders, bypassing Reynolds. One regimental commander recalled that Thomas told him, "Form your men at once and charge the enemy in your front. Do not wait for orders from your brigade commander, but go at once; every minute is precious." Another officer remembered that Thomas simply pointed to the woods to the north and shouted, "They are there; clear them out."[32]

Forming quickly into line of battle, the division charged forward, taking the Confederates by surprise and pushing them back. Reynolds became separated from his men during the movement, and Thomas took charge of the division while Reynolds was unavailable. Thomas ordered one brigade to take up a position guarding the road that the army would use in its retreat and had the other two establish a firm anchor to the army's northern flank.[33] When Reynolds returned, Thomas ordered him to take command of the northern half of the army and coordinate its withdrawal. Thomas hurried back to Snodgrass Ridge, and the Union troops in the northern part of the line began their withdrawal. As soon as the Union troops left the cover of their defensive works, the Confederate infantry rushed forward after them, and the Confederate artillery opened up a heavy fire. The retreating Union soldiers suffered heavy casualties, and some regiments panicked and ran. Fortunately for the Union soldiers, the Confederates did not continue their pursuit once they gained the Union entrenchments, and the retreat was able to continue in safety.[34]

As he approached Snodgrass Ridge, Thomas saw that the divisions of
Jefferson C. Davis and Philip Sheridan had come up to reinforce him and
were drawing close to the front. However, it was too late in the day to
deploy them. If the two divisions kept moving forward, they would block
the road that Thomas wanted to use for his retreat. Thomas ordered the
two divisions to march away from the front.[35] The situation at Snodgrass
Ridge was now desperate. Many of the soldiers had run out of ammunition completely and were defending their positions with the bayonet
alone. At one point, the men of two regiments discovered a wagon
overturned by the road that contained two boxes of ammunition. There
was only enough to provide each man with a few cartridges, and as one
officer remembered, "the scramble by each for his share of it was greater
than I ever saw for rations." Thomas ordered the two newly supplied
regiments to the front, to cover the retreat of the rest of the army.[36]

The retreat began after sunset and continued after darkness fell. Heavy
smoke covered the field, both from rifle fire and from brush fires that
had been started by the fighting. The smoke, along with the fading
daylight, made it impossible for Thomas's men to see more than a few
yards in any direction. In the confusion a Confederate division advanced
quietly against the Union position and surprised and captured three
Union regiments. A few minutes later, their captors were thrown into
confusion by firing from another Union regiment, and many of the
captured men escaped. The Confederates made one last attack but were
driven back, and then it was too dark for them to continue. In the
darkness, Thomas's men completed their withdrawal from the field.[37]

As his soldiers retreated, Thomas rode back to Rossville, where he
meant to establish a new line of defense for the next day. He met up with
Philip Sheridan on the road to Rossville, and the two men rode to the
town together, arriving at around 10:00 P.M. They dismounted, and
Sheridan made a seat for them from a fence rail. After they sat down,
Sheridan waited for Thomas to say something, but Thomas just sat, staring
in silence, as Sheridan's troops marched by them on the road. According
to Sheridan, Thomas "looked very much exhausted, seemed to forget
what he stopped for, and said little or nothing of the incidents of the day
... his quiet unobtrusive demeanor communicating a gloomy rather than
a hopeful view of the situation."[38] Thomas's aides lit a campfire, and
Thomas sat by it thinking. When Col. Benjamin F. Scribner, a regimen-

tal commander, stopped by the fire to warm himself, Thomas spoke to Scribner for a while about the weather and other small topics but said nothing about the day's battle. After a few minutes, Scribner got up, leaving Thomas alone with his thoughts.[39]

Thomas let his guard down with Sheridan and Scribner, but he kept up a positive front before the men. One officer recalled seeing Thomas at Rossville just after dawn on September 21. "Someone said 'Here comes Pap Thomas,'" the officer recalled, and "the sleepy heads sprang to their feet and gathered around the 'Old Hero,' and impeded his progress. He drew reins, and looking over the men, said: 'Well, you don't look so few; if it hadn't been for some unauthorized person to order our ammunition trains to the rear, we would be out there still.'" The men cheered as Thomas rode on.[40]

Thomas even played a practical joke that night on one of his fellow officers, the notoriously foul-tempered Maj. Gen. Gordon Granger. Captain Woodcock, an officer on Rosecrans's staff, had become separated from the army headquarters while delivering one of his orders on the morning of September 20th and had spent the rest of the day wandering around the confusion in the army's rear, searching for Rosecrans. He finally made his way to Rossville, where he walked into Thomas's headquarters late at night. According to Woodcock, Thomas was still awake when Woodcock arrived, while all of Thomas's staff officers were stretched out on the ground around him, sleeping by the fire. Since there were no adjutants or clerks awake to report to, Woodcock went to speak directly to Thomas. The General received Woodcock "without red-tape, pomp, or show, in a business-like, companionable way."

Woodcock had a dispatch to deliver to General Wilder, whom he had not seen since that morning, and he asked Thomas if he knew where Wilder was. Thomas said he would ask his adjutant, who was asleep on the ground nearby. "This person would not awake, even with repeated shaking, so the general took him by the collar with both hands, raised him up, and stood him on his feet and shook him while standing until he got awake enough to talk." Woodcock then asked Thomas where General Granger was, and Thomas pointed out Granger's tent, which was a little distance away. Captain Woodcock noticed a "peculiar smile" on Thomas's face as he pointed to Granger's tent, which he did not understand until he arrived there. Granger had been sleeping in his tent and was furious at being awoken. Thomas, who had not engaged in "devilment," or hazing, while a West Point cadet, was willing to play a practical joke on the notoriously ill-tempered Granger.[41]

After resting for a while by the fire, Thomas got back to work. If the Confederates advanced the next day, Thomas had to stop them before they reached Rossville, because the majority of the troops at Rossville were in no condition to fight. John Beatty, one of Thomas's divisional commanders, wrote in his diary that evening, "At this hour of the night (eleven to twelve o'clock), the army is simply a mob. There appears to be neither organization nor discipline. The various commands are mixed up in what seems to be inextricable confusion. Were a division of the enemy to pounce down upon us between this and morning, I fear the Army of the Cumberland would be blotted out."[42] According to another officer, "The confusion and disorder was great at Rossville, the retreating troops seeing others here stopped, and being tired and worn out threw themselves down anywhere, there was no head to, no order in, the mass. I truly believe that a charge of one regiment of cavalry suddenly made would have routed the whole mass, but thanks to General Thomas they were kept too busily occupied for any such movement."[43]

While most of the army was still disorganized on the 22nd, enough units remained in good order for Thomas to construct a defensive line around Rossville. He placed two divisions from his own corps in the front line, bolstered by the divisions of Granger's Reserve Corps and some units from McCook's and Crittenden's commands that had managed to reorganize. He placed two divisions of his corps in reserve and guarded the flanks and rear of his position with cavalry. Bragg did not attack that day, as he felt his own army was too disorganized and exhausted by the previous two days of fighting. However, Confederate cavalry under Gen. Nathan Bedford Forrest raided north of Rossville, pushing back the cavalry guards that Thomas had posted there and threatening to cut off Thomas's force from Chattanooga. Deciding that the Rossville line was untenable, Thomas asked Rosecrans for permission to retreat to Chattanooga, and Rosecrans agreed. The withdrawal began at 9:00 P.M. on September 21, and by the morning of September 22 the entire Union army was posted behind the strong fortifications at Chattanooga.[44]

When Thomas entered Chattanooga on September 22, he was greeted by the cheers of the soldiers who had gone there before him, all of whom recognized that Thomas's defensive stand on September 20 had saved the army. Thomas also learned what had happened to the rest of the Union army on the second day of the battle. That morning, Rosecrans had ordered General Brannan's division out of line in the Union center so that it could go north to reinforce Thomas. To fill the gap left by Brannan, Rosecrans ordered Wood's division, which was stationed south of Brannan's, to "close up on Reynolds," meaning that he should spread out and cover the ground between his division and Reynolds's division, stationed north of him in the line. In the meantime Brannan had decided that it was too dangerous for him to take his division out of line, as it looked like the Confederates were getting ready to attack. With Brannan deciding to stay where he was, Rosecrans's orders to Wood to "close up on Reynolds" made no sense, as there was no gap between Wood's division and Reynolds's. Wood should have asked Rosecrans to clarify the order, but instead he pulled his entire division out of line and marched it behind Brannan's division, intending to put it back into line between Brannan and Reynolds.[45]

Just after Wood withdrew his division, the Confederate army launched a major attack. Lt. Gen. James Longstreet, commanding the southern wing of the Confederate army, had spent the morning getting his forces aligned for a single, concentrated attack against one segment of Rosecrans's line. In a stroke of terrible luck for the Union, Longstreet's assault centered on the portion of the line that had been held by Wood's division, and began just after Wood's men left their entrenchments. Longstreet's men poured into the space left vacant by Wood.[46] Hardly able to believe their good luck, Longstreet's soldiers charged forward, soon overrunning Rosecrans's headquarters and fanning out to outflank and attack the Federal line on either side of the breach. Finding themselves simultaneously attacked from the front, flank and rear, the Union soldiers fled in panic. A few brigades tried to make a stand, but soon finding themselves surrounded by the advancing Confederates, they were forced to retreat. By 12:30 P.M. the entire southern and central part of the Union line was routed and in flight to Chattanooga. Rosecrans, Crittenden, and McCook all retreated to Chattanooga to plan a last-ditch defense of the city.[47]

While Davis and Sheridan eventually rallied their divisions and marched back toward the battlefield, one of Thomas's divisional commanders, General Negley, continued to retreat to Chattanooga. Negley also ordered Thomas's ammunition wagons, along with most of the artillery that Thomas had originally placed on Snodgrass Ridge, to retreat to

Chattanooga. Negley later argued that he did so in order to prevent the artillery and ammunition wagons from being captured. While this decision may have been justifiable, given the knowledge that Negley had at the time, it placed Thomas in a bad position on Snodgrass Ridge.[48]

The Union army suffered terribly in its defeat at Chickamauga, but the Confederates fared little better. In terms of the proportion of casualties to the total number engaged, Chickamauga was the bloodiest battle of the Civil War. The Union army suffered 16,179 casualties, or 28 percent of its total force of 57,840 men; and the Confederates suffered about 18,000 casualties, 26 percent of their total force of 68,000. While the Confederate army held the field after the battle, it had suffered more casualties than the Union army, making the victory an extremely costly one. Bragg had almost succeeded in destroying at least part of the Union army, and if he had succeeded, he could have altered the course of the war. Thomas's leadership had saved the Union cause from disaster.[49]

While the Army of the Cumberland eventually recovered from its defeat at Chickamauga, its commander did not. On September 20, after Rosecrans retired to Chattanooga, he did little to reorganize his forces and took no action to support Thomas. On September 21 one of Thomas's divisional commanders sent an aide to report to Rosecrans in Chattanooga and to ask him for instructions on what to do next. The aide observed that Rosecrans "looked worn and exhausted and was laboring under excitement. He heard my statement but in doing so showed want of one requisite of a great military commander, firmness and self-reliance under adverse circumstances. He was evidently crushed under the weight of his disaster; skillful, energetic, and brave, his nervous temperament overbalanced all and exposed his one weakness."[50]

Thomas, for his part, became a national hero. While the initial newspaper reports of the battle were confused and inaccurate, within a few days Thomas's role in saving the Union army from destruction became clear. The *Chicago Tribune* stated that Thomas "filled every soldier with his own unconquerable firmness." The *Cincinnati Commercial* called Thomas "glorious," and "the tower of strength that saved the army." Describing Thomas's calm demeanor during the fighting, the *Commercial*'s correspondent characterized him as "a picture of ineffable courage, tempered with wisdom and gentleness," and "the incarnation of manly majesty." William Shanks's eyewitness account of the fighting on Snodgrass Ridge, which he entitled "Thomas Saves the Army," was reprinted in a number of other newspapers, and the account brought Thomas national recognition.[51]

Secretary of War Edwin Stanton sent a telegram to Charles Dana saying that "the merit of General Thomas and the debt of gratitude the nation owes to his valor and skill is fully appreciated here and I wish you to tell him so. It is not my fault that he was not in command months ago."[52] Abraham Lincoln also praised Thomas's performance at Chickamauga, although Thomas did not learn of his praise until after Lincoln's death. Shortly after the battle, Lincoln received a telegram from a mentally ill man named Robert A. Maxwell, who often wrote Lincoln with criticisms or speculations about Rebel conspiracies. This telegram accused Thomas of disloyalty. In response, Lincoln wrote, "[N]othing could be more ungracious than to indulge any suspicion towards Gen. Thomas. It is doubtful whether his heroism and skill exhibited last Sunday afternoon, has ever been surpassed in this world." Lincoln decided not to send his response, commenting that he "can't afford to answer every crazy question asked me," but the telegraph operator saved Lincoln's telegraph slip, and in 1867 he presented it as a gift to Thomas.[53]

Lincoln and Stanton were as critical of Rosecrans, McCook, and Crittenden as they were complimentary of Thomas. Stanton was particularly harsh. As he listened to the reading of a dispatch from Rosecrans explaining the reasons for the Chickamauga defeat, Stanton interrupted the reading and snapped, "I know the reasons well enough. Rosecrans ran away from his fighting men and did not stop for thirteen miles." Rosecrans's report placed some of the blame on General McCook, and this angered Stanton even more. "No, they need not shuffle it off on McCook," Stanton said. "He is not much of a soldier. I never was in favor of him for a Major General. But he is not accountable for this business. He and Crittenden made pretty good time away from the fight to Chattanooga, but Rosecrans beat them both."[54]

Stanton dismissed Crittenden and McCook from their commands, consolidated their men into a single corps, and placed this new corps under the command of Gordon Granger. Stanton also recommended that Lincoln remove Rosecrans from command, but political considerations caused Lincoln to hesitate. Gubernatorial elections were scheduled to take place in Ohio on October 9, and Lincoln feared that the election would be a close one. The Democratic candidate, Clement Vallandigham, was an outspoken opponent of the war, and if he were elected, he could do much to undermine the war effort. Rosecrans was still popular in his native state of Ohio, and removing Rosecrans from command might place the election at risk, so Lincoln postponed taking any action against Rosecrans until after the election.[55]

Thomas is best known today as "the Rock of Chickamauga," and his fame is well deserved. On the first day of the battle, he commanded the bulk of the Union forces actually engaged in fighting. His defensive actions prevented Bragg from breaking through the Union lines, but more importantly, his willingness to make attacks and counterattacks kept Bragg off balance, causing him to cede the initiative early in the day. During the morning of the second day, Thomas's careful defensive preparations and good use of artillery and terrain completely frustrated Bragg's plans, as the Confederates wore themselves out in fruitless attacks on heavily fortified positions.

Only Rosecrans's error in creating a gap in his own line, and the Confederates' good fortune in attacking just as the gap opened, made the Confederate victory at Chickamauga possible. While Rosecrans and the other corps commanders fled to Chattanooga, Thomas stayed on the field, reacting swiftly and correctly to a series of tactical challenges. He not only made intelligent command decisions but also commanded with great courage, intervening personally to lead counterattacks and to encourage his men to hold fast. Thomas's leadership was not perfect, however. He failed to use his forces well on the morning of the second day, in sending too few men to extend his line northward and sending them too late, and in waiting for Negley's division to extend his line even though he had adequate troops available in his own reserves. In hindsight, it seems that he should have remained on the field until nightfall, as the late afternoon retreat caused the loss of many men. These mistakes are minor, however, compared to his successes. Perhaps Lincoln's statement should be the final word on Thomas's performance at Chickamauga, as the heroism and skill that Thomas demonstrated there remain an example of front-line leadership that has rarely, if ever, been surpassed.

The Thomas family plantation, from a photo taken in the 1930s. The house was much smaller when Thomas was born, and his family added this front section while he was a child. Courtesy of the Library of Virginia.

Thomas had this daguerreotype made around 1853, possibly for his wife to keep while he was apart from her on military assignments. Courtesy of the National Portrait Gallery.

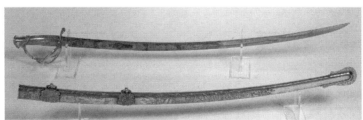

Thomas's neighbors in Southampton County commissioned this sword in recognition of his distinguished service in Florida and Mexico. The grip and hilt are of engraved silver, and the pommel of the sword holds an amethyst. The scabbard is engraved with the words *Florida*, *Fort Brown*, *Monterey*, and *Buena Vista*, and a small picture of the Battle of Buena Vista. Courtesy of the Virginia Historical Society.

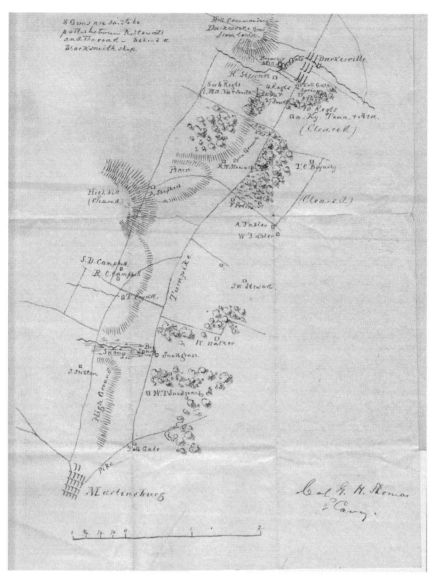

Thomas drew this reconnaissance map of the approaches to Martinsburg, Virginia (now West Virginia), in 1861, while serving as chief of cavalry for Maj. Gen. Robert Patterson during the Manassas campaign. Courtesy of the National Archives.

Two posed photos, probably taken shortly after the Civil War. Courtesy of the United States Army Military History Institute.

191

Thomas designed this wagon for his topographical corps. The awning and map shelves folded up into the body of the wagon when it moved. Courtesy of the United States Army Military History Institute.

This photo was taken near Ringgold, Georgia, at the start of the 1864 Atlanta campaign. Courtesy of the National Archives.

Thomas Nast drew this caricature of Thomas for sale at a charity ball. Nast drew an appealing picture of Thomas, but exercised his satirical wit on Johnson, pictured here kicking over the Freedmen's "bureau" due to his recent veto of the bill to establish the institution. Courtesy of the University of Virginia.

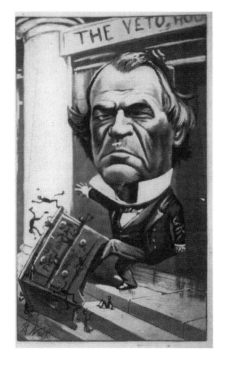

This photo, taken in the late 1860s, shows how Thomas put on weight toward the end of his life. Courtesy of the Library of Congress.

This cartoon shows President Johnson using a promotion as bait to trick Thomas into endorsing his policies and opposing Grant. Thomas refused to allow Johnson to use him for political purposes and declined the promotion. From *Harper's Weekly*.

This contemporary illustration shows the immense crowd and procession at Thomas's funeral in Troy, New York. From *Harper's Weekly*.

A portrayal of the crowd at the unveiling of Thomas's statue. From *Harper's Weekly*.

This illustration from the late 1860s or 1870s shows the pantheon of the four Union heroes of the war. Today, Grant and Sherman remain well known, while Sheridan and Thomas are largely forgotten. Courtesy of the Library of Congress.

CHAPTER ELEVEN

Chattanooga

I will hold the town till we starve.

To assist the Army of the Cumberland, trapped in Chattanooga, Lincoln promoted Grant to overall command of the armies in the West, and Grant went to Chattanooga to command in person. Grant relieved Rosecrans of command, putting Thomas in his place, and reinforced Chattanooga with a force commanded by William T. Sherman. While Grant and Thomas got along well at first, Grant came to think of Thomas as excessively slow and cautious, and this perception intensified throughout the Chattanooga campaign. While Thomas served Grant well at Chattanooga, Grant came away from the campaign with a low opinion of Thomas's generalship. Convinced that Thomas was too slow and unaggressive for independent command, Grant would pass over Thomas for promotion consistently in the future. Thus, while the campaign for Chattanooga was a successful one for the Army of the Cumberland, the fact that Thomas lost Grant's confidence during the campaign was extremely detrimental to Thomas's career.

Rosecrans retreated into Chattanooga after the Battle of Chickamauga because the strong defensive works around the town would make his army virtually invulnerable to assault. While this was true, the geographic features of the position turned Chattanooga into a trap for the Union army. Chattanooga is located on the southern bank of the Tennessee River, in a valley surrounded by steep mountains. When the Union army retreated into the city, the Confederates moved to occupy all the high ground to the south, and from these heights blocked the Union routes of

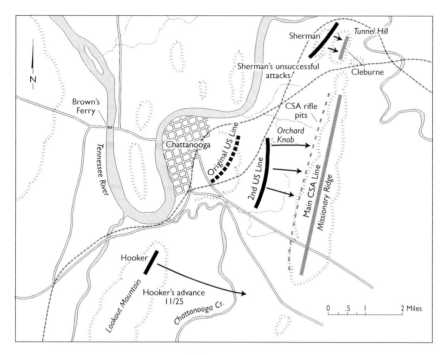

Chattanooga

supply. Normally, an army in Chattanooga could draw supply from the river, the railroad running along the river's southern bank, or the wagon road running along its northern bank, but Confederate artillery and sharpshooters occupying the high ground southwest of the city closed off all these supply lines. The Union army could draw supply only from a long, difficult road that ran through the mountains north of the city, and only a trickle of supplies made it through. Confederate cavalry raids reduced the quantities of supplies even further, and the Federal soldiers in Chattanooga soon faced the threat of starvation.[1]

While the Union army was low on ammunition and other supplies, the soldiers were sure they could resist any frontal attack. Recognizing the strength of the Union position, Bragg declined to attack and settled for a siege instead. The Confederate army shelled the city from its positions on Lookout Mountain and Missionary Ridge, but these positions were so far away that the shelling did little damage. When one of Thomas's officers asked him what he thought of the threat, he commented that the shelling was hurting the enemy more than it was hurting them. After all, he said, the damage the shells inflicted was "trifling," while the artillery shells were expensive, and "the Southern Confederacy had no money to throw away."[2]

On September 30 a light rain began to fall, and the rain worsened into a downpour the next day. It rained during nineteen of the next fifty-four days, making the troops in the front line miserable, and making the mountain roads nearly impassable with mud. The soldiers were put on reduced rations, supposedly receiving two-thirds of their normal ration, but in actuality receiving much less. Soldiers were reduced to stealing feed corn from the army's pack animals; many horses and mules died for lack of forage, while others were sent out of the city to prevent them from starving. With most of the draft animals gone, the army could not transport its artillery and supplies, meaning that it was trapped in Chattanooga. If Bragg decided to move around Chattanooga and head for Nashville, Knoxville, or Kentucky, Rosecrans would not be able to follow him.[3]

As Rosecrans tried to deal with his supply problem, the War Department worked to send him reinforcements. Secretary of War Edwin Stanton sent twenty thousand troops from the Army of the Potomac to Chattanooga, placing these soldiers under the command of Gen. Joseph B. Hooker. Stanton arranged for them to move over the railroads from northern Virginia to Tennessee, and this movement went quickly and successfully, rushing reinforcements to Rosecrans's aid. The War Department also arranged for reinforcements to be sent from Grant's army, which had been relatively inactive since the fall of Vicksburg in July.[4]

William T. Sherman commanded the detachment of reinforcements from Grant's army, and soon Grant himself headed for Chattanooga to take command. Lincoln had become dissatisfied with Rosecrans's performance, stating in private that he thought Rosecrans was acting "confused and stunned, like a duck hit on the head." Rather than simply replacing Rosecrans at the head of the Army of the Cumberland, Lincoln decided to appoint an overall commander for the entire western theater. This commander would be better able to coordinate the actions of forces engaged in different areas, making it easier to send reinforcements to the area around Chattanooga and to coordinate their actions once they arrived. The obvious choice for this command was Ulysses S. Grant, who had a long record of successes, culminating in his recent capture of Vicksburg.[5]

Lincoln left the decision of what to do with Rosecrans to Grant. Lincoln had retained Rosecrans earlier because he did not want to endanger the chances of the Republican gubernatorial candidate in Ohio, Rosecrans's home state. The elections were now over, and the Republican candidate had won, but Lincoln still could not bring himself to fire Rosecrans. Instead, he left the choice to Grant, giving him the discretion either to retain Rosecrans or to replace him with Thomas. It did not take Grant long to make up his mind. Receiving Lincoln's instructions on the morning of October 18, he sent Rosecrans a dispatch that same evening, ordering him to turn over his command to Thomas.[6]

Grant's orders did not come as a surprise. Ever since Chickamauga, rumors had begun circulating throughout the army that Rosecrans would be removed and Thomas put in his place. Earlier, Stanton had asked Dana to sound Thomas out on the prospect of replacing Rosecrans. Dana did so, and wrote Stanton that Thomas had responded by sending a friend to tell Dana that "while he would gladly accept any command out of this department to which [Stanton] might see fit to assign him, he could not consent to become the successor of General Rosecrans, because he would not do anything to give countenance to the suspicion that he had intrigued against his commander. Besides, he has as perfect confidence in [the] capacity and fidelity of Rosecrans as he had in those of General Buell." Thomas also spoke to Garfield, asking him to tell Rosecrans that Thomas did not support the "intrigues" to have Rosecrans removed from command. According to Rosecrans, Thomas spoke to him through an intermediary because he felt uncomfortable speaking about the matter in person.[7]

The order relieving Rosecrans arrived on October 19. Rosecrans read the dispatch and immediately sent for Thomas; when he arrived, Rosecrans gave him the dispatch and sat silently as he read it. "At the conclusion," Rosecrans recalled, "Thomas drew a long breath and turned pale." Thomas began to protest that he would not take command of the army at Rosecrans's expense, but Rosecrans cut him off. He insisted that Thomas take command of the army for the good of the nation and assured Thomas that "there is no misunderstanding that can come between you and me" over the matter. Reluctantly, Thomas agreed to take Rosecrans's place.[8] Rosecrans told Thomas that he intended to leave early the next morning, without addressing his troops, as he could not bear to see them after being relieved of his command. He then stayed up late that night conferring with Thomas, making sure that his successor was familiar with the details of the command. Rosecrans wrote an address to be read to the soldiers after his departure, which praised them and their officers, and particularly praised Thomas.[9]

Thomas resisted taking command of the Army of the Cumberland in part due to loyalty to Rosecrans, who had treated him well throughout his tenure. Thomas was also reluctant to put himself in the same position that Rosecrans and Buell had occupied, being responsible for an army over which he did not have complete control. In an 1862 letter to Andrew Johnson, Thomas had stated that he did not want command of an army if he did could not give orders without interference from politicians. The main reason, however, was almost certainly his sense of honor.[10]

Thomas's reluctance to replace Rosecrans, like his reluctance to replace Buell, was an error. While Thomas was probably sincere in his support of Rosecrans's leadership, he was also incorrect in his assessment of Rosecrans's fitness for command. Rosecrans had led a brilliant campaign until the capture of Chattanooga, but afterward he had erred badly. He had taken too many risks in his pursuit of Bragg, averting disaster only through a combination of luck, Thomas's caution, and a last-minute concentration of his forces. He had managed his forces poorly during the Battle of Chickamauga, and after the Confederate breakthrough he had ceased to exercise command at all. Even after the crisis passed, Rosecrans had remained emotionally unstable and erratic. Several observers commented that after the battle he had become indecisive, moody, and ineffectual, and his official reports from Chattanooga in September and October demonstrate his frequent swings from optimism to despair. Thomas, who must have been aware of Rosecrans's unstable mental state, should have agreed to take over an army that Rosecrans was no longer fit to lead.

Thomas's expectation that an army commander would be able to make decisions free from political interference was unrealistic. The Civil War was a political as well as a military conflict, and it was inevitable that civilian authorities would take an active part in directing the conduct of the war. The duty of a general officer in such a war was to assume the burden of command, despite the frustrations and risks that such a burden would entail. Thomas's concern about his honor was equally inappropriate, as he placed his concerns about how others might perceive him over his duty to command where needed. Only after Rosecrans pushed him to accept command did he agree to do so.

Many of the soldiers still held confidence in Rosecrans, even after Chickamauga, and were sorry to see him go. The men also loved and respected Thomas, and it was fortunate for the morale of the Army of the Cumberland that Rosecrans talked Thomas into staying, as those men who opposed Rosecrans's removal were assuaged by the fact that Thomas replaced him.[11] One officer's recollections seem to accurately represent the general feeling of the men:

> The boys never throw up their hats for Thomas, [although] I believe, in spite of his modest ways, he would rather like it if they did, but in a fight, they are always glad to see "Old Pap" looking after things, and will stay with him to the end. Thomas is always cool and his men can't be stampeded. To a casual observer, "Rosy" would seem to be the idol of the army, but if officers and men were to choose a commander by vote, I believe Thomas would be elected.[12]

As Thomas took command of the Army of the Cumberland, Grant prepared to travel to Chattanooga, where he would take personal command of the forces in and around the city. On October 19 Grant received a desperate telegram from Charles Dana, describing the terrible supply situation in the city and implying that the army might soon retreat. In response, Grant wired Thomas asking him about the amount of supplies he had on hand, and ordering him to "hold Chattanooga at all hazards." Thomas responded, "Two hundred and four thousand four hundred and sixty-two rations in store-houses; ninety thousand to arrive tomorrow, and all the trains were loaded which had arrived at Bridgeport up to the 16th—probably three hundred wagons. I will hold the town till we starve."[13]

After sending the telegram, Thomas began to put into effect plans to reopen the supply lines to Chattanooga, plans that Rosecrans had considered but not acted on. Thomas directed Gen. Joseph Hooker, who commanded the two corps that had been detached from the Army of the Potomac, to bring his force by rail to Bridgeport, Alabama, and then march quickly up the south bank of the Tennessee River clearing the area of Confederate artillery and sharpshooters. Hooker delayed in complying, explaining that he had to wait for his supply wagons to arrive before he could advance. Hooker still had not moved by the time Grant arrived.[14]

This was only half of Thomas's plan. Even if Hooker's advance cleared the enemy from the south bank of the Tennessee River, the Confederates would still retain control of Lookout Mountain, from which they could fire artillery shells on any boats attempting to traverse the last few miles of the supply route. The chief engineer of the Army of the Cumberland, William F. "Baldy" Smith, had thought of a way to avoid this artillery fire, by transporting the supplies across a hilly spit of land called Moccasin Point. Moccasin Point was located just downriver from Chattanooga, at a point where the Tennessee River made a hairpin curve to the north before flowing west again toward Bridgeport. Smith thought it would be possible to land supplies on the western side of the point, transport them across, and carry them over a bridge into the city, as the hills on Moccasin Point would shelter the entire route from Confederate artillery fire. The Confederates currently occupied Moccasin Point, but they had not realized its strategic value and had posted only a small force there to defend it. By launching a surprise attack from Chattanooga, Thomas's men could capture the point and then link up with Hooker's troops advancing upriver from Bridgeport. Some of Thomas's officers criticized the plan, but Smith was able to answer their questions and objections, and Thomas approved it. Thomas told Smith to ready his assault force and be prepared to move the moment Hooker was ready.[15]

Grant arrived in Chattanooga on the night of October 23. He was still recovering from a leg injury he had suffered during a fall a few weeks before, and he had spent the last two days traveling over terrible roads in a driving rainstorm. The meeting between Grant and Thomas did not go well at first. Shortly after Grant's arrival, Lt. Col. James H. Wilson, of Grant's staff, walked into the room where they were meeting, where he saw Grant "sitting on one side of the fire over a puddle of water that had run out of his clothes. Thomas, glum and silent, was sitting on the other," while the members of Grant's staff "were scattered about in disorder." Wilson asked, "General Thomas, General Grant is wet and tired, and ought to have some dry clothes, particularly a pair of socks and a pair of slippers. He is hungry besides, and needs something to eat. Can't your officers attend to these matters for him?" At once Thomas began hurrying about, doing things to make Grant comfortable. Thomas had initially reacted to Grant as a commander and had waited for his orders. Wilson's request made Thomas think of Grant as a guest, and Thomas reacted immediately to show Grant hospitality.[16]

After Grant had eaten and changed clothes, he listened to Thomas and his staff officers' briefings on the current situation at Chattanooga. At first he just listened, sitting "as immovable as a rock and as silent as the sphinx," but then he sat up and "began to fire whole volleys of questions at the officers present." From his questions and instructions, it became clear that he planned to open a new supply line, bring up reinforcements, and then go on the offensive as soon as possible. Grant was interested in Smith's plan to capture Moccasin Point, but he wanted to look over the ground himself before approving it. After doing so the next day, Grant approved Smith's plan and put Smith in charge of carrying it out. Grant ordered Hooker to begin his advance from Bridgeport as soon as possible, and he also ordered Sherman to hurry his march from Mississippi. As soon as Sherman's and Hooker's troops arrived, and the Army of the Cumberland was resupplied, Grant planned to attack Bragg's army and break out of Chattanooga.[17]

On October 27 Smith's forces crossed the river before dawn and surprised and defeated the small force of Confederate defenders at Moccasin Point. Now Thomas had to make sure that Hooker advanced quickly enough to link up with Smith's force, before the Confederates counterattacked and dislodged it. Hooker had opposed the advance from Bridgeport, and he had a reputation for being slow to obey orders he disagreed with, so Thomas kept a close watch on him. Thomas gave Hooker very specific orders designating the movement of his troops and sent an officer from Grant's staff to ensure they were carried out. Hooker's advance met little opposition, and by that evening Hooker's forces had linked up with Smith's. The Confederates counterattacked during the night but were driven back. By the next day, the Union troops were fully reinforced and had entrenched their positions, and the Confederates did not try again to dislodge them.[18]

During the night battle of October 27–28, some mules, panicking from the noise of firing, broke free from their harnesses and stampeded toward a Confederate unit. The Confederates, unable to see and confusing the sound of the mules' hooves with a cavalry charge, panicked and ran away. Some Union soldiers who witnessed the action dubbed it the "Charge of the Mule Brigade," and the story soon became the subject of a number of jokes. One officer wrote a mock-heroic poem praising the mules' bravery, and another requested that the mules be given brevet promotions to the rank of horses. As one regimental historian recalled, Thomas partic-ipated in the joke as well. One day, a private came up to Thomas as he was sitting outside of his headquarters tent and asked him to write out an order to the quartermaster for a quart of shelled corn. Thomas, "who always looked very carefully after his soldiers," asked the man if he had received his ration of corn from the quartermaster the previous day. "Yes, I did," the man answered, "but last night I was on guard, and getting very hungry I borrowed a quart of corn off a mule and promised to pay him back this morning. . . . You see, General, I am up a stump, and the whole Mule Brigade will be kicking if I don't pay up." Thomas "smiled," "took in the situation," and wrote the soldier an order for an extra quart of corn.[19]

By October 30 the supply line through Moccasin Point was fully open, and soon two steamboats were making regular supply runs between Bridgeport and Chattanooga. The soldiers named the new supply line the "Cracker Line," after that staple of army rations, which they had now begun to receive in adequate quantities. Two ferryboats could bring only a limited amount of supplies, so Thomas personally monitored the supply runs to make sure they were done as efficiently as possible. As food, ammunition, and other necessities came into the city, the soldiers' morale and the army's combat readiness improved.[20]

During all this time, as the Union force reopened its supply lines and brought up reinforcements, the Confederate army did little. Bragg had hoped to starve the Union army into submission, but it was clear now that this would not occur. Bragg was unsure what to do, and while he tried to make up his mind, he did nothing. This inaction gave the Union army time to gain in strength and carry out its plans.[21]

While Thomas waited for his army to return to strength, he restruc-tured the officer corps he had received from Rosecrans. He brought many of his own staff aides with him when he was promoted but retained Rosecrans's adjutant general, Brig. Gen. William D. Whipple. Like Thomas, Whipple was a reserved, serious, and formal career officer. The two men set high standards for the Army of the Cumberland's officers, requiring them to be punctual, organized, businesslike, and efficient. The choice was a good one for Thomas's army, but it led to some tension with Grant's staff, who were used to Grant's informal way of doing business. According to James Wilson, Whipple was particularly difficult to work with and had "a disposition . . . to raise technical objections, amounting in several instances to personal rudeness." Tensions between the two generals' staff officers exacerbated the tension that was beginning to build between Thomas and Grant.[22]

Thomas also reorganized his unit commanders, promoting some and relieving others of their commands. Stanton had already removed McCook and Crittenden and had consolidated their corps under the more capable Gordon Granger. Thomas promoted Maj. Gen. John Palmer, a volunteer officer who had demonstrated his ability on the battlefield, to his own former command, the Fourteenth Corps.[23] Thomas also made changes among his divisional and brigade commanders and among the staff officers of the Army of the Cumberland. On October 27 Thomas learned that he had been promoted to the rank of brigadier general in the regular army. Thomas already had the rank of major general of volunteers, but this rank was only a temporary one that would last for the duration of the war, while his rank of brigadier general would hold after the war ended. In two and a half years, Thomas had progressed from the rank of major to the second-highest rank the army then conferred.[24]

While Grant was in overall command of the forces at Chattanooga, Thomas had extensive responsibilities as the new commander of the Army of the Cumberland. These ranged from consulting with Grant on large questions of tactics and strategy to dealing with the tedious details of personnel, supply, and discipline. A typical day for Thomas would include monitoring reports on the quantity of food, supplies, ammunition, horses, wagons, and pack animals possessed by each of his brigades and regiments and coordinating the delivery of additional supplies to ensure that the most needed items were transported first. He might engage in a personal inspection or review of one or more of his regiments and consult with his subordinate officers about the condition of their commands. Thomas reviewed correspondence and reports from cavalry and scouts, maintaining a close watch on the movements of Bragg's army outside the city. He replied to the correspondence of commanders of other armies, who needed to coordinate their movements with the Army of the Cumberland's actions, and made frequent reports to his supervisors in Washington. Thomas's staff officers handled many of the details of this work, but he had to supervise and remain informed of the progress of each of these areas of army management.[25]

So far, all had gone well since Grant's arrival. The army was steadily regaining strength, the men's morale had improved, and the commanding officers worked well together. On November 14 Grant wrote his wife, "The best of feeling seems to prevail within the army since the change" in commanders, and "Thomas has the confidence of all the troops of Rosecrans' late command." Thomas had worked well with Grant in the campaign to open the Cracker Line, providing Grant with advice when needed but deferring to his authority and following his orders. Grant and Thomas were also on friendly personal terms, at least at first. As Wilson recalled, Thomas, Grant, and the other generals often gathered around the fireplace at Grant's headquarters, "all official cares thrown aside and all formality discarded." The men cracked jokes, told stories, and called each other by their West Point nicknames. "Even Thomas unbent and told his reminiscences with wit and good feeling," Wilson wrote. Both Thomas and Grant, though known for their taciturnity, "were interesting if not brilliant conversationalists upon such occasions."[26] Joseph J. Reynolds, who served under Thomas for years, recalled that "there was no [bad] feeling between Thomas and Grant" at Chattanooga. After Grant's arrival, Thomas instructed Reynolds, "Tell Grant to have no hesitancy about giving me orders. I will be ready to obey his every wish." According to Reynolds, the only criticism Grant ever made against Thomas was that he was slow, but Reynolds considered this criticism justified, as "it's the God of Mighty's truth that he *was* slow."[27]

Despite Reynolds's claim that there was no conflict between Thomas and Grant, other observers reported that there was some hostility, never overtly expressed, between the two men. Thomas never criticized Grant, but as time went on he came to treat Grant with a cool reserve that seemed to mask some underlying resentment. Wilson later speculated that Thomas, "having graduated higher at West Point, entered a more scientific arm of service and served generally with great distinction, regarded himself as a better soldier than Grant, and that he thereby, perhaps unconsciously, resented Grant's assignment to duty over him." Thomas "doubtless believed to the end that while Grant had put him in Rosecrans' place, it was not because he loved Thomas more, but because he distrusted Rosecrans too much to keep him in command at all."[28]

Thomas and Grant had their first open disagreement in early November. The Cracker Line first opened on October 30, but it took some time before adequate supplies could be brought up, and the men and animals of the army were slow to recover from their weeks of low rations. Grant grew impatient during the wait, and he also began to worry about Ambrose Burnside's force at Knoxville, Tennessee, about 100 miles to the northeast. Grant feared that if he remained inactive at Chattanooga, Bragg would realize that Grant's army was too weak to move and would send a large detachment to attack Knoxville. Grant wanted to make some sort of demonstration against the Confederate army, to discourage Bragg from sending a force against Knoxville.[29]

Grant and Thomas discussed the possibility of launching a demonstration but could not agree on a plan. William F. "Baldy" Smith favored making a limited attack against the northern end of Missionary Ridge, but Thomas thought Missionary Ridge too difficult a target and wanted to postpone the attack until Sherman arrived with reinforcements. Instead, Thomas favored using Hooker's troops to attack Lookout Mountain. On November 6 Grant learned that Longstreet's men had left their entrenchments and seemed to be moving east, and he also received information that a force was moving toward Knoxville from Virginia. Fearing that this combined force would overwhelm Burnside, Grant decided to take action immediately. On November 7 Grant ordered Thomas to attack Missionary Ridge the following morning, using "all the force you can bring to bear against it."[30]

Thomas was appalled by Grant's order. He did not have enough men to successfully attack the steep ridge, and he worried that his men were too weak from their long period of deprivation to fight effectively. So many of his draft animals had died or been sent away during the siege that there were not enough left to move artillery and supplies in support of an attack. Realizing that this might be a problem, Grant had offered the unrealistic suggestion that Thomas could borrow mules from the ambulance service, or use officers' horses to move artillery. Assuming that the attack would succeed, Grant had even given Thomas instructions for a pursuit, telling him to advance after the battle and cut the Confederates' rail supply line in Georgia.[31]

When he received Grant's order, Thomas called for Smith and told him, "You must get that order for an advance countermanded; I shall lose my army." Smith agreed with Thomas and explained that he had only envisioned a demonstration, not an all-out assault, when he had recommended the attack. Thomas and Smith made another reconnaissance of the ground in their front and then reported to Grant that an attack on Missionary Ridge would be impossible, as Bragg's army was too strongly entrenched. They both recommended waiting for Sherman's troops to arrive before attempting an attack on the ridge.[32]

While opposing the Missionary Ridge attack, Thomas recognized that the army should do something to prevent Bragg from moving against Knoxville. He recommended that they begin shelling Lookout Mountain with heavy artillery, in preparation for an assault by Hooker. The threat might convince Bragg to keep Longstreet's forces at Chattanooga, and if Hooker's men captured Lookout Mountain, they would displace the Confederate artillery that blocked the river to boat traffic between Brown's Ferry and Chattanooga. Later, Thomas proposed crossing ten thousand troops over the Tennessee River east of Chattanooga to cut Longstreet's supply line, but Grant did not accept this suggestion. He did accept Thomas's suggestion to shell Lookout Mountain and agreed to wait for Sherman to arrive before assaulting the northeastern end of Missionary Ridge. He did so reluctantly, however, and the incident led him to view Thomas as unaggressive. When Sherman did arrive, Grant would entrust the main offensive effort to him.[33]

Sherman's army had left September 22, but they encountered problems with river transport and the roads and did not reach Bridgeport until November 13.[34] Leaving his army at Bridgeport for the moment, Sherman came to Chattanooga to confer on strategy, and Thomas, Grant, Sherman, and Smith spent the next few days examining the terrain around the city and discussing a plan of attack. Grant decided that Sherman's force should march from Bridgeport to the valley beneath Lookout Mountain, deceiving the rebels into thinking that the main attack would occur there. Sherman's men would then cross the Tennessee River, march along the mountain roads north of Chattanooga, and cross back over the river east of the city. If the movement went undetected, Sherman's men would have the advantage of surprise when they attacked the far northern end of Missionary Ridge. Once they gained a foothold on the ridge, Thomas's troops would advance to support them, and the Federal army would roll up the Confederate right flank and center on Missionary Ridge.[35]

Grant wanted the attack to take place as soon as possible, so planned for it to begin on November 22. Thomas did not share Grant's sense of urgency. In a November 19 letter to Rosecrans, Thomas stated that his men in Chattanooga had sufficient food and ammunition, but that he was still worried about the condition of the army's draft animals and the poor state of the railroads. "If, however, we can hold out for a month longer," he stated, "our position will be entirely secure." While Grant wanted to go on the offensive immediately, Thomas wanted to remain on the defensive for at least another month. There is no written record of the statements Thomas made in his conferences with Grant and Sherman, but if Thomas made similar remarks to Grant, it is not surprising that Grant perceived Thomas to be overly cautious and slow.[36]

Sherman's troops began to march out of Bridgeport on November 18, but they moved much more slowly than Grant or Sherman had expected. Sherman had underestimated the delays that would be caused by the poor quality of the roads, and the bottlenecks that would develop from moving large bodies of troops over narrow pontoon bridges. On November 20 and 21 a heavy rain fell, which made the roads nearly impassable. Sherman made another error in ordering that each division's baggage wagons should stay with the division's infantry. This slowed the march considerably, and Sherman should have ordered all the baggage wagons to move behind the entire army.[37]

Although Grant grew increasingly restless and frustrated as the delays mounted, he did not blame Sherman for his mistakes. Dana wrote Stanton, "Grant says the blunder is his; that he should have given Sherman explicit orders to leave his wagons behind. But I know that no one was so much astonished as Grant on learning they had not been left, even without such orders."[38] Unwilling to blame his friend for the delays, Grant found a scapegoat in Thomas. On November 20 Thomas had to borrow horses from Sherman's army, as his own draft animals were still too weak to haul artillery. Grant complained to Halleck, "I ordered an attack here two weeks ago, but it was impossible to move artillery. Now Thomas's chief of artillery says he has to borrow teams from Sherman to move a portion of his artillery to where it is to be used. Sherman has used almost superhuman effort to get up even at this time, and his force is really the only one that I can move. . . . I have never felt such restlessness before as I have at the fixed and immovable condition of the Army of the Cumberland."[39]

Bragg observed Sherman's movements and shifted some forces to meet them. Seeing movement in the Confederate lines, Grant suspected that the Confederates might be retreating and ordered Thomas to find out whether Bragg's army actually was falling back.[40] Thomas could have obeyed this order in a number of ways, such as by sending out scouts, making a reconnaissance with cavalry, or advancing a line of skirmishers to probe the enemy line. Instead, he chose to launch a massive attack on the Confederate position.[41] Thomas never stated why he chose to make this attack, but several explanations are likely. His men had been cooped up in Chattanooga for two months, all the while stinging from their defeat at Chickamauga, and were eager for revenge, but Grant had given the major roles in the upcoming attack to Sherman's and Hooker's forces. Thomas was just as anxious as his soldiers to redeem the Army of the Cumberland from its defeat at Chickamauga, and he may also have wanted to show Grant that he was capable of taking the offensive. In any case, the next day saw the occurrence of one of the more unusual events of the war: an attack made in broad daylight, involving a long period of preparation and the marshaling of nearly twenty-seven thousand men, which nevertheless came as a surprise to the enemy.[42]

On the afternoon of November 24, Thomas and Grant stood at Thomas's command post, watching as four divisions assembled. Two divisions were set to attack the Orchard Knob position, and the other two were held in reserve, ready to assist if the attack ran into trouble.[43] After taking a long time to assemble, the troops marched about in formation in the manner of a grand parade. As one observer recalled, "[T]he quick earnest steps of thousands beat equal time. The sharp commands of hundreds of company officers, the sound of the drums, the ringing notes of the bugle," and "the bright sun lighting up ten thousand polished bayonets . . . all looked like preparations for a peaceful pageant, rather than for the bloody work of death."[44] While the preparations for the attack were impressive, its goals were modest. Thomas told his divisional commanders to advance only as far as the enemy's skirmish lines, to force the Confederates to deploy their troops in defense. Once they did so, making it possible to ascertain how many men the Confederates had in their front line, they were supposed to retreat.[45]

The attack went forward at two o'clock. The northern part of the line was defended by two Confederate regiments, but these regiments did not form in time to put up an effective defense. Lulled into a false sense of security by nearly two months of inactivity, the Confederates watched the Union troops assemble with great interest but no sense of alarm, as they considered all the marching and aligning to be nothing more than a grand review. When the Union troops began marching toward them, they scarcely had time to get into position before the attackers were upon them. One regiment broke and ran for the safety of the second Confederate position, at the base of Missionary Ridge, while the other regiment stayed and fought, shooting down more than 150 Federal soldiers before being overwhelmed. Of the defenders, 40 were killed and 150 were captured.

On the southern portion of the line, the Union troops encountered almost no opposition and easily occupied the Confederate skirmish line. Thomas signaled his divisional commanders to entrench their positions and hold on, and he ordered the two reserve divisions forward to reinforce them and extend the line. The captured position, which now formed the Union front line, ran along a low ridge south of Chattanooga, with its highest point running across the hill called Orchard Knob.[46]

Thomas was delighted with his soldiers' performance. He told the commanding officer of the Forty-first Ohio Infantry, which had seen the heaviest fighting, to pass along his thanks to the men, calling the action "a gallant thing, Colonel, a very gallant thing." The soldiers' performance also impressed Grant, who wrote to Halleck that "the troops moved under fire with all the precision of veterans on parade."[47]

Ironically, while the attack had succeeded in terms of capturing territory, it failed in its original purpose of discovering the location and intent of the enemy, as it was not clear whether the small number of defenders on the Orchard Knob line represented the rearguard of a retreating army or the skirmish line of an army still in place.[48] Meanwhile, Sherman's troops crossed the Tennessee River during the early morning hours of November 24 and moved quickly southward, meeting little resistance. They reached what they thought was the northern end of Missionary Ridge that afternoon but realized the next day that a steep, wooded ravine still lay between them and their object. To get at the Confederate army, Sherman's men would have to descend into the ravine and attack uphill against fortified positions. Worse, the Confederates now knew Sherman was there, so he had lost the advantage of surprise.[49]

The situation was better for the Union forces at the other end of the line. In the late afternoon of November 23, Thomas's signal officers, who had broken the Confederate signal code, intercepted a message from the Confederate commander on Lookout Mountain. This officer had noticed the Union army's movements in Chattanooga but had misinterpreted what he saw, and he had signaled Bragg to expect an attack on Lookout

Mountain. Thomas suggested that Hooker's force, which was currently idle, make an attack on Lookout Mountain to divert Confederate attention away from Sherman. Grant liked the idea but was concerned that Lookout Mountain might be too steep and well fortified to attack. He ordered Hooker to make only a demonstration attack against Lookout Mountain but gave him discretion to turn his demonstration into a full-scale attack, if the situation seemed favorable.[50]

Hooker's men easily captured the lower slope of Lookout Mountain on November 24 and dug in. The Confederate counterattack failed to dislodge Hooker's troops, and skirmishing went on throughout the evening and night. When dawn broke the next day, the troops in the valley saw the United States flag flying from the peak of Lookout Mountain.[51] Bragg had decided to abandon the mountain, for fear that the garrison there would be surrounded, and pulled back his line to Missionary Ridge.[52]

While Bragg's decision was a sound one, the Confederate retreat boosted the morale of the Union soldiers in Chattanooga, while dampening the spirits of Bragg's own men. The Union troops had spent the last two months living under the threat of Confederate shelling and in the shadow of the Confederate flag, and they viewed the capture of Lookout Mountain as an important victory. The mountain's capture also caused Grant and Thomas to change their plans. Grant had originally planned for Thomas to advance toward the base of Missionary Ridge on the morning of November 25, primarily to ascertain whether the Confederates were still there. The dawn light showed clearly that the Confederates still occupied their entrenchments at the base of Missionary Ridge, so there was no point in continuing with Grant's original plan. Instead, Thomas proposed to send Hooker forward from Lookout Mountain and across West Chickamauga Creek, to get behind Missionary Ridge. Grant adopted Thomas's suggestion. If everything worked as planned, Sherman would attack the Confederates to the north, while Hooker got behind them to the south, and the two forces would crush the Confederate army between them.[53]

Grant and Thomas now had little to do but wait for Sherman and Hooker to attack. They spent the day on Orchard Knob, observing the fighting through field glasses and listening to the news from the front. Also present on Orchard Knob were Gordon Granger, Charles Dana, Thomas Wood, and a number of other officers. A civilian observer on the hill remarked that Orchard Knob was dangerously close to the firing line and wondered out loud why the Confederates were not shelling their position. Thomas remarked that if the Rebels knew who was there, they would have certainly paid more attention.[54] Later, the Confederates did begin firing at the command post. As Dana recalled, "The enemy kept firing shells at us, I remember, from the ridge opposite. They had got the range so well that the shells burst pretty near the top of the elevation where we were, and when we saw them coming we would duck—that is, everybody did except Generals Grant and Thomas and Gordon Granger. It was not according to their dignity to go down on their marrow bones."[55]

Grant and Thomas could see activity in the far distance, along the northern end of Missionary Ridge, so they knew Sherman was attacking. Sherman sent no word, however, of how his attack was progressing. The morning turned to afternoon, and Sherman still did not send Grant any news about his progress. At 12:45 Sherman sent a three-word message: "Where is Thomas?" Thomas answered that he was still in his original position. Something was clearly going wrong with Sherman's attack. From Orchard Knob, the generals could see that his troops were not advancing, and some of them seemed to be falling back in disorder. Hooker had also run into trouble, his advance temporarily blocked by the swollen waters of West Chickamauga Creek.[56]

Grant wanted to achieve some kind of success before the end of the day, and his thoughts turned to Thomas's army, the only force that had not been committed to the fight. Despite his impatience, Grant was reluctant to order them forward. Thomas was not supposed to attack until Sherman had already gained the top of Missionary Ridge. Missionary Ridge was considered too steep to take by direct assault, and if Thomas advanced before Sherman was on the scene, his men might find themselves stuck at the base of the ridge, vulnerable to rifle and artillery fire from above but unable to move forward.

Unsure of whether he should order an attack on Missionary Ridge, Grant first approached Gen. Thomas J. Wood, a divisional commander, and hinted that the Army of the Cumberland should do something to take the pressure off Sherman. Wood agreed, and Grant went to talk to Thomas, who was peering through field glasses at the ridge. Wood saw Thomas respond but could not hear what he said, and Grant walked away and continued to wait. Another half hour passed without any news from

Sherman or Hooker, and John Rawlins, Grant's chief of staff, urged Grant to attack. Grant now went to Thomas and gave him a direct order to attack the rifle pits. Thomas went to Granger and spoke to him for a few minutes, and then Granger walked off. This seemed to indicate that an attack was about to start, but time passed and nothing happened. Finally, Grant went to Wood, whom Granger commanded, and asked him, "Why is your division not in motion?"

"We have received no such orders, sir," answered Wood.

Grant then went to Thomas. "General Thomas, why are not these troops advancing?"

"I don't know," Thomas replied. "General Granger has been ordered to move them forward."

Grant looked for Granger and found him at a nearby artillery battery, personally aiming and firing the pieces. Granger's habit of playing with cannons during battle was well-known, but was generally considered a harmless, childish idiosyncrasy. But this time Granger's foolish behavior had delayed the progress of an entire army. "If you will leave that battery to its captain," Grant scolded, "and take command of your corps, it will be better for all of us." Granger immediately set the attack into motion.[57]

The strange sequence of events on Orchard Knob that afternoon demonstrates that the command relationship between Grant and Thomas had already become quite poor. Thomas disagreed with Grant's decision to attack Missionary Ridge, but he did not discuss the matter openly with Grant. With Buell and Rosecrans, Thomas had felt free to argue at length when he disagreed with his commanders' decisions, but with Grant Thomas only stated briefly his opposition to the movement and then returned to watching the battle in silence. When Grant ordered the attack to take place, Thomas expressed his opposition by taking a passive role, leaving the planning of the attack to Granger and taking no action himself. Thomas was reasonable to view an attack on Missionary Ridge as overly risky, but he should have expressed his objections directly to Grant, not indirectly by passively resisting Grant's orders.

The attack involved four divisions of infantry, or about twenty-four thousand men, and began at 3:40 P.M. At the prearranged signal of six cannon shots, the divisions advanced quickly across the open field between the Union front line and the base of Missionary Ridge. Confederate artillery opened fire on the advancing troops, and Union artillery fired back at the Confederate guns. The Confederates on the ridge above,

who had a good view of the advance, were impressed by the size of the
force moving against them. Brig. Gen. Arthur Manigault, commanding
one of the brigades on the ridge, estimated the size of the Union force
at fifty thousand men. "Such a sight I never saw either before or after,
and I trust . . . never to see again. . . . I noticed some nervousness among
my men as they beheld this grand military spectacle."[58]

By contrast, the Union troops were confident and eager for action. As
one officer later remembered, "We had been held in restraint so long . . .
that our enthusiasm knew no bounds." In some parts of the line the
Confederate defenders put up a resistance, but in most places the Confederates retreated in haste up the ridge. The Union troops soon held the
entire lower line, but they now found themselves subject to a heavy fire
from the artillery and infantry at the top of the ridge. The Confederate
breastworks that the soldiers now occupied offered no protection from
fire from this direction, and the soldiers could not fire back effectively up
the steep hill.[59]

Their position at the bottom of the hill being untenable, the Union
troops had only two choices: retreat across the open field behind them,
which was still being shelled by Confederate artillery, or advance up the
mountain in front of them. The soldiers soon decided to advance, in some
cases on the orders of their officers, and in some cases on their own initiative. The Union soldiers were encouraged by the quick retreat of the
Confederates at the base of the mountain, and in the heat of battle, with
their spirits fueled by adrenaline, the soldiers did not think too much
about what they were up against. "We had no orders and no distinct
purpose," wrote one soldier. "The enemy were fleeing up the slopes and
we were bound to follow them. We didn't stop to think whether we
could carry the crest or not—we didn't think at all! Each man just
crowded on." As some soldiers began to ascend the ridge, others saw them
moving up and began climbing the ridge also. Soon, the entire Union line
was advancing up the ridge, with Sheridan's and Wood's divisions leading
the way.[60]

Thomas and Grant watched the assault unfold from their observation
post on Orchard Knob. Grant was angry, as he had not ordered this attack,
and he feared that it would end in disaster. He turned to Thomas and
demanded, "Who ordered those men up that ridge?"

Slowly, Thomas replied, "I don't know. I did not."

Grant asked Granger, "Did you order them up?"

"No," Granger replied. "When those fellows get started all hell can't stop them."[61]

Grant grumbled that someone would pay for it if the attack failed and returned to observing the battle in silence.[62] He and Thomas watched as their men climbed the ridge. The soldiers formed in groups behind their regimental colors, trailing in two lines behind their flags in an inverted V formation. Men fell as bullets and artillery shells hit them, and some of the color-bearers fell, dropping their flags, only to have others take up the colors and continue the ascent. As the men reached the top, Grant and Thomas watched intently, wondering whether their tired men would be able to overcome the Confederate defenders.[63]

The struggle was fierce but brief, and the generals on Orchard Knob watched in wonder as the Confederates ran away in panic. After gaining the top, victorious Union troops moved north and south along the ridge, attacking the remaining defenders from the flank while their comrades, still climbing the ridge, attacked them in front. The Confederate soldiers could not maintain their positions against this pressure, and soon almost the entire ridge lay in Union hands. Dana sent a triumphant telegram to Stanton: "Glory to God. The day is decisively ours. Missionary Ridge has just been carried by a magnificent charge of Thomas's troops, and rebels routed."[64]

Grant wired Sherman with news of Thomas's success and ordered him to launch a follow-up attack, but Sherman's men were in no condition to comply. They had spent the day assaulting the strong Confederate positions on the northern end of Missionary Ridge and had been driven back repeatedly. Sherman had managed his forces badly, sending them forward in piecemeal attacks against strongly fortified Confederate positions. Sherman had not reported to Grant because he kept hoping that the next attack would succeed, and he could report good news. His earlier message "Where is Thomas?" reflected his expectation that Thomas would attack immediately, with the hope that it would draw defenders away from his own sector and make some sort of victory possible.[65]

That evening, Grant, Thomas, Granger, and Smith rode up to the top of the ridge to survey the field and talk to their men. Everywhere they went, they saw rebel prisoners and captured guns. The men cheered as they rode along the ridge, and the line officers reported their regiments' exploits to the generals. Thomas recalled later, "I fell among some of our old soldiers, who always took liberties with me, who commenced talking and giving their views of the victory. When I attempted to compliment them for the gallant manner in which they had made the assault, one man very coolly replied, 'Why, general, we know that you have been training us for this race for the last three weeks.'" Thomas was embarrassed at the attention and at a loss for a response. He saw a steamboat coming into Chattanooga down below, and he fell back on his habitual concern for logistics and the men's welfare. "We have trained you as long as we want to," Thomas replied; "there come the rations."[66]

While the capture of Missionary Ridge seemed like a miracle at the time, military historians have demonstrated that a combination of factors explains the Rebel defeat on the ridge. The Confederates had done little to fortify the top of the ridge, counting on the natural strength of the position for defense. The artillery at the top of the ridge was poorly situated and did not have a clear field of fire against troops assaulting the ridge. The advancing Union troops followed close behind the Confederates retreating from the rifle pits at the bottom of the ridge, meaning that the defenders at the top of the ridge had to hold their fire, for fear of hitting their own men. The Union troops were also able to use the uneven terrain of the hill to their advantage, taking shelter from enemy fire by hiding in ravines, and climbing up these ravines to the top of the ridge.[67]

The morale of the defenders was low. Bragg's army suffered from a constant lack of food, clothing, and supplies and had been living in the open in the cold, wet weather for months. On November 23 they had watched the Union army capture the Orchard Knob line, and the next morning they saw that the Union had captured Lookout Mountain. They were frustrated with Bragg's inaction and had little confidence in their commander. By contrast, the Union soldiers were well fed and supplied and had recently received extensive reinforcements. They were encouraged by their successful attacks on Orchard Knob and Lookout Mountain and had confidence in the skill of their commanders. The men of the Army of the Cumberland had suffered under the taunts of Sherman's troops, fresh from their victory at Vicksburg, who had looked down on the Army of the Cumberland after its defeat at Chickamauga. Now they felt exhilarated and confident after their capture of the Confederate line at the base of Missionary Ridge and were pursuing closely behind a fleeing enemy. When they reached the top of the ridge, they had the courage and confidence to fight, while the Confederates, discouraged and pessimistic, fled before them.

On November 26 Hooker, Thomas, and Sherman all advanced their forces in pursuit, capturing some stragglers and wagons but failing to catch up to the main body of Bragg's army. That evening, Hooker asked Thomas if his command could lead the pursuit the following day. Hooker's men had seen less fighting on November 25 than Thomas's or Sherman's and were in the best condition to undertake the pursuit, so Thomas gave Hooker permission to take the lead.[68] On November 27 the Confederate rearguard fought an effective delaying action and prevented Hooker from catching up to the rest of the army, and Grant called off the pursuit the next day. His men were short of supplies and rations, the roads were too muddy for rapid travel, and the army still did not have enough draft animals to haul supplies. Most of the cavalry was absent, having been ordered out of Chattanooga weeks ago so that the cavalry horses could get enough forage, and it seemed unlikely that infantry would be able to move fast enough to catch up with Bragg.[69]

Instead, Grant sent a force to relieve Burnside, who was still under siege in Knoxville. For days, Burnside had been sending desperate messages to Grant claiming he was badly outnumbered and short on supplies, and would have to retreat soon if he did not receive assistance. On November 27 Grant ordered Thomas to send two divisions under Granger's command to Knoxville as quickly as possible. When Grant returned to Chattanooga on November 28, he was furious to discover that Granger had not yet left. Thomas had not received Grant's orders until the evening of November 27, and Granger let his men, who were tired from their assault on Missionary Ridge, rest and prepare before leaving on their long march. While Grant was most angry with Granger, it seems likely that he took this as further evidence of Thomas's inability to move quickly. Grant sent part of Sherman's army to Knoxville instead, and Sherman soon drove off the besieging Confederates. With Knoxville and Chattanooga safe, Grant let his army settle into winter quarters.[70]

Grant received accolades from all quarters for his victory at Chattanooga. On December 8 Lincoln wrote Grant, "I wish to tender you and all under your command my more than thanks, my profoundest gratitude for the skill, courage, and perseverance with which you and they, over so great difficulties, have effected that important object. God bless you all." On December 17 Congress passed a resolution of thanks and ordered that a gold medal be presented to Grant for his victory. Inside the army, officers knew that the battle had been won by luck and the performance of individual soldiers. James Wilson, then on Grant's staff, wrote in his memoir that "the victory was quite as surprising to those who won it as to those who lost it."[71]

While the Chattanooga campaign won glory for the Army of the Cumberland, it left Grant with a negative impression of that army's commander. Thomas had actually done Grant excellent service during the campaign, advising in favor of successful tactics such as the Brown's Ferry attack and Hooker's assault on Lookout Mountain, and advising against Grant's unrealistic plan to attack the Confederate line on November 7. Thomas had served as an effective subordinate commander during the Brown's Ferry operation and had captured the Confederates' outer defense line on Orchard Knob. While he had advised against the attack on Missionary Ridge, the efforts he had made to train his men, provide them with supplies, and keep up their morale all contributed to their eventual success.

Despite these contributions, Grant perceived Thomas's role in the campaign as a negative one. On four different occasions—the canceled attack on November 7, the attack on Missionary Ridge on November 25, Hooker's pursuit on November 26, and Granger's delayed start to Knoxville on November 28—Grant had found Thomas and his subordinates to be unaggressive and slow. In Grant's eyes, Thomas compared poorly with Sherman, who was always willing to take risks and eager to go on the offensive. Even though Sherman had failed to achieve his goals throughout the Chattanooga campaign, Grant knew that Sherman had tried his best to carry out his orders, move quickly, and stay on the offensive. Grant had no such confidence in Thomas.

Grant and Thomas also communicated poorly. Both men were known to be taciturn, and when working they failed to communicate well. While Thomas had been able to disagree openly with Buell and Rosecrans, and discuss his disagreements with them, he tended to take a more passive stance with Grant. By contrast, Sherman's talkative, expressive personality complemented Grant's, and the two men worked well together. Grant enjoyed Sherman's company and felt like he always knew where Sherman stood, but his polite, formal relationship with Thomas left Grant unsure of Thomas's real opinion.

As Grant was promoted to overall command of the Union armies, he had his choice of commanders to work with, and he consistently chose

Sherman over Thomas. He chose Sherman not only out of friendship but also because he worked more effectively with Sherman and considered him a better general. While Thomas had been promoted from corps to army command, he would spend yet another year as a subordinate officer, first under Grant, and then under Sherman. Several months would pass before Thomas resumed active campaigning. In the meantime a series of military and political duties awaited him in his new role of commander of the Department and the Army of the Cumberland.

CHAPTER TWELVE

The Army of the Cumberland

The pressure always brought to bear against the commander of the Army of the Potomac would destroy me in a week.

After the Battle of Chattanooga, the Union army settled in to winter quarters. Thomas spent the next few months further improving his army's organization and performance, and carrying out the administrative and political tasks that came to him as commander of the Department and the Army of the Cumberland. One of the most important of his political tasks involved deciding how to treat escaped slaves who came into Federal lines. At this point in his career, Thomas was still conservative in his racial views, and he did little to assist escaped slaves. He supported the recruitment of African American soldiers as a measure necessary for the war effort, but he viewed escaped slaves as potentially dangerous and advocated keeping them under strict white control, either in military units or in labor camps. He also thought African Americans made inferior soldiers, and he did not use them in frontline service. His racial views did not change until a year later, when he commanded African Americans in battle.

The purely military aspects of Thomas's command role were the easiest, as Thomas had inherited an efficient military organization from Rosecrans and did not have to make any major changes. Thomas improved on the hospital train system established by Rosecrans, allocating the best locomotives, cars, and railroad employees to the transportation of the wounded.[1] He also made improvements in the army's mapmaking section, worked with the Sanitary Commission to improve his soldiers' health, and supervised the construction of a national cemetery at Chattanooga.

Thomas made several improvements in the Army of the Cumberland's already excellent mapmaking department. Thomas supervised the development of a specially equipped wagon for the topographical engineers, which traveled with Thomas's headquarters. The wagon had sides that folded down into desks, and awnings that folded out to keep maps and papers dry. Thomas also kept a personal map book, which contained tables of distances between strategic points, lists of roads and their quality, and his own campaign sketches and plans. Under Thomas, the Army of the Cumberland's mapmaking department became the most sophisticated such organization in the war, superior to any other topographical department in either the Union or the Confederate army.[2]

Thomas cooperated with the Sanitary Commission and other groups in providing his men with the best possible medical care. In January 1864 Thomas complied with a New York chapter's request for an autograph, which they auctioned off to raise funds. He also sent the auction a set of carved wooden napkin rings, which he had obtained in an unusual way. During the slow days of the winter encampment, the soldiers of the Army of the Cumberland passed the time by whittling, and some of them became quite expert at it. Nicholas Phieffer, a private, carved two dozen napkin rings out of laurel root, which were so good that his friends suggested that he present them to General Thomas for his personal use. According to the historian of Phieffer's regiment, the private easily obtained an interview with Thomas, who praised the soldier's "exquisite taste and skillfulness, as he turned the rings over and over in his hands" and called members of his staff over to admire them. Stating that he "could hardly dare" to use "such beautiful and valuable articles" in his own mess service, Thomas proposed to send them instead to be auctioned by the Sanitary Fair in New York. Phieffer agreed, and Thomas shook his hand and sent him back to camp. The napkin rings sold for twenty-five dollars each, raising a total of six hundred dollars.[3]

Thomas's main innovation during this period was the establishment of a national cemetery at Chattanooga. Previously, soldiers who fell in battle were commonly buried on or near the battlefield where they fell. They were often buried hastily in shallow and unmarked graves, and some were not buried at all. Contemporary soldiers' diaries and letters mention the horror they felt at seeing pigs dig up the bodies and eat them, or of returning to a battle site months afterward to find that rain had washed away the graves, leaving bones and remnants of clothing lying exposed.

On December 25, 1863, Thomas placed Thomas Van Horne, the chaplain of the Army of the Cumberland, in charge of establishing a cemetery at Chattanooga.[4] Thomas personally chose the site of the cemetery, a beautiful location on a ridge south of the city, and Van Horne recalled that Thomas "manifested great interest in the work, and frequently rode out from the town to note the progress and make suggestions." Van Horne proposed having the dead buried in lots according to their state of origin, but Thomas disagreed. "No, no," he said, "Mix them up; mix them up. I am tired of state-rights." Thomas did segregate soldiers by race, however, designating a separate place in the cemetery for the dead from African American regiments.[5]

Thomas also worked to overcome the problem of expiring enlistments that the Union army faced that winter. Most Union soldiers had volunteered in 1861 for three years, and their terms of service were due to expire. These early volunteers formed the backbone of the Union army, and the government desperately needed them to reenlist. The War Department offered rewards to the individual soldiers of regiments in which more than three-quarters of the men reenlisted. The men would be granted a furlough and a cash bounty, and their regiments would be labeled "veteran volunteers" and allowed to remain single units. Regiments in which less than three quarters of the men reenlisted would be broken up, and the men would be assigned to other regiments. The plan capitalized on the men's loyalty to and pride in their regiments, and on the pressure that men who had already reenlisted would bring to bear on holdouts. The plan worked, and the majority of the regiments in the army met their quotas.[6]

In one case, Thomas intervened personally to make sure a regiment reenlisted. Maj. Thomas Taylor, the acting commander of the Forty-seventh Ohio Infantry, had just begun getting his men to reenlist in early February, when he learned that his regiment was ordered to report to active service in Chattanooga. If the regiment went on active duty, the men would not be eligible to use their thirty-day furloughs, which would virtually guarantee that the regiment would not meet its quota. Taylor pleaded with his commanding officers to allow his regiment to stay off active duty. They refused, but they gave Taylor permission to speak with Thomas.

Taylor set out immediately for Thomas's tent. Upon entering, Taylor immediately noticed an officer in a well-pressed uniform who seemed to be in charge; this man turned out to be Thomas's chief of staff, Gen.

William D. Whipple. He also saw several staff officers and clerks busily copying documents, writing letters, and discussing official business. Taylor asked Whipple where Thomas was and was answered by a man sitting quietly in a corner, who had previously escaped Taylor's notice. Taylor looked the man over, "saw his two stars," and realized it was Thomas. After hearing his request, Thomas assured Taylor that his regiment would be excused from the coming campaign so that his veterans could take their furloughs. Much relieved, Taylor returned to his camp.

Taylor wrote his wife about his meeting with the general, describing Thomas as "apparently fifty-five years old" (Thomas was actually forty-seven) and "hale and vigorous," with a fair complexion and almost white hair. While many officers found Thomas intimidating, Taylor wrote that "his countenance indicates a hopeful disposition and a love of sport. Eyes are almost laughing and a pleasant expression hovers over his face all the time, voice mild; is easily approached and speaks earnestly and, I would swear, is a good liver and enjoys a 'punch' as greatly as any man."[7]

Another request for a furlough gave rise to a comic story about Thomas that was repeated widely through the army. Different versions of this story were recorded in different regimental histories and memoirs, but the earliest published version of the story is that of William B. Shanks, a journalist who traveled with the Army of the Cumberland throughout 1862 and 1863. Shanks recounted that a private from an East Tennessee regiment spotted Thomas riding in the camps around Chattanooga and hailed Thomas by calling out, "Hey mister! You! I want to speak with you!" Ignoring this breach of military etiquette, Thomas rode over to talk to the man. The soldier asked for a furlough to visit his wife.

"How long since you saw your wife?" Thomas asked.

"Ever since I enlisted—nigh on to three months," the soldier replied.

"Three months!" exclaimed the general, good-naturedly. "Why, my good man, I haven't seen my wife for three years."

According to Shanks, "The East Tennessean stopped whittling the stick which he had in his hand, and stared for a moment incredulously at the general. 'Wall, you see,' he said at length, with a sheepish smile, 'me and my wife ain't that kind.'" In Shanks's version of the story, Thomas laughed and rode away without a reply, but in other versions Thomas granted the furlough.[8]

The men also liked to tell a story about Thomas catching an Irish private with a butchered pig, clearly foraged from a nearby farm in violation of orders. Thomas was ready to send the private to the stockade, when the soldier protested, "You see, general dear, he was eating our corps badge [an acorn], and it was for that I killed him." Amused by the private's bold response, the general did not punish him.[9]

The popularity and humor of these stories lay in the contrast between the patrician general on the one hand and the simple, rustic private and the quaint Irish soldier on the other. The stories were also popular because Thomas, despite his reputation for strict discipline, let the backwoods private get away with insubordination, and let the Irish private get away with foraging. The soldiers told these stories as a way of democratizing Thomas, bringing him down to their level, and showing that they knew a kind heart lay behind his gruff exterior.

Thomas's kind heart led him to take a personal interest in the youngest soldier of the Army of the Cumberland, an eleven-year-old drummer boy named Jonathan Clem. Clem had run away from home in 1862 and had joined the drum corps of the Twenty-second Michigan Infantry. During the Battle of Chickamauga, Clem disobeyed orders to stay in camp and went into the field with his regiment. The Twenty-second Michigan was one of the last regiments to retreat from Snodgrass Ridge, and in the darkness and confusion many of the regiment's men were captured. Clem was apprehended by a Confederate officer, who ordered Clem to surrender, but Clem turned on the man and shot him. Historical evidence indicates that Clem probably shot a staff officer, but Clem thought he had killed a Confederate colonel. Word of his exploit traveled through the army and reached the newspapers, making "the Drummer Boy of Chickamauga" a national hero. His regimental commander gave him an unofficial promotion to the rank of sergeant, and the officers of his regiment chipped in to pay him a sergeant's salary. In October 1863 Rosecrans awarded Clem the Badge of the Roll of Honor.[10]

Clem was captured later that month and spent almost five weeks in a Confederate prison camp before being exchanged. In January 1864 Thomas appointed Clem to be an orderly on his staff, apparently as a way of keeping him out of danger. Thomas's staff officers acted as tutors for Clem, and Thomas intended to send him to West Point or the Naval Academy as soon as he became old enough. As an orderly, Clem carried messages and performed other errands at headquarters, performing work that seemed less dangerous than service in a regiment. Thomas did not succeed in keeping the boy safe, however, as Clem was slightly wounded while carrying a message for Thomas during the Atlanta campaign.

In August 1864 Thomas made sure Clem would stay safe by mustering the boy out of the service and sending him to a private boarding school in Indiana. In September Clem wrote to Sanford Kellogg, Thomas's nephew and staff aide, and asked Kellogg about Thomas, adding that he had not written to Thomas himself "as I am afraid that he would not answer me."[11] Thomas responded to Clem's letter and continued a correspondence with Clem over the years to come. An extract from an 1866 letter to Clem shows Thomas taking the role of a strict but affectionate surrogate father. Thomas told Clem he was "very much pleased" to hear from the headmaster that Clem was doing well at the school, and that he saw "a very evident improvement in your letters. The letters are well made and the words and sentences correctly spelled and constructed." Thomas advised Clem not to disappoint the "many kind friends" who were helping and encouraging Clem, "but study hard [and] fill your head with knowledge."

To encourage Clem Thomas told him about James Garfield (the future U.S. president), whom Clem had met while Garfield was Rosecrans's chief of staff. Garfield "worked on a canal," Thomas wrote, "and educated himself by buying his textbooks which he studied at every leisure moment whilst the canal was frozen up." Despite Garfield's humble origins, he "greatly distinguished himself" as a soldier, and is now "one of the most distinguished of our representatives in Congress." "In time," he wrote Clem, "you will doubtless stand as good a chance for honorable distinction" as Garfield, or "as many of our distinguished men, who commenced life in many instances without any encouragement whatever."[12]

Thomas also wrote to a Presbyterian minister who was helping to oversee Clem's education in Indiana. "I was indeed very much pleased to get the letter of my manly little friend," Thomas wrote, "which exhibited unmistakable signs of the frankness of character that has always made him friends wherever he has been known, and gratified to learn from you that he was in such good hands, where he has every opportunity of receiving a good moral and religious training." No other letters from Thomas to Clem survive, but these excerpts provide an interesting glimpse into Thomas's character. Thomas enjoyed children, and he evidently regretted not having children of his own. With Clem Thomas acted the role of a nineteenth-century father, expressing love through attention, discipline, and encouragement to hard work, rather than through open affection. Thomas also took a paternal role with his soldiers and subordinate officers, and the men's favorite nickname for Thomas was "Old Pap," in recognition of the fatherly concern Thomas felt for them.[13]

Throughout Thomas's command of the Army and Department of the Cumberland, he had political duties to uphold, working with Tennessee's military governor to maintain law and order in the state. In 1862, as a first step toward reconstructing Tennessee, Lincoln had appointed Andrew Johnson as the state's military governor. Johnson had feuded often with Buell and Rosecrans, but Thomas had developed a good working relationship with Johnson during his service in Kentucky in 1861–62, and Thomas continued to maintain good relations with Johnson now that he was governor.[14]

Another of Thomas's military duties was the supervision of a Board of Claims that paid compensation to residents whose property had been destroyed or appropriated by the army. Some of the applicants to the board were actually secessionists and Confederate sympathizers, so Thomas changed the rules of the board to ensure that only loyal Unionists could make good on their claims. Thomas was much more strict than Rosecrans had been in denying the claims of secessionists; as a Southerner who had suffered greatly for his decision to remain loyal to the Union, Thomas evidently felt especially resentful of former secessionists who now professed loyalty.[15]

Thomas also cracked down on guerrilla activity in the department. On December 23, 1863, Confederate partisans operating near the town of Mulberry, Tennessee, attempted to murder five Union prisoners. Three of the prisoners were killed, but the other two escaped and made it back to Union lines. Thomas levied a fine of $30,000 on all citizens living within ten miles of where the men were captured, and he ordered that the money collected be distributed to each of the murdered men's families. Thomas felt that the fine against civilians was justified by the "atrocious" and "cold-blooded" nature of the murders, and by the fact that the civilian population was supporting and hiding the guerrillas. While punishing all of the civilians in an area for the activities of a few guerrillas may seem unduly harsh or unfair to a modern reader, this response to guerrilla activity had become common practice by this point in the war. Other commanders went further, burning to the ground entire towns as punishment for the sheltering or assisting of guerrillas.[16]

In another case, Thomas was more lenient. A military tribunal gave Frank B. Gurley, a Confederate partisan, a death sentence for the 1862 murder of Robert L. McCook, a Union colonel who was shot while trying to surrender. Gurley admitted killing McCook but claimed that he did so by mistake, acting in the heat of battle. Thomas believed Gurley and commuted his sentence to five years in prison, and Gurley was later pardoned by Andrew Johnson. Commuting Gurley's sentence was unpopular with East Tennessee loyalists, including a number of Thomas's troops, but Thomas followed his own sense of what was right.[17]

The most controversial responsibility that Thomas had as a department commander was dealing with the issue of how to treat escaped slaves who fled to Federal lines. Early in the war, escaped slaves were treated as property and returned to their owners; later, they were returned only when their owners could prove they were sympathetic to the Union. At the time Thomas took command of the Department of the Cumberland, federal policy toward escaped slaves was not clearly defined, and field commanders had considerable leeway in deciding how escaped slaves were treated. The Second Confiscation Act, passed by Congress in July 1862, declared that all secessionists' slaves who came within Federal lines would be considered free men, and the Emancipation Proclamation of January 1, 1863, declared all slaves owned by secessionists to be free. Rosecrans had issued orders telling his subordinates to accept able-bodied men into Federal lines, as they would be useful as laborers, but not to allow in women, children, or men incapable of labor. Many of Rosecrans's subordinates disobeyed these orders out of compassion for the slaves, and Rosecrans did not force the issue.[18]

Thomas was much stricter than Rosecrans. When Thomas first took command of the department, he ordered his men to enforce the policy of excluding women, children, and unemployable men from Union lines. Thomas also revoked an order made by a subordinate commander at Gallatin, Tennessee, that required the white trustees of plantations in the area under his command to pay their slaves wages and supply them with clothing. Thomas considered master-slave relations to be a matter of civil law, and he scolded the Gallatin commander for overstepping his author-ity, by intervening in "a matter which he, as a military commander of the district, is not called upon to adjust." Thomas emphasized that "military authorities should have as little to do with the Negro as possible, it being considered best to let the masters and slaves settle their own affairs without military interference." Thomas had enacted a similar policy while commanding the Nashville garrison in August 1862. He had impressed slaves to construct fortifications around the city and had then returned them to their owners after the work was completed.[19]

While Thomas's orders to the Gallatin commander might indicate only a concern for proper subordination of military to civilian authority, his decision to strictly enforce the policy barring women, children, and men unsuitable for labor from Union lines indicates that his racial views were still not especially sympathetic to the slaves' desire for freedom. The policy excluding most blacks from Union lines was a military policy, not a civilian one, and Thomas was free to revise or overturn Rosecrans's prior orders. In any case, Thomas's policy did not last long. When Lorenzo Thomas, the army's adjutant general, heard about Thomas's orders, he countermanded them and told Thomas to establish a contraband camp in his department for men, women, and children. Lorenzo Thomas also overruled George Thomas in regards to the black laborers at the Gallatin plantation, reinstating the policy that required the plantations' trustees to pay wages and provide laborers with clothing.[20]

Thomas considered escaped slaves to be a potential threat to white society, and while he complied with Lorenzo Thomas's orders, he also took steps to make sure that the slaves would remain under close white control. He ordered Col. Thomas J. Morgan, the commander of the Fourteenth Regiment of U.S. Colored Troops, to send out patrols to arrest all African American men in the area who did not possess passes, and to send them either to the recruiting service or to labor camps.[21]

Where issues of security were not involved, Thomas could be generous in his treatment of African Americans. In October 1863 one of Thomas's subordinates complained that black laborers working on the fortifications at Fort Donelson, Tennessee, were not being paid. Under the policy in effect at that time, slaves of disloyal owners could be paid directly, but the wages of slaves with loyalist owners were paid directly to their owners. There was no way to tell whether the former owners of the escaped slaves laboring at Fort Donelson were loyal or disloyal, and as a result none of the former slaves were being paid. Thomas decided to pay wages to all of the escaped slaves at the fort, and he forwarded the matter to the Adjutant

General's Office in Washington. The adjutant general approved Thomas's plan, setting a precedent for other military jurisdictions.[22] On another occasion, Thomas intervened to help a runaway slave whom Thomas had hired as a personal servant. When one of his cavalry officers went on a raiding expedition in the area where the former slave had lived, Thomas instructed the officer to free his servant's wife and children and bring them back to camp. Thomas's actions were consistent with his kind personality and traditional, paternalistic attitude toward blacks. While he could be generous and kind in his treatment of African Americans, he still did not trust them and felt it necessary to keep them under close supervision by whites.[23]

Thomas strongly supported the government's policy of recruiting African American soldiers, but this was not unusual. Many white Unionists, including some with extremely racist views, supported the recruitment of black soldiers as a necessary step to win the war. Thomas worked well with Col. Robert D. Mussey, the senior recruiting officer for African American troops in Thomas's department, and intervened on several occasions to make sure Mussey could carry out his recruitment efforts. In March 1864 Mussey complained that the district commander at Nashville was not allowing black soldiers out of camp unless accompanied by an officer, which was interfering with the regiment's ability to maintain courier lines. Thomas "promptly ordered that no distinctions should be made in this matter between Black and White troops." Later, at Mussey's request, Thomas arrested and sent to military trial a local mayor who had ordered a black schoolteacher to be flogged. Another officer in charge of recruiting black troops, Maj. George Stearns, praised Thomas for "giving his most hearty aid and cooperation" in the recruitment efforts. Thomas also allocated a section of the National Cemetery at Chattanooga for African American soldiers. Thomas knew that people might suspect him of not supporting the policy of recruitment, and he was quick to defend himself against such accusations. When a subordinate officer was quoted in a newspaper as accusing Thomas of not supporting the recruitment policy, Thomas called the statement "slander" and wrote the officer to demand a retraction.[24]

While Thomas supported the recruitment and fair treatment of black troops, he did not trust them to perform well in combat, and this led to some friction with Mussey. On June 6, 1864, Mussey wrote Adj. Gen. Lorenzo Thomas complaining, "[T]hat the Negro is to be made a man by first being made a soldier, does not seem to be comprehended by the commanding Generals." Mussey had a valid point, given that six black infantry regiments had been recruited but none had yet been given combat duties. At the time, four of the new regiments were working as laborers, while two guarded the railroads in the army's rear. Mussey also complained to the adjutant general that Thomas had gone back on a months-old promise to establish a hospital for black soldiers. The African American soldiers had to go to an overcrowded, poorly equipped hospital, which they shared with black refugees and civilian laborers, and which had a much higher mortality rate than the hospitals for white soldiers.[25]

When Thomas learned of Mussey's report, he had Mussey arrested for insubordination. Mussey quickly recanted, explaining that he did not mean to criticize Thomas, but admitting that "the careless phrase, 'commanding generals,' could be so interpreted." Thomas promptly released Mussey from arrest. The incident does not seem to have injured their working relationship, as Mussey continued to write favorable reports on Thomas to the adjutant general. While Mussey apologized for part of his statement, he did not take back his complaint about the lack of a hospital for black soldiers, and on this issue he prevailed. On June 28, 1864, Thomas ordered the construction of a separate hospital for the African American troops.[26]

Thomas also clashed with Col. Thomas J. Morgan, the commander of the Fourteenth Regiment of U.S. Colored Troops. Morgan resented Thomas's refusal to use black troops in combat and wrote Thomas twice to ask that his regiment be assigned to combat duty. Thomas refused both of Morgan's requests, stating Morgan's men were still needed for labor duty at Chattanooga, and adding, "[W]hen you shall have learned cheerfully to perform your duty to the best of your abilities in such a position as may be assigned you, then shall you have learned the final lessons of the discipline which apparently you are so anxious should be taught your regiment."[27]

Morgan apparently did not resent Thomas's criticism, as he later described Thomas as a "singularly fair-minded, candid man." Morgan continued to train his men for combat, hoping that they would someday get the chance to use their skills. During the 1863–64 winter encampment, Thomas reviewed Morgan's regiment at drill and remarked that he "never saw a regiment go through the manual [at arms] as well as this one." Thomas asked Morgan whether he thought his troops would fight, and Morgan answered that he knew they would. Thomas agreed that they might fight behind breastworks but doubted that they would have the courage to stand firm on the open field of battle.[28]

While Thomas's racial opinions were conservative by today's standards, by 1863 he was already demonstrating more flexibility on racial issues than most other Southern Unionists, and more tolerance than many Northern whites. A large number of Southern white Unionists bitterly opposed the Emancipation Proclamation and the recruitment of African American soldiers. Having joined the war effort to support the preservation of the Union with slavery intact, they now felt that the Lincoln administration had betrayed them. Many Southern white Unionists feared that putting arms in the hands of blacks would lead to a race war and other atrocities against white civilians. They also felt that allowing African Americans to become soldiers insulted the honor of white soldiers by placing blacks on the same social level.[29]

Thomas's role as the commander of African American troops and his post as the commander of the Department of the Cumberland brought him into occasional political controversy, which he disliked intensely. When rumors spread that he might be made commander of the Army of the Potomac, he immediately took steps to prevent the transfer, realizing that the commander in the East would be subjected to political controversy far beyond what he had experienced in Tennessee. In Virginia, George Meade had made little progress against Lee since his victory at Gettysburg and was coming under increasing criticism. James Garfield, who was now an influential congressman, had begun a campaign to replace Meade with Thomas and was supported by Edwin Stanton, the secretary of war, and Charles Sumner, an influential senator.[30] Garfield told Thomas that he was being considered for the command of the Army of the Potomac, and Thomas wrote Garfield on December 17, 1863, that he did not want the command:

> You have disturbed me greatly with the intimation that the command of the Army of the Potomac may be offered to me. It is a position to which I am not the least adapted, and putting my own reputation entirely aside I sincerely hope that I at least may not be victimized by being placed in a position where I would be utterly powerless to do good or contribute in the least toward the suppression of the Rebellion. The pressure always brought to

bear against the commander of the Army of the Potomac would destroy me in a week without having advanced the cause in the least. Much against my wishes I was placed in command of this army—I have told you my reasons—now, however, I believe my efforts will be appreciated by the troops and I have reasonable hopes that we may continue to do good service.[31]

Thomas truly believed he could not function in the political environment of the eastern theater, and he preferred to stay in the West, where the authorities in Washington paid less attention to military affairs. Thomas may have underestimated his abilities to interact with politicians, as he later performed well as a departmental commander in the difficult political environment of Reconstruction. In any case, Thomas was not offered the command. In March, Lincoln decided to bring Grant to the eastern theater to take overall command of the Union armies, and Grant, also wary of the political intrigues in Washington, decided to command in the field, becoming both general in chief and senior commander of the Army of the Potomac.

Meanwhile, Thomas returned to active field service in February 1864. Grant had sent Sherman to Vicksburg to lead a raid into Mississippi, and he ordered Thomas to make a reconnaissance in force against the Confederate army in northern Georgia, to prevent the Confederates from detaching troops from this force to send to Mississippi. Braxton Bragg had resigned after Chickamauga, and Jefferson Davis had replaced him with Joseph E. Johnston. Johnston was a skillful but unaggressive commander, who fought carefully on the defensive, establishing strong lines and rarely making counterattacks.

On February 24 Thomas attacked the main Confederate line, which lay along a steep line of hills called Rocky Face Ridge. After several days spent probing the Confederate defenses, Thomas's men found the line to be nearly impregnable and retreated before taking serious losses. Thomas told Grant that he had called off the attack for several reasons: he lacked supplies and transportation, too many of his men were absent on furloughs, and Johnston's position was too strong. Thomas was correct not to press the attack, but Grant was disappointed that Thomas had called the movement off completely, as he feared that Johnston would now be able to detach troops to oppose Sherman in Mississippi. The episode reinforced Grant's perception of Thomas as slow and unaggressive.[32]

Despite Thomas's retreat, Johnston did not send reinforcements to Mississippi, and Sherman's campaign succeeded.[33]

During the Rocky Face Ridge campaign, Thomas's men discovered that a pass to the south of the main Confederate line, called Dug Gap, was lightly defended. The Union force nearly captured the pass, but it was driven back by Confederate reinforcements. Thomas did not press the attack, as it was only meant to be a demonstration, but the episode gave Thomas an idea for the upcoming spring campaign.[34] Thomas's scouts had discovered a second pass farther south, called Snake Creek Gap, which was also lightly defended. Thomas proposed to send a large force, perhaps the entire Army of the Cumberland, through Snake Creek Gap, with the goal of cutting Johnston's railroad supply line at the town of Resaca. This would compel Johnston to retreat from Rocky Face Ridge and would enable the larger Union army to engage the Confederates in the open, where it would have the advantage. Thomas's plan was risky, as it involved dividing the Union army in half, but Thomas felt the risk was worthwhile, as the maneuver held the possibility of inflicting a crippling defeat on the Confederate army. Sherman later adopted Thomas's plan with one key change, deciding to make the move with his own former command, the Army of the Tennessee, instead of with Thomas's army.[35]

In March Lincoln called Grant to Washington, promoted him to the rank of lieutenant general, and placed him in command of all of the Union armies. Grant decided that he would not command from Washington, as Halleck had done, but would join the Army of the Potomac in the field, retaining Meade in command of that army while directing the movements of all the forces in the eastern theater. Grant promoted Sherman to take his place as overall commander in the West.[36] Some of Thomas's officers, and many of his biographers, have criticized Grant's decision to promote Sherman over Thomas to command the armies of the West. Thomas had seniority over Sherman, and his command record was more successful, so by these standards Thomas appeared a more appropriate choice. However, an important part of Grant's offensive plan was the coordination of movements in the East with movements in the West, and Grant needed to promote someone he trusted and with whom he worked well. From this standpoint, Sherman was the obvious choice. Grant worked well with Sherman and considered him a close friend, but he had a distant and conflict-ridden relationship with Thomas. Moreover, Grant had grown to think of Thomas as slow and unaggressive and preferred Sherman's energetic, aggressive, and improvisational style of leadership.

While Grant favored Sherman to command the western armies, he continued to consult with Thomas about his eastern campaign. Grant told Thomas about a plan he was considering to land an army of sixty thousand men either at Suffolk, Virginia, or at New Bern, North Carolina. The force would then move west to cut the railroads leading to Petersburg and Richmond. Grant favored the landing at Suffolk, which was just east of Southampton County, and he proposed a line of march that would probably take the army through Southampton. Knowing that Thomas was a native of that area, Grant asked for his views.[37]

Thomas advised against the Southampton County route because of the "great difficulties" inherent in crossing the county's swamps and rivers. He suggested that Grant advance through the area north of Southampton, where the ground was drier and the Union army would find "large plantations, well supplied with forage and cattle." An even better alternative, Thomas suggested, would be to march through North Carolina, along the southern bank of the Roanoke River, just south of the Virginia line. An army following this route would avoid Southampton's swamps and could use the Roanoke River to cover its movements.[38]

Southampton County local legend holds that Thomas made this recommendation to protect his home county from attack, but Thomas's motives seem to have been military, not personal. It was true that Southampton County was swampy and crossed by many rivers; in 1862 McClellan's army had crossed similar terrain during the Peninsular Campaign and had met with many difficulties as a result. The difficulty of the terrain probably explains why Grant eventually avoided a landing at Suffolk, and instead chose a landing site on the James River between Richmond and Petersburg.[39]

After consulting with Thomas, Sherman, and others about his plans, Grant formulated his strategy for the 1864 campaign. Grant wanted to launch simultaneous offensives in the East and West, maintaining constant pressure in both theaters so the Confederates could not shift troops from one sector to the other. The main offensive would take place in Virginia and would consist of three simultaneous advances: a main effort against Lee's army; a subordinate campaign in the Shenandoah Valley; and another subordinate advance up the James River toward Petersburg. In the West, Sherman was to maintain pressure on Johnston's army. If possible,

Sherman should defeat Johnston's army and capture Atlanta, but his main goal was simply to keep Johnston busy and prevent him from sending men to reinforce Lee.[40]

Sherman spent the next few months improving his army's supply, transportation, and logistics, as he knew that the success of his advance on Atlanta would depend on his ability to keep his army in supply. There was only a single railroad connecting Chattanooga and Atlanta, and only two railroads connecting Chattanooga with the main Union supply depot at Nashville. In March and April Sherman arranged for huge amounts of supplies to be stockpiled at Nashville and Chattanooga, supplies he would need during the upcoming campaign. He impressed a number of civilian locomotives and their rolling stock into service, raising the total number of engines under his control to more than one hundred. He placed severe restrictions on civilian use of the railroads, even restricting the travel of Sanitary Commission agents and members of religious societies. He had his engineers build fortified blockhouses along the railroads, particularly at vulnerable points such as trestles and bridges, and he posted infantry garrisons where they could best protect the railroads from cavalry raids. Finally, he increased the size of his engineer corps, so that when enemy cavalry did damage the railroads, they could be quickly repaired.[41]

Sherman relied heavily on the logistical and engineering departments of the Army of the Cumberland, the largest single force under his command. As commander of this army, Thomas naturally had an important role to play in assisting Sherman in his preparations for an advance. Thomas and Sherman were old, close friends, and Sherman trusted Thomas and respected his judgment. As he had previously done for Rosecrans, Thomas became a senior adviser to Sherman, and Sherman came to depend on his advice. According to William Shanks, Sherman commented on how much he missed Thomas when he commanded without him during his March to the Sea. At one point, when he had difficulty making up his mind about his next move, Sherman turned to an aide and exclaimed, "I wish old Tom was here! He's my off-wheel horse, and knows how to pull with me, though he don't pull in the same way."

It is doubtful that Thomas was as happy as Sherman with his role as Sherman's "off-wheel horse." While he preferred working under Sherman than working under Grant, he would have doubtless preferred overall command in the West. During the campaign to come, Thomas frequently disagreed with Sherman over tactics and strategy, and he felt frustrated when Sherman ignored his advice. The resulting tension, combined with Sherman's tendency to blame Thomas for the campaign's setbacks, proved to be very detrimental to their friendship.[42]

The period between the Battle of Chattanooga and the Atlanta campaign was an important one for Thomas, despite the fact that the Army of the Cumberland was engaged in little fighting. His position as commander of the Department of the Cumberland placed him squarely in the middle of a number of political disputes, including many having to do with the Union policy toward escaped slaves and African American soldiers. While Thomas was still conservative on racial issues at this point in his life, the events of the war had led him to accept emancipation and the recruitment of African American soldiers as necessary, his value of obedience to law had led him to accept the guidance of the political authorities on this issue, and his sense of fairness had led him to protect African Americans from abuse. Thomas was beginning to make the transformation from slave owner to civil rights defender, but the most significant change in his attitudes on race and politics lay well in the future. With the coming of spring, the Atlanta campaign occupied all of his attention, and he did not return to the issue of African American troops until the end of the year.

CHAPTER THIRTEEN

The Atlanta Campaign

One or two more such assaults would use up this army.

As 1864 began, Thomas prepared the Army of the Cumberland for action in the spring and summer campaign against the Confederate Army of Tennessee, guarding the approaches to Atlanta. Grant had designated Sherman's campaign as a secondary effort, and Sherman's primary goal was to keep the Confederate army under constant threat, so that the Rebel commander, Joseph E. Johnston, could not detach reinforcements to Lee's army in Virginia. While Sherman kept Johnston occupied, Grant would launch a three-pronged attack in Virginia, designed to defeat Lee's Army of Northern Virginia and capture the Confederate capital.

Thomas and Sherman worked together effectively during the campaign, but they frequently disagreed over tactics and strategy. While Sherman preferred a campaign of limited engagements and maneuver, Thomas sought to deliver a knockout blow that would take the Army of Tennessee out of action. On two occasions, at the beginning and the end of the campaign, Thomas suggested tactics that might have achieved this goal, but Sherman declined Thomas's suggestions. Sherman did not want to engage his force in an all-out battle, in part because he did not want to take the risk of losing so badly that Johnston could safely reinforce Lee, and in part because Sherman was a more cautious general than Thomas and preferred a strategy of maneuver and limited fighting. As a result, Sherman missed two important opportunities to defeat Johnston. Sherman captured Atlanta but left the Confederate army intact.

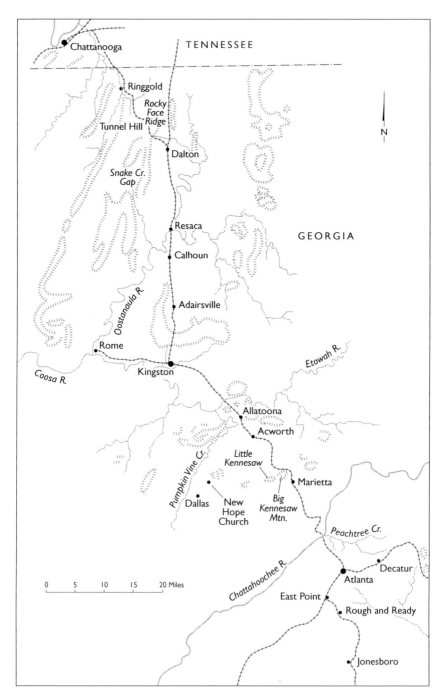

TENNESSEE

Chattanooga

Ringgold

Rocky Face Ridge

Tunnel Hill

Dalton

Snake Cr. Gap

GEORGIA

Resaca

Calhoun

Oostanaula R.

Adairsville

Rome

Etowah R.

Kingston

Coosa R.

Allatoona

Acworth

Little Kennesaw

Pumpkin Vine Cr.

Marietta

Dallas

New Hope Church

Big Kennesaw Mtn.

Peachtree Cr.

Decatur

Chattahoochee R.

Atlanta

East Point

Rough and Ready

Jonesboro

N

0   5   10   15   20 Miles

Atlanta Campaign

240

Sherman had an army of nearly 100,000 men assembled for the spring campaign, as compared to Johnston's force of about 65,000. The Union force consisted of three armies of unequal sizes. The largest army, Thomas's Army of the Cumberland, consisted of approximately 61,000 men, divided into three infantry corps and one cavalry corps, and 130 guns. Thomas's corps commanders were Maj. Gen. Otis O. Howard, commanding the Fourth Corps; Maj. Gen. John M. Palmer, commanding Thomas's old Fourteenth Corps; Maj. Gen. Joseph Hooker, commanding the Twentieth Corps; and Brig. Gen. Washington L. Elliot, commanding the cavalry. The second-largest force was the Army of the Tennessee, Sherman's former army, which was now commanded by a protégé of Sherman and Grant, Maj. Gen. James McPherson. The Army of the Tennessee was less than half the size of the Army of the Cumberland, having only 24,000 men in the field, divided into two corps, and ninety-six artillery. The third "army," the Army of the Ohio under Maj. Gen. John Schofield, was actually a single infantry corps of 13,000 men and was accompanied by twenty-three cannons.[1]

In March and April Sherman consulted with Thomas and his other generals about his plans for the spring offensive. Sherman liked Thomas's suggestion to advance through Snake Creek Gap to Resaca, but he decided to make the movement with the Army of the Tennessee instead of the Army of the Cumberland. Sherman thought Thomas's army would be too large to move quickly, whereas McPherson's army would be small enough to move quickly and achieve surprise, but large enough to capture and hold Resaca. Sherman ordered Thomas to engage the Confederate main position, while Schofield's Army of the Ohio would move as if it were trying to maneuver around Johnston's northern flank. While these two forces distracted Johnston, the Army of the Tennessee would advance through Snake Creek Gap and cut the Confederate line of communications and supply at Resaca.[2]

Grant wanted his offensive and Sherman's to begin simultaneously, and the two armies began moving in early May. The move through Snake Creek Gap caught Johnston completely off guard, and McPherson could have easily overwhelmed the small garrison at Resaca. However, McPherson hesitated when he reached the town, worried that Johnston had anticipated his movement and had moved a large force to oppose him. By the time McPherson brought reinforcements up, Johnston had retreated from Rocky Face Ridge and dug in along a new line at Resaca.[3]

Since surprise had been lost, there seemed no point of fighting a battle at Resaca, and Thomas advised a second flanking move. Sherman rejected this proposal, and on May 14 he ordered a general assault on the Confederate lines instead. By this time the Confederates were strongly entrenched, and the Union troops were repulsed with heavy casualties. Encouraged by this success, Johnston launched a counterattack against the northern end of the Union line, which was held by Howard's Fourth Corps. Howard asked Thomas for assistance, and Thomas rushed another division to Howard's support, which arrived just in time to drive back the Confederate assault.[4]

On May 15 Sherman tried again, ordering Thomas to attack from his position on the railroad line north of Resaca. Thomas sent Howard's Fourth Corps and Hooker's Twentieth Corps to make the attack. Their men became disoriented in the heavy woods north of the town and then ran into heavily fortified Confederate positions. The two corps attacked the Confederate positions but were driven back with heavy casualties, and the Confederates counterattacked but were driven back in turn. While the battle raged around Resaca, a small force of Union troops managed to cross the Oostanula River on Johnston's flank. Thinking that Sherman had sent a large force to outflank him, Johnston withdrew across the river during the night and set up a new line near the town of Calhoun.[5]

While this initial phase of the campaign was not as successful as Sherman had hoped, the results were certainly not bad. In ten days Sherman had driven Johnston's troops out of their strong fortifications near Dalton, Georgia, and had gotten about twenty miles closer to Atlanta. His army had suffered about 3,000 casualties, only slightly more than those suffered by the Confederates. During the same period, Grant's army had suffered approximately 35,000 casualties to Lee's 20,000 in the Battles of the Wilderness and Spotsylvania and had advanced a similar distance toward Richmond. In comparison to Grant's progress in the East, Sherman's campaign was a success.[6]

In his *Memoirs*, Sherman blamed the failure of the Resaca campaign on McPherson's excessive caution, but Sherman also bears some of the blame. Even if McPherson had not lost his nerve before Resaca, the Army of the Tennessee may not have been large enough to block Johnston's retreat. The Army of the Cumberland was the only force large enough to do the job properly, and Sherman should have adopted Thomas's original suggestion and sent the Army of the Cumberland through Snake Creek Gap.[7]

After letting his army rest for several days following the Battle of Resaca, Sherman went back on the offensive. He first maneuvered the Confederates out of the line they had established near the town of Calhoun, pushing them back to Cassville. This left the town of Rome, Georgia, undefended, the site of an important iron works and cannon foundry, and one of Thomas's divisions captured the town and destroyed its factories. Sherman then flanked Johnston out of his Cassville position, and Johnston withdrew across the Etowah River, establishing a new line near the town of Allatoona.[8]

On May 20–22 Sherman paused before Allatoona to repair the railroad, bring supplies forward, and let his men rest. He then set out on another move around Johnston's western flank, striking for the town of Dallas, in Johnston's rear. Sherman moved nearly his entire force around Johnston's line, with McPherson's Army of the Tennessee traveling the farthest west and south, Thomas's Army of the Cumberland in the middle, and Schofield's Army of the Ohio staying to the northeast, close to the railroad. Sherman wanted to repeat the Snake Creek Gap strategy, either forcing a battle under favorable conditions or driving Johnston far back toward Atlanta. Johnston anticipated the move, however, and shifted his forces to block Sherman's path.[9]

With Johnston parrying his flanking movements, Sherman was unable to gain much territory. Sherman attacked Johnston's army near New Hope Church on May 25, and again at Pickett's Mill on May 27, but both attacks failed with heavy losses. Frustrated with these setbacks, and lacking the supplies to continue, Sherman decided to cut his flanking movement short and work his way back to the railroad. The proximity of the Confederate army and the wooded, hilly terrain made this move difficult, and it took Sherman over a week to get back to his supply line. On June 3 Sherman's advance troops occupied the town of Acworth, just five miles south of the former Confederate line at Allatoona. It had taken Sherman two weeks to advance less than ten miles, and he lost three thousand men during the campaign, as compared to a Confederate loss of only one thousand.[10]

Throughout these maneuvers, Thomas worked actively to reconnoiter the terrain and coordinate the operations of his army, often riding far ahead of his men. One of his staff aides, Henry Stone, recalled that Thomas "invariably made his way along to the head of the column. If, when he was at the rear, the sounds indicated contact with the enemy, he pushed on to the very front, where he often dismounted and walked to the outer skirmish line, to reconnoiter." Thomas remained considerate of his men, however. "Nobody ever saw him, with an escort trailing behind him, dashing past a moving column of troops, throwing up dust or mud, and compelling them to leave the road to him. If anybody had the right of way it was they, not he. He would break through the woods, or flounder across a swamp, rather than force his men from the road, and so wear them out by needless fatigue."[11] At one point in the campaign, the men of one exhausted company fell asleep in the road. As an enlisted man later recalled, he was abruptly awoken by his fellows, who were shouting, "Move out of the road. General Thomas is coming." When Thomas saw them getting up, however, he moved off of the road, stating, "Let them rest. I can find my way to the top of the hill."[12]

On one occasion, Thomas and his staff went too far forward and came under fire from enemy pickets while they were dismounted and far from their horses. His staff officers ran to their horses and galloped off, but Thomas walked slowly and deliberately to his mount, despite the target he presented to enemy sharpshooters. Van Horne, who reported this incident, took it as evidence of Thomas's courage, but it is also possible that Thomas's back injury left him unable to run. On another occasion, Thomas and Gen. Jefferson C. Davis discovered a field of blackberries during a reconnaissance and dismounted to eat some of the fruit. A Confederate cavalry patrol discovered them and began to fire on them, but by this point in the war Thomas was so used to being shot at that he stayed where he was. He continued to pick blackberries, even as the bullets flew around them, only acknowledging the bullets with the statement, "Davis, this is eating blackberries under difficulties."[13]

As Sherman's men moved back to the rail line at Acworth, Johnston dug in at another strong position along a mountain ridge north of Marietta. After spending a week drawing supplies and repairing the railroad, Sherman pushed forward. Sherman hoped to maneuver Johnston across the Chattahoochee River, but the Confederates fell back only a few miles, to a much stronger position along the ridge of Kennesaw Mountain. Sherman then tried another flanking move, but this one was even less successful than the one before it. Heavy rains had turned the roads into mud, and Johnston, who could observe the Union movements from his vantage point on Kennesaw Mountain, easily shifted his forces to block Sherman's movements.

Sherman first tried sending Hooker's corps and Schofield's Army of the Ohio in a movement around Johnston's western flank, and Johnston responded by sending the corps of Gen. John Bell Hood to block them. When Hooker came into contact with Hood on June 22, near a place called Kolb's Farm, he overreacted, reporting to Thomas and Sherman that he had three Confederate corps in his front. Thomas reassured him that this was impossible, as Johnston's entire army only had three corps, and he told Hooker to dig in and hold fast. Hood did attack Hooker's line, but the result was a slaughter, as the Confederates suffered nearly 1,500 casualties and Hooker lost only about 250 men. The victory failed to affect the strategic picture, however, as Hood simply withdrew down the road to Marietta and set up a new defensive line.[14]

By this point, Sherman felt extremely frustrated. Johnston was getting better and better at parrying Sherman's attempts to outflank him, and the Union army seemed unable to carry out a successful maneuver or attack. Sherman mistakenly blamed this on a "lack of offensive spirit" among his officers and men, but the truth was that the Union army's problems were unavoidable. The mountains and forests of northern Georgia made quick maneuvering difficult, and the tactics and weapons of the time favored the defender. Nevertheless, Sherman blamed his officers and men for the slow progress. In a private letter to Grant, he placed particular blame on Thomas:

My chief trouble is with the Army of the Cumberland, which is awful slow. A fresh furrow in a ploughed field will stop the whole column, and all begin to intrench. I have again and again tried to impress on Thomas that we must assail and not defend; we are on the offensive, and yet it seems the whole Army of the Cumberland is so habituated to be on the defensive that, from its commander down to its lowest private, I cannot get it out of their heads. I came out without tents and ordered all to do likewise, yet Thomas has a headquarters camp in the style of Halleck at Corinth; every aide and orderly with a wall-tent, and a baggage train big enough for a division. He promised to send it all back, but the truth is everybody there is allowed to do as he pleases, and they still think and act as though the railroad and all its facilities were theirs.[15]

This was the most severe criticism of Thomas that Sherman ever wrote, and the least justified. All three of the armies under Sherman's command moved slowly, and all three were reluctant to attack enemy fortifications, because of their correct perception that such tactics were not likely to succeed. To single out Thomas and the Army of the Cumberland was unfair. His charge that Thomas had brought too much baggage with him was also unfair, but at least this charge had some justification. Thomas had ignored Sherman's order at the beginning of the campaign not to carry tents or other significant headquarters baggage, and the complex of tents around Thomas's headquarters was so extensive that Sherman called it "Thomas' circus." But Thomas had disobeyed Sherman's order for a good reason. Headquarters tents were necessary to accommodate the mapmaking, planning, administrative, and logistical functions of directing the army, and Thomas felt that the tents were too useful to leave behind. Besides the headquarters tents, however, Thomas's army had only a minimum amount of equipment, and there was little difference between the size of the baggage train of the Army of the Cumberland and the baggage trains of Sherman's other two armies.[16]

There was a second reason for Thomas's reliance on headquarters tents. With his back injury, Thomas needed a good tent to sleep in if he were to be able to command at all. However, other than making sure he slept in a camp bed, Thomas did not grant himself extra comforts on the campaign. One of his soldiers recalled seeing Thomas on the march, looking like "some good old farmer" in a battered army hat, and eating hard bread for dinner, just like his men.[17]

After seeing his advance blocked at Kolb's Farm, Sherman considered extending his line farther to the left, but he decided against the move, concluding that the Confederates would just observe what he was doing and extend their lines as well. Thomas recommended that Sherman try to outflank Johnston to the east, varying the pattern of western moves that Sherman had used since the beginning of the campaign. Sherman rejected this strategy as too risky, as it might give Johnston the chance to cut the Union army off from its supply line.[18]

Having rejected plans to advance on either flank, Sherman had only two other options: to take the Kennesaw Mountain line by slow, siegelike advances, or to break the line through a frontal assault. Rejecting the siege strategy as too slow, Sherman decided to risk a direct attack. His army was larger than the Confederate army, and Johnston had extended his lines widely to block Sherman's flanking maneuvers and threats. Perhaps the Confederates were stretched too thin, making it possible for a direct assault to pierce the center of their line. Thomas opposed this tactic, as frontal assaults rarely succeeded against entrenched opponents, but Sherman, perhaps recalling the success of the assault on Missionary Ridge, decided to risk it.[19]

Sherman ordered an attack on the Confederate line at its left center, on the ridge of Kennesaw Mountain just south of its peak. Sherman selected the Army of the Tennessee and the Army of the Cumberland to make the attack and left it to McPherson and Thomas to determine the details. Although Thomas had opposed the attack, he now tried his best to make it succeed, choosing a division from Howard's Fourth Corps and a division from Palmer's Fourteenth Corps to lead the assault. He let Howard plan the Fourth Corps' attack and directed the movements of the Fourteenth Corps personally. Thomas reconnoitered the Confederate lines, looking for a weak point, but he found none.

With no good choices available, Thomas decided to attack at a place a few miles south of Kennesaw Mountain, where part of the Confederate line bulged outward to accommodate a hill. Thomas's men would have to march uphill, across rocky and brush-covered ground, to get to the Confederate line, but at least the Confederates had not yet erected log abatis on top of the hill. If the attackers could actually reach the Confederate position, they might be able to take it. This was not an especially good chance, but it was the best that Thomas could hope for, as the Confederate line was equally strong or stronger everywhere else. Thomas ordered the divisional commander, Jefferson C. Davis, to assault the hill by sending two of his brigades forward in densely packed columns. This formation was commonly used when attacking fortified positions, with the idea that the troops in the front of the column would weaken the defense, and then the troops in the rear would reinforce them and overwhelm the defenders. McPherson and Howard used similar tactics in their assaults.[20]

The attack began at around 8:00 A.M. on June 27. After overwhelming the outer line of Confederate rifle pits and pickets, the Union troops came up against a severe fire from the main Confederate line. While the

Confederates had not yet constructed log abatis, they were still extensively entrenched, and in many places the Union soldiers could not even see the enemy. The steep ground, the underbrush, and the entanglements erected by the defenders slowed the advance of the Union soldiers, who had to pick their way toward the Confederate line while exposed to a killing fire from above. When the Union troops approached the Confederate line, they hesitated to climb over the log barricades and engage the Confederates in hand-to-hand combat. In most places, the attackers simply halted and traded shots for a few minutes before retreating. In a few places the attackers did climb over the enemy works, only to be killed or captured when they reached the other side. Two Union brigade commanders, Charles Harker and Daniel McCook, were mortally wounded in the battle.

At ten o'clock Thomas got a message from one of Howard's regimental commanders, Col. Emerson Opdycke, stating that the Confederate line in his front had weakened, and might break if the attack were reinforced. Thomas ordered the brigade of Brig. Gen. Nathan Kimball forward. As it turned out, Opdycke's assessment was overly optimistic, and the commitment of Kimball's brigade did nothing but increase the number of Union casualties. Thomas called off the attack at about 10:45 A.M., and McPherson called off his assault at around the same time. In less than three hours, the Union army had lost nearly three thousand men killed or wounded, while inflicting only seven hundred casualties on the Confederates.[21]

Not wanting to concede defeat, Sherman asked Thomas whether there was any point at which the Confederate line could be successfully broken. Thomas replied, "The division commanders report the enemy's works exceedingly strong; in fact, so strong that they cannot be carried by assault except by immense sacrifice, even if they can be carried at all. I think, therefore, the best chance is to approach them by regular saps, and if we can find a favorable position to batter them down. We have already lost heavily today without gaining any material advantage; one or two more such assaults would use up this army."[22]

Sherman had to agree that a direct assault was impossible, and he decided to try another flanking move, despite the risk that this would take him too far from his supply base. He telegraphed Thomas with questions about the terrain on Johnston's western flank, and Thomas responded with information and questions of his own. Thomas endorsed the new plan, adding with some exaggeration that it seemed "decidedly better than butting against breastworks twelve feet thick and strongly abatised." Sherman sniped back that wherever the army went, "we will find the breastworks and the abatis, unless we move more rapidly than we have heretofore."[23]

Sherman began moving again on July 1. He forced Johnston to retreat to a point just north of the Chattahoochee River and then forced him across the river, and into the fortifications of Atlanta. After two months of fighting, Sherman had driven the Confederates back to the outskirts of Atlanta, nearly one hundred miles from his starting point. His army had suffered 12,000 casualties and had inflicted about 9,000 casualties on the Confederate force. Grant's army had suffered 65,000 casualties during the same period, while inflicting about 35,000 on the enemy, in the course of driving Lee's army back to Richmond. Sherman had made some serious mistakes during the last two months, but his campaign had been a success overall.[24]

As Sherman approached Atlanta, he received news from Halleck that the goal of his campaign had changed. On the one hand, Lee's supply situation at Richmond was so poor that he could barely feed the troops he had, so Sherman no longer had to worry about preventing Johnston from sending Lee reinforcements. On the other hand, it was clear that there was going to be a long siege at Richmond before Grant would be able to capture the capital. If the Union were to gain a victory before the fall presidential election, it would have to be Sherman who won it. The outcome of the election might depend on the Atlanta campaign.[25]

As the fortifications around Atlanta were too strong to assault, the only way to capture the city would be to cut the three rail lines that brought in supplies: the Georgia Railroad to the east of the city, the Atlanta and West Point Railroad to the west, and the Macon and Western Railroad to the south. Sherman sent a small part of his force to cut the Atlanta and West Point Railroad and moved the main part of his army around the eastern edge of Atlanta, trying to cut the Georgia Railroad while maintaining contact with his own supply line.

While Sherman put this plan into action, the president of the Confederacy was making plans of his own. Disgusted with Johnston's constant retreats, Jefferson Davis decided to replace him with a more aggressive commander, and after much consideration, he chose John Bell Hood. Davis selected Hood because of his reputation as a fighter, a reputation that he certainly deserved; his abilities as a strategist and tactician were less certain. Hood had studied under Thomas at West Point, graduating in 1853 with a rank of forty-fifth out of a class of fifty-five students. He served under Thomas in Texas, where he first gained his reputation as a fighter by attacking a force of Comanche Indians that greatly outnumbered his own, defeating the Indians but at a heavy cost to his own men. During the Civil War, Hood had served under Lee in Virginia, gaining fame for his bold assaults at Gaines's Mill, Second Manassas, and Gettysburg. He fought under Longstreet at Chickamauga and moved west permanently in March 1864 to serve as a corps commander under Johnston. He had been wounded at Gettysburg, which cost him the use of his left arm, and again at Chickamauga, which had caused his right leg to be amputated at the thigh. He still suffered from these wounds, and the pain, along with the morphine-based medicines he took to combat it, sometimes affected his ability to command.

Hood took charge of the Confederate army on July 18. He planned to fight an active defense, using his interior lines to transfer troops quickly from sector to sector, with the goal of attacking an isolated segment of Sherman's army and defeating it before the rest of the army could come to its support. Hood's hero, Robert E. Lee, had used a similar strategy against McClellan in his 1862 defense of Richmond, and Hood hoped to achieve equally successful results. Hood's first attack came on July 20, just two days after he assumed command. The Union army was moving around the eastern edge of Atlanta toward the Georgia Railroad, and its components were separated from one another and disorganized as they undertook the march. Hood decided to attack Thomas's Army of the Cumberland while it crossed Peachtree Creek, with the goal of catching Thomas's lead units in the open and alone, separated by the creek from the rest of the army. He planned to drive Thomas's soldiers westward into the angle formed by Peachtree Creek and the Chattahoochee River, where they would have no line of retreat, and force them to surrender.[26]

Hood wanted the attack to begin at 1:00 P.M. on July 20, but at the last minute he had to send part of his attack force east to block Schofield and McPherson, who were marching toward Atlanta almost unopposed. As Hood's men moved closer to the Union army, Thomas's scouts detected their presence, and Thomas ordered Brig. Gen. John Newton's division to move forward and ascertain the enemy's location and strength. Thomas ordered Hooker's Twentieth Corps and John Palmer's Fourteenth Corps

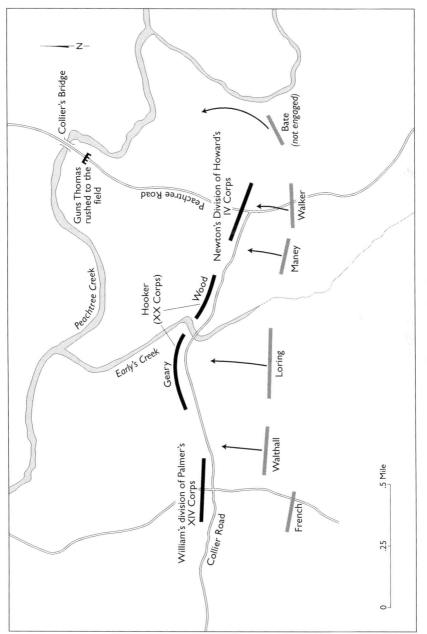

Collier's Bridge

Guns Thomas
rushed to the
field

Peachtree Creek

Early's Creek

Peachtree Road

Hooker
(XX Corps)

Wood

Newton's Division of Howard's
IV Corps

Geary

Bate
(not engaged)

Walker

Maney

Loring

Walthall

William's division of Palmer's
XIV Corps

Collier Road

French

0   .25   .5 Mile

Peachtree Creek

to move forward and make contact with the enemy, but both commanders balked. Suspecting a Confederate trap, neither commander wanted to be the first to advance, and the two corps stood still as their commanders argued over who should move first. Thomas stayed with Newton's division and sent his chief of staff, William Whipple, to get Palmer and Hooker to cooperate. Sherman had told Thomas to move quickly, and Thomas did not want to delay before a Confederate threat that might turn out to be imaginary.[27]

As Newton moved forward, he discovered that there actually was a large Confederate force in his front, so he ordered his men to stop and entrench. Hooker and Palmer continued to argue, and both failed to dig in as carefully as Newton did. The Union line ran westward along a ridge just south of Peachtree Creek and was divided into two parts by Early Creek, a tributary of Peachtree Creek. Newton's Fourth Corps held the easternmost part of the line, followed by Hooker's Twentieth Corps, on the other side of Early Creek, and then Palmer's Fourth Corps, farther west.

Hood's attack began at 4:00. He ordered the assault to take place in echelon, meaning that his easternmost units would attack first, then the next in line to the west, and so on down the line. If the tactic succeeded, Hood's men would turn Thomas's easternmost brigade, then the next brigade, and the next, eventually rolling up the entire Union line. Hood's last-minute realignment to meet the threat caused by Schofield's and McPherson's advance had not cost him anything, as Hooker and Palmer had not used the time to strengthen their defense. In fact, the realignment helped Hood's army, as his line now extended past Thomas's to the east, giving him the chance to attack Newton's division from the front, flank, and rear.

The easternmost of Hood's divisions got lost in some heavy thickets and did not engage the enemy, but the next division in the line, commanded by William Walker, connected with Newton's division and came close to defeating it. While some of Walker's men attacked Newton's division in front and in flank, others moved around Newton's position and headed for the bridge over Peachtree Creek, in Newton's rear. If Walker's men captured this bridge, they would block Newton's line of retreat and prevent reinforcements from reaching him. Newton had guarded against this possibility by posting artillery where it could cover the bridge, and Thomas quickly brought up more artillery to join them. Thomas led the guns forward himself, using the flat of his sword to spur the artillery horses to a faster pace, and then personally directed their fire. The artillery drove the infantry back, and the bridge was saved. Thomas then turned his guns on the rest of Walker's division, and these artillery and Newton's infantry drove off the Confederate attackers.[28]

Once Walker's attack failed, the rest of Hood's plan had little chance of succeeding. The next division in the Confederate line, that of George Maney, failed to make a dent in the fortified Union position and soon retreated. William Loring's division, the next in line, attacked near Early's Creek and broke through one segment of the Union line, but it was stopped temporarily by a Union counterattack. Hooker then personally rallied the men of two brigades and sent them back against the enemy, plugging the breach in the Union lines. An attack on Palmer's corps also succeeded at first but was then repulsed. As the fighting died down along the front, the Union soldiers entrenched in preparation for a second Confederate assault, and Thomas rushed infantry and artillery forward. Hood did not attempt another assault, however. The day's fighting resulted in about 1,900 Union and 2,500 Confederate casualties and only temporarily halted Thomas's advance.[29]

Two days later, on July 22, Hood attacked the Army of the Tennessee, in a battle that caused 5,500 Confederate and 3,700 Union casualties but did little to slow Sherman's progress. The army's commander, John McPherson, was killed in the fighting, and Sherman chose Maj. Gen. Oliver Otis Howard to replace him. In promoting Howard, Sherman passed over Joseph Hooker, who had seniority, and Hooker turned in his resignation in protest. After consulting with Thomas, Sherman accepted it.[30]

By this time, Sherman had succeeded in cutting the Georgia Railroad, which ran into Atlanta from the east. Two more railroads remained to be cut: the Atlanta and West Point Railroad to the west, and the Macon and Western Railroad to the south. Sherman spent the next two months trying to disable these railroads, through a combination of small-scale infantry movements and cavalry raids, but he never completely committed his army. His motive, again, was caution. To move with his whole force against Hood's supply lines, Sherman would have to separate from his own supply line, a move that involved some risk. Sherman also tried a heavy artillery barrage of Atlanta, which caused damage to the city and inflicted some civilian casualties but had little effect on Hood's army.[31]

By late August Sherman had accepted that he had to take a risk if he ever hoped to force Hood out of Atlanta. On the night of August 25–26

Sherman pulled all of his troops out of their fortifications, posted one corps on the Chattahoochee River to guard his own supply line, and marched the rest of his army west and south around Atlanta. Hood at first concluded that a recent Confederate cavalry raid had damaged Sherman's supply line so badly that Sherman had to retreat, and he failed to react to the Union movement. On August 28 Sherman's army reached the Atlanta and West Point Railroad, and Sherman had his men spend the entire day of August 29 destroying it. This was an unnecessary delay, as the Confederates no longer used this railroad extensively for supply, and it could have given Hood more time to react. Hood failed to move, however, and Sherman continued his advance on August 30. Howard's Army of the Tennessee reached the Macon and Western Railroad at Jonesboro that afternoon, but Howard hesitated, fearful that the Confederate force defending Jonesboro was too large for him to attack. The garrison there was actually quite small, and Howard probably could have taken the town that day. His caution gave Hood another chance to save Atlanta.[32]

By this time, Hood had finally realized the danger he was in, and he rushed the corps of Stephen D. Lee and William Hardee to Jonesboro, with orders to drive the Union army away from the railroad. It took Lee and Hardee until the afternoon of August 31 to get into position, and Howard, anticipating their attack, had his men dig in. Lee and Hardee lost about two thousand men in the battle, and inflicted only about two hundred casualties on Howard's troops. Meanwhile, Schofield's Army of the Ohio reached the railroad north of Jonesboro and cut the last supply line to the city. The Fourth and Fourteenth Corps of the Army of the Cumberland soon joined Schofield's army, placing a force on the railroad too large to drive away. Hood would now have to abandon Atlanta.

At this point, Sherman had another opportunity to cripple Hood's army, the best since his missed opportunity at Snake Creek Gap. Two of Hood's corps were at Jonesboro, the third was in Atlanta, and three Union corps occupied the railroad between them. Thomas urged Sherman to close the trap by moving the Fourth and Fourteenth Corps forward to surround Lee and Hardee, but Sherman directed Thomas to leave these corps where they were and continue to destroy railroad track. Sherman finally did attack Lee and Hardee in the late afternoon of September 1, but the delay, along with another overly cautious performance by Howard, gave the Confederates time to escape. Hood withdrew from Atlanta on the night of September 2–3 and united his army about five miles south of Jonesboro.

On September 3 the mayor of Atlanta surrendered the city to Sherman. Sherman began a pursuit of Hood's army but halted when he saw that the Confederates had taken up strong defensive positions along a ridge. For the time being, the capture of Atlanta was enough.[33]

In the North, the public was overjoyed with Sherman's accomplishment. Atlanta was seen as secondary only to Richmond in importance, and its capture was considered a major blow to the Confederate war effort. This success in the western theater made up for the failure of Union operations in the East, and it reflected well on the Lincoln administration's handling of the war. Some historians have asserted that the capture of Atlanta made the difference between victory and defeat for Lincoln in the 1864 election, perhaps even the difference between victory and defeat for the entire Union cause.[34]

While Sherman's campaign was a success, in that he prevented Johnston from reinforcing Lee and captured Atlanta, Sherman failed to cripple or destroy the Confederate army. The implications of his failure became evident soon after the capture of Atlanta, as Sherman was pinned down by having to protect Atlanta and his supply lines, while Hood was free to operate as he wished. Sherman later solved this problem by cutting loose from his supply lines and raiding through Georgia, but it is possible that he could have avoided the problem entirely if he had defeated the Confederate army in a major battle. At Resaca and at Jonesboro, Thomas gave Sherman advice that could have led to a major victory, and Sherman ignored it. While historians of the campaign differ on their assessment of whether Thomas's tactics would have succeeded, at least Thomas would have attempted the defeat of the Confederate army.[35] Sherman's failure to do so left a sizable Confederate army free to operate in the Union rear, and this army remained in operation until the end of 1864.

CHAPTER FOURTEEN

Nashville

Dang it to hell, Wilson, didn't I tell you we could lick 'em? Didn't I tell you we could lick 'em?

By capturing Atlanta but leaving intact the Confederate Army of Tennessee, Sherman placed his army in a difficult situation. The Union army now had to defend both Atlanta and its supply line, while Hood, relieved of the need to protect the city, was free to move wherever he wanted. Furthermore, there was no obvious next objective for Sherman to pursue. The nearest target of importance was Macon, Georgia, the site of a number of factories and depots, but it would be difficult for Sherman to attack Macon while maintaining his hold on Atlanta.[1]

Sherman proposed a bold solution to this problem: destroy all buildings of military value in Atlanta, abandon the city, and go on an extended raid through Georgia, cutting the army loose from its supply lines and living off the country during the campaign. The autumn harvest season was approaching, making it the ideal time of year for an army to live off the country. During his march, Sherman would attack Southern cities and military targets and destroy the Confederate army's food supplies at their source. At the same time, the raid would damage Southern morale by showing that a Union army could roam at will through the Confederate heartland, destroying property as it went. Sherman wanted to "make Georgia howl," destroying the Confederate army's supplies and the Southern people's will to fight.[2]

At first Sherman's superiors opposed his plan as too risky, particularly with the presidential election coming up in November. Grant proposed a cavalry raid instead of a raid by the entire army, an idea that Thomas supported. Halleck proposed that Sherman make an infantry raid through Georgia and Alabama to Mobile. This was a shorter distance than the path to the Atlantic, and Sherman would be able to draw supplies at the end of this path from Union boats on the Alabama River. Grant and Halleck also wanted Sherman to defeat Hood's army before beginning his raid, so as not to leave Hood active as a threat in his rear.[3]

While the Union leadership discussed strategy, Hood took advantage of his new freedom of movement. He marched his army north to threaten Sherman's supply line, attacking the Union railroad garrisons at Acworth, Allatoona, Dalton, and Resaca. When Sherman pursued him, Hood moved away to the west, and Sherman was unable to catch him. After returning to Atlanta, Sherman wired Grant and Halleck, pointing out that Hood could repeat this maneuver indefinitely. This argument convinced Grant, and Grant convinced Halleck, Stanton, and Lincoln to approve Sherman's plan.[4]

Sherman abandoned Atlanta on November 12, four days after Lincoln's victory in the presidential election, and moved southward. There were two ways that Hood could respond: he could follow Sherman through Georgia, contesting his advance, or he could turn away from Sherman's army and invade Tennessee. The evidence suggested that Hood might do the latter. The president of the Confederacy had recently made a speech announcing that the Confederacy would invade Tennessee, and Hood had moved his army to Tuscumbia, Alabama, one hundred miles west of Atlanta, and had established a bridgehead on the north side of the Tennessee River.[5]

Despite these indications that Hood planned to go north, both Thomas and Sherman believed that Hood would follow Sherman's army once his march began. The rainy, cold weather and the problem of transporting supplies would make an advance into Tennessee difficult, and it seemed unlikely that the Confederate government would allow Sherman's invasion of the Confederate heartland to proceed unopposed. Sherman sent Thomas to Nashville with instructions to prepare for both contingencies. If Hood turned north, Thomas was to concentrate his forces and defend against Hood's advance. If Hood went south, Thomas was to follow him.[6]

Thomas's forces in Tennessee included the 14,000 men of David Stanley's Fourth Corps, the 10,000 men of John Schofield's Twenty-third Corps, and 15,000 cavalry, divided among a number of different commands. Thomas had also been assigned Andrew J. Smith's Sixteenth Corps, part of the Army of the Tennessee, but Smith's men were in Missouri, where they had just assisted in driving back a Confederate invasion of the state. Smith's corps left Missouri for Nashville at about the same time Sherman left Atlanta. There were 5,000 men posted at Nashville, and another 15,000 men in different garrisons and posts around the state, making about 50,000 infantry and 15,000 cavalry in all of Thomas's command. Since many of these men were dispersed in various garrisons, only about 25,000 infantry and 5,000 cavalry were available for active operations against Hood.[7]

Some historians have criticized Sherman for taking the army's best troops with him into Georgia, leaving Thomas with a second-rate, disorganized force for the defense of Tennessee. With hindsight, knowing how little resistance Sherman was to face, it seems strange that Sherman took so many of his best troops with him. At the time, however, Sherman did not know what Hood would do, and Sherman was taking a significant risk in moving away from his supply base and communications. If Thomas met with difficulty in Tennessee, he could receive reinforcements from other theaters, but if Sherman met with difficulty in Georgia, he would be on his own. Thus, it made sense for Sherman to take the best troops with him, thus minimizing the risk to the force that would be in the most potential danger. Thomas did not complain about being left with inadequate troops, and he assured Sherman that he was satisfied with the size of his army and would be able to hold out against Hood.[8]

Thomas arrived at Nashville on October 3. He apparently did not expect his duties to be too difficult, as he sent his nephew, Sanford Kellogg, to New York to bring Frances Thomas to Nashville for a visit. This was the first time Thomas had seen his wife in three years, and she stayed for about a month. Unfortunately, the couple probably did not get to spend much time together, as Thomas soon found himself busy attempting to capture the Confederate cavalry raider Nathan Bedford Forrest, who had been operating in middle Tennessee since late September. From Nashville Thomas attempted to coordinate the movements of his troops by telegraph to capture Forrest, but he was unsuccessful. Forrest captured a number of prisoners and destroyed a great deal of Union supplies before rejoining Hood's army in early November.[9]

On November 12 Sherman sent his last communication to Thomas and then marched off into Georgia. Like Sherman, Thomas expected that

Hood would follow Sherman's army, so when reports of Confederate activity near the Tennessee-Alabama border began to come in, Thomas suspected that the reports merely indicated a small-scale raid. Thomas remained at Nashville and instructed Schofield to take his own Twenty-third Corps, based at Pulaski, and Stanley's Fourth Corps and respond to the Confederate movement.[10]

As more information came in from the Union scouts, Schofield began to suspect that he was not facing a raiding force, but Hood's entire army. By November 20 Schofield was almost sure of it. His position at this point was difficult. Hood's force outnumbered Schofield's greatly, with 40,000 infantry to Schofield's 24,000, and 7,000 cavalry to 3,500 for the Union. With such a disadvantage in cavalry, it would be difficult for Schofield to correctly ascertain Hood's movements. Thomas instructed Schofield to delay Hood as long as possible, gaining time for Smith's corps to reach Tennessee, and for the forces currently posted in small garrisons throughout the state to concentrate at Nashville. Thomas told Schofield to keep his army as far forward as possible, while being careful not to allow Hood to move around his flank and block his retreat to Nashville.[11]

Over the next ten days, Schofield slowly withdrew before Hood's advance, trying to slow Hood's progress without being surrounded or cut off from Nashville. He retreated to Columbia on November 24 and then retreated to the northern bank of the Duck River on November 27.[12] Hood followed the same strategy that Sherman had used during the Atlanta campaign, using his numerical superiority to execute a series of flanking moves. While Hood succeeded in forcing Schofield to retreat, what he really wanted was to get between Schofield's force and Nashville, thus forcing them into a fight on open ground where Hood's larger army would have the advantage. On November 29 Hood almost managed to block Schofield's retreat at the town of Spring Hill, but stiff resistance from a small force of Union defenders, combined with a series of errors and miscommunications on the part of Hood and his corps commanders, allowed Schofield's army to escape. Hood's men went into bivouac only a few hundred yards from the Columbia–Nashville Turnpike, and Schofield's army marched past it in the night, reaching the town of Franklin the next day.[13]

Schofield had to stop at Franklin because he had no way to cross the Harpeth River, which blocked his path just north of the city. Schofield had destroyed his own pontoon bridge during his retreat from Pulaski, because he had inadequate transportation for it. He had asked Thomas to send another pontoon bridge from Nashville, but Thomas had failed to do so. Ordering his men to stop and entrench, Schofield set about finding a way to bridge the river. His men were in a potentially dangerous position, with the enemy in their front and the river at their back, but they had strong artillery support and plenty of time to build fortifications. It seemed unlikely that Hood would attack Schofield's strong defensive line.[14]

Hood did attack, however. He was furious about Schofield's escape from his trap at Spring Hill, and he was convinced that his officers' and troops' lack of offensive spirit was to blame. Hood ordered an attack at Franklin despite the fact that the Union troops there were well entrenched, that Hood's own men were exhausted, and that his artillery had not yet reached the field. The resulting battle was a slaughter: in little over an hour, more than seven thousand Confederates were killed, wounded, or captured, compared to a Union loss of only twenty-five hundred. Among the Confederate dead were six generals, including the Confederates' best divisional commander, Patrick Cleburne. Five other generals were wounded, and one was captured. Hood's foolish and wasteful attack had crippled the army in terms of its numbers, its leadership, and its morale and had caused Hood to lose the confidence of his soldiers.[15]

After the victory at Franklin, Thomas wanted Schofield to hold his ground, but Schofield advocated a withdrawal. Schofield still felt his position was too vulnerable, as Hood could cross the river above or below the town and block his line of communications with Nashville. This argument convinced Thomas, and Schofield retreated from Franklin during the night of November 30. Meanwhile, Thomas was becoming extremely anxious about the delays in the arrival of Smith's corps. Now that Hood had crossed the Harpeth River, Thomas feared Hood might move artillery to the south bank of the Tennessee River and block the transport boats that were to bring Smith's corps to Nasvhille.[16]

When Schofield arrived in Nashville the following evening, Thomas greeted him politely but unenthusiastically and congratulated him on the success of his campaign. Shortly afterward, Andrew J. Smith walked in, and according to one eyewitness, Thomas was so glad to see him that he "literally picked him up in his arms and hugged him." Schofield took offense at the cool treatment he had received from Thomas and recalled the incident bitterly in his memoirs. Schofield later criticized many of

Thomas's actions during the retreat to Nashville; the one criticism that had the most validity was his statement that Thomas should not have remained at Nashville during the retreat but should have come to the front to take charge of Schofield's force personally.[17] Thomas's reasons for staying at Nashville are unclear. Perhaps he thought that it was more important for him to coordinate the concentration of his forces at Nashville for eventual offensive action against Hood. He may have underestimated the threat to Schofield, or overestimated Schofield's ability to handle it. In hindsight, it seems that it would have been better for Thomas to command at the front in person. Not only was Thomas a more experienced officer, but Thomas's personal presence would have bolstered the morale of his men. Before Sherman had left Atlanta, Thomas had written Sherman that he planned to command in the field. It is not clear why Thomas changed his mind.[18]

Now that Schofield's and Smith's forces were at Nashville, Grant wanted Thomas to go on the offensive, but Thomas did not feel that his army was ready. He was particularly concerned about the condition of his cavalry. Because Wilson's cavalry had been campaigning actively for the last two weeks, many of the horses had broken down, and his men needed rest as well. Wilson had sixty-five hundred cavalry on hand, but he estimated that Forrest had twice as many cavalry as he did and thought that only half of his own force could be considered effective, due to the lack of mounts. Schofield agreed that Wilson's force was "far inferior" to Forrest's and complained to Thomas that Wilson was "entirely unable to cope with him." Actually, Forrest's cavalry was about equal in number to Wilson's, and Forrest was having just as much trouble finding mounts as Wilson. On the one hand, given how common a mistake it was for commanders to overestimate the size of the enemy force they faced, perhaps Thomas should have been more skeptical of Wilson's and Schofield's reports. On the other hand, Forrest had outmaneuvered Wilson throughout the last week's campaign, so it was clear that Wilson would benefit from having a larger effective force.[19]

By December 1 all of Smith's and Schofield's forces had reached Nashville, and Thomas had pulled in men from his outlying garrisons. He had more than 50,000 soldiers under his command, which were divided into five groups. About 4,000 of these were reserve troops, garrison soldiers, or other units not normally used in the front lines, which Thomas planned to use as reserve troops, manning the Nashville fortifications while Thomas's other troops attacked. His best troops were the 9,000 men in Smith's Sixteenth Corps, the 14,000 men in Schofield's Twenty-third Corps, and the 10,000 men in Thomas J. Wood's Fourth Corps. The men in these corps were all veterans, who had fought extensively under Thomas, Grant, and Sherman.[20]

The fourth group of infantry were 8,500 men taken from the Tennessee garrisons. Thomas named these "the Detachment of the District of the Etowah" and placed them under the command of Maj. Gen. James B. Steedman. While Thomas had evacuated most of the smaller garrisons in middle Tennessee and northern Alabama, he had left garrisons at the larger towns, including Murfreesboro, Chattanooga, Stevenson, and Bridgeport. When Hood had first started moving north, Thomas had ordered Steedman to use some of his garrison troops to attack Hood's supply line, and to burn his pontoon bridge at Tuscumbia, Alabama. When Hood's advance went more quickly than Thomas expected, he canceled these orders, telling Steedman to bring his men directly to Nashville. Many of Steedman's troops were African Americans, and Thomas had little confidence in their fighting abilities. He placed them on the far western flank of his line and did not plan to use them in the upcoming offensive.[21]

In addition to these five infantry groups, Thomas had a little over two hundred pieces of artillery and about seven thousand cavalry. Wilson was still having difficulties finding new mounts. Grant and Stanton gave Thomas the authority to impress into service any and all horses his men were able to find in and around Nashville, but the countryside had been so depleted by the war that Wilson's men were unable to find many. They had more success in Nashville itself, where they commandeered every horse they could find, including a show horse owned by a traveling circus and the carriage horses owned by the governor, Andrew Johnson. While Thomas later used Wilson's cavalry as an offensive weapon, at this point his main concern was defensive. He was convinced that Forrest's cavalry outnumbered Wilson's two to one and wanted to make sure that he had enough cavalry to cover his army's flanks.[22]

Despite Grant's orders to attack immediately, Thomas was in no hurry. Thinking that Hood's force posed no immediate threat, he assumed he could take as long as he wanted to prepare. From a military standpoint, Thomas was correct. The Union force at Nashville outnumbered Hood's and were posted behind strong fortifications, so it would be foolish for Hood to attack him. As a precaution, however, and as a stepping-off point for his upcoming attack, Thomas had his men construct a second line of fortifications, farther out from the city than the first one. Thomas was not worried that Hood would bypass Nashville and raid north into Kentucky. The bad condition of the roads made movement difficult, and Hood had already advanced beyond the point where he had good access to his supplies. Federal gunboats controlled the Cumberland River, and they would make it difficult or impossible for Hood to effect a crossing. If Hood did somehow manage to cross the river, Thomas could follow him, cutting off his line of supply and retreat as he went, and attack him in the open. This would be such a risky move on Hood's part that Thomas did not worry about his attempting it.[23]

Instead, Thomas assumed Hood would wait outside of Nashville until Thomas was ready to attack him. Thomas explained in an 1867 letter to Dennis Hart Mahan, the professor of engineering and strategy at West Point, that he considered it foolish to attack in early December, as he was not adequately equipped to follow up on a victory. Since Thomas's soldiers were well supplied and Hood's were not, Thomas reflected, every day's delay "strengthened my command and in a like proportion weakened Hood."[24]

While waiting made sense from a military standpoint, it did not make sense in political terms. Thomas's retreat had left most of middle Tennessee under Confederate control. Political leaders, as well as the general public, did not understand that logistical considerations made it impossible for Hood to advance farther northward, and they feared that Hood would bypass Nashville and invade Kentucky. In addition, the mere fact that a Confederate army was besieging Nashville, a city that had been captured over two and a half years before, was humiliating for the Lincoln administration. Lincoln and his cabinet were desperate to see Thomas drive Hood out of Tennessee.

On December 1 Thomas told Halleck that he did not plan to attack right away but would instead stay behind the fortifications at Nashville until Wilson could get his cavalry equipped. Halleck met with Stanton and Lincoln that evening to discuss this news. The president objected to Thomas's strategy of waiting behind the fortifications "for an indefinite period of time," and Stanton opined that Thomas's strategy "looks like the McClellan and Rosecrans strategy of do nothing and let the Rebels raid the country." Stanton told Grant to push Thomas into action. On December 2 Grant reprimanded Thomas for not attacking immediately after the Battle of Franklin and ordered him to attack at once. Thomas responded that he would attack as soon as he received the last of his cavalry reinforcements, which he expected to arrive in the next two or three days.[25]

Several days passed, and the cavalry reinforcements arrived, but Thomas still did not attack. Thomas learned that Confederate cavalry raiders had crossed the Cumberland River and were attempting to interfere with his supply line, so he sent the new cavalry force after them. He then continued to wait for Wilson to remount his cavalry. When Grant sent Thomas direct attack orders on December 5 and 6, Thomas stated that he would comply but protested that the lack of cavalry would make the movement "hazardous." He then discovered that he could not even mobilize the cavalry he had, because so many of Wilson's men were scattered throughout the countryside looking for mounts. Stanton wired Grant, "Thomas seems unwilling to attack because it is hazardous, as if all war was anything but hazardous. If he waits for Wilson to get ready, Gabriel will be blowing his last horn."[26]

Thomas kept a close watch on Hood during this period, but Hood seemed to be doing little but fortifying his position and waiting for Thomas to attack. This was, in fact, Hood's strategy. Hood knew that Thomas's forces outnumbered his own, and that attacking the fortifications at Nashville would be suicidal. It would also be too dangerous to bypass Nashville and invade Kentucky. Hood's plan was to wait outside of the city until Thomas attacked him and then hope for a tactical success that would allow him to counterattack and destroy Thomas's army. This was a desperate strategy, with little chance of succeeding, but Hood felt this was the only plan that held even the slightest hope of saving the Confederacy.[27]

When Thomas did not attack right away, Hood grew impatient. He detached a force to attack the Federal garrison at Murfreesboro, with the hope that this would provoke Thomas to march out of his fortifications and come to the garrison's assistance. The Murfreesboro garrison, numbering eight thousand men, was commanded by Maj. Gen. Lovell Rousseau, an experienced officer who had fought under Thomas at Stones River. On November 30 Thomas had ordered Rousseau to hold on at Murfreesboro until Thomas went on the offensive against Hood, which Thomas stated he planned to do within five days. Confederates had cut the telegraph wires to Murfreesboro on December 2, and the Union garrison remained out of communication for over a week.

Thomas regained contact with Murfreesboro on December 11. Rousseau reported that he had been besieged by a force of roughly eight thousand Confederate infantry and cavalry since December 4, but that he was not in danger of surrendering. His foraging parties were able to operate without hindrance from the enemy, and he had even defeated the Confederate force in a sortie on December 7, capturing two hundred prisoners and two cannons. Unknown to Thomas, Hood had further weakened his force at Nashville by sending nearly all of Forrest's cavalry away, to assist with the siege of Murfreesboro and on raiding missions. Already outnumbered, Hood had foolishly reduced his army still further with these auxiliary campaigns.[28]

Grant and Halleck continued to send Thomas daily orders to attack. Thomas responded on December 9 with a promise to attack in the immediate future but did not specify an exact date. He told Halleck that he had done all in his power in preparation, but "that the troops could not have been gotten ready before this." To Grant he stated that his preparations were "nearly completed" and promised to attack soon. Acknowledging Grant's dissatisfaction with his performance, Thomas stated, "If you should deem it necessary to relieve me I shall submit without a murmur."[29] Grant wired Halleck telling him to replace Thomas with Schofield, but Thomas sent another message that afternoon that caused Grant to change his mind. Thomas stated that he had planned to attack the next day, but that a tremendous storm of snow and ice had descended on Nashville, making the attack impossible. Reluctantly, Grant suspended the order relieving Thomas from command. Grant informed Thomas that he had nearly relieved him and explained that he had suspended the order only on the condition that Thomas act as soon as possible.[30]

This telegram upset Thomas greatly. As one of his staff officers recalled, Thomas did not tell anyone about Grant's message at the time, but "it was very evident that something greatly troubled him. While the rain was falling and the fields and roads were ice-bound, he would sometimes sit by the window for an hour or more, not speaking a word, gazing steadily out on the forbidding prospect, as if he were trying to will the storm away." During this period, Thomas was often visited by citizens and officials of the city, including Governor Johnson. As the officer recalled,

Johnson used to "unfold to him with much iteration his fierce views concerning secession, rebels, and reconstruction. To all he gave a patient and kindly hearing, and he often astonished Governor Johnson by his knowledge of constitutional and international law. But underneath all, it was plain to see that General Grant's dissatisfaction keenly affected him."[31]

On December 11 Grant ordered Thomas to attack immediately, despite the icy weather, and Thomas tried to comply. Wilson's cavalry were stationed north of the river, where the forage was better, and Thomas ordered him to bring his men and horses across the river in order to be ready to attack the next day. He also had his men deploy in combat positions near the front. But the icy roads and bridges were so treacherous for the horses that it took all day for Wilson to get his cavalry to the front, and many men and horses slipped on the ice and were injured.[32]

Thomas called his corps commanders to headquarters for a conference that evening. He asked each of them whether they favored an immediate attack on Hood or thought it best to wait. Nearly all of them agreed that he should wait for the snow to thaw.

Eyewitness accounts differ on how Schofield reacted. Schofield claimed that he spoke up immediately to support Thomas, as he had guessed that Grant might appoint him to replace Thomas and did not want to seem to be scheming for Thomas's command. Wilson wrote that Schofield remained silent during the meeting, while Wilson himself enthusiastically endorsed Thomas's decision to wait. James Steedman stated that Schofield did not speak until last and then stated only that he would obey orders. It is impossible to tell at this remove which account is true, but Steedman's seems the least self-serving and the most plausible.[33]

Some of Thomas's officers later accused Schofield of plotting against Thomas, by sending secret dispatches to Grant from Nashville, complaining of the failures of Thomas's generalship. According to Frances Thomas, George Thomas also suspected that Schofield was doing this but never said anything about it in public.[34] Schofield and Grant both denied these allegations, and no copies of telegrams from Schofield to Grant have ever been found. While Schofield's biographer states there is "strong circumstantial evidence" to support the allegations that Schofield communicated secretly with Grant, there is no direct proof. In any case, Grant had his own reasons for being critical of Thomas and did not need Schofield's encouragement to contemplate removing Thomas from command.[35]

Wilson recalled having dinner with Thomas after the December 11 meeting, during which Thomas spoke with emotion and resentment of his treatment by his superiors. He complained that his superiors treated him "like a boy," and acted as if he were incapable of making decisions on his own. Thomas noted that Sherman had taken most of the Army of the Cumberland's best corps on his Georgia expedition, leaving Thomas to confront Hood with second-rate troops. Thomas was particularly annoyed by Grant's impatience with him at Nashville, given that Grant himself had been stalled before Richmond for months.[36]

Feeling more confident after the council of war, Thomas wired Halleck that he would not attack until the snow and ice thawed, since to act immediately "would only result in a useless sacrifice of life." Thomas did not send a message to Grant, although he knew Grant would soon hear of his decision. This action seems to indicate that Thomas expected to be relieved of command and avoided communicating directly with Grant in the hope of delaying Grant's reaction.[37] Grant did decide to relieve Thomas from command, choosing Maj. Gen. John A. Logan, who was temporarily without a command, to replace him. Grant wrote out orders naming Logan to command of the army at Nashville and instructed him to go there immediately. If Thomas had not moved against Hood by the time Logan arrived, Grant stated, Logan should take over the army and launch an attack on Hood. A few days after sending Logan, Grant decided to go to Nashville himself.[38]

Some historians, and many of Thomas's biographers, have attributed Grant's decision to remove Thomas to jealousy or personal animosity. It is true that Grant's decision is difficult to understand in purely military terms. Grant was experienced enough to know that the commander in the field has a much better idea of conditions and tactics than any commander observing from a distance. Thomas had shown himself to be less quick and aggressive than Grant, but his record did not justify Grant's lack of confidence. Grant's biographers attribute his decision to frustration over his stalled Virginia campaign and anxiety over Sherman's progress in the Carolinas, not to malice. Grant feared that Thomas's inaction would make it possible for the Confederates to transfer troops from western garrisons to Georgia, where they could oppose Sherman. While there was little basis for this fear in reality, as the Confederates had already sent all the troops to Georgia that they could, Grant seems to have considered this a real possibility, and for this reason wanted Thomas to attack.[39]

By comparison, Grant was much more generous in his relationship with George G. Meade, the commander of the Army of the Potomac. Stanton and others considered Meade too slow and unaggressive and recommended that Grant relieve him from command when Grant transferred to the Virginia theater in 1864. After talking to Meade, Grant decided to leave him in command of the Army of the Potomac. The two worked fairly well together, and Grant gave Meade a fair amount of freedom in directing the army's operations. What seems to be different in Meade's case is that Grant was present in Virginia and could intervene when he disagreed with what Meade was doing. Also, Meade always obeyed Grant's orders, even when he disagreed with them, and thereby retained Grant's confidence.[40]

The weather around Nashville began to improve on December 13, and Thomas told Halleck he would attack soon. Thomas ordered his corps commanders to keep a close watch for any changes in Hood's dispositions that might affect Thomas's plans. The temperature rose on December 14, melting the ice, but leaving a sea of mud in its wake that made it impossible for Thomas to attack that day. Thomas called his corps commanders to his headquarters that afternoon, and explained his plan for an attack the next day.[41]

Hood's army was stationed along the ridges and hills just south of the city. His line went from east to west and bent back to the south on either flank. Thomas's line curved in an arc around Nashville and was anchored by the river at both ends. The eastern end of Thomas's line was held by James Steedman's provisional force, the Detachment of the District of the Etowah. Next in line to the west was John Schofield's Twenty-third Corps, then Thomas Wood's Fourth Corps, and then Andrew J. Smith's Sixteenth Corps. James Wilson's cavalry, having just moved into the city from its encampments on the north bank of the Cumberland, was available for service wherever Thomas saw fit.

Thomas explained that Smith's infantry would make the main attack, striking the western part of Hood's line, while Wilson's cavalry would go around Hood's western flank to participate in Smith's attack and to cut off Hood's retreat. Wood's corps, in the center, would attack in coordination with Smith. Thomas did not assign Schofield's and Steedman's troops an active role and told them only to remain in their positions until

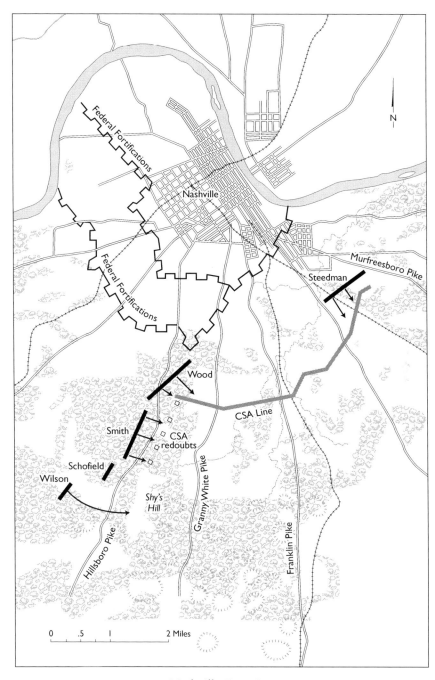

Nashville, Day One

called on. Thomas also planned to post garrison and quartermaster troops in the inner lines of the city's fortifications, as a last line of defense in case the attack on Hood met with disaster.[42]

Both Schofield and Steedman expressed their displeasure with the passive role Thomas had assigned them. Steedman proposed that he launch a limited attack against the eastern flank of Hood's line early in the morning. This attack, Steedman argued, would distract Hood's attention from the main effort and would keep him from transferring men from the eastern part of his line to the west. Schofield also wanted an active role, and he suggested that his portion of the defensive line could be held with garrison troops while his corps could be sent to assist with the main attack. Thomas agreed to both changes and set the attack to begin at dawn the next day.[43]

Thomas was confident of defeating Hood. In the predawn hours of December 15, he checked out of his room at the St. Cloud Hotel, confident that by nightfall his front line would be far south of the city. A soldier who saw him that morning remembered his "quiet dignity" and military bearing, which had "no haughtiness nor ostentatious show." Thomas had "an air of 'business' about him," the soldier recalled, "which boded no good for Mr. Hood." Thomas was looking forward to the culmination of his military career. After learning his trade through decades of regular service and years of Civil War command, Thomas finally had the opportunity to command his own campaign. While his superior officers and the politicians in Washington had tried to interfere with his plans, Thomas had successfully resisted them. While he was not as fully prepared as he would have liked, his force readiness was adequate for battle and pursuit, and he knew he was in a position to destroy Hood's army completely. It is no wonder that Thomas looked confident and satisfied that morning; he was sure of his talents and confident of success.[44]

Thomas's chaplain and biographer, Thomas Van Horne, wrote, "Seldom has a battle been fought in more exact conformity to plan than the Battle of Nashville," a claim that some historians have repeated. In reality, the battle did not go at all as Thomas had planned. The first problem Thomas encountered was a heavy morning fog, which limited visibility so much that his officers could not even get their regiments into formation. It took until 8:30 A.M., two and a half hours after he originally intended, for Thomas's soldiers to begin their march. Wilson's cavalry, which had the farthest distance to travel, were supposed to march first, but when the fog began to clear they found their road blocked by a division of infantry from Smith's corps who had begun its march prematurely. Wilson had to wait another hour and a half for the infantry to get out of the way.[45]

As Wilson waited for the infantry to clear the road, Steedman began his diversionary attack on the eastern portion of the line. Thomas was at the western point of the line at this time, overseeing the preparations for his main attack, and he could hear the sounds of firing off to the west but did not know how the battle was progressing. At about ten o'clock, the Union artillery in the west prepared for the infantry by launching a tremendous barrage of shelling, which lasted for over two hours. At 12:30 Smith's corps and Wood's corps moved forward to attack Hood's line. From his observation post, Thomas watched as Wood's men moved forward, meeting with only minor resistance from the defenders. Wood halted his men when they had drawn close to the Confederate fortifications, adjusted part of his line, and charged the fortifications, capturing them with ease.[46] This grand victory seemed too good to be true, and it was. Thomas soon learned that the fortifications he had just captured had only held a few skirmishers, as Hood had moved his main defense line back a few days before. Thomas's massive artillery barrage had fallen on nearly empty ground.[47]

It was now 2:00 P.M. Wood wanted to move forward and engage Hood's main line, but a problem with the alignment of Smith's corps forced him to wait. Smith's advance had brought his corps closer to Wood's corps than Thomas had originally anticipated, and there was a large gap between the end of Smith's line and the beginning of Wilson's. Thomas ordered Schofield's corps to fill the gap. The change would increase the pressure brought to bear on Hood's western flank and give Wilson more freedom to move into the rear of Hood's army, but it meant still further delay. Meanwhile, Wilson's men were having problems of their own. After dismounting in preparation for their attack, they found that they still had a long distance to travel before reaching Hood's line. Their slow advance on foot was slowed even more as they came into contact with Hood's skirmishers.[48]

While Thomas waited for Wilson and Schofield to move up, he received a report from Steedman about that morning's attack. Steedman stated that he had "pressed [the enemy's] right strongly" but had withdrawn after coming under fire from the enemy's artillery. While the report gave few details, it seemed that Steedman's attack had served its purpose in deceiving Hood and in keeping his troops pinned down on the eastern flank. That evening, Steedman gave Thomas a more lengthy report, in which he stated that he had occupied one portion of the enemy's breastworks and had suffered only 250 casualties.

Steedman's report was not accurate, however. Disobeying Thomas's orders to launch only a limited attack, Steedman had ordered a major assault and had sent his men into a Confederate trap. The defenders had devised their lines carefully, hiding an artillery battery at a point where it could fire down a railroad cut. The gunners held their fire during the Union advance, waiting until Steedman's men were crowded into the ravine. They then opened fire on the crowd, and a brigade of Confederate infantry moved forward to open fire as well. While a brigade of white soldiers ran away, Steedman's black troops bravely tried to continue forward, but they could not make any progress in the face of the overwhelming enemy fire. Hundreds of men died, having done little damage to the Confederates. Their defeat was so total that the Confederate corps commander, Benjamin F. Cheatham, felt sure that the attack would not be repeated and sent two brigades to reinforce the western part of Hood's line. While these brigades arrived too late in the day to be of any use, Steedman's attack more than failed to prevent Hood from transferring troops away from the eastern part of his line. Thomas apparently never learned the full truth about Steedman's attack. In his final report of the battle, written on January 20, 1865, Thomas wrote that Steedman's advance met with "great success and some loss," and forced Hood to move men away from his western flank.[49]

Thomas's second attack on Hood's western line began at 2:15 P.M. Hood's army had been reduced so much in the Battle of Franklin that he did not have enough men to defend his entire line. While he maintained a continuous line in the center, Hood had resorted to using a system of redoubts on each flank. These redoubts were small forts, manned by infantry and artillery, placed in such a way that they could support one another. If one redoubt was taken, the other redoubts could fire on it and make the position too dangerous for the attackers to hold. The western flank of Hood's line had five of these redoubts, which extended southward in a line along the high ground near the Hillsboro Pike.[50]

Thomas watched as Smith's men, supported by a portion of Wilson's dismounted cavalry, moved forward to attack the redoubts. The men captured the southernmost fort, advanced through a heavy fire, and took the next redoubt to the north. Inspired by their success, one of Smith's brigade commanders attacked and captured the next two redoubts in the line. Hood pulled a division out of the center of his line to counterattack, but they arrived too late, and the Union men turned the captured Confederate artillery pieces around and used them to drive back the attackers. Wood then ordered his men forward against the last remaining redoubt, which they captured easily, completing the rout of the Confederates' western line.[51]

At five o'clock, as Wood's men were attacking the last Confederate redoubt, Thomas ordered Wilson to advance eastward to the Granny White Pike and the Franklin Pike to cut off the Confederate line of retreat. He also ordered his infantry to pursue the enemy directly, but this pursuit was ineffective. Schofield's men were too far behind the main line to catch up to the Confederate army, while Smith's and Wood's corps had been disorganized by the difficult assault, and their men were busy guarding hundreds of prisoners. Wilson's cavalry made better progress, but did not quite manage to block the Confederate retreat. They did not reach the Granny White Pike until 6:00, nearly an hour and a half after sunset. The Confederates had rallied to defend the road, and Wilson did not have time to deploy his men before the dusk turned to total darkness. The Granny White Pike and Franklin Pike stayed in Confederate hands, and Hood used them during the night to fall back and reorganize his army.[52]

Looking back on the day's fighting, Thomas could take satisfaction in a partial victory. The delays had been frustrating, but Thomas had remained patient, making sure that all of his men were in place and aligned before launching his attack. His patience had paid off, as the assault, when it came, was so well coordinated and overwhelming that it crushed Hood's line. Because of the delays and the shortness of the winter day, night had fallen before Thomas could completely destroy Hood's army, but he hoped to continue the fight the next day. Also, by interrogating prisoners he had learned that Forrest's cavalry was not at Nashville. He could safely assign a more aggressive role to Wilson's cavalry the next day, either in battle if Hood stayed to fight, or in pursuit if Hood retreated.[53]

As night fell, Thomas arranged for the prisoners captured that day to be escorted into Nashville. Some of the guards were African American soldiers, and some of the Confederates objected to being held prisoner by blacks. One group of prisoners appealed directly to Thomas, saying they would rather die than be taken to Nashville under the guard of "nigger" soldiers. "Well, you may say your prayers, and get ready to die," Thomas responded, "for these are the only soldiers I can spare." The prisoners thought better of their request and marched off under guard to Nashville. Thomas had come a long way in his views of African American soldiers. In 1861 he might have agreed that being guarded by former slaves was a dishonor, but by 1864 he had little sympathy for Southern racial sensitivities.[54]

Upon returning to his headquarters, Thomas allowed himself one indulgence in his victory, using the official military telegraph lines to inform Frances, "We have whipped the enemy, taken many prisoners and considerable artillery." He sent a more detailed account of his victory to Washington, which arrived at an opportune time.[55] Grant had written orders just that day to relieve Thomas, putting Schofield in command until Grant could come to Nashville to take charge in person. The telegraph officer on duty had intentionally delayed sending Grant's telegram, to give Thomas a little more time, and was relieved when Thomas's report of the battle arrived shortly after 11:00 P.M. The officer rushed out the door with the telegraph and ran to give the good news to Stanton and Lincoln. Stanton came out of his house and cheered the good news, and his wife and children came out and cheered with him. At the White House, Lincoln came out in his nightshirt, candle in hand, and read the dispatch.[56]

Grant wired Thomas at 11:30 stating, "I was just on my way to Nashville," but now that he had news of Thomas's "splendid victory," he did not intend to go. "Push the enemy now, and give him no rest until he is entirely destroyed," Grant urged. "Do not stop for trains or supplies, but take them from the country, as the enemy has done. Much now is expected." A few minutes later, Grant sent a second telegram, more congratulatory and less lecturing in tone. Lincoln's congratulatory message, sent the following day, also contained both admonishments and praise. "Please accept for yourself, officers, and men, the nation's thanks for your good work of yesterday," Lincoln wrote. "You made a magnificent beginning. A grand consummation is within your easy reach. Do not let it slip."[57]

Thomas had no intention of stopping with his victory of December 15, but his plans for the next day would depend on what Hood did. The intelligence from Wilson's scouts indicated that the Confederates were retreating,

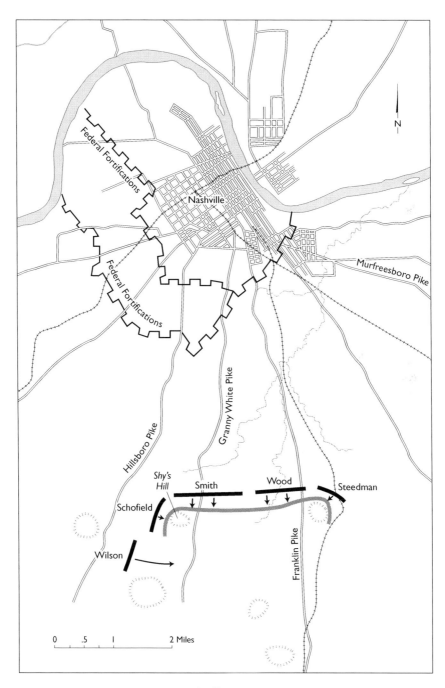

Nashville, Day Two

which would certainly be Hood's most sensible move. Schofield thought Hood would stay and fight and was afraid that if the Union army advanced too carelessly, they might fall victim to a counterattack. Thomas prepared for both contingencies, telling his commanders to make a cautious advance the next day while they gathered what information they could. Once Thomas learned where Hood's army was, Thomas would either pursue or attack him.[58]

The morning of December 16 was foggy, but not as foggy as the previous day, and most of the fog burned off by 8:30 A.M. The day was unseasonably warm, almost springlike. The morning light revealed that Hood had only retreated about a mile and had set up a new defensive line farther south. This new line was similar in shape to the old one, running east–west in the center with each flank bent southward at a nearly ninety-degree angle. The Confederates occupied a line of steep hills, which they had worked all night to fortify. Hood's army had recovered from the defeat of the previous day, and attacking them in their fortified positions would be difficult.[59]

Thomas's forces were aligned as they had been the day before, with Steedman's force holding the far eastern end of the line, Wood and Smith in the center, Schofield in the west, and Wilson at the far end of the line, west and south of Schofield. During the evening of December 15, Schofield had expressed his concern that his infantry was in a vulnerable position, on the end of Thomas's main line with only Wilson's cavalry on their flank. He asked Thomas to send him reinforcements, and Thomas complied by sending him a division from Smith's corps.[60]

Once he ascertained that the Confederates had only fallen back about a mile, Thomas ordered his own line forward. Smith's and Schofield's corps soon made contact with the enemy, and their infantry took cover while the artillery fired on the Confederate works. Meanwhile, Wilson reported that large numbers of Confederate infantry and cavalry were moving toward Hood's far western and southwestern flank. Wilson also told Thomas that the terrain in his front was "too difficult for cavalry operations" and recommended that his cavalry move all the way around the Union rear to operate on the opposite, eastern flank. Thomas went to Wilson at about 10:30 A.M. to consult with him. After a short discussion, Thomas declined to send Wilson to the other flank of the army and ordered him to continue his advance around Hood's western flank.

Thomas then rode off to check on Wood's division, which had still not reached the enemy line.[61]

Both Wood and Steedman took much longer to reach Hood's main line than Smith and Schofield. Their corps had a greater distance to travel, and their advance was contested by Confederate skirmishers. They did not make full contact with Hood's line until shortly after noon and did not finish getting their men into position until one o'clock. Thomas did not want to attack until all his troops were in contact with the enemy, so he had little to do but wait as Wood and Steedman inched forward. An orderly later recalled seeing Thomas sitting alone on a log outside of his tent with his elbow on his knee, nervously running his fingers through his beard as he watched their progress. The men in Schofield's and Smith's corps also waited impatiently, unaware of the reason for the delay. At noon a light rain began to fall, and the rain soon turned into a heavy downpour.[62]

As Wood's soldiers began to make contact with the enemy, Thomas conferred with him about his next move. Thomas still wanted the main effort to come on the western flank, but he told Wood that he could attack if he found "any opening for a more decisive effort." Thomas then rode off to the western flank to set the main attack in motion. He did not realize that Wood, impulsive and eager for glory, would take advantage of Thomas's grant of discretion and launch a major attack. The Confederate line in Wood's front was well fortified, heavily defended, and anchored on a steep rise called Overton Hill, but Wood soon convinced himself that his men could capture it. Wood then asked Steedman to support him with his troops, and Steedman, who was equally ambitious, agreed. At 2:45 their men went forward.[63]

Steedman's and Wood's men crossed hundreds of yards of open ground, under a heavy enemy fire, slogging slowly through the mud and then up Overton Hill. As they neared the summit of the hill, they had to work their way past the fallen trees, abatis, and ditches that the Confederates had constructed the previous night. The soldiers fought bravely, particularly the African American troops, but their efforts were in vain. Over a thousand Union soldiers died in the brief assault, nearly one-third of the casualties that the Union suffered during in the entire two days of battle. The Confederate losses were slight. One of the Confederate commanders, Brig. Gen. James T. Holtzclaw, was so astonished by the black soldiers' bravery that he commended them in his report. "They came only to die," he stated. "I have seen most of the battle-fields of the West, but never saw dead men thicker than in front of my two right regiments."[64]

After leaving Wood, Thomas rode back to his western flank and found Smith and Schofield in the midst of a disagreement. When Schofield heard Wilson's report about Hood shifting forces toward his western flank, he took this as further evidence that Hood was preparing to attack him. Schofield requested a second division from Smith's corps, and Thomas granted his request, but Smith, protesting that he had already weakened his own line too much, refused to send the division to Schofield. At 1:30 P.M., Schofield sent Thomas a message stating that his forces were too weak to attack Hood that day. As Thomas rode toward Smith's headquarters, he heard the noise of Wood and Steedman's attack, but he did not have time to investigate. He had to get Smith and Schofield's attack under way.[65]

Thomas spoke first to Smith, who felt that he was too weak to attack now that he had sent one of his divisions to Schofield. While the two generals were talking, an important message came in from one of Smith's brigade commanders, Brig. Gen. John McArthur. McArthur's brigade was positioned in front of where the Confederate line occupied a steep hill. This hill later came to be known as Shy's Hill, after a Confederate general, William M. Shy, who was killed there during the day's fighting. McArthur had examined the Confederate position closely and had discovered that it was not as strong as it seemed. The steepness of the hill actually worked to the Union advantage, as the Confederate gunners would be unable to depress the barrels of their cannons far enough to fire at troops climbing the slope. The Confederate fortifications, which had been constructed hastily the night before, were placed on the topographical summit of the hill, not the "military" summit, the place where the defenders would have the best field of fire. In short, the conditions were similar to those at Missionary Ridge, and McArthur thought he could achieve similar results. He had spent the last two hours trying to convince Smith to give him permission to attack.[66]

After listening to McArthur's message, Thomas gave him the permission he wanted, asking him only to wait so Thomas could make sure Schofield attacked at the same time. Smith ordered his other brigades to attack along with McArthur. Thomas rode over to tell Schofield to attack when Smith's corps did, but Schofield resisted the order, insisting that he did not have enough men. As they were talking, Wilson rode up and asked why Schofield had not advanced. His cavalry had defeated their opponents on

Hood's far western flank, he said, and were now ranging into Hood's rear. From Schofield's command post, Thomas could see Wilson's men through his binoculars, moving behind Hood's lines. This settled matters for Thomas. As Wilson recalled, Thomas turned to Schofield and, "as calmly as if on parade, directed him to attack with his entire corps."[67]

Now that he had committed his troops to battle, Thomas once again had little to do but wait. He watched as the lines of blue infantry climbed Shy's Hill, under fire from the Confederates at the top. As his men reached the summit, the position became wreathed in smoke, and it was difficult to see what was going on. From Schofield's headquarters, Thomas rode back to Smith, wanting to hear how his assault had progressed. When he arrived at Smith's headquarters, Thomas saw crowds of gray-coated infantry walking down Shy's Hill, advancing toward the Union position. The movement was not a counterattack, however, but crowds of Confederate prisoners being herded to the rear. The attack on Shy's Hill had succeeded.[68]

As McArthur had guessed, the Confederate artillery was badly positioned on Shy's Hill, making it possible for the Union troops to advance without suffering many casualties. When McArthur's men reached the top, most of the defenders fired a single volley and ran, and the few who stayed and fought were quickly killed or captured. Hood, judging Shy's Hill to be so steep as to be unassailable, had left the position lightly defended and then weakened it further by detaching two divisions from the hill as reinforcements for his eastern and western flanks. The remaining defenders were so few in number and so widely dispersed that they were unable to resist the Union attack.

Once Smith's men breached the Confederate line, the rest of the line crumbled. To the west of Smith, one of Schofield's brigades participated in the successful assault on Shy's Hill, but the rest of his men advanced too late to participate in the fighting. With their flank turned by Wilson, and their center broken by Smith, the Confederates had fled before Schofield's men even reached them. Wood's men, seeing Union flags flying from the Confederate works to their west, spontaneously moved forward to attack the Confederate line, and Steedman's men went forward in turn. By the time they reached the Confederate fortifications, most of the defenders had already retreated, but they managed to capture a number of stragglers and abandoned cannons. The morale in Hood's army was so poor that some of the Confederates did not even attempt to run away but stayed and gave themselves up as prisoners, and some Union regiments took so many prisoners that they found themselves outnumbered by the men they were guarding.[69]

Thomas ordered Wilson to continue forward to block Hood's retreat, and he ordered Schofield to advance west and south in cooperation with Wilson. Schofield moved slowly and provided little assistance to Wilson, who pursued the fleeing Confederates until just after sunset. At 10:00 P.M. rain began to fall once again, and it soon turned into a raging storm. The Federal soldiers encamped on the field, while the Confederates marched south through the night, placing miles between themselves and the Union army.[70]

As he was directing his cavalry's pursuit, Wilson met up with Thomas, who had ridden out to confer with him. Elated with his success, Thomas galloped up to Wilson and shouted, so loud that "he might have been heard a quarter of a mile" away, "Dang it to hell, Wilson, didn't I tell you we could lick 'em? Didn't I tell you we could lick 'em?" Wilson wrote later that Thomas, who "was famed as one of the most reserved" and "most dignified men," and who "never used profane language," "on this occasion he said 'dang it' with all the vehemence of an old dragoon." Thomas's near profanity on this occasion showed how "deeply wounded" he had been by the impatience and lack of trust showed him by Grant, Halleck, and Stanton. Thomas ordered Wilson to continue the pursuit as long as he could that evening, and to resume it as early as possible the next day. Thomas then rode off to Nashville.[71]

CHAPTER FIFTEEN

Victory and Frustration

Gentlemen, the question is settled; Negroes will fight. . . . This proves
the manhood of the Negro.

Thomas's victory at Nashville was one of the most complete battlefield
victories of the Civil War and should have been the crowning triumph
of his career. But Thomas almost immediately ran into problems. Failing
to cut off Hood's army during its retreat, he thus crippled the Army of
Tennessee but did not quite destroy it. His performance in managing the
pursuit and his decision to put his army into winter quarters convinced
Grant that Thomas was too slow and unaggressive to be trusted with
further commands. Thomas spent the rest of the war as a departmental
commander in Nashville, with no field command of his own, while his
soldiers went on missions under other commanders.

The initial results of the Battle of Nashville were all positive. On
December 16 Thomas reported that he had captured so many prisoners
and cannons that he had not yet been able to count them all, and that "the
woods, fields, and entrenchments are strewn with the enemy's small arms,
abandoned in their retreat." When Thomas was able to tally the results of
the battle, the numbers were impressive. The Confederates lost 1,500 men
killed and wounded, and the Union army captured 4,400 Confederate
prisoners and fifty-three pieces of artillery, while suffering losses of about
3,000 killed, wounded, and missing.[1]

Thomas's victory was lauded by Northern newspapers. The *Chicago
Tribune*'s headline announced, "Glorious Victory at Nashville—Hood's
Army Completely Routed by Thomas." The *New York Herald* called the

battle "the handsomest victory of the war," and the *New York Times* called Thomas's attack "splendidly successful." The *Chicago Tribune* praised Thomas's decision to wait at Nashville until he was ready, stating that "Thomas did indeed get Hood where he wanted him." "Long will the rebels rue the day," the paper proclaimed, "that Hood set out to cross the Cumberland and carry the war into Tennessee." The *Louisville Journal* compared "the cool and hardy old veteran" to a chess-master, directing the battle from the heights around Nashville with ease and coolness. "It was military science employed to perfection," wrote the *Journal*, "it was a hero who had reputation and honor at stake. . . . it was a mind filled with more plans than a clock with wheels, and final, decisive victory the key."[2]

A group of Nashville's prominent citizens tried to present Thomas with a gift of silver plate as recognition of his victory, and groups in Cincinnati and Louisville tried to collect money to present him as a gift. Thomas thanked them for their appreciation but refused the gifts, telling them they should use the money instead to establish a relief fund for disabled soldiers and the widows and orphans of men killed in the war. Thomas made a general practice of declining private gifts, although he did accept a few gifts from colleagues in the military. These included a ceremonial sword given to him by one of the regiments that fought with him at Mill Springs, a pair of silver spurs sent to him by Gen. William Landrum, and a jeweled badge of the Army of the Cumberland that a group of volunteer officers presented to him shortly after the end of the war.[3]

Stanton praised Thomas for his "admirable skill" in bringing about a "great and decisive victory," and the Union armies at Richmond and in the Shenandoah Valley each gave Thomas a two-hundred-gun salute.[4] On December 24 Lincoln nominated Thomas for the rank of major general in the regular army. Thomas was still bitter, however, at the lack of confidence the administration had shown him before the battle. According to one source, when Thomas received the dispatch announcing his promotion, he cast it aside in disgust. According to another, he stated, "I suppose it is better late than never, but it is too late to be appreciated; I earned this at Chickamauga." A fellow officer wrote in January 1865 that Thomas "feels very sore at the rumored intentions to relieve him, and the Major-Generalcy does not cicatrize the wound. You know Thomas is morbidly sensitive, and it cut him to the heart to think that it was contemplated to remove him." Thomas later told Van Horne, "I thought, after what I had done in the war, that I ought to be trusted to decide when the battle should be fought. I thought I knew better when it should be fought than any one could know as far off as City Point, Virginia."[5]

Sherman congratulated Thomas in a letter written from Savannah on December 25. "I do not believe your own wife was more happy at the result than I was," Sherman wrote. "Had any misfortune befallen you I should have reproached myself for taking away so large a proportion of the army and leaving you too weak to cope with Hood. But as events have turned out my judgment has been sustained, but I am none the less thankful to you, and to Schofield, and to all, for the very complete manner in which you have used up Hood." Sherman urged Thomas to pursue Hood as rapidly as possible, and to advance into Alabama, where his army could live off the country. He added a few personal notes, reminiscing about the time he and Thomas had served together at Charleston in the 1840s, and giving Thomas news of some of their army friends. "Whilst you are freezing to death in Tennessee," Sherman joked, "we are basking in a warm sun, and I fear I did you personal injustice in leaving you behind whilst I made my winter excursion. But next time, I will stay at home and let you go it."[6]

Thomas did not rest after his victory at Nashville but immediately turned his attention to the pursuit of Hood's defeated army. Because he was tired, after the days of preparation and fighting, he made a significant error in coordinating the pursuit. On the night of December 16, Thomas wrote an order for the pontoon train to move south from Nashville on the Murfreesboro Pike, and head for Brentwood and Columbia. Since the Murfreesboro Pike did not go to Brentwood and Columbia, Thomas had clearly meant to write the Franklin Pike, but he had just awoken from a deep sleep when he wrote the order, and his fatigue caused him to err. Neither Thomas's staff officers nor the officer in charge of the pontoon trains caught the mistake, and the next day the pontoon train marched off along the Murfreesboro Pike. During the day the officer in charge of the pontoon train realized he was going in the wrong direction, and he tried to use a small country road to cross over to the Franklin Pike. The heavy rains had made the road impassable, and the pontoon wagons got stuck in the mud. It took some time to get the wagons out, and they then had to backtrack to Nashville and start over again down the Franklin Pike. The pontoons did not reach the front of the army until December 21.[7]

Thomas never mentioned his error with the pontoon train in his final report. Instead, he ascribed the delay in crossing the Harpeth River to the poor quality of the roads, the poor quality of the pontoon bridge, which had been "hastily constructed at Nashville," and the "incompleteness of the [pontoon] train." He added that "the splendid pontoon train properly belonging to my command, with its trained corps of pontoniers, was absent with General Sherman." This evasiveness and dishonesty, which was out of character for Thomas, indicates how embarrassed he was by his mistake.[8]

Thomas gave Wilson's cavalry the main role in pursuing the Confederate army, and they began their pursuit early on the morning of December 16. At 9:00 A.M. Wilson reached the Franklin Pike at Hollow Tree Gap, about five miles north of Franklin, and fought his way past the Confederate rearguard. He arrived at the Harpeth just in time to see the Confederate rearguard destroy the bridge over the river after the last of the Confederate supply wagons moved across it. His men eventually found a ford over the river and fought another battle with the Confederate rearguard just south of Franklin. Thomas had sent Wood's infantry to support Wilson, but by the time the foot soldiers reached the river, the heavy rains had raised the level, making it too high to ford. Wilson was also deprived of the part of his command he had sent along the Franklin Pike, in accordance with Thomas's orders. As Wilson had feared, the troops that took this longer route did not catch up with his main force until the end of the day. Wilson continued southward and fought a third battle with the Confederate rearguard that afternoon but could not reach the main Confederate army.[9]

Thomas moved his headquarters to Franklin on December 17 and tried to send infantry to support Wilson's. But with the pontoon train stuck near the Murfreesboro Pike, the infantry had to wait the entire night of December 17–18 for the engineers to construct a temporary bridge over the Harpeth. Another heavy rainfall began on the afternoon of December 18, which further delayed the Union pursuers. On December 19 Wilson had to stop to construct a temporary bridge across Rutherford Creek, a tributary of the Duck River, and on December 20 he was blocked by the Duck River and had to wait for the pontoon bridge. This arrived on December 21, but the assembly of the bridge was delayed by the weather and by Nathan B. Forrest's cavalry, which fired on the pontoon engineers from the south side of the river. Wood's infantry and Wilson's cavalry did not complete their crossing of the Duck River until December 24.[10]

Meanwhile, Thomas's superiors in Washington had become frustrated with his failure to catch Hood's army. On December 21 Halleck urged Thomas to move more quickly, and Thomas responded angrily. "Pursuing an enemy through an exhausted country, over mud roads, completely sogged with heavy rains, is no child's play," he wrote, "and cannot be accomplished as quickly as thought of." The next day, Stanton and Grant assured Thomas of their confidence in him, although Grant did urge Thomas to "push and do all we can."[11]

After crossing the Duck River, Wilson hurried to catch up with the Confederate army but fell into a series of ambushes laid for him by Forrest, the commander of the Confederate rearguard. After being defeated by Forrest on December 25 and 26, Wilson called off his pursuit. His men were tired, cold, and hungry, and their horses were exhausted. They had pushed far ahead of the infantry, only to find that they were not able to handle Forrest without infantry support. By the time the infantry caught up with Wilson, the main Confederate army was too far away to reach.

Thomas still had two more chances to catch Hood before he crossed the Tennessee River. He had earlier sent a force of gunboats, under the command of Admiral S. P. Lee, to destroy Hood's pontoon bridge at Florence, Alabama, and prevent him from crossing the Tennessee. This attempt failed, as Lee found the too low to be navigable. Thomas also sent Steedman's force on a roundabout route that he thought might enable it to get ahead of Hood's army. He sent Steedman's men by road and rail through Murfreesboro to Decatur, Alabama, from whence Thomas intended them to travel by boat down the Tennessee River and get in the rear of Hood's army. Steedman's advance was delayed by the bad weather and poor roads, just as Wilson's was, and he did not arrive at Decatur until December 27. He was too late. On December 28 Hood's army crossed the Tennessee River near Florence, fifty miles downstream, and reached safety.[12]

Thomas blamed Hood's escape on the weather, and on the fact that he had been forced to attack prematurely, before he could organize his forces properly and mount his cavalry. In a January 9, 1865, letter to William S. Rosecrans, Thomas stated that "nothing but the intolerable weather and imperfect organization of my forces prevented me from destroying Hood's army entirely." He told James Garfield that he blamed the inadequate preparation of his cavalry, and the pressure that forced him to attack prematurely, for Hood's escape. "Having sufficient stores in Nashville," he explained, "I felt perfectly easy, and was working hard to get up a cavalry force of sufficient strength to completely destroy Hood's army. . . . But in this instance, as in all others during my military life, I was not permitted to exercise my best judgment." The deficiency in cavalry prevented Thomas from getting a large enough force in Hood's rear during the battle, and this made it possible for Hood's army to escape. "I regret this very much," Thomas concluded, "for besides the satisfaction I should have felt at the success, the enemy would have lost their most formidable army in the Southwest."[13] Thomas's explanation is unconvincing, as it is difficult to see how one or two thousand more cavalry would have made much of a difference in the campaign, and equally difficult to imagine Thomas getting many more additional cavalry mounted than that, regardless of how long he waited in Nashville.

Thomas made different comments about his pursuit of Hood after Nashville at different times. In an 1867 letter to Dennis Hart Mahan, Thomas claimed that he had enough time to prepare his army for the pursuit, and as a result, "Hood's army, broken and demoralized by his defeat in front of Nashville, was pursued and harassed for a greater distance than any other Confederate Army was during the war."[14] Thomas later concluded that he made his most significant error on the battle's first day. In an informal lecture before a small group of officers and politicians in Washington, Thomas explained that he could have captured Hood's army despite his deficiencies in cavalry if he had detached a large force from his main army on the first day of battle and sent it into Hood's rear to cut off his retreat. One of the audience members, Senator L. F. S. Foster, urged Thomas not to be so critical of himself, pointing out that if Thomas had weakened his attacking force in this way, he would not have been assured of carrying Hood's line. The senator stated that Thomas "did not at all yield to my suggestions; he said that a general must be prepared to take some risks, and that Hood's army ought all to have been captured."[15]

In reality, Thomas's pursuit failed in part due to his own errors, in part due to the poor weather and roads, and in part due to the same difficulty that all Civil War armies had in exploiting battlefield victories. Pursuing and retreating armies moved at the same pace, a walk, and retreating armies could slow their pursuers by destroying bridges and fighting delaying actions with cavalry. Furthermore, a retreating army fell back on its own supply line, while a pursuing force tended to outrun its own supplies. While Thomas did make some mistakes in his pursuit, his record is not

VICTORY AND FRUSTRATION 287

worse than that of other Civil War generals. There are very few examples of successful pursuits after victory in any theater of the Civil War.[16]

While Thomas did not trap the Confederate army, by pressing the pursuit he inflicted further damage on Hood's force. The rain and icy weather slowed the Union pursuers, but it took a terrible toll on Hood's hungry, poorly clothed soldiers. Many soldiers threw away their muskets along the route, and some units lost all cohesion and degenerated into numerous small bands of stragglers. Hundreds of soldiers deserted or surrendered during the march, and others died of illness, cold, and exhaustion. By the time Hood's men reached Alabama, his army had ceased to function as an effective force. Union control over Tennessee was now certain, and Mississippi, Alabama, and Georgia were almost undefended.[17]

After Hood crossed the Tennessee River on December 28, Thomas called a halt to the campaign. Hood moved the remnants of his command to Tupelo, Mississippi, while Thomas put his army into winter quarters and reoccupied the garrisons in Tennessee. Hood had left Alabama in November with 38,000 men, and he returned with fewer than 14,000. He lost 8,600 killed and wounded at Franklin and Nashville, and 17,000 more to illness, capture, and desertion during his advance and retreat. Hood submitted his resignation in January, and Jefferson Davis sent Lt. Gen. Richard Taylor to replace him.[18]

The Battle of Nashville had a decisive impact on the war. By defending Tennessee from invasion, Thomas validated Sherman's strategy of ignoring the Confederate army and raiding through Georgia and the Carolinas. Thomas nearly destroyed the Confederacy's second-largest army, which left Georgia, Mississippi, and Alabama undefended. The Union took advantage of this vulnerability in the spring, sending cavalry and infantry forces to raid throughout these states and capture the port of Mobile.

The Battle of Nashville also had a decisive impact on Thomas's view of African Americans, both as soldiers and as human beings. Thomas had supported the recruitment of African American troops, but thought they lacked the courage and discipline to make first-rate soldiers. At Nashville his lack of white troops forced him to use African American troops in battle, and their courageous performance forced Thomas to rethink his opinions.[19]

On December 17 Thomas rode over the battlefield with James Steedman and Thomas Morgan, reviewing the events of the previous two days.

He had not been to this portion of the battlefield on December 15 and 16 and had not seen the African American soldiers in action. What he saw on December 17 affected him strongly. The bodies of black Union soldiers lay in heaps along the battlefield, mingled with the bodies of white soldiers who had also participated in the assault. Many of the corpses lay in piles before the Confederate works, indicating that the black soldiers had died while trying to capture the enemy position. Turning to his staff officers, he said, "Gentlemen, the question is settled; Negroes will fight." Later, Thomas remarked, "This proves the manhood of the Negro."[20]

While the bravery of African American soldiers caused many white Unionists to change their views on race, this reaction was by no means universal. How individuals interpreted and reacted to the achievements of black soldiers depended partly on the attitudes they held before the war began, and partly on their ability to abandon old prejudices in the face of new evidence. For those white Unionists who did not serve directly with black soldiers, the newspapers they read were also an important factor. Republican newspapers tended to emphasize the bravery and success of black soldiers, while Democratic newspapers focused on the soldiers' failures. Overall, African Americans performed well during the Civil War, but there were some examples of atrocities, poor discipline, and poor battlefield performance by black troops. Racial conservatives, who sought confirmation of their prejudices, were generally able to find it.

By the end of 1864, black soldiers had fought bravely in a number of engagements, including the battles of Port Hudson and Milliken's Bend in Louisiana, the attack on Fort Wagner in Charleston Harbor, and a series of battles in Florida, but they had performed poorly in other situations, such as the Battle of the Crater in Petersburg. Historical evidence indicates that their failure at the Battle of the Crater was the fault of poor leadership, not of the soldiers, but contemporary observers who wanted to believe that blacks made poor soldiers seized on this battle as evidence. Like many whites, Thomas was initially skeptical of the claims that some journalists and politicians made for black military success. Only after seeing the evidence with his own eyes was he willing to acknowledge the discipline and courage of African American soldiers.[21]

Thomas's change of heart was late in coming, but it was significant, lasting, and profound. The scope of his change of views is demonstrated by his actions during Reconstruction, years in which Thomas took an extremely active role in protecting the rights of freedmen. Thomas's change of heart was also unusual, as most white Southern Unionists remained conservative on racial issues throughout the war.[22] Part of the difference between Thomas and other Southern Unionists was his direct contact with black troops. As Southern Unionists usually did not get along well with African American soldiers, most commanders kept African American regiments and Southern Unionist regiments separated, and very few line officers in black regiments came from the South.

The other difference between Thomas and other Southern Unionists stems from the values he held as a career army officer. As a professional soldier, Thomas valued courage, self-discipline, and devotion to duty, and he considered these virtues to be among the highest moral qualities that a person could possess. His low opinion of blacks, and his reluctance to use black soldiers in combat, had resulted from his opinion that they lacked these qualities, a view common among Southerners but particularly strong with Thomas because of his experience of Nat Turner's Rebellion. Turner's men had murdered white civilians but had dispersed and run away when they met with organized resistance. Thomas viewed blacks as violent and dangerous, but not capable of discipline and courage under fire.

At Nashville, however, black soldiers not only met white standards of discipline, courage, and duty, but exceeded them. Some of the white units involved in Steedman's attack broke and fled, but all of the black regiments continued the attack, despite suffering extremely heavy casualties. The soldiers' courage and discipline proved to Thomas that blacks possessed the moral attributes that he considered fundamental to full humanity. While some of Thomas's later comments may indicate that he still thought blacks were inferior to whites intellectually, he also seemed to attribute this inferiority to the effects of slavery, not to innate racial differences. In any case, Thomas came to think that African Americans had shown themselves, through military service, to be true men, and that they therefore deserved to be treated as full citizens. For the rest of his life, Thomas strongly supported civil, political, and legal equality for African Americans.

As the year 1865 began, Thomas began to consider his army's next offensive, planning to rest his men and rebuild his supply lines in preparation for a decisive campaign in the spring. Since Grant and Sherman had done the same thing the previous winter, Thomas did not expect to be criticized for his decision. But the war was different now, and neither Grant nor Sherman had stopped campaigning during the winter months. Grant was still actively trying to break through Lee's fortifications around Richmond, and Sherman was raiding northward through the Carolinas. Both Sherman and Grant were concerned that if Thomas did go into winter quarters, the Confederates would be able to move men from Hood's army to Richmond or the Carolinas. This actually did happen, as Jefferson Davis sent two of the Army of Tennessee's three corps by rail to South Carolina, where they later formed part of a force that opposed Sherman. The two corps left Mississippi in late January, leaving behind only a single corps of infantry and Forrest's cavalry to oppose Thomas's entire army.[23]

Halleck, Grant, and Sherman all pushed Thomas to continue active operations during the winter. Halleck wrote Thomas on December 31 telling him to get his forces in readiness to continue southward as soon as possible. Thomas replied that he would comply as best he could but stressed that his army needed to rest and refit before beginning a new campaign. Halleck then wrote Sherman, praising Thomas for his success against Hood, but stating that Thomas was "too slow for an effective pursuit" and incapable of living off the enemy's country. Grant agreed and also criticized Thomas for remaining in the rear of the army after the Battle of Nashville and not directing the pursuit personally from the front. In late December Schofield wrote to Grant and Sherman to state that Thomas had more troops than he needed, and to ask that his own corps be sent east where it could fight with Grant or Sherman.[24]

Halleck, Grant, and Sherman all agreed that Thomas's army should be broken up into smaller forces and sent on raids throughout the western Confederacy. During the months of January and February, the three generals discussed how best to do this, leaving Thomas out of their discussions, and agreeing that Thomas should not be given personal command of any of the raids. They decided that some of Thomas's men should be sent to support Gen. Edward R. S. Canby's campaign against Mobile, and that others should be sent on an extended raid through Alabama, targeting the cities of Selma and Montgomery.[25]

In mid-January Grant ordered Schofield's corps to leave Thomas's army and go to Annapolis, from whence he planned to send his corps to North Carolina by sea and have it meet up with Sherman. This order came as a surprise to Thomas, who had recently ordered Schofield's corps to

Eastport, Mississippi, in preparation for a new campaign. Later that month, Grant ordered Thomas to send Smith's infantry corps and a division of Wilson's cavalry to General Canby, for use in his Mobile campaign, and to send three thousand cavalry, under the command of General Stoneman, on a raid into western Virginia and the Carolinas.[26] Unaware that Grant, Sherman, and Halleck were making plans without him, Thomas wrote Sherman on February 5 and proposed either to lead his army against Selma and Montgomery or to march through western North Carolina to Richmond, depending on Grant and Sherman's plans. While he was "as anxious as anybody to strike crushing blows to the enemy," Thomas did not want to start his advance until March 1, as he felt that the poor conditions of the roads made it pointless to attempt anything before then.[27]

On February 14 Grant instructed Thomas to send a force of five thousand cavalry, under Wilson's command, on a raid into northern Alabama that would coincide with Canby's advance on Mobile.[28] Grant thus divided Thomas's army into three offensive forces, none of which would be commanded by Thomas himself. Despite Grant's constant urging for these expeditions to begin as soon as possible, none of them started until the middle of March, due to supply difficulties, a shortage of horses, and rainy weather. In a March 16 letter to Sherman, Grant excused his own inaction around Richmond by saying that the roads there were impassable, but blamed the delays in the western campaigns on Thomas, whom he called "slow beyond excuse."[29]

While Grant's criticisms of Thomas were unfair, his decision to divide Thomas's command was justified by the strategic situation at the time. Thomas had defeated Hood so thoroughly that his army had almost ceased to exist as an effective force, and in January two-thirds of the remnants of that army had been sent to the Carolinas. With no large Confederate army in the area, there was no reason to keep Thomas's army together. In effect, Thomas had become a victim of his own success, as he had defeated Hood so soundly at Nashville that there was no longer anything in his department for a large army to do. Thomas did not see things this way, however, and deeply resented having his command taken from him.[30]

For the next three months Thomas remained at Nashville, supporting and coordinating the movements of Wilson and Stoneman. In February and March he arranged for the cavalry leaders to get the horses, supplies, and equipment they needed, and he consulted with them about the goals of their campaigns. While Grant had suggested that Wilson undertake his raid with five thousand men, Thomas proposed to double that number. Wilson wanted to take an even larger force, and after consulting with Wilson in person, Thomas agreed that he should make his raid with a force of fourteen thousand men, nearly all of the cavalry in the theater.[31]

On March 7 Grant told Thomas to move infantry to East Tennessee, in preparation for a possible move eastward into Virginia or North Carolina. Grant anticipated that Lee might evacuate Richmond and head west, with the goal of joining Johnston's army in North Carolina, and he wanted Thomas to be ready to block him. On April 2 Lee did abandon Richmond and march westward, but Grant was able to intercept him without Thomas's assistance. On April 9 Lee surrendered his army at Appomattox Court House, ending the war in Virginia.[32]

In the meantime, Wilson raided into Alabama and Georgia, destroying property and military supplies in Selma, Montgomery, and Macon. He was opposed by Forrest's cavalry, but Forrest's command had been so weakened by protecting Hood's retreat that December that it could offer little resistance.[33] Stoneman's raid into western Virginia and North Carolina went almost unopposed and inflicted extensive destruction on the railroads and supplies in the area. Canby's attack on Mobile met with tenacious opposition, but on April 12, after several days of heavy fighting, he captured the city. By this time it was clear that the war was over. Wilson and Stoneman stopped destroying railroads and property, and Canby stopped at Mobile instead of advancing northward into Alabama. When the forces opposing Sherman in North Carolina surrendered on April 26, the war east of the Mississippi came to an end.[34]

Thomas spent the next month making arrangements for the surrender of the numerous small Confederate forces in his department. He also coordinated the efforts to capture Jefferson Davis, who had fled Richmond with his cabinet and the Confederate treasury. Davis was attempting to flee to Florida or Texas to continue the struggle, and either escape route would take him through the area under Thomas's command. Thomas warned his subordinate officers to look out for Davis, adding that if he escaped, "he will prove himself a better general than any of his subordinates." A detachment of Wilson's cavalry captured Davis near Irwinville, Georgia, on May 10. Three weeks after Davis's capture, the Confederate forces in the trans-Mississippi theater surrendered, and the defeat of the Confederacy was complete.[35]

As Thomas's military duties drew to a close, the scope of his civil and political duties expanded. The collapse of the Confederate government had left the South in anarchy, and the federal government had not come up with a policy for the administration of the conquered South. In the absence of clear guidance, Thomas made a series of temporary decisions, with the goal of restoring order and alleviating suffering in the area under his command. On April 13 Thomas issued an order stating that local judges, sheriffs, commissioners, and justices of the peace in his department should continue to perform their duties according to the laws that existed in their states prior to the state's secession. He also promised local civilian authorities military assistance and protection. Where there were vacancies in local governments, Thomas authorized the "loyal people" of a county or town to hold elections.[36]

Lincoln was assassinated on April 14, and his vice president, Andrew Johnson, was elevated to the presidency. There is no record of Thomas's reaction to Lincoln's assassination, although one can assume that he shared the feelings of shock and sorrow that most Americans felt. Thomas knew Johnson well, having worked with him throughout the war, and Johnson liked and respected Thomas.[37] As the nation's postwar president, Johnson would have great influence over the policy taken toward the conquered South, and his record indicated that he would treat former secessionists harshly.

Self-educated, and from a poor family, Andrew Johnson had risen through the ranks of Tennessee politics, serving before the Civil War as a state congressman and senator, as a U.S. congressman and senator, and as the governor of Tennessee. At the time the Civil War broke out, Johnson was one of Tennessee's senators, and he was the only senator from a seceded state to remain loyal to the Union. Johnson was known for his tendency to become involved in factional fights within his own party, and for the vicious attacks he made on his enemies. Thomas was one of the few people who had managed to disagree with Johnson but still retain his friendship.[38]

Johnson's political base lay in East Tennessee, and his political opinions were similar to those of his constituents. East Tennessee is a mountainous area, where plantation agriculture was not productive and few people owned slaves. Johnson and his constituents resented the domination of the white planter class over Southern politics, but their dislike of slave owners did not translate into an affection for blacks. On the contrary, they resented slave owners for bringing blacks, whom they considered inferior and dangerous, into white communities. Johnson had opposed secession, and he blamed the Civil War on the slaveholding aristocracy who, in Johnson's view, had forced their views on the poor white men of the South. During the war Johnson had often spoken in favor of punishment for the secessionist "traitors," and most people expected that his Reconstruction policy would be harsh.

The last months of the war were a frustrating time for Thomas personally, despite the success of the Union cause. Instead of being rewarded for his defeat of Hood, Thomas found himself shunted aside in discussions of strategy and saw his army broken up to serve under other commanders. With the Confederate surrender, he faced a new set of tasks under a new president. His new role as military commander in the conquered South would involve him increasingly in politics, putting his commitment to civil rights to a series of tests. While he knew the future would be difficult, Thomas was convinced that military defeat had shown Southerners the error of their ways and that they would now obey the national authority. Thomas looked to the future with optimism, convinced that the nation's worst trial was over.

CHAPTER SIXTEEN

Occupation

In all civil proceedings hereafter, the Negro must be regarded and treated as a free man.

As the war ended in April and May of 1865, Thomas found himself thrust into an overtly political role as the commander of the Department of the Cumberland, entrusted with maintaining order and protecting citizens in a violent and politically contentious environment. His experience commanding African American troops at Nashville had profoundly changed his views of blacks, as their courage and discipline under fire convinced him that African Americans fully deserved the rights and protections of citizenship. Thomas tried to protect blacks from white oppression despite the fact that the new president, Andrew Johnson, held blacks in contempt and did little to help them. Thomas struggled during this period between his own idea of what was right and his duty as a military officer to obey civilian authority.

In the chaotic weeks after Lincoln's assassination, President Johnson did not establish a formal Reconstruction policy, and Thomas followed his own judgment in administering the territory under his control. On April 29, 1865, Thomas wrote Stanton that the condition of the people in the area under his command was "deplorable" and asked that the government adopt a consistent program of administration and reconstruction of the conquered South. Thomas wanted to send one of his subordinate officers, George Stoneman, to Washington, to explain Thomas's views on how the South should be governed. On May 2 Thomas recommended to Stanton that military governors be appointed for Georgia and Alabama, and that local elections be allowed for county offices in those states.[1]

While Thomas supported letting Southerners hold local elections, he also wanted to ensure that the rights of blacks would be protected. In the absence of a federal policy, Thomas temporized, issuing an order to the people of Georgia advising them that their local officers should continue in office and should enforce the laws of the state as they existed before the war. He made one significant exception, however, by invalidating the laws dictating different treatment to blacks. "In all civil proceedings hereafter," Thomas ordered, "the Negro must be regarded and treated as a free man."[2]

Thomas worked to alleviate the suffering of the people living in the area under his command, many of whom were now destitute and starving. He had his soldiers distribute the food that had been kept in Confederate government storehouses but directed his subordinates to remind the Southern people that they had lost all rights to this food when they gave it to the Confederate government. Southerners "should be thankful," he stated, "that the United States Government elects to distribute this corn, rather than to require them to divide with the poor of their section what of subsistence they still have in their private possession." Thomas also distributed food from U.S. government stores.[3]

Thomas's friendship with Sherman had been strained by his interactions with the War Department after Nashville, as he suspected that Sherman had supported the decision to deny Thomas a significant command. In a May letter to Sherman, Thomas wrote that his "only desire" was "to have a sufficient duty assigned to me to perform, that I may not tread on the toes of anybody, and be enabled to keep within my own bounds." Thomas complimented Sherman on the success of his campaign through Georgia and the Carolinas. "Although you may consider my congratulations on your brilliant campaigns against Savannah and Raleigh rather late," Thomas wrote, "they are nevertheless offered with the greatest sincerity and pleasure, and would have been given before had I deem[ed] it at all necessary to give you any additional evidence of my friendship." While Thomas's letter asserts his friendship, the polite, formal language contrasts strongly with the chatty and informal nature of the two men's earlier correspondence, indicating that Thomas knew Sherman had undercut his position within the army.[4]

In May 1865 Johnson asked Thomas to come to Washington and share his views on Reconstruction. Before he left, Thomas held a grand review of the forces at Nashville. This review was a farewell ceremony for

Thomas's men, most of whom were being mustered out of volunteer service. An officer at the review wrote his wife, "I never knew that cheering was allowed on review, but this time we gave full play to our lungs. General Thomas is liked by the men and they can cheer him with a will. . . . I think that General Thomas' ears are ringing yet with cheers that we gave him."[5]

As Thomas traveled to Washington, Johnson issued two proclamations outlining his plan for Reconstruction. The first proclamation set out the procedures by which participants in the rebellion could be granted pardons and amnesty. The second appointed a provisional civilian governor for North Carolina and set out rules by which loyal North Carolinians could hold a constitutional convention, ratify a new state constitution, and hold elections. In the weeks that followed, Johnson recognized the provisional governments already set up by the Lincoln administration in Arkansas, Louisiana, Virginia, and Tennessee and issued Reconstruction proclamations for the six other seceded states, with terms similar to those established for North Carolina.[6]

Johnson's Reconstruction policy turned out to be much more lenient than most people had anticipated. While his proclamations deprived many Southerners of their right to vote and hold office, they allowed secessionists to regain these rights if they received amnesty from the president, and Johnson granted amnesty to nearly every person who applied. Johnson also refused to use federal power to protect blacks' economic and political rights, and allowed Southern state governments to pass laws that discriminated against African Americans.

Johnson ordered the military to remain strictly subordinate to state authorities.[7] In July Johnson wrote to Tennessee governor William Brownlow assuring him that he could call on Thomas to provide military assistance whenever needed for "the execution of the law," "the protection of the ballot box," and "to sustain the civil authority of the state."[8] For states that had not been reconstructed under a loyalist government, Johnson appointed civilian provisional governors, who had the authority to call on the military to provide assistance.[9]

In June 1865 the War Department restructured its command system to accommodate the change from an active war footing to the occupation and rebuilding of the South. A rumor went around that Thomas was going to be transferred out of Tennessee, and the Unionist government appealed to Johnson to keep Thomas in the state. Governor Brownlow wrote Johnson that he regretted the departure of "noble old Thomas," who was "vastly popular" with loyal men in Tennessee, and was also respected by former rebels "for his ability, integrity, and manly bearing." On June 12 the Tennessee legislature drew up a resolution honoring Thomas, which announced that the state would now "adopt him as a Tennessean."[10]

On June 27 the War Department redrew the boundaries of all the U.S. military commands, setting up five military districts: the Atlantic, the Gulf, the Tennessee, the Mississippi, and the Pacific. Thomas was assigned the District of the Tennessee, which included the states of Kentucky, Tennessee, Georgia, and Alabama. At the same time, the government greatly reduced the size of the army, in particular reducing the cavalry, as this was the most expensive branch of the army to maintain and supply. While a reduction in the size of the army was inevitable, the extent of the reduction in force made it difficult to maintain order in the occupied South. Still, Thomas was optimistic about the prospects of Reconstruction, and he wrote to Grant that "with judicious management," he expected "but little trouble in restoring perfect order."[11]

Thomas's first task was putting a stop to the bands of guerrillas and bandits who operated throughout the South. The breakdown of civil order and the constant violence of the war had made it possible for these groups to operate with impunity. While many of the groups called themselves "guerrillas," the Union army considered resistance to be illegal now that the Confederate armies had surrendered, and Thomas and the other generals prosecuted all of the groups as bandits. Thomas gave orders to attack the "bushwhackers" and "drive them out of the country," which one of his subordinates, George Stoneman, interpreted to mean that his men should take no prisoners. Thomas intervened to correct Stoneman, ordering his officers not to execute guerrillas and bandits without a trial, no matter how terrible their crimes had been.[12]

Thomas also took action to protect discharged Union soldiers from arrests and lawsuits. Throughout the occupied South, and particularly in Tennessee, Union veterans returning to formerly secessionist areas faced harassment from their neighbors. Many of them were arrested on charges of murder, theft, or the destruction of property, or were sued for civil damages, for actions they had undertaken while serving in the Union army. Since many of the judges and jury members were former Confederates or Confederate sympathizers, it seemed likely that many former soldiers would be convicted or found liable. To prevent this, Thomas issued an order on September 21, 1865, that prohibited the arrest, imprisonment, or trial of former Union soldiers for any acts committed while performing their military duties.[13] In January 1866 Grant published orders extending similar protections to former Union soldiers throughout the South, and in May 1866 Congress passed a bill protecting former Union soldiers from prosecution, which President Johnson signed into law.[14]

Thomas intervened personally to help two former Union soldiers whose possessions had been seized in an unjust lawsuit. The soldiers could get their property back if they paid a bond, but they did not have enough cash on hand and could not find anyone to loan them the money. In desperation one of them went to Thomas for assistance. Thomas had never met the men, but the knowledge that they were former soldiers of the Army of the Cumberland was enough to get them a personal interview. The soldiers had hoped Thomas would use his military authority to intervene in the civil suit, but Thomas instead went to the office of the justice of the peace in Nashville and pledged his own money toward the bond. "Now, boys, don't get me into any scrape about this," Thomas remarked, as they walked out of the justice's office.[15]

Another one of Thomas's tasks was to preserve peace and order during elections. Tennessee held its first postwar congressional election in late July, in which Unionists ran as Republicans and former secessionists ran as candidates of the new Conservative Party, which later merged into the Democratic Party. Many Conservative candidates condemned the state's Reconstruction constitution as unconstitutional, which condemnation the Republican governor, William Brownlow, considered to be treason. Brownlow had one of the Conservative candidates arrested, and Thomas kept him in jail until the election was over.[16] On Brownlow's request Thomas sent troops to preserve order at the polls in the pro-Confederate areas of middle and western Tennessee, and the election proceeded without violence. Despite Brownlow's efforts the results of the election were discouraging for the Union cause. While voters in Unionist East Tennessee elected Republican congressmen, most of the rest of the state voted for Conservatives.[17]

Thomas's most difficult duty during Reconstruction was the maintenance of peace and order between whites and blacks. Thomas believed that the freedmen had been greatly degraded by the institution of slavery, and that it would take some time for them to recover from its effects. At the same time, he did not believe that blacks were intrinsically incapable of living as free men. In a personal letter to a former colleague, Thomas wrote, "It will take time for the regeneration of the Negro, but he will come out purified by the terrible ordeal to which he has been subjected, and assume an honorable position in the ranks of humanity." While some African Americans would be "too thoroughly infected with the poisonous influence of slavery" to survive, "the remnant will be found to be men, and discharge their duties as citizens in our midst."[18]

Thomas's officers were sometimes called on to help mediate labor disputes between blacks and whites, and Thomas gave instructions to one of his subordinate officers on how to handle these situations. Thomas agreed with his subordinate that the freedmen were "restless," accustomed to "lying and deceit," and unwilling to commit themselves to labor contracts. However, Thomas thought that the freedmen's refusal to work under white supervision was understandable, given "the suspicion and distrust excited in the mind of the Negro by the knowledge that their old masters are bitterly opposed to their emancipation and would, were it in their power, again reduce them to slavery." The problem lay in the unfair terms of the contracts, not in "any inability or indisposition on the part of the Negro to support himself." "It has been demonstrated," Thomas added, "that most slaves, when removed from the influence of their former masters and subjected to the restraints of law and military rule, are found to be not only able but willing to work for their own support."[19]

Thomas looked to the newly established Bureau of Freedmen, Refugees, and Abandoned Lands to formulate rules and regulations to manage black-white relations in the occupied South. Until the Freedmen's Bureau had time to formulate and implement its policies, Thomas recognized that the military had the responsibility to maintain order, punish crime, and provide relief to the needy. As an intermediate measure, Thomas established military commissions to regulate criminal and contract disputes between blacks and whites. He emphasized that the military should "protect with force the Negro in the full enjoyment of his rights as a freeman," but at the same time "compel him to the performance of his engagements to his employer." The military commissions should conform to the laws of the state as they existed prior to the war, with the exception that they should ignore the "barbaric black codes of slavery," and "place all upon the same platform as the white man."[20]

Thomas's views were quite progressive for his time. While he considered blacks to be inferior, he considered their inferiority a result of the effects of enslavement, not necessarily an intrinsic racial characteristic. Whether or not they were inferior, however, Thomas believed that blacks should be treated as equals under the law. He realized that the racial conflict then prevalent was more the fault of the whites than the blacks, and he advocated strong measures to ensure that blacks' economic and political rights would be protected. Some other officers were not as progressive and enforced labor contracts in favor of the white employers, thus forcing blacks to work long hours for subsistence wages, under conditions little better than slavery. While Thomas was not the most progressive of all the Reconstruction commanders, he was well above average in his treatment of the former slaves.

Thomas not only told his subordinates to protect blacks from white injustice but also intervened personally to protect blacks from abuse. In July 1865 local authorities in Columbia, Tennessee, arrested two black schoolgirls on trumped-up charges of trespassing and assault and battery. The two black girls and a white friend had entered a white man's garden to steal some plums. The owner had thrown a rock at them, and the girls had thrown rocks back at the owner, but nobody had been hurt. While the white girl was not charged with any crime, the two black girls were placed in solitary confinement with their bail set at $500, double the maximum allowed by state law.

Thomas surmised that the true purpose of the criminal prosecution was to force the closure of the local freedmen's school by intimidating its students. He responded by arresting the two attorneys who had initiated the charges and suspending from office two of the public officials involved in the case. He then published an order condemning all four of them for their "persecution of the weak and helpless," and their "malignant rebellious spirit." Thomas justified the attorneys' arrest and the officials' suspension by stating that they were "persons dangerous to the peace of the community," and that they would remain in detention or suspended from office until they demonstrated that "they possess a little humanity and a willingness to conform to the laws."[21]

Thomas was strict in his treatment of racist local white authorities, but diplomatic in his interactions with President Johnson. Johnson trusted Thomas and respected his opinion, and by intervening diplomatically with Johnson on behalf of the blacks in his department, Thomas was able to protect them from Johnson's tendency to side with their white persecutors. Throughout 1865 Johnson received many complaints from his former Tennessee constituents about the behavior of freedmen, black soldiers, and Freedmen's Bureau agents. These complaints were largely unfounded, but Johnson credited them, as he habitually took the word of a white Southerner over the word of a black man. Thomas handled Johnson's complaints carefully and sent trusted officers to investigate each of the complaints.

Thomas nearly always concluded that the whites' complaints were unfounded and convinced Johnson that no action was needed. In August, for example, Johnson wrote Thomas that Freedmen's Bureau agents in Nashville and Pulaski were overstepping their authority and abusing the local whites. Thomas investigated the situation and informed Johnson that the complaints were not justified by the facts.[22] In September Johnson wrote Thomas that he had "information of the most reliable character" that black troops in Greenville were "committing depredations through the country," and that they had taken over Johnson's own house in Greenville and turned it into a Negro brothel. After investigating the matter, Thomas once again reported to the president that the allegations were not true.[23]

Johnson wrote Thomas several times to object to having black troops serve in the occupied South, and the president asked Thomas to assign only white troops to occupation duty. Johnson had heard whites complain about the behavior of black troops and also feared that the freedmen were planning an insurrection and that the black soldiers would take their side. Thomas explained to Johnson that the continued use of black troops was unavoidable, because so many white volunteers had been mustered out of service that there were simply not enough white soldiers available. There was not "the least foundation" for fearing a black insurrection, or for fearing that black troops would participate if an insurrection did occur. Thomas wrote this in September, but at the end of the year he did send a contingent of white troops to Memphis in response to widespread rumors that local blacks were going to rise up in an insurrection after Christmas. No insurrection took place, and Thomas never again gave credence to these kinds of rumors.[24]

In his correspondence with Johnson, Thomas asserted that his black soldiers were under excellent discipline, and that when conflicts arose it was usually the case that "the white man has attempted to bully the Negro, for it is exceedingly repugnant to the Southerners to have Negro soldiers in their midst, and some are so foolish as to vent their anger upon the Negro because he is a soldier." Employing only white troops in the South would not put an end to conflict, Thomas wrote, because these troops tended to be hostile to black freedmen. In conclusion, Thomas warned Johnson not to believe the complaints of Southern whites. While the majority of Southern whites were satisfied with the state of affairs, "there are always, in every community, evil-minded persons to whom nothing seems right except when they can have all their whims and caprices satisfied. These, I find, are always ready to misrepresent and exaggerate every event, however trifling, that does not in some manner benefit them."[25]

Thomas's repeated assurances about the conduct of black soldiers seem to have reassured Johnson, as he eventually stopped writing Thomas about the complaints of white Southerners.[26] Thomas's tactful handling of Johnson's complaints also preserved their good working relationship, and on September 8, 1865, Johnson told Thomas that he, along with "the whole South," had confidence in his leadership. Thomas's careful handling of Johnson was important both for his own career and for the fate of the African Americans in his department. Throughout his presidency, Johnson removed commanders that he considered too radical on racial issues and replaced them with more-conservative officers. Thomas was as radical as many of the commanders Johnson removed, but he retained the president's confidence. In doing so, Thomas ensured that he remained in command of the Department of the Cumberland, where he could continue to protect blacks from white violence.[27]

While Thomas disagreed with Johnson's racial prejudices, he followed presidential orders because he believed in the subordination of the military to civilian control. Thomas made independent decisions about political matters during the first chaotic months after Appomattox, but he did so only as an emergency measure. Once Johnson established a policy and appointed civilian governors, Thomas instructed his subordinates to follow the orders of the civil authorities.[28] Thomas was willing to make exceptions, however, where the local authorities were clearly defying the law. In Gallatin, Tennessee, guerrilla bands continued to operate as late as September 1865, with assistance and protection from local residents and officials. Thomas instructed the local commander that he could demand the cooperation of the local sheriff in arresting the guerrillas. He warned the commander, however, to maintain the appearance of cooperation with the sheriff, and not to allow his men to commit any "outrages" or "depredations" against innocent whites.[29]

Thomas did overstep his authority in two controversial cases involving churches in the area under his command. In September 1865 Richard Wilmer, the Episcopal bishop of Alabama, intentionally omitted the customary prayer for the president and the government from his worship service. Thomas deemed this an act of treason, suspended the bishop and all of the clergy under him from office, and ordered all of their churches closed. Thomas stated that this suspension would remain in place until the Episcopal clergy in Alabama resumed prayers for the president and took an oath affirming their allegiance to the United States. Thomas's action created an outrage in the South and considerable opposition in the North, as people considered Thomas to be interfering unlawfully in the free exercise of religion. Refusing to admit he had made a mistake, Thomas kept Wilmer's suspension in force while the bishop appealed the decision. On December 22, 1865, shortly before Wilmer's appeal was to reach President Johnson, Thomas revoked his order, apparently because he was certain that Johnson would take Wilmer's side.[30]

Thomas's order revoking Wilmer's suspension, which he arranged to be published, was not apologetic. Thomas criticized Wilmer for interfering with "the spread of popular approbation and grateful appreciation of the magnanimous policy of the President in his efforts to bring the people of the United States back to their former friendly and national relations with one another." Wilmer had used "the sanctity of his position" to mislead his congregation "back into the labyrinths of treason," and in doing so, Wilmer was "animated with the same spirit through which temptation beguiled the mother of men to the commission of the first sin—thereby entailing eternal toil and trouble on earth." Thomas denied that he was revoking his original order because he considered it incorrect but stated that the order was now unnecessary, as Alabamans had proven themselves able to withstand Bishop Wilmer's treasonous influence. In conclusion, Thomas left Wilmer to "that remorse of conscience consequent to the exposure and failure of the diabolical schemes of designing and corrupt minds."[31]

Thomas also intervened in the affairs of the Methodist church in Georgia. The Methodist leadership removed one of their ministers, John H. Caldwell, after he denounced slavery in his sermons. In September

1865 Thomas ordered the Methodists to reinstate Caldwell. The Methodist elders complained to President Johnson, but Johnson left the matter to Thomas's discretion. In November the Georgia Conference of the Methodist Church upheld the decision to dismiss Caldwell, and Thomas let the matter drop.[32]

Later in November, Thomas went to New York and brought Frances back to live with him in Nashville. Frances had visited in October and November 1864, and again in May 1865, but had been separated from George since that time. Frances stayed with George in his various commands throughout the rest of his life.[33] Thomas was also reunited with Ellen, the slave he had bought in Texas and had left with his family in Virginia. According to Van Horne, Ellen brought with her a husband and children and insisted on staying on as Thomas's servant, despite his efforts to encourage her to live independently. Eventually, Thomas sent Ellen to live with his brother Ben in Vicksburg, Mississippi.[34]

In late 1865 President Johnson asked Thomas to assist him in lobbying the new Southern state governments to support his plan for Reconstruction. This placed Thomas in an awkward position. He believed he had a duty as a military officer to support the president, but at the same time he was personally opposed to Johnson's policies. Johnson had allowed the formerly seceded states to write new constitutions and elect new governments and had allowed most former Confederates to vote and run for office. The secessionist-dominated conventions adopted Constitutions with racially discriminatory provisions, including the denial of black suffrage, and the new state legislatures passed openly discriminatory laws, or "black codes." Many of the new state legislators and governors were former secessionists, including a number of individuals who had held high positions in the Confederate government and army.[35]

Two of the states under Thomas's command did not go through this process. Kentucky had never left the Union, and the Tennessee state government had already been reconstituted during the Lincoln administration. In Tennessee former secessionists were not allowed to vote in state elections, and the state government was controlled by Unionists. However, many county and municipal officials were Conservatives, and the Unionist hold on the state government seemed unlikely to last once the voting rights of former secessionists were restored.[36]

Toward the end of 1865, Johnson sent Thomas to Mississippi, Alabama, and Georgia on a mission to encourage the new state governments to cooperate with Johnson's Reconstruction plan. Johnson wanted the governors and legislatures of these states to guarantee suffrage and basic civil rights to blacks, and to ratify the proposed Thirteenth Amendment abolishing slavery. Thomas advised the governors and legislatures of Mississippi and Alabama to cooperate with Johnson's plan, arguing that they had no choice but to agree to these measures if they expected to be readmitted to representation in Congress. Despite Thomas's efforts, the Mississippi legislature refused to ratify the Thirteenth Amendment, and neither Alabama nor Mississippi passed laws that gave equal status to blacks. Thomas cut his trip short and did not visit Georgia, telling Johnson that he feared that his visit would only cause "uneasiness" among the members of the legislature and hinder the president's efforts.[37]

Throughout 1865 Johnson had implemented his own Reconstruction policy without consulting Congress, because Congress had gone out of session in March and did not meet again until December. At first Johnson's conciliatory policy met with approval in the North, but the election of former Confederates to government positions, and the passage of the Black Codes, caused a change in Northern public opinion. When Congress met again in December, it established the Joint Committee on Reconstruction to consider Johnson's policy and the admission of former Confederate states to representation in Congress. The Committee called on a wide range of witnesses, including Thomas and a number of other senior generals, to testify about conditions in the South.[38]

In December 1865 Thomas was introduced to the House of Representatives by the Speaker of the House, Schuyler Colfax. This was the first time the congressmen had seen Thomas, and they greeted him with an ovation. Colfax, noticing that Thomas's hands "were trembling like an aspen leaf," was surprised to see that Thomas "could bear the shock of battle, but he shrank before the storm of applause."[39]

Thomas testified before the Joint Committee on Reconstruction, speaking mainly about the state of affairs in Tennessee. He reported that Tennessee had largely returned to loyalty to the Union and attributed the violence in the region to "personal animosities and hatreds," not opposition to Federal rule. Thomas predicted that as former secessionists returned to their farms and businesses, they would resume the ways of peace and become loyal citizens once again. Despite his optimism, Thomas warned that affairs were not yet settled. He advocated the

continuation of martial law, the maintenance of a strong Federal occupation force, and the continued suspension of the writ of habeas corpus.[40]

Thomas was also optimistic about race relations and the situation of
Tennessee's freedmen. He reported that the former slaves' condition was
"very favorable at this time," and stated that "there is a general understanding among the Negroes and among the whites" to make fair labor
contracts and to comply with them. He also praised the work of the
Freedmen's Bureau in Tennessee and Kentucky. Thomas's testimony
differed from that of some Union officers who testified before the
committee, a slight majority of whom testified that white employers
treated black laborers unfairly.[41] At Grant's request, Thomas also prepared
a detailed report on instances of interracial violence in the area under his
command, showing that the number of murders and assaults by whites
against blacks greatly exceeded the number of murders and assaults by
blacks against whites.[42]

Thomas's testimony indicated that he expected Reconstruction to
proceed peacefully and quickly, as former Confederates accepted their
defeat and returned to the peaceful, law-abiding ways they had followed
before the war. His optimistic attitude could also be seen in his
recommendation that Federal troops be withdrawn from Alabama. In his
visit to Alabama during early December, Thomas had come away with the
impression that the Alabama legislature was eager to cooperate with
federal policies on Reconstruction. On December 30, 1865, the governor
of Alabama wrote Thomas asking that the federal government provide
the state militia with arms and ammunition, and Thomas forwarded his
request to Grant. As the governor had pledged to defend equally the
rights of "all classes" in the state, Thomas favored granting his request, "as
soon as there can be a perfect understanding between the Freedmen's
Bureau and the civil authorities as to the civil rights and duties of the
Freedman." Grant was less optimistic that the state authorities would treat
the freedmen fairly, and he denied the governor's request.[43]

Thomas left Washington in December 1865 and went to Nashville,
but Grant called him back in January to discuss a bill that would establish
the size and form of the postwar army. George G. Meade and William T.
Sherman were also part of the discussion, and the four generals wrote
the Senate proposing a number of minor, technical changes to the bill.
The law that Congress passed in June authorized an army of slightly fewer

than sixty thousand men, a much larger force than the prewar regular army, but not large enough for the tasks set before it. The law authorized an increase in the number of generals the army could appoint, thus confirming Thomas's promotion to the rank of major general. His superiors included Grant, the only full general in the army; Sherman, a lieutenant general; and Halleck, Meade, and Sheridan, all of whom were major generals with seniority over Thomas.[44]

Thomas found his meeting with Grant, Sherman, and Meade to be frustrating, and he wrote Rosecrans shortly afterward that he expected to have "little if any thing to say or do in the reorganization of the army." He approved of Rosecrans's intention to leave the army and return to private enterprise. "I do not know but that a man in this country does better by remaining out of the army than in it," Thomas wrote, because "generally speaking, officers have attained higher position in the army [entering it] from civil life than from [within] the army." For his own part, however, Thomas added, "I have been so long in the army that I could not live happily out of it, and therefore expect to adjust myself as well as possible." "If I can retain my present rank," he concluded, "I shall be content," as he had become accustomed to his ideas "not [being] considered when they conflict with predetermined plans."[45]

After the Joint Committee on Reconstruction finished hearing testimony about conditions in the South, Congress established its own Reconstruction policy, which differed dramatically from Johnson's. In February 1866 Congress passed a law that expanded the powers of the Freedmen's Bureau, creating special Bureau courts that would hold jurisdiction over cases in which local courts did not provide blacks with fair and equal treatment. The law also provided for the distribution to freedmen of some of the land confiscated from secessionist plantation owners. The bill was considered relatively uncontroversial, and most congressmen had expected Johnson to sign it. When Johnson vetoed the bill, calling it unconstitutional, his action shocked many Republicans.

Congress also passed a civil rights bill, which allowed blacks to bring suit in federal courts for violations of their rights, and designated the military as the agency that would assist U.S. Marshals and other federal officials in serving warrants from federal courts. Johnson also vetoed this bill, but Congress passed it over his veto in April, marking the first time in American history that Congress had overridden a presidential veto of an important piece of legislation. The supporters of the Freedmen's

Bureau Act had a more difficult time achieving a two-thirds majority, and they ultimately had to drop the provision of the law that would grant land to former slaves. The reduced Freedmen's Bureau Act finally passed in July.[46]

Nearly a year passed between the end of the Civil War and the beginning of Congressional Reconstruction. During this period, Thomas had implemented Johnson's lenient Reconstruction policy, and he had intervened with Johnson in defense of the freedmen. Despite numerous setbacks to the cause of blacks' civil and political rights, Thomas still hoped that the Southerners of both races would learn to settle their differences peacefully, once they became accustomed to the new order of things. He was also hopeful that the new Reconstruction Acts passed by Congress would encourage whites to cease resistance to the federal government and obey the law. A peaceful settlement was not forthcoming, however. Whites' violence against blacks escalated in the years to come and became more organized. Thomas found himself fighting a second war in Kentucky and Tennessee against the Ku Klux Klan and other white-supremacist groups, only this time he lacked the military force and political backing to win the fight.

CHAPTER SEVENTEEN

Reconstruction

Everywhere in the states lately in rebellion treason is respectable, and loyalty odious.

The years 1866 to 1868 were difficult ones for Thomas, as he commanded in a region beset by violence and had to cope with the conflict between President Johnson and the Republican Congress over Reconstruction policy. The conflict between the executive and legislative branches presented Thomas with a series of difficult decisions. Thomas had always believed in the subordination of military to civilian authority in political matters, but he now was uncertain of which competing civilian authority to follow. The president and Congress disagreed strongly on Reconstruction policy and gave Thomas conflicting orders. Even within the executive branch, Grant and Stanton often disagreed with the commander in chief. Matters were further complicated once Tennessee was readmitted to the Union, as the state government sometimes disagreed with the federal government, the governor and legislature were often at odds, and local officials, many of whom were former secessionists, defied state and federal authorities.

Thomas felt that it was his duty to follow the orders of the commander in chief of the armed forces, and he did so despite his strong disagreement with Johnson's Reconstruction policy. As time went on, and as the negative consequences of Johnson's Reconstruction policy became clear, Congress began to oppose Johnson more openly, and Grant began to implement Congress's Reconstruction policy instead of Johnson's.

Encouraged by this opposition to Johnson, Thomas, too, began to follow congressional policy as well as his own judgment in enforcing the law.

Political matters became simpler for Thomas when Grant became president, as the Congress and the president then implemented a consistent policy, but matters on the ground became more difficult, as the Ku Klux Klan began systematically to abuse and intimidate freedmen in Tennessee and Kentucky. Thomas attempted to protect African Americans from the Klan, but a lack of resources and the complicity of white local authorities made Thomas's job impossible. As the year 1868 ended, Thomas despaired of ever bringing law and order to the South.

Thomas's difficulties in deciding which civil authority to follow began in the spring of 1866. On April 2 Johnson issued a proclamation declaring the insurrection to be over and the rebellion suppressed. The wording of this proclamation did not specify what the effects of the end of the rebellion would be, but many took it to mean that martial law, the suspension of the writ of habeas corpus, and the use of military courts to try civilians would no longer be allowed. Shortly after issuing the proclamation, Johnson instructed Stanton that martial law was still in place and that military tribunals could still be used, but only as a last resort.[1]

Thomas interpreted Johnson's proclamation to mean that he had very limited authority to implement military law, and his communications to subordinates after April 2 contain repeated instructions not to "interfere" in civil affairs.[2] In any case, the reduction in the size of the army had left Thomas with so few men that it was difficult for him to undertake any effective action. When 1866 began, Thomas had more than twenty-five thousand soldiers under his command. By May all of Thomas's volunteer regiments had been mustered out, leaving him with only four thousand troops to maintain order in the five states of his command.[3] By the middle of 1866 Thomas felt that he lacked both the authority and the manpower to be effective. In a letter to a woman whose Unionist husband was being persecuted by former secessionists, Thomas wrote that he regretted "as much as you can" the current state of affairs, but was "powerless" to correct it. "It is and has been the policy of the President to return to the people of the Southern States all their privileges of citizens," Thomas wrote, "and in furtherance of that policy has removed nearly all the military from them, just sufficient being left to guard the public property."[4]

With the weakening of federal authority, violence against blacks increased throughout the South. On May 1 a race riot broke out in Memphis, sparked by an incident in which black Federal soldiers intervened to prevent the local police from arresting a black civilian. The local whites retaliated, and soon a mob of white civilians, aided by the local police and firemen, invaded and burned the black neighborhood of South Memphis. Over the next three days forty-six blacks and two whites were killed, at least five black women were raped, and hundreds of black homes, churches, and schools were destroyed.[5] The local commander, George Stoneman, badly mishandled the incident, neither reporting the violence to Thomas nor taking action to stop it. By May 3 Thomas had heard about the riot from the newspapers, and he sent a sternly worded telegram to Stoneman ordering him to stop the fighting immediately and disarm all parties. The rioting died down once Stoneman's soldiers intervened.[6]

The Memphis riot, along with other incidents of violence against blacks, aroused widespread anger in the North. These events also encouraged the military leadership to defy Johnson's wishes and take a more active role. On July 3 Grant issued General Order No. 44, which authorized the army to arrest violators of blacks' civil rights whenever the local authorities did not take action.[7] This order gave Thomas more authority to act, and he did so by sending soldiers to arrest guerrillas in Georgia and Mississippi. His efforts were not successful, as he needed cavalry to catch the guerrillas, and he had only one regiment of cavalry in his entire district.[8] Thomas also moved to arrest guerrillas in Tennessee, and he asked Governor Brownlow to call out the Tennessee militia to assist in these efforts.[9]

Thomas favored using military tribunals, as authorized by General Order No. 44, to prosecute the perpetrators of the Memphis riot. He wrote the War Department on August 15 that the leaders of the riot were known, but the local grand jury was not taking any action to indict them. Thomas asked for permission to bring the perpetrators before a military court. Thomas's request went to Johnson, who decided that the civil courts should retain exclusive jurisdiction over the rioters. Thomas was angry, but there was nothing he could do, and the perpetrators of the Memphis riot went unpunished.[10]

Thomas faced another difficult question of civil and military authority when the Tennessee legislature voted on ratification of the Fourteenth Amendment, which would write into the Constitution civil rights protections for blacks. The state senate ratified the amendment, but a number of state representatives absented themselves from the voting, preventing the Tennessee house from achieving a quorum. Governor Brownlow asked Thomas to arrest the absent representatives and force them back to the chamber, and Thomas, unsure whether he had the authority to arrest members of the state legislature, asked Grant for guidance. Thomas criticized the absent representatives for having acted "in a very refractory manner" but did not make it clear whether he favored using Federal troops to arrest them. Grant referred Thomas's question to President Johnson, who directed Thomas not to intervene. In the meantime state authorities located two of the absent representatives and forced them back to the Capitol, thus achieving a quorum and securing the amendment's ratification. Shortly afterward, Congress recognized and seated Tennessee's congressional delegation, completing the state's readmission to the Union.[11]

In August a race riot took place in New Orleans, in which thirty-four blacks and three whites were killed and more than one hundred people were injured.[12] The violence in Memphis and New Orleans discredited Johnson's conciliatory policies and convinced many Northerners that Southern whites were continuing to rebel against the national authority. As a result, Radical Republican candidates did well in the 1866 elections, winning enough seats to gain a majority in Congress.[13] The violence also motivated Grant to adopt a stricter policy toward the South, following congressional intent instead of President Johnson's wishes. Grant's change in policy made it easier for Thomas to take an active role in protecting blacks and white Southern Unionists.[14]

In October Thomas had responded to the criminal prosecution of two black veterans in Murfreesboro, Tennessee, by ordering the Freedmen's Bureau to intervene if the veterans did not receive a fair trial.[15] Later that month, Thomas learned that white local officials in Nashville had begun to arrest African American adults and teenagers for vagrancy and then contract them out as prisoners for forced labor on plantations. Thomas sent his chief of staff, William Whipple, to investigate and take action. The city officials at first refused to cooperate, but when Thomas threatened them with military detention, they changed their minds and let the prisoners go.[16]

On December 15, 1866, the second anniversary of the battle of Nashville, the Tennessee legislature honored Thomas with a ceremony to commemorate his victory. They presented Thomas with a gold medal, which had a picture of Thomas on one side, and a picture of the state capitol on the other, and was inscribed with the words of Thomas's 1863 dispatch from Chattanooga, "I will hold the town till we starve." The legislature also commissioned a portrait of Thomas and displayed it prominently in the capitol building.[17]

Thomas managed to overcome his fear of public speaking and deliver a gracious acceptance speech. He recalled graduating from West Point and receiving an officer's commission almost thirty years before and referred to the oath that he took as an officer to uphold the United States Constitution. "I have faithfully endeavored to keep that oath," he explained, and a vow that he regarded as "a solemn pledge on my part to return to the Government some little service for the great benefit I had received in obtaining my education at the Academy." Thomas briefly recounted the events of the Battle of Nashville, placing less emphasis on his own generalship than on the "gallant assaults" made by his men. "While I cannot venture to speak of myself, without fear of being accused of egotism," Thomas stated, "I can, with pleasure, sincerity, and pride, speak of the brave soldiers and officers" who left civilian life and volunteered for military service. "No other country on earth ever produced such another army as that which assembled to put down the rebellion."[18]

The ceremony celebrating the Battle of Nashville was one of the few bright spots in a difficult year. As 1866 came to an end, Thomas found himself baffled by the lawlessness and violence that persisted in the South. Gangs of armed guerrillas and bandits still operated with impunity, and friends and sympathizers helped them hide from the army while loyal citizens were afraid to get involved. While many of the victims of violent crimes were black, Thomas still considered the motives of the offenders to be personal or monetary, not political or racial. Thomas had always thought of his fellow Southerners as basically honorable, law-abiding people, and he had expected they would return to peaceful activities now that the rebellion had ended. Thomas could not yet understand why the Southern people persisted in violence, and it was only during the following year that Thomas came to understand fully the racial and political motives behind their actions.[19]

Thomas was equally frustrated by white Southerners' continued insistence that secession had been legal and their cause, though lost, had been a just and honorable one. In November 1866 Thomas forbade a series of public ceremonies scheduled for the funeral of former Confederate general Roger W. Hanson in Louisville, Kentucky. Thomas wrote that these ceremonies, which he suspected would take the character of a military parade, would be "insulting to loyal citizens" and "would tend to a breach of the peace." Also, many of the participants in the ceremonies would be former Confederate soldiers, and Thomas considered their participation in a public demonstration that had a military character to be a violation of their paroles. Thomas issued an order prohibiting any "military display" during the funeral ceremony, particularly any display of the Confederate flag.[20]

In January 1867 the citizens of Rome, Georgia, held a public funeral for General Hanson, in which they displayed the Confederate flag. When Thomas heard of the event, he had the men who displayed the flag arrested, and Rome's mayor and city council protested, claiming that the men meant no disrespect or treason to the national government. Thomas wrote an answer on February 9 and arranged for the response to be published in the newspapers:

> In your letter you state that no disrespect was intended to the United States Government by the exhibition of the Confederate flag. . . . If that is the case, it can only be supposed, presuming that they possess ordinary intelligence, that they misunderstand the present "status of affairs," which is that the rebellion has been decided to be a huge crime, embodying all the crimes of the Decalogue, and that it has been conquered and disarmed; and that its very name and emblems are hateful to the people of the United States, and he must be indeed obtuse who expects without offense to parade before the eyes of loyal people that which they execrate, and that their abhorrence of which they have expressed in the most emphatic language in which it is possible for a great nation to utter its sentiments.

Thomas went on to express his own feelings about the nature of the recent war, and his objection to the "Lost Cause" version of the war's history that was already being formulated in the South:

> The sole cause of this, and similar offences, lies in the fact that certain citizens of Rome and a portion of the people of the states

lately in rebellion, do not and have not accepted the situation, and that is that the late civil war was a rebellion and history will so record it. Those engaged in it are, and will be pronounced rebels; rebellion implies treason, and treason is a crime, and a heinous one too, and deserving of punishment, and that traitors have not been punished, is owing to the magnanimity of the conquerors. With too many of the people of the South, the late civil war is called a "revolution," rebels are called "Confederates," loyalists to the whole country are called "d——d Yankees," and "traitors," and over the whole great crime, with its accursed record of slaughtered heroes, patriots murdered because of their true hearted love of country; widowed wives and orphaned children; and prisoners of war, slain amid such horrors as find no parallel in the history of the world, they are trying to throw the gloss of respectability, and thrusting with contumely and derision from their society the men and women who would not join hands with them in the work of ruining their country. . . . Everywhere in the states lately in rebellion treason is respectable, and loyalty odious. This the people of the United States, who ended the rebellion and saved the country, will not permit, and all attempts to maintain the unnatural order of things, will be met by decided disapproval.[21]

Having made his point, Thomas released the men from confinement. Thomas's words were in vain, however, as neither reasoned argument nor the military defeat of the Confederacy would change the minds of most Southerners about the rightness of their cause. Similarly, Southerners considered themselves justified in defying the federal government on matters of civil rights for the freedmen, if the law did not agree with their own views of what was legitimate. Thomas found this attitude toward the law abhorrent and was even more unforgiving of Southern defiance of national law in 1867 than he had been at the time of secession.[22]

A number of observers noted Thomas's hardened attitudes toward Southerners during a trip to Washington he made in January 1867 to confer with Grant on Reconstruction affairs.[23] Rutherford B. Hayes, a Republican congressmen from Ohio, wrote one of his constituents that Thomas was "now known to be all right," and one of Grant's aides observed that Thomas had become a "radical."[24]

Throughout 1867 Thomas worked hard to protect blacks from white violence, exercising considerable independence and initiative in doing so. In a May 6, 1867 letter to a subordinate officer, Thomas detailed his new policy for dealing with racial violence. The officer had asked for guidance on how to prosecute a white terrorist group operating near Fort Donelson, Tennessee, who called themselves "Ghouls." Thomas gave two sets of instructions, depending on whether the "Ghouls" were former Confederate soldiers. If the criminals were former Confederate soldiers, the officer should arrest them and send them to a military trial, on the grounds that they had violated the terms of the paroles they had signed upon the surrender of the Confederate armies. If they were not, the officer should first attempt to assist the local authorities in prosecuting the nightriders. If the local authorities would not cooperate, the officer could place the perpetrators under military arrest and prosecute them under General Order No. 44.[25]

Thomas used this parole violations tactic in several other cases that spring and summer. The legality of Thomas's arrests was uncertain, as it could be argued that the Confederate paroles were no longer binding after Johnson's April 1866 proclamation that the rebellion had ended.[26] In August a man arrested for violating his parole challenged his arrest on these grounds by filing a writ of habeas corpus in federal court.[27] The arrested man, a former Confederate soldier named William A. Milliken, had accused a former Union officer of helping blacks organize politically and had threatened to kill him. A local court convicted Milliken but punished him with only a five-dollar fine, so Thomas placed Milliken in military detention. The federal attorney, a Johnson loyalist who was hardly sympathetic toward blacks' lack of political rights, wanted to drop the charges against Milliken instead of opposing his habeas petition, but Thomas wanted to establish a precedent and insisted on going forward.[28] Realizing that the federal attorney would not be zealous in prosecuting the case, Thomas hired Barbour Lewis, one of the most prominent attorneys in Memphis, to act as primary counsel.[29]

The Milliken case attracted national attention, and many prominent Memphis attorneys attended the hearings. Despite extensive efforts by Lewis, the U.S. district court judge ruled in Milliken's favor, stating that paroled Confederate soldiers were no longer under military court jurisdiction after Johnson's proclamation of April 2, 1866. Thomas wanted to appeal the federal court's decision to the U.S. Supreme Court, but the attorney general, acting on the orders of President Johnson, refused to file an appeal.[30] Thomas was actively involved in the prosecution of the Milliken case, and his letter to the adjutant general arguing that the judge had ruled incorrectly and encouraging the government to appeal shows that Thomas had a sophisticated understanding of legal procedure.[31] Thomas's judge advocate, Col. Gates Thruston, once wrote that when he began serving with Thomas, he was surprised at the extent of Thomas's knowledge of military law. Thomas explained to Thruston that he had researched the subject extensively earlier in his career, when he had served as a juror on a large number of courts-martial. While Thomas's legal knowledge did not help him achieve his goals in the Milliken case, it helped him perform many of his other duties during Reconstruction.[32]

Despite the difficulties of his Tennessee service, Thomas felt comfortable in the state, having served there through most of the war, and he tried to avoid serving in the Deep South, where Reconstruction was even more contentious. In March 1867 Congress passed legislation to restructure the army's system of command, dividing the ten states still out of the Union into five military districts. Johnson wanted Thomas to command the Third District, which comprised Georgia, Alabama, and Florida, but Thomas did not want the job. Thomas recommended the appointment of Brevet Maj. Gen. John Pope instead, stating that Pope would be "much more acceptable to the inhabitants" of the district than himself. Grant still thought Thomas would be the best man for the job, but President Johnson appointed Pope to the Third District and left Thomas where he was. Thomas's command was still called the Department of the Cumberland, but now consisted of the states of Tennessee, Kentucky, and West Virginia. As all three states were full members of the Union, with loyalist state governments, it probably seemed to Thomas that this assignment would require fewer political duties than a command in the unreconstructed South.[33]

Johnson tried again to assign Thomas to a Deep South command in August. Johnson wanted to get rid of Philip Sheridan, who commanded in Louisiana and Texas, because he considered Sheridan's administration too radical. In reality, Thomas was at least as committed to the protection of blacks as Sheridan, but he was more diplomatic than Sheridan in his interactions both with local politicians and with Johnson. The president continued to view Thomas as a moderate, despite Thomas's record of support of radical policies. Thomas heard rumors of this reassignment in

July and wrote Stanton to object, stating that the "politico-military duties" that came with commanding in one of the Reconstruction districts were "repugnant" to him. Thomas added that removing Sheridan from command would only "revive the hopes and energies of the opponents of reconstruction in those states." Thomas felt that he could exercise "but little influence" on the citizens of the district, as they viewed him as less strict than Sheridan, and replacing Sheridan with himself would only cause "their hopes of success [to] be doubled."[34]

Grant intervened on Thomas's behalf, writing Johnson that "the services of General Thomas in battling for the Union entitle him to some consideration" in choice of commands. Johnson still insisted on appointing Thomas, whom he praised for his "great ability, sound discretion, and sterling patriotism." Thomas's doctor then wrote the War Department, apparently without Thomas's knowledge, stating that Thomas had a serious liver ailment. This ailment would be aggravated by the stress of command and the Louisiana climate, making it a "great risk" for Thomas to serve at New Orleans. Johnson finally relented and appointed Winfield Scott Hancock instead.[35]

Thomas did suffer from serious illness during the years after the Civil War, a recurring pain that his doctors diagnosed as "neuralgia," a disease of the liver. Photographs from this period show that Thomas gained a great deal of weight after the end of the war, probably because he was no longer actively serving in the field. The available evidence suggests that Thomas did not suffer from liver disease but from high blood pressure and cardiovascular disease, which were complicated by his weight gain and the stress of command.[36]

While Thomas had hoped that service in Tennessee, Kentucky, and West Virginia would involve fewer political duties than a command in the Deep South, this did not turn out to be the case. While West Virginia remained relatively quiet, there was an explosion of racial and political violence in Kentucky and Tennessee in 1867 and 1868. Tennessee also experienced a series of power struggles between the Republican-controlled state government and Conservative county and municipal governments. In some ways, the fact that these states were full members of the Union made Thomas's job more difficult, as the relationship between military and civilian authority was even more complex than in the Deep South. Deep South states, which had not been readmitted to the Union, were ruled by federally appointed civilian governors, so both civilian and military authority followed federal policy. In Kentucky, West Virginia, and Tennessee, the state and local governments followed their own policies, and made their own demands on the military. When state, local, and federal civilian officials came into conflict, Thomas had to decide which of the three civil authorities to follow.

The conflict between state, local, and federal authority came to a head during the congressional elections in August 1867 and the Nashville mayoral election in September. Many white voters were disqualified from voting in these elections because they had supported the Confederacy, while black freedmen were able to vote for the first time. Furious that blacks could vote while they could not, the disqualified whites threatened to disrupt the elections with violence. At the governor's request, Thomas sent soldiers to a number of localities to keep the peace. Thomas wrote to Grant that another riot was feared in Memphis on election day, and Grant told Thomas to go there in person to maintain order. Through personal diplomacy, Thomas negotiated a peace settlement between the Unionist police chief of Memphis and the pro-Confederate sheriff of the surrounding county, and the election took place without violence.[37]

Maintaining order in the September municipal election in Nashville was more difficult. Nashville's Conservative mayor set up his own voter registration boards, allowing disenfranchised whites to register but denying the vote to African Americans. Governor Brownlow declared the mayor's registration lists to be invalid and created his own list of registered voters. Brownlow asked Thomas to send troops to make sure only state-registered voters participated in the election, while the mayor persisted in running the election his way, asserting that the state government had no authority over a municipal election. Unsure of which civil authority he should obey, Thomas asked Grant for instructions. Grant told Thomas not to take sides, as "the military cannot be the judge of which set of election judges have the right to control" the election, but merely to preserve order at the polls. When Thomas pointed out that there was no way he could avoid supporting one side or the other, Grant just repeated his instructions to "preserve the public order."

Deciding to support the governor, Thomas went to Nashville in person to negotiate with the city's mayor, W. Matt Brown. At first Brown threatened that federal intervention would bring about "unpleasant consequences," and that he would "yield up the city to a state of organized anarchy never paralleled." After several days of personal negotiations, involving many notes and personal visits to Brown, Thomas convinced the mayor to back down. The election went forward peacefully under the governor's rules.[38]

Despite these successes, Thomas was deeply frustrated by the events of 1867. In his yearly report to headquarters, he complained that the people were still bitterly opposed to "the hated Yankee and anything represent-ing loyalty to the Union," and that they defied the government whenever they could. Throughout the area under his command, blacks and white Unionists were threatened, murdered, or driven from their homes, and government employees were fired on, while the civil authorities did little or nothing to protect them. These problems had been the most severe in Mississippi and Georgia, but even within the supposedly loyal states of Tennessee and Kentucky, the conditions in rural areas were "most deplorable." "Murders, robberies, and outrages of all kinds" were commit-ted against Union men and blacks, "without any effort on the part of the civil authorities to arrest the offenders." In both states "the administration of justice depends in a great measure upon the personal character of the judge, sheriff and jurors, the laws seemingly making but little difference." When a black man was injured by a white man, redress was difficult or impossible to obtain. "But when the reverse complaint comes into court, the utmost zeal and energy is displayed in bringing the Negro offender to justice." In these cases, Thomas sarcastically observed, "the efforts of the civil authorities are then worthy of the highest admiration."[39]

While 1867 had been a difficult year, Thomas felt guardedly optimistic about the future. The reduction of the area under his command combined with the augmentation of his forces with the Tennessee militia made it possible for him "partially to hold in check the disloyal tendencies of the people, and to punish if not to prevent unlawful proceedings." While outrages against blacks and white Union men had not ceased, and "the feeling of the people does not warm in love for the government or the flag," Thomas hoped that matters might improve in the near future. "The present prospect of a good harvesting of the corn and cotton crops, bringing with it the soothing influence of money earned," meant that soon "the prevailing animosity in Tennessee and Kentucky may be diminished in strength."[40]

Thomas's prediction was not borne out. While the harvest was good in 1868, and the economy improved, the effect was the opposite of what Thomas had anticipated. "It would appear," Thomas complained in his yearly report, "that with the increased means, the spirit of lawlessness is more actively exhibited." Thomas was now investigating "a mysterious organization known as the Ku Klux Klan . . . whose acts were shown to be of a lawless and diabolical nature." The Klan targeted white Unionists but was most violent toward educated and politically active blacks, and its violence took place on an unprecedented scale and level of organization.[41]

The Ku Klux Klan was founded in Pulaski, Tennessee, in May or June 1866, by six young former Confederate soldiers. The Klan's founders claimed that it was begun as a harmless social club, but by 1867 the group had begun to harass and intimidate local blacks. It remained a small local group until the spring of 1867, when a new group of leaders expanded and restructured the Klan. The group worked quietly at first, concentrating on recruiting new members and engaging in relatively little violence. At the time, white Conservatives thought they could convince blacks to vote for Conservative candidates, and had not yet begun to practice systematic violence and intimidation to keep blacks from the polls. When blacks voted overwhelmingly in favor of Republican candidates in the 1867 elections, white Conservatives gave up courting the black vote. The Klan, along with other white terrorist groups, began a campaign of violence designed to prevent blacks from engaging in any political activity.[42]

Violence broke out all over Tennessee in late 1867 and early 1868. In March 1868 two members of the state legislature wrote Thomas to ask for help in suppressing the Klan, stating that the organization was too powerful for the militia to oppose alone. Thomas asked Grant whether he could comply with their request, as it did not come from the governor, or from the legislature as a whole. For his part, Thomas thought the state authorities should deal with the matter first, as Tennessee was a fully reconstructed state. Grant referred the matter to Johnson, who agreed that Thomas should not act until the state government as a whole had asked him to do so.[43]

By April Klan violence had increased to the point that the legislature and governor of Tennessee called on Thomas for assistance. Thomas sent soldiers to support the Tennessee militia and also sent troops out of his district to fight Klan violence in Georgia.[44] Governor Brownlow asked for more assistance in June, but Thomas did not have adequate forces to comply with his request. Washington sent reinforcements in August, which Thomas distributed to localities threatened by the Klan, as directed by the governor.

Throughout 1868 Thomas pursued the Klan with vigor, collecting information on its activities and arresting Klan members whenever he could.[45] He publicly objected to the position of some newspapers, which denied that the Klan even existed, and he also disputed white allegations that the Klan's actions were merely a defensive response to the activities of the Loyal League, an organization of black voters. While Thomas conceded that some of the Loyal League's actions may have been "impolitic" or "unwise," he stated that "there has been reported to me no one instance of any outrage or unlawful act having been committed by them." Thomas criticized local authorities for their ineffectiveness and complicity, stating that their failure helped the Klan expand from a small, informal organization to "grand political society" around which "the adherents of the late rebellion, active or passive, might safely rally." Thomas's criticism was accurate, as the complicity of Tennessee civil authorities had made possible the Klan's success in Tennessee and had facilitated its spread to the rest of the South.[46]

Thomas's zeal in prosecuting the Klan was energetic by any standard, and he worked much harder than many other Reconstruction commanders in pursuing them. The officer who replaced Thomas as commander in Tennessee, Henry Halleck, did nothing to fight the Ku Klux Klan. He claimed that violence was not more common in the state than it had been before the Civil War, and that what violence existed was ordinary crime, not racially or politically motivated. Just a year after Thomas wrote that the Klan had become a "grand political society" with thousands of adherents, Halleck concluded that "no such general organization" existed.[47]

While Thomas's efforts to prevent and prosecute Klan violence were partially successful, Klan members were generally able to avoid capture by Federal troops. One of the main reasons for this was Thomas's shortage of soldiers, particularly cavalry. By September 1868 he commanded only eighteen hundred men, and these were all infantry, as the cavalry in his department had been sent to fight Indians on the Great Plains.[48] Thomas's effectiveness was also hampered by the support and aid that the whites in Kentucky and Tennessee gave the Klan. For example, in May 1868 Thomas sent a company of infantry to Columbia, Tennessee, a center of Klan activity, with the hope that the troops might have a "moral effect in preventing disturbances and outrages" in that "lawless district." While he hoped his men could have a moral effect, he knew they would be "of but little service physically, as they can only aid the civil authorities, who do not appear to be zealous in their duties as conservators of the peace."[49]

By the end of 1868, Thomas's initial optimism about the prospects of Reconstruction had turned to despair. He had always viewed his fellow Southerners as a people who respected the rule of law, but the events of the previous year had led him to view his former countrymen with disgust. It was "mortifying," he stated in his 1868 annual report, to admit that public opinion had rendered the rule of law invalid. "A criminal who is popular with the mob can set law at defiance," he stated, while a man whom the community opposes for his black skin or Unionist political views "is likely to be hung to the nearest tree, or shot down at his own door."[50]

In Tennessee, Thomas stated, white hostility to blacks and Union men might be traced to the continued disenfranchisement of former secessionists. In Kentucky, however, there were no such reasons for white resentment, since whites were not disenfranchised and blacks did not yet have the right to vote. Even so, violence against blacks was the rule in Kentucky, and white "ruffians" there were able "to tyrannize over them without fear of punishment."[51] Unable to stop the violence, Thomas documented it, providing forty-two pages of attachments to his annual report that detailed the atrocities that had occurred in Tennessee and Kentucky. He also directed the commissioners of the Freedmen's Bureau for Kentucky and Tennessee to prepare a list of murders that had occurred in their states, together with reports on whether the murderers had been prosecuted. These reports helped demonstrate that the civil courts were not protecting blacks.[52]

Thomas felt that the cause of Southern whites' violence and lawlessness lay in their failure to recognize that secession from the Union was illegal, and their feeling that their cause had been a just one. Thomas wrote in his 1868 report:

> The controlling cause of the unsettled condition of affairs in the Department is that the greatest efforts made by the defeated insurgents, since the close of the war, have been to promulgate the idea that the cause of liberty, justice, humanity, equality, and all the calendar of the virtues of freedom, suffered violence and wrong, when the effort for Southern independence failed. This

is of course intended as a species of political cant, whereby the crime of treason might be covered with a counterfeit varnish of patriotism, so that the precipitators of the rebellion might go down in history hand in hand with the defenders of the Government, thus wiping out with their own hands their own stains, a species of self-forgiveness amazing in its effrontery, when it is considered that life and property justly forfeited by the laws of the Country, of War, and of Nations, through the magnanimity of the Government and people, was not exacted from them. Under this inspiration, the education of the great body of the people, moral, religious, and political, has been turned into channels where all might unite in common. The impoverishment of the South resulting from War and its concomitants, the emancipation of the slaves, and the consequent loss of substance, the ambiguity and uncertainty of political rights, and financial values as well as personal rivalries, have all combined to strengthen the efforts of pernicious teachers. The evil done has been great, and it is not discernable that an immediate improvement may be expected.[53]

This statement was Thomas's last word on the secessionists, and it expresses his bitterness over the outcome of the war. Military defeat had not led white Southerners to admit their guilt and to reform but had instead reinforced their feeling that they were victims and that their cause was just. Southerners had little choice but to acquiesce in the abolition of slavery, but they refused to allow blacks any civil and political rights and resorted to extremes of violence to keep blacks subordinate. Organized white opposition to federal rule and the limited resources allocated him by the national government had made it impossible for Thomas to maintain peace and security in the area under his command. As the year ended, Thomas welcomed the opportunity to leave the South and perform more useful service elsewhere.

CHAPTER EIGHTEEN

Late Career and Death

To attend to the equipping of this force, as well as to be able to correspond with General Sherman, Thomas was compelled to remain in Nashville, while he placed Schofield in immediate charge of the troops engaged in watching the movement of Hood and retarding his advance on Nashville. This necessity existing until the army fell back to Nashville, gave Schofield the opportunity to fight the battle of Franklin. This was a very brilliant battle, most disastrous to the enemy, and as the writer in the [*New York*] *Tribune* says, no doubt contributed materially to the crowning success at Nashville....

A number of politicians attempted to recruit Thomas to their cause in 1868, as Johnson attempted to use Thomas to undermine Grant's candidacy, and both the Democratic and Republican parties considered Thomas as a presidential or vice presidential candidate. Thomas refused to participate in any of these campaigns. Thomas left Kentucky at the end of 1868 to serve on a court-martial in Washington, D.C., and returned to the Department of the Cumberland only briefly before traveling to San Francisco to command the Department of the Pacific. Thomas enjoyed his service at this post, as it took him away from the politics and violence of his Tennessee command and gave him the chance to travel through the newly acquired territory of Alaska. Thomas looked forward to a long term of service in command of this peaceful district, but he did not get to enjoy his service for long. John Schofield, Thomas's former subordinate, arranged for an aide to write an anonymous critique of Thomas's generalship during the Nashville campaign, which angered Thomas so much that he set out to write a rebuttal. His intense anger caused his blood pressure to rise, and he suffered a stroke in the course of writing his response. He died later that day, March 28, 1870.

The year 1868 was an election year, and politicians from both parties attempted to recruit Thomas to support their cause. Andrew Johnson was the first. Hoping to serve a second term as president, and perceiving Grant to be his most dangerous rival, Johnson tried to undermine Grant's status by promoting one of his subordinates to replace him as general in chief. Johnson first proposed this scheme to Sherman, but Sherman refused to have anything to do with it, and Johnson then tried Thomas. In February 1868 Johnson nominated Thomas for promotion to the rank of brevet full general, which would have given Thomas a brevet rank equal to Grant's permanent rank. Once the Senate confirmed Thomas's promotion, Johnson intended to replace Grant with Thomas as general in chief. Thomas did not want to be involved in this dispute, nor did he want the political responsibilities that would go with such a command. He wrote to Johnson and the Senate on February 22, thanking Johnson for the nomination but asking him to recall it. "I have done no service since the war to deserve so high a compliment," Thomas wrote, "and it is now too late to be regarded a compliment if for services rendered during the war." Johnson withdrew Thomas's nomination.[1]

As a successful Union general, who was considered a political moderate, Thomas was considered by both parties in 1868 as a potential presidential or vice presidential nominee. Thomas refused to run for either office. In a letter to his friend and former subordinate James Negley, Thomas explained that he did not want anything to do with politics, which, since the time of Andrew Jackson's presidency, had become a matter of "personal intrigue and faction."[2] Thomas gave a more detailed explanation in a letter he wrote to Henry Cist, a former general and Ohio politician. Thomas cited six reasons for his refusal to run for the presidency:

First: I am wholly disqualified for so high and responsible a position, being but a mere tyro in the science of statesmanship.

Second: I have not the necessary control over my temper, nor have I the faculty of yielding to a policy, and working to advance it, unless convinced within myself that it is right and honest.

Third: My habits of life, established by a training of over twenty years, are such as to make it repugnant to my self-respect to have to induce people to do their duty by persuasive measures.

If there is any thing that outrages me more than another, it is to see an obstinate and self-willed man oppose what is right morally, and under the law, simply because, under the law, he cannot be compelled to do what is right.

Fourth: I can never consent voluntarily to place myself in a position where scurrilous newspaper men and political dema-gogues can make free with my personal character and reputation with impunity.

Fifth: I have no taste whatever for politics, and, besides, restric-tions have recently been thrown around the President by Con-gress, which virtually deprive him of his just powers and rights under the Constitution. I could never consent to be deprived of rights and privileges guaranteed the President by the Constitu-tion, as long as the Constitution remained unaltered.

I could cite many more equally valid reasons for not wishing the office. I will name only one more and not the least. I am poor and could not afford it.[3]

In January 1868 the Tennessee Republican Convention passed a resolution stating that their first choice for presidential nominee had been Thomas, but as he had already refused the office, they nominated Grant instead. Many other state conventions also nominated Grant, seeing him as a nonpartisan moderate who would bring integrity and balance to Washington after the years of factional squabbling between Johnson and Congress. Grant's nomination was confirmed by the Republican National Convention in May. Thomas was also considered by a few members of the Democratic Party leadership as a potential vice presidential candidate, but they never became serious enough to contact Thomas about the office. If they had, it seems certain that he would have refused.[4]

Thomas declined to make a public endorsement of either presidential candidate. In an August, 1868 letter, he explained that he considered it not "becoming" of a military officer to "meddle" in politics. Since the army and navy were departments of the government, he wrote, military officers "should therefore especially refrain from giving public expression of their political sentiments." He also considered his involvement unnecessary, as the soldiers and former soldiers of his army were "intelligent, and much more interested personally than an officer of the army can be in the result of the elections. . . . My confidence in the general intelligence of the people is so firm that I have no fears but they will elect the best men and best measures to preserve the peace and prosperity of the country." Given the events of the last decade, Thomas may not have had so much confidence in the will of the people as he stated. He expected that his letter would be published, however, so he was careful to express himself as tactfully as he could.[5]

Thomas still had a role to play in the elections of 1868, that of protecting voters and maintaining order at the polls. On March 28 there was a special election for local offices in Gallatin, Tennessee, a center of Ku Klux Klan violence. Thomas ordered the local commander to guard the polls, preventing violence by the Klan and by disaffected individuals, and also preventing clashes between the Unionist state militia and the Conservative local police. The election took place without trouble. In September Thomas sent troops to maintain order during local elections in Brownsville and Nashville, and these elections went peacefully as well.[6]

During the November elections, Thomas sent troops to all the cities and larger towns of Tennessee. Conditions remained peaceful wherever Federal troops were present, but there was widespread violence and intimidation in rural areas. When Federal troops were recalled from the larger towns after the election, violence broke out once again, forcing the governor to declare martial law and call out the militia. In Kentucky the election went off peacefully, largely because secessionist whites had not been disenfranchised and blacks did not have the right to vote.[7] Ulysses S. Grant was elected to the presidency, signaling an end to the conflict between Congress and President Johnson and the beginning of a more unified Reconstruction policy.

In the months that followed Grant's election as president, Thomas and the governor of West Virginia agreed that conditions there had become peaceful, and Thomas withdrew nearly all Federal troops in the state.[8] Thomas reported that the conditions in his department had improved after the election, and that the opinion of the newspapers, if not of the general public, was beginning to turn against the Ku Klux Klan. While Thomas recommended maintaining Federal troops in the region, he admitted that they were "of little use" in areas where the civil authorities would not perform their duties. In this respect, matters had not improved over the previous year.[9]

In November 1868 Thomas was called to Washington to preside over a court of inquiry for Maj. Gen. Alexander B. Dyer, who had served as the head of the army's Ordnance Department during the war. While in Washington, Thomas and his staff aide, Alfred L. Hough, paid a social call on President-Elect Grant, and Grant discussed with Thomas the possibility of assigning him to command the Division of the Pacific. Grant stated that he was going to send either Thomas or Sheridan, and Thomas stated that he would prefer to remain in the East, for the sake of his wife. Mrs. Grant joked, "Your having a wife is one reason why you should go there instead of Sheridan, as he ought to stay here, where he can get one." After the meeting, Thomas told his aide, "Hough, we are going to California; that was settled tonight."[10]

Later, when Grant made his decisions about the division commands, Thomas was surprised and angry to find that John Schofield, a brigadier general, had been assigned the Division of the Pacific, while Thomas was left in charge of the Department of the Cumberland. "Very naturally," Thomas wrote to Hough, "I came to the conclusion that I was intentionally slighted." When Thomas went to Grant to object, "Grant protested he had no intention of the kind, and had me assigned to the Pacific." Grant ordered Halleck, then commanding the Division of the Pacific, to take over Thomas's Department of the Cumberland, but then elevated the department to division status. Thomas was now even more angry. He had not wanted to move in the first place but had only wanted a command commensurate with his rank. Thomas complained to Van Horne that, for reasons unknown to himself, Grant simply did not like him and treated him poorly. To Hough, Thomas wrote, "[T]he whole transaction only confirms me in my previous estimate of the petty mind we have at the head of office."[11]

While in Washington, Thomas received a letter from his friend and former subordinate officer Benjamin F. Scribner. During the war, Thomas had often teased Scribner about his large and ever-increasing family and had joked that Scribner should name one of his children after himself. Scribner's letter announced the birth of a son, with the words, "George Henry Thomas Scribner has this day reported in person for duty." In reply Thomas sent a letter addressed to Scribner's son, "bearing all the official marks of special orders." The letter read, "George Henry Thomas Scribner, having reported in person for duty, is hereby assigned to the care of his mother until further orders."[12]

Thomas took part in a number of Washington social events, including a party given in honor of the Battle of Mill Springs, which was attended by nearly thirty of the officers who had participated in the battle. Thomas also went to a reception at the home of Benjamin F. Butler, a politician and former general who was now an influential Republican senator. Butler was a leading supporter of a bill reducing the size of the army, and he also supported the continued use of paper money, or "greenbacks." Butler's military record was not distinguished, and he had a shady reputation as a politician. Thomas wrote Hough that the lavish party, with its expensive flowers and other decorations, was "all very fine in appearance, but to me had a strong and disagreeable odor of dirty greenbacks." Thomas expressed his concern over Butler's attempt to reduce the army but was confident that "Ben can't crush the army. . . . The more he attacks us, the more friends we find." Butler's bill did pass in March 1869, however, and the reduction in the army made controlling the occupied South even more difficult than it had been previously.[13]

In December 1868 Thomas was elected to preside over a grand reunion of the Armies of the Cumberland, the Tennessee, the Ohio, and Georgia, held in Chicago. Thomas opened the proceedings by having the drum corps sound the reveille. The former soldiers had heard this sound every day during their military service, but never since then, and the sound brought back powerful memories. At first the assembly grew silent and stood at attention; then they broke into cheers. Thomas gave a few short speeches during the reunion but left most of the speaking to his more eloquent colleagues. One of them, Gen. William Belknap, praised Thomas and called him the "Rock of Chickamauga," which brought the assembly to a standing ovation. The next day, Thomas spoke to Scribner about his feelings on seeing his former soldiers again. "I can't make it out," Thomas said. "I can't recognize these brilliant and elegant gentlemen or these eloquent orators as the same men who served under me as soldiers." After a pause, Thomas continued, "But then I saw them at a disadvantage; I saw them in their blouses, unshaven and unshorn, awkward in a new role in which they had had no experience."[14]

When Thomas returned to Washington for court duty, he found that much of his time was taken up by visits from many former soldiers, who sought recommendations from Thomas that they could use to gain political appointments. Since thousands of soldiers had served under Thomas during the war, he did not even recognize many of the men who asked him for recommendations. At first he tried to accommodate them, but he soon found himself overwhelmed with the sheer number of people asking for his help. Finally, he announced that he would no longer write letters of support for anyone, no matter how distinguished their services had been. By April he was joking that he missed them, as the hour between breakfast and the commencement of the court seemed "rather heavy" without "half a dozen visits from office-seekers."[15]

The Dyer court of inquiry finally wound up in early May. Dyer, a native of Virginia, was a regular army officer who had sided with the Union in 1861. He had served with great distinction, first as assistant chief and then as chief of the Ordnance Department, and was best known for his zeal in cracking down on corrupt contractors. Many of these contractors were connected with their home-state congressmen and senators, and these politicians had accused Dyer of malfeasance. Dyer had called the court of inquiry to clear his name. After five months of testimony, Thomas and the other board members found in Dyer's favor, and their findings were endorsed by President Grant.[16]

After finishing with the court of inquiry, Thomas had time to stop only briefly in Tennessee before traveling on to San Francisco. In his final report on his service in the Department of the Cumberland, Thomas admitted that he had not been successful in his attempts to maintain peace and protect black freedmen and white Unionists. His task had indeed been impossible, as the local authorities consistently supported the Klan, and Thomas lacked the troops and the legal authority to succeed without their cooperation.[17]

The 1869 Tennessee state elections were the first in which a large number of former secessionists were allowed to vote, and the governorship and legislature passed to the control of conservative candidates.[18] The new government quickly returned Tennessee to white rule, recalling the militia and ending the campaign to prosecute the Ku Klux Klan. The newly elected legislators also turned on Thomas, whom many of them despised due to his support of blacks' political rights. One legislator proposed to sell the portrait of Thomas that the previous assembly had commissioned. Thomas's supporters in Nashville offered to buy the painting, and Thomas's brother Benjamin offered to buy it as well. Thomas, deeply offended, wrote to the legislature and offered to buy the painting himself, also stating that he would return the gold medal that the previous government had given him. The sponsor of the resolution to sell the portrait apologized to Thomas, explaining that he had not really wanted to sell the painting but had only made the proposal as a satirical critique of the economizing measures then being considered by the legislature. Despite this apology, Thomas remained offended, particularly when the assembly as a whole did not vote to repudiate the proposal. In a February 21, 1870, letter to James Wilson, Thomas stated that he still intended to return the medal but had been as yet unable to do so because he had placed it in storage when he moved to San Francisco.[19]

Thomas arrived in San Francisco on June 1, 1869, and spent two weeks at his headquarters learning about his new command. He then set off on an extended inspection tour, traveling eastward overland to Silver City, Nevada, then north to Boise, in present-day Idaho, and west to Umatilla, Oregon. After traveling by boat down the Columbia River to Portland, he inspected the forts along the Pacific coast. While in Portland, Thomas received word of a threatened outbreak of violence against Chinese laborers in Nevada. Thomas sent two companies of cavalry to the territory, and no disturbance occurred. On July 6 Thomas set out by boat for Alaska, stopping over at Vancouver and arriving at Sitka, Alaska, on July 22.[20]

The U.S. government had acquired Alaska only two years before, and the territory was temporarily under military rule. Sitka, with just nine hundred residents, was the territory's capital and largest town. Sitka's population was composed of Russians who had stayed on after the sale of the territory to the United States and American adventurers who had recently moved there in the hopes of profiting from land speculation or commerce. The cold, wet climate made farming nearly impossible, and Alaska's gold and mineral resources had not yet been discovered, so what little commerce did exist in Alaska mainly involved trading with the native inhabitants for furs.[21]

Thomas made a grand tour of Alaska, traveling first to Sitka and then to Kenay, on the mainland near the present-day city of Anchorage, where he investigated the region's coal deposits. From there he sailed west to Kodiak Island and then to Unilaska Island in the Aleutians, where a trading company mined ice for shipment to San Francisco for sale. Thomas then visited St. Paul's and St. George's Islands, which are north of the Aleutians and five hundred miles west of the mainland. Trading companies had contracted with natives living on these islands to hunt fur seals for sale to the traders. The islands had military outposts, placed there to prevent the traders from selling whisky to the natives and to ensure that the traders did not cause overhunting by buying too many seal pelts.

Thomas enjoyed his trip through Alaska, as it gave him the opportunity to see new places and research the geology, biology, and Native American cultures of the region. In a private letter, Thomas remarked that Alaska was "a beautiful country," too cold to be of any economic value besides as a source of furs, but strategically useful as a way of "crowding England out of British Columbia."[22] Upon his return to San Francisco, Thomas sent samples of coal and some walrus bones he had collected to Spencer F. Baird, a naturalist at the Smithsonian Institution who later became the institution's director. Thomas wrote Baird, "Alaska would have been an excellent purchase had it been made in '61 and used thereafter as a kind of water and cold air cure for the hot-headed Southerners who fell into our hands as prisoners of war. Three months in Alaska are sufficient to cool down the most heated brain." In another letter, Thomas estimated that he had traveled about eight thousand miles on his two-month journey, which, he joked, was "fast traveling for a slow man."[23]

On March 8 Thomas responded to his cousin, John Tyler, Jr., who had written him to encourage him to run for President in 1872. In his reply, Thomas expressed approval of Grant's record and emphasized that he would never run for president, no matter what the circumstances. On March 14 Thomas wrote Sherman, who was now the general in chief of the army, asking him to intervene with Congress in regards to a proposed bill that would reduce the number of officers in the army. Thomas wanted the bill to be modified to include pensions for officers who had been disabled due to wounds or illness suffered during their military service.

On March 12, 1870, the *New York Tribune* published a letter that severely criticized Thomas's generalship during the Nashville campaign. The letter also claimed that Schofield deserved credit for the victory at Nashville, because his defeat of Hood at Franklin had made the victory at Nashville possible. The letter was signed, "One who fought at Nashville," and Thomas suspected that Schofield himself had written it. Thomas's suspicions were essentially correct, as the letter was written by one of Schofield's aides, from notes prepared by Schofield and with Schofield's approval. The previous year, Halleck had told Thomas that Schofield had tried to get Thomas removed from command before the

Battle of Nashville. Now Thomas had further evidence of Schofield's desire to discredit him.[24]

A second writer, who signed himself "Another Man," rebutted Schofield's contentions in the March 19 issue of the *New York Tribune*. Thomas approved of the rebuttal but decided that he would write his own response.[25] Thomas's staff aide, Alfred Hough, saw him working on his reply on the morning of March 28, 1870. Thomas seemed to be in good health when Hough left Thomas's headquarters at 10:30 A.M. Later that morning, Thomas came out of his office, said, "I want air," and collapsed. When Hough returned at 1:45 P.M., he found Thomas lying on a couch, with several doctors attending him.

At first the doctors thought Thomas was just suffering from a fainting fit, perhaps brought on by indigestion. As the afternoon wore on, Thomas developed a headache, but he managed to get up briefly and walk around. Frances came to see him, and the couple spoke briefly. Then, according to Hough, Thomas began to struggle, "with a convulsive movement about his chest, and try to rise, which he could not do." The doctors were called again, but by the time they returned Thomas had already lost consciousness, and he remained unconscious until the time of his death, 7:25 P.M. The cause of death was diagnosed as "apoplexy," or a stroke. No autopsy was performed, but when Thomas's body was embalmed the arteries leading from his heart were found to have fatty deposits. It seems likely that similar arterial blockage caused his fatal stroke.[26]

Thomas was fifty-three years old when he died. He had always been inclined to stoutness and had gained considerable weight in his final years. During most of his career Thomas had been physically active, spending much of the day riding in the field. During his postwar service, his work became more sedentary, and he spent long hours in his office writing letters, orders, and reports. Always a heavy eater, he exercised less than before and gained weight. He may have shown symptoms of arterial disease before 1870, as the illness that prevented Thomas from being transferred to New Orleans in 1867, which his doctor diagnosed as a liver ailment, may in fact have been a cardiovascular problem.

Frances Thomas held a small, private memorial service in San Francisco, and she remained behind to wind up their affairs, while Thomas's body was shipped east for a public funeral. William T. Sherman asked Frances to bury George at West Point, but Frances preferred that

George be buried in her family plot in Troy, New York. Frances asked Sherman to take care of the arrangements for the public service.

Thomas was the first well-known Union general to pass away after the war, and his death came as a shock to the country. The officers and men of the army, along with the general public, expressed their respect and affection for him in a series of mourning activities.[27] As Thomas's coffin passed through the towns along the rail line in the West, people came out to pay their respects. In larger cities, Thomas's funeral train stopped and was greeted with military honors, and in smaller towns people came out to watch as the train went past. An honor guard came out from Chicago to meet the train in Omaha and to escort the train to the city. When Thomas's train arrived in Chicago, Philip Sheridan and Winfield Scott Hancock presided over a procession that accompanied Thomas's coffin from one train station to the next. Thousands of people lined the streets to watch the procession go by.[28]

Public memorial ceremonies were held in Boston, St. Paul, Washington, and Philadelphia. On April 6 memorial services were held at the Capitol, attended by President Grant, the justices of the Supreme Court, the members of Grant's cabinet, and many senators and members of Congress. Salmon P. Chase, William T. Sherman, James Garfield, and a number of former Union generals all made speeches in Thomas's honor. Meanwhile, Thomas's funeral train passed through the cities of Toledo, Cleveland, Erie, and Buffalo, and it was met in each city by large crowds. The train arrived in Troy in the early morning hours of April 7.[29]

Thomas's casket lay on display at St. Paul's Episcopal Church throughout the day of April 7 and the morning of April 8, and hundreds of people came to pay their respects. The casket was draped with an American flag and adorned with flowers, and Thomas's sword and a recent photograph were placed on the casket for the public to view. The funeral service began at 11:30 on April 8 and was followed by a procession to the Kellogg family vault. George Meade, William S. Rosecrans, John Schofield, Joseph Hooker, Gordon Granger, John Newton, William B. Hazen, and Andrew J. Mackay acted as pallbearers. President Grant led the procession, followed by Secretary of War Belknap, General in Chief Sherman, a committee of senators and congressmen, the governor of New York, and a committee of legislators from Indiana. Many ordinary citizens joined the procession, which the *New York Times* estimated to number four thousand people and 140 carriages. At Mrs. Thomas's request, there was no eulogy, but Stewart L. Woodford, the lieutenant governor of New York and a former Civil War general, gave a speech in Thomas's honor that evening.[30]

Frances Thomas did not attend the public service. She left San Francisco several days after George's funeral train and traveled separately to Troy, arriving there after the April 8 ceremony. At a small, private service, her husband's remains were taken out of the Kellogg family vault and buried in the cemetery of her church. Later that month, Frances wrote Sherman to ask him to provide employment for Thomas's former staff officers, including her nephew, Sanford Kellogg. Frances feared that Kellogg and Thomas's other aides, who were now without commands, might be forced to resign due to reductions that were being made in the size of the officer corps. Sherman made sure that Thomas's aides were given new assignments.[31]

While Northerners mourned Thomas as a fallen hero, the reaction of Southerners varied. The *New Orleans Picayune* presented the most negative view of Thomas, describing him as a traitor and an opportunist. The paper asserted that Thomas had been violently prosecession before the war, but had abandoned the South because of the influence of his Northern wife and his hopes of rapid promotion in the Union army. The *Richmond Dispatch* ran a much more positive obituary, speaking respectfully of Thomas's achievements and character. The *Dispatch* asserted that Thomas had been uncertain of his loyalties at the beginning of the war but stated that this was commendable, since only a person with a "heart of stone" would be able to oppose his native state without hesitation.[32]

Frances Thomas outlived her husband by nearly twenty years. She lived in Troy, New York, with her sister, often visiting Washington, D.C., and spending the winters in Florida. She kept up with what was published about her late husband and was greatly concerned with how he would be remembered in history. She also corresponded with Thomas Van Horne in regards to his biography of Thomas, providing him with some information that he used in the book. Frances carried out George's wishes in regards to his personal papers, making sure that they remained private and were destroyed after her death.[33]

Frances declined to attend the unveiling of the Thomas monument in Washington in 1879, apparently out of a desire to avoid public attention, but she did visit the statue privately a few months later. She wrote Alfred Hough that "the likeness is excellent, the figure and position of General Thomas life-like to a degree I did not suppose the artist could get." She found the pose to be particularly accurate. "General Thomas so often in driving out, would, on going up an elevation, take off his hat and look over the country," she wrote. "It was the first thing that struck me as I approached the statue."[34]

After George Thomas's death, Frances Thomas lived off of their savings and the inheritance she had received from her father. In 1879 she applied for the $30 per month pension she was entitled to as George Thomas's widow, and in 1885 Congress passed a special bill increasing her pension to $2,000 per year. Frances Thomas died peacefully on December 25, 1889. After spending a pleasant Christmas evening with her family and some friends, she went to bed in apparent good health. She was found dead in her bed the next morning.[35]

Thomas's siblings also survived him, and his sisters Frances and Judith lived the longest, dying around 1903. While their circumstances were reduced by the war and the liberation of their slaves, they lived comfortably on the income they received from renting their lands to black farmers. Judging from a letter written by Frances Thomas in 1900 to her cousin, Mattie Tyler, it seems that Frances and Judith enjoyed a happy and active old age.[36] It was rumored in Southampton County that Judith and Frances had turned George's photograph to the wall after he decided to fight for the Union and that they remained angry at him throughout their lives, but this rumor is almost certainly not true.[37] According to William Blount Barham, the sisters' doctor and a close family friend, Thomas's decision gave his sisters "more a feeling of mortification, disappointment and sorrow than anger." Years after George's death, Judith showed Dr. Barham a picture of George in *Scribner's* magazine, in which he was portrayed lying on his side, with his face resting on the palm of his hand. "She spoke affectionately of him," Barham recalled, "of how often she had seen him, after coming in fatigued from work or walking, assume this position." George's brothers had reconciled with him during his lifetime, but his sisters had not, which they regretted. As a gesture of reconciliation, Judith sent some acorns from an oak tree on the Thomas family plantation to be planted around his monument in Washington. "I am not sure that they ever sprouted," Barham wrote, and it seems that the acorns were never planted.[38]

Of all Thomas's siblings, only his brother Benjamin had children, so Judith and Frances willed the plantation to Benjamin's children when they died. They lived in Louisiana and Mississippi and did not want to move to Southampton, so they sold the plantation to a local buyer. The Thomas plantation is currently in private hands; while the house is listed in Virginia's guide to "Civil War Trails," it is not open to visitors. The sisters gave George's sword, some of his letters, and the rest of the Thomas family papers to a friend of the family, William Shands, who later donated them to the Virginia Historical Society. While they acted too late to reconcile with George during his lifetime, Frances and Judith Thomas did manage to preserve some of the records of his life for posterity.[39]

CHAPTER NINETEEN

Thomas in Historical Memory

The day is coming, gentlemen of Virginia, of North Carolina, of South Carolina, of Alabama, when you and your fellow-citizens will be making their pilgrimage to this magnificent monument . . . and say that there was a man who, under the tumult and excitement of the times, stood true and firm to his country, and that he is a hero, and that brave George Thomas will become the idol of the South.

—*William Tecumseh Sherman, speaking in 1879 at the dedication of the Thomas monument in Washington, D.C.*

Sherman's prediction that Thomas would become a hero in the South has yet to come true. Robert E. Lee, Thomas "Stonewall" Jackson, and J.E.B. Stuart are household names in both the North and the South, while Thomas, at one time a Northern hero, is now virtually unknown. How did Thomas's reputation diminish so drastically? While there are a number of answers, the most important lies in the rise of the nationalist or reconciliationist Civil War history of the twentieth century. This historical approach described the Civil War as a conflict between two equally honorable groups of white soldiers, while glossing over the issues of race and slavery. With secession and racism no longer seen as immoral, Thomas's Unionism and commitment to civil rights were not viewed as particularly praiseworthy, and his reputation thus suffered.

In the decades following the Civil War, Northerners and Southern Unionists celebrated Thomas one of the war's greatest heroes. Linus P.

Brockett's 1865 work, *Our Great Captains: Grant, Sherman, Thomas, Sheridan, and Farragut*, and William Shanks's 1866 book, *Personal Recollections of Distinguished Generals*, both accorded Thomas the third-highest place in the pantheon of Union generals, just after Grant and Sherman. Shanks, Brockett, and other Northern authors had special praise for Thomas's moral qualities, portraying him as particularly admirable because he was a Southerner who made the morally correct decision to remain loyal to the Union.[1]

So long as the memory of the Civil War was a living memory, Thomas's reputation remained high. Union veterans, particularly veterans of the Army of the Cumberland, revered Thomas's memory and continued to speak and write about him. The Society of the Army of the Cumberland honored Thomas by placing a draped and vacant chair on the rostrum during each of its meetings and by offering a toast to Thomas's memory every year. Veterans wrote many articles about Thomas and the battles in which he fought, which appeared in the publications of veterans' societies and in popular journals.[2]

Between 1881 and 1898, four biographies of Thomas appeared, all of which portrayed Thomas as exemplary both in moral character and military skill. Thomas's biographers were Richard W. Johnson, who served under Thomas in Texas and during the Civil War; Henry Coppee, who served at West Point during Thomas's tenure as an instructor; Thomas B. Van Horne, Thomas's former chaplain and the author of *The History of the Army of the Cumberland*; and Don Piatt, a journalist and former volunteer officer. In accordance with the standards of biography prevalent at that time, the books portrayed Thomas in heroic terms, which made Thomas seem admirable and flawless, albeit a little dull.[3]

Thomas's postwar reputation reached its height in 1879, with the unveiling of a monument in his honor in Washington, D.C. The monument was funded by voluntary donations, most of which came from former soldiers of the Army of the Cumberland. Stanley Matthews gave the main address, and James Garfield, Stewart Van Vliet, William S. Rosecrans, and a number of other former generals also spoke. A crowd estimated at from twenty to sixty thousand people attended the unveiling.[4]

The diminution of Thomas's reputation began with the publication of Sherman's memoirs in 1875, and Grant's memoirs in 1885–86. Like many Civil War memoirists, Grant and Sherman exaggerated their own achievements, and in some cases they did so at Thomas's expense. Grant praised Thomas for his courage, moral character, and skill as a defensive general but criticized him as slow and unaggressive. Sherman made the same criticisms and also distorted the factual record, retelling the story of the Atlanta campaign so that Sherman seemed responsible for all the campaign's successes, while Thomas and others seemed to bear responsibility for its failures. For example, Sherman did not mention that Thomas had originated the idea to outflank Johnston's army through Snake Creek Gap and Resaca. He falsely claimed that Thomas supported his plan to make a frontal assault at Kennesaw Mountain, and that Thomas opposed the plan to outflank the Confederates from the Kennesaw position.[5]

Grant and Sherman had different motives for discrediting Thomas in their memoirs. While some authors have attributed Grant's criticisms to jealousy or malice, this does not actually seem to be the case. Grant honestly thought Thomas was slow and unaggressive, and his memoirs reflect this opinion. Grant did give a misleading account of the operations around Chattanooga, but his inaccuracies are not particularly damaging to Thomas. By contrast, Sherman's account of the Atlanta campaign contains numerous inaccuracies, many of which elevate his own reputation at Thomas's expense. In the same book, however, as well as in other writings and speeches, Sherman professed to admire Thomas and described himself as Thomas's lifelong friend.

This mix of positive and negative in Sherman's comments about Thomas is difficult to explain. Some historians have seen Sherman's criticism of Thomas as a malicious betrayal, but Sherman's biographer, John Marszalek, offers an interpretation that makes more sense. As Marszalek explains, Sherman was an insecure person, who felt the need to exaggerate his own importance and accomplishments in order to protect his fragile ego. As Albert Castel has stated, acknowledging Thomas's true role in the Atlanta campaign "would have required Sherman to reveal how much he owed to Thomas's counsel and to admit that by so often ignoring it he wasted opportunities to achieve a quicker, easier, and more complete victory." Since Sherman could not tolerate the idea that he made significant mistakes, he convinced himself over the years that the events of the Atlanta campaign had occurred as he wished they had, not as they actually had. The false statements in Sherman's memoirs represented Sherman's actual but inaccurate memory of the events, not an intentional and malicious fabrication. This still does not excuse Sherman's actions, as he could have easily checked the records and corrected his errors, but it does help to explain them.[6]

Marszalek's explanation better explains Sherman's actions than any assumption of malice on Sherman's part. Sherman continued to correspond amicably with Frances Thomas after George Thomas's death, and Sherman often praised Thomas in speeches and writings. In an 1887 article in the *North American Review*, Sherman called Thomas the second-best general of the war, after Grant, and argued that Thomas was a better general even than Robert E. Lee. If Sherman had truly felt malice toward Thomas, it is unlikely that he would have spoken so frequently in praise of him.[7]

John Schofield was also critical of Thomas in his memoir, but Sherman's and Grant's memoirs were much more widely read, and their books had a much greater impact on the decline of Thomas's reputation.[8] Some writers pointed out Sherman's and Grant's errors, but these critics were not prominent military figures, and their words did not carry as much weight. Sherman's and Grant's memoirs strongly influenced the writings of historians, and only in recent decades has new scholarship made possible an accurate accounting of Thomas's role in the western campaigns.[9]

While Sherman's and Grant's memoirs were one cause of the diminution of Thomas's reputation, a more significant cause relates to changes in the way the war has been remembered by historians. Southern historians wrote about the war in what has been termed the "Lost Cause" view of Civil War history, and Northern historians, largely accepting and accommodating Southern views, eventually adopted a "nationalist" or "reconciliationist" view of the war. In both of these traditions, the role of Southern Unionists was given little attention.

The Lost Cause movement in Southern history gets its name from Edward A. Pollard's 1866 book, *The Lost Cause: The Standard Southern History of the War of the Confederates*. The Lost Cause movement was both a historical school and a popular movement, and it generated books, articles, monuments, parades, ceremonies, speeches, and other commemorative events. The movement was most active in the late nineteenth and early twentieth centuries and diminished somewhat in importance as the North and South reconciled and the Civil War passed from living memory. The Lost Cause tradition had a strong influence on academic historical writing about the war, and even today it remains an influence on popular accounts of the conflict.[10]

The Lost Cause tradition arose out of white Southerners' need to understand and cope with their defeat. The Southern states seceded from the Union to protect what Southerners saw as their freedom, their right to own slaves, and their way of life, but their decision caused them to lose their slaves, their prosperity, and, for a while, their right to self-government. Unionists expected that the magnitude of Southerners' defeat would force them to admit that secession was an error. Instead, former Confederates constructed their own interpretation of the events of the war, which absolved them from blame for both the start of the war and their defeat. Lost Cause historians claimed that Northern intransigence and tyranny had given Southerners no choice but to secede, and that Northern aggression had made war inevitable. They claimed that the underlying cause of the Civil War was not slavery, but cultural differences, economic issues, and states' rights. Lost Cause historians stated that most slaves were well treated and happy before the war, and their accounts of slaves' actions during the war focused on those slaves who remained loyal to their masters, not those who escaped and joined the Union army. Lost Cause histories idealized the moral character of Confederate leaders and soldiers and described the Confederate home front as uniformly loyal and supportive of the war. They portrayed Southern military prowess as superior to that of the North and explained their defeat by reference to unfortunate battlefield contingencies and the superiority of Northern resources and manpower.[11]

Since a central premise of Lost Cause histories was that white Southerners had no choice but to fight for the Confederacy, the existence of Southern Unionists threatened the entire historical enterprise. Lost Cause historians both minimized the number of Southern Unionists and denigrated their motives, describing them as poor, uncultured, and unethical individuals who supported the North for financial gain. While these strategies could explain away the Unionism of some Southerners, they could not be easily applied to Thomas, who was too famous to ignore, and from too wealthy a family to dismiss as a financial opportunist. Southern writers tended to adopt two strategies to explain Thomas's actions. The first strategy blamed Thomas's Northern wife, stating that she used her feminine influence to induce him to side with her section. The second strategy called Thomas a career opportunist, who sided with the Union due to the greater scope for advancement in the Federal army.[12]

These accusations began during the Civil War itself, particularly as Thomas's career brought him to public attention. Shortly after Thomas's promotion to command the Army of the Cumberland, the *Richmond Examiner* published a letter from an anonymous correspondent who claimed to have served with Thomas in Texas. The writer stated that before the war, Thomas "expressed himself loudly as a strong Southern man of the Calhoun school." After Fort Sumter, Thomas went to Richmond to apply for a position with the Virginia State Guard, but he first went to New York to visit his wife. After this visit, the writer claimed, Thomas "threw his puny weight in the scale against the South." The secessionist writer Edmund Ruffin wrote in his diary that Thomas was strongly pro-Southern before the war, but "a business-like calculation, and comparison of the chances of promotion and profit in his profession," no doubt led him "to remain in the service of the Yankee government, rather than to defend his principles and his native country."[13]

These attacks continued through the Civil War and Reconstruction. Thomas never responded to them in public, but he did respond to one attack in a private letter. In 1868 the *Lexington Gazette* printed a letter that claimed Thomas had applied for a commission in the Confederate army in 1861 but had changed his plans when he found better opportunities in the Union army. An officer forwarded the article to Thomas, and Thomas sent the officer a carefully worded denial:

> No one can truthfully say that I ever belonged to the States Rights Party, or that I ever expressed more than the usual disapprobation of such conduct as John Brown was guilty of in his raid into Virginia, or that I threatened to resign my commission in the army and join Gov. Wise to take Virginia out of the Union, if such a thing was reported. Nor can any person truthfully say that I ever applied by letter or verbally to any person private or official in the Southern Confederacy for a commission in their army or for any position in their Government, nor that I ever received any propositions from any person private or official in the Confederacy relating to my acceptance of a commission either civil or military under that government.[14]

This convoluted and legalistic response fails to mention that Virginia's governor, John Letcher, once offered Thomas the position of chief of ordnance of the state militia. The response is misleading but not actually false, since Virginia had not yet joined the Confederacy when Letcher made the offer. As the historian Francis MacDonnell has pointed out, Thomas probably neglected to mention the offer in order to be sure that his opponents did not learn about it. Thomas did not know his correspondent personally and may have feared that the officer would publish Thomas's reply. Since none of Thomas's critics had yet mentioned Governor Letcher's offer of a position in the Virginia militia, Thomas did not want to volunteer this information in a letter that might become public.[15]

While scattered attacks on Thomas's reputation occurred during his lifetime, concerted efforts to discredit him began after his death. The first of these attempts came less than a month after Thomas died, when the April 23, 1870, *Richmond Dispatch* published a letter by Fitzhugh Lee. Fitzhugh Lee, a nephew of Robert E. Lee, served under Thomas in the Second Cavalry in Texas and served as a general in the Confederate army. Lee wrote that Thomas's political views before the war "were Southern to almost the bellicose degree," and that in early 1861 Thomas had told Lee that he intended to fight for the South. Lee also claimed that Thomas had written to the governor of Virginia in early 1861 offering his military services to the state.[16] Thomas's staff aide, Alfred Hough, denied Lee's statement in a public letter, and this letter was widely printed in Northern newspapers.[17]

On December 31, 1875, the *New York Herald* published a letter from Francis Smith, the superintendent of the Virginia Military Institute, that Thomas had written him in January 1861 to inquire about a teaching position. Smith now stated that Thomas had also applied for a position in the Confederate army in 1861 and claimed to have documentary proof of Thomas's application. Smith's allegations made Frances Thomas so angry that she departed from her usual policy of ignoring criticisms of her husband and wrote the *New York Herald* in response. In her letter Frances claimed that Thomas's loyalty to the Union had never wavered, and that her influence had had no effect on his decision. She explained that Thomas had applied for the position at VMI because he thought his back injury had left him incapable of military service, not because he wanted to avoid serving in the Union army. Frances concluded by criticizing Smith and Thomas's other "enemies" for not making their accusations when Thomas was alive and able to respond.[18]

In 1883 Simon Cameron made a public statement that Thomas had wavered in his loyalty in 1861. Cameron had been Lincoln's secretary of war during the first months of the Civil War and was now a senator from Pennsylvania. He spoke about Thomas as part of his testimony before a court of inquiry that Fitz John Porter had called to clear his record, two decades after being dishonorably discharged in 1862. In April 1861 Cameron had sent Porter to Pennsylvania with instructions to send units to the capital, and during this time Porter came into contact with Thomas. Cameron claimed that Thomas had hesitated at first to fight for the Union, but that Porter had convinced him to remain loyal.[19]

Cameron's statement made it into the newspapers at the time, and it was reprinted by the Southern Historical Society, whose members were happy to find evidence that Thomas had considered siding with the secessionists. Fitz John Porter wrote Frances Thomas to assure her that he had not had any such conversation with George Thomas, and that he had not prompted Cameron to make his statement. Frances wrote Cameron and asked him to retract the statement, but Cameron never replied. The motive for Cameron's testimony is unclear, as it does not seem that he had any reason to be hostile to Thomas. Perhaps he made the statement as a way of supporting Porter, without thinking about how it would affect Thomas's reputation.[20]

As time passed, Southern writers gradually stopped trying to discredit Thomas's reputation. In 1876 Dabney H. Maury, a former Confederate general and the secretary of the Southern Historical Society, wrote positively about Thomas in his review of Van Horne's *History of the Army of the Cumberland*. While Maury condemned Thomas's decision to fight for the Union, he admitted that Thomas's decision was a huge loss for the South and stated that Thomas was "a tower of strength" for the Union side. An early twentieth-century historical survey, *The South in the Building of the Nation*, called Thomas "one of the ablest of the Union generals," adding that Thomas was "said to have contemplated resigning from the United States army" but that unspecified "influences" prevented him from doing so. A 1901 article in the *Richmond Times* repeated the charges that Thomas had originally planned to fight for the South and that his wife's influence changed his mind but concluded with praise for Thomas's skill as a general and the statement that "we of this generation can be proud of him as a Virginian." An issue of the 1907 *William and Mary Quarterly* also praised Thomas, stating that without the contributions of

Thomas and other Southern Unionists, the Union cause "would have been 'the lost cause.'" William Squires's 1928 book of Virginia history, *The Days of Yester-Year in Colony and Commonwealth*, devoted a full chapter to Thomas, praising his character and military achievements. Squires speculated that the influence of Thomas's wife led him to side with the North, but he also stated that Thomas considered secession unwise and unconstitutional.[21]

The twentieth century also marked the return of Thomas to South-ampton County local history. When Judith and Fannie Thomas died, they left Thomas's sword from the war with Mexico to William Barham, their doctor and friend. In 1915 Barham donated Thomas's sword to the Virginia Historical Society, and in 1932 he published an article about the Thomas family in the *Virginia Magazine of History and Biography*. The official county history, published in 1978 by the Southampton County Historical Society, devotes six pages to Thomas, including a fair and accurate analysis of Thomas's motives for deciding to side with the Union. In recent decades the Southampton County Historical Society has published two articles about Thomas in its newsletter, and in 1985 the county recognized Thomas with the erection of a historical roadside marker. The Thomas family plantation has also been registered on Virginia's "Civil War Trails" list of historical sites.[22]

Thomas has also received some recognition in the capital of the former Confederacy. The Virginia Historical Society, which possesses Thomas's ceremonial sword and papers, has placed his sword on display as part of an exhibit on how Virginians made varying decisions about secession. The exhibit contrasts Thomas and Winfield Scott with Robert E. Lee and explains the ethical reasoning behind each of their decisions. The president of the Virginia Historical Society, Charles Bryan, wrote an article in the April 11, 2004, *Richmond Times-Dispatch* that described Lee and Thomas as highly moral individuals who struggled with their consciences over secession and came to different but equally ethical decisions. More than a century after the end of the Civil War, Southamp-ton County and the state of Virginia have finally chosen to recognize Thomas as one of their own.[23]

While it is understandable that Southerners once wanted to disparage or forget Thomas, the eclipse of Thomas's reputation in the North is less easily explained. One reason has to do with the lack of sources. Thomas had his personal papers destroyed, and he never wrote a memoir. His siblings and neighbors in Southampton County declined to talk about him to journalists and historians. Grant and Sherman, by contrast, each wrote memoirs, left extensive personal papers, and were written about by many people who knew them, which gave biographers much more material to work with. Dozens of biographies of Grant and Sherman have been written over the years, while only nine have been written of Thomas.[24]

A second reason for Thomas's fall from prominence has to do with how Northerners have chosen to remember the Civil War. In the decades immediately after the war's conclusion, Northern historians wrote highly partisan accounts of the war, with Unionists cast as heroes, and secessionists as traitors. Southern Unionists were seen as particularly important and admirable, and Thomas occupied a high place in the pantheon of loyal Southerners. As time passed, however, Northern writers came to accept the South's Lost Cause view of history as valid and adjusted their own historical writing in response. In this new version of Civil War history, called the nationalist or reconciliationist school, Northern historians began speaking of the war as a national tragedy, in which neither side was to blame. Instead of characterizing Southern secessionists as traitors, Northern writers began to portray both sides as equally honorable. With this change in perspective, Southern Unionists were seen as less important and thus were given a less prominent role in historical accounts. Thomas's status as one of the most prominent loyal Southerners became less important, and his reputation faded.[25]

Historians writing in the reconciliationist or nationalist school of the Civil War tended to focus on the details of military campaigns and on the courage, suffering, and honor of the white soldiers of both sides, while glossing over the political, social, and racial issues that surrounded the war. Many of today's popular histories of the Civil War still follow this strategy. In these accounts, Thomas is described as a skillful Union general and an admirable human being, who incidentally happened to come from Virginia. This approach downplays Thomas's importance as a Southern Unionist and ignores his change of views on racial issues, taking away two of the most important and historically significant aspects of his career.[26]

During the last several decades, historians have adopted new perspectives on the Civil War, perspectives that give a renewed importance to George Thomas. First, the military significance of the western campaigns in bringing about a Union victory has been recognized. A large number of new studies of these battles have appeared, and these books accurately describe Thomas's contributions to the Union cause. Second, scholars have become interested once more in the role of Southern Unionists and have begun to recognize their crucial contribution to the Union victory. Finally, scholars have given new consideration to the role of race and slavery in the Civil War and Reconstruction, overcoming the racial biases of their predecessors and adopting a more balanced view. In all three of these areas, Thomas's role is significant.

Of these three issues, Thomas's role as a military commander in the western campaigns has been the most widely discussed. Many writers have cast this debate in terms of a sort of competition among Thomas, Grant, and Sherman for the title of best Union general. Asking the question in this way makes coming up with an answer impossible, as the three men commanded in very different circumstances, and one cannot make an accurate comparison. Furthermore, the three generals had very different leadership styles, so each writer ranks them differently, according to what criteria the writer adopts to judge them. Instead of comparing the three generals, it is more productive to evaluate Thomas independently and assess how his efforts contributed to Union victory.[27]

It is also necessary to address the claims of those historians and biographers who argue that Thomas was unfairly discriminated against, and not allowed to reach the prominence that he deserved. Thomas's partisans have based their claims of discrimination on three arguments: that Thomas was discriminated against on account of being a native of Virginia; that he was persecuted out of jealousy and personal animosity by a clique made up of Grant, Sherman, and their associates; and that Thomas's superior officers unfairly labeled him as "slow."

The claim that Thomas was discriminated against on account of being a native of Virginia has little foundation in fact. Thomas ascended quickly through the ranks in 1861 and 1862, and there is no reliable historical evidence to indicate that Lincoln, Stanton, or anyone else of importance in the War Department doubted Thomas's loyalty, once Winfield Scott vouched for him. On the contrary, Lincoln often promoted officers from Upper South states as a way of encouraging Southern Unionists. One of the reasons that Thomas was assigned to the crucial theater of Kentucky in late 1861 was that he was a Southerner; Robert Anderson and Ormsby

M. Mitchel were assigned to Kentucky for the same reason. However, the fact that Thomas came from a seceded state may have hurt his career later in the war, not because anyone doubted his loyalty, but because there was no state political constituency to lobby for his promotion. Grant had the backing of Illinois politicians, and Sherman and Rosecrans had the backing of their Ohio congressional delegations. In Sherman's case, his brother, John Sherman, was one of Ohio's senators. Thomas's lack of state political backing did put him at a relative disadvantage.

The second claim, that Thomas was discriminated against by a clique made up of Grant, Sherman, and their followers, also has a limited foundation. As Grant rose to overall command of the Union forces, he gained the power to choose officers for promotion, and he consistently favored other officers over Thomas. This was most noticeable when Grant promoted Sherman instead of Thomas to overall command in the Atlanta campaign, despite Thomas's seniority and better field record. Grant's preference for Sherman was not simple favoritism, though. Grant thought that Sherman's ideas about strategy were similar to his own, and Grant trusted Sherman to move quickly and keep Johnston's army under pressure, something that he did not trust Thomas to do. While Grant liked Sherman and disliked Thomas, he did not promote Sherman out of personal sentiment, but because he honestly thought that Sherman was the better man for the job.

The third issue, whether Thomas was "slow" at Nashville and elsewhere, has been debated for decades. Schofield, Sherman, and Grant all criticized Thomas for waiting too long at Nashville before attacking Hood, and for moving too slowly in the pursuit. Sherman also alleged that Thomas was too slow during the Atlanta campaign. Following them, a number of historians have portrayed Thomas as a good defensive general but too cautious and unaggressive to be an effective offensive general.

It is difficult to evaluate the charge that Thomas was slow. Many people described Thomas as slow, but they meant different things by the word. Thomas had a deliberate, careful personality; he spoke slowly, moved slowly, and even rode his horse slowly. An intelligent but deliberate thinker, he lacked Sherman's quick wit or Rosecrans's creative genius. Braxton Bragg, writing in 1856, praised Thomas's abilities and character but described him as "not brilliant." In an 1860 letter, before the two men had any reason to be rivals, Sherman characterized Thomas as "reliable" but "maybe a little slow." Joseph Reynolds, who liked and respected Thomas, stated that "it's the Lord of Mighty's truth that he *was* slow."[28]

But slowness of speech and action are not the same as slowness on the battlefield, and in this regard the record is less clear. It is true that Thomas was less quick and less aggressive than Grant or Sherman. Grant and Sherman pushed their men hard, made risky frontal attacks, and improvised their plans as they went. Thomas was more careful of his men's welfare, made few frontal attacks, and planned his movements carefully. However, one cannot place Thomas in the same category as Henry Halleck, Don Carlos Buell, or George McClellan. Thomas did not shrink from fighting when the conditions were right, as Buell and McClellan did, and he did not move as slowly as Halleck had done before Corinth.

Advocates of Thomas have pointed out that he never lost a battle, and while this is true, there is more to good generalship than not losing. Thomas's method, and the method of Grant and Sherman, each had advantages and disadvantages. On the one hand, Thomas never ordered his men to make disastrous frontal assaults, as Sherman did at Kennesaw Mountain and Grant did at Cold Harbor. On the other hand, Thomas never improvised his way to quick, unexpected victories, as Grant did at Forts Henry and Donelson and at Missionary Ridge. Grant lost more battles than Thomas did, but he won more battles as well. A comparison of the three generals is made even more difficult by the fact that Thomas only held independent command twice in his career. If Thomas had received the command of the Army of the Cumberland after Buell, or command of the western armies after Grant, historians would have good basis for comparison. As it is, Thomas did not hold independent command long enough for others to know how aggressive he would have been in an entire offensive campaign.

Turning to Thomas's actual record, there is little evidence that his more careful command style caused him to miss any opportunities that Grant or Sherman might have gained. Thomas's delay before attacking Hood at Nashville did not create any military disadvantage for the Union—in fact, it helped the Union cause—as Hood's army was weakened during the delay. Thomas did not succeed in capturing Hood's army intact after his victory at Nashville, but it is difficult to find an example of a Civil War pursuit that was more successful. Only at Appomattox did a Union army manage successfully to block the escape of a retreating Confederate army, but this was possible only after a months-long siege, the near destruction of the Confederate rail and supply network, and a great disparity in the numbers of the two forces. Thomas's failure to trap Hood's army after Nashville was typical for a Civil War battle, and his pursuit seems to have been at least as effective, if not more so, than most comparable examples.

Thus, many of the criticisms made of Thomas by Grant, Sherman, and the historians who sympathize with them seem to be unfounded. For the most part, many of the extremely laudatory statements made by Thomas's partisans seem to be equally unsupported by the historical record. For example, Thomas's biographer Francis McKinney and the historian Thomas Buell give Thomas credit for nearly every one of the Army of the Cumberland's successes, while blaming Grant, Sherman, and Rosecrans for its failures. They do so without making a careful analysis of the role of each of these generals in making specific decisions and instead simply assert that Thomas made the good decisions and that the other three generals made the bad ones.

In addition, some writers have been too generous in their praise of Thomas's conduct of the Battle of Nashville. In his *History of the Army of the Cumberland*, Van Horne stated that the battle went exactly according to Thomas's plans, and some historians have echoed Van Horne's analysis.[29] In reality, there were so many setbacks, delays, and unexpected developments during the two days of the battle that most of Thomas's original plan had to be abandoned, and Thomas improvised adjustments on the spot. This was hardly unusual. As the historian Paddy Griffith has pointed out, the communications technology available to Civil War commanders was inadequate to the size of the armies involved, so that once battle was joined, army commanders lost effective control of their units. This happened at Nashville, as Thomas was forced to leave Wood and Steedman unsupervised, while riding continually to and from Wilson's, Schofield's, and Smith's command posts trying to coordinate their actions. Thomas did not win the battle because he devised a perfect plan, but because of his persistence and improvisation in the face of frequent changes and setbacks. His performance at the Battle of Nashville was indeed impressive, but not for the reasons cited by Van Horne.

In conclusion, an evaluation of Thomas's generalship finds him to be somewhat less brilliant than the exaggerated portrait painted by Van Horne, McKinney, and Thomas Buell but nevertheless deserving of his reputation as a great general. Thomas was well organized, conscientious, and effective in providing his men with adequate food, clothing, supplies, and armaments, and these factors contributed to the great morale of his army. He was strict but fair in training and disciplining his men. Along with Rosecrans and Sherman, Thomas presided over important innovations in the engineering, medical, and mapmaking departments of the Army of the Cumberland. His battlefield leadership was equally impressive. He served capably as a subordinate commander under Buell, Rosecrans, Grant, and Sherman, contributing greatly to the success of their campaigns. As an independent commander, his defensive stand at Chickamauga probably saved the Union army from destruction, and his offensive victory at Nashville nearly destroyed a Confederate army. Most military historians place Thomas either second or third in the pantheon of Union generals, behind Grant, and sometimes behind Sherman. All agree that Thomas's generalship contributed greatly to the success of the Union cause.[30]

Most biographies of Civil War generals stop after assessing their subject's skill as a general and contribution to the war effort of his side. In Thomas's case, however, his military accomplishments constitute only one aspect of his importance. Thomas was also the war's most prominent Southern Unionist and was one of the few white Southerners whose views on race and slavery changed as a result of the war.

As a Unionist, Thomas is representative of thousands of others. William W. Freehling has argued that the decision of many white Southerners to remain loyal to the Union was one of the most important turning points of the war. Southern white Unionism took two forms: the decision of individuals from seceded states to join the Union army, and the decision of Southerners living in Maryland, Delaware, Kentucky, and Missouri to keep their states in the Union. While the majority of Southern Unionists were nonslaveholders from highland or mountainous regions of the Confederacy, such as western Virginia and North Carolina, eastern Tennessee, and northern Alabama, a sizable minority of Southern Unionists were slaveholders, and Thomas can be seen as representative of this group.[31]

While Thomas's Unionism is illuminating in that it is representative, his change of views on race is even more instructive in that it was so unusual. Many Northern whites changed their views on race and slavery as a response to African Americans' military service, but few Southern white Unionists did so. While some Southern white Unionists formed alliances with black voters during Reconstruction, this was an alliance born more of pragmatism than idealism. Most white Southern Unionists opposed black suffrage during the early years of Reconstruction and only allied with black voters once Congress had made blacks' political rights an unavoidable reality.

As a former slave owner who became a strong supporter of blacks' political rights, Thomas was extremely unusual. Why he came to such a profound change of views on this point is the most interesting question of Thomas's character, and the most difficult to answer. Discovering the answer is important, however, as our understanding of the racial views of most white Southerners can be increased by an examination of how Thomas's views came to differ from them.

One answer to the question of what made Thomas different could be that Thomas was an unusually good person. Thomas did have a reputation as a kind, honest, and morally upstanding person, and his moral character evidenced itself in a variety of ways unrelated to the issue of African Americans and slavery. Also, Thomas had an unusually legalistic, rule-oriented sense of morality. In 1861 this particular moral sense led him to side with the Union, where he felt that his duty lay, instead of with Virginia, where his affections lay. Similarly, Thomas's sense of justice led him to believe that black former soldiers, and blacks in general, deserved rights and protections, regardless of whether Thomas liked blacks personally or sympathized with them emotionally. Perhaps Thomas was able to change his views on race, while other white Southerners were not, because of these exceptional moral qualities.

This examination of Thomas's personal moral character does provide some clues to his unusual decision to support blacks' political rights, but it is of little use as a historical explanation, as it tells us nothing about the racial views of nineteenth-century Southern whites in general. Thomas differed from other Southern white Unionists in two important and illuminating respects: he was a career army officer, and he saw with his own eyes the evidence of black courage and discipline under fire. Thomas's career as a regular army officer led him to consider courage and discipline under fire to be essential moral qualities, virtues that defined one's manhood. More so than other whites, Thomas considered combat veterans who had borne themselves with discipline and courage to be deserving of rights and protection from the government, regardless of their race. Both Thomas Van Horne and Thomas J. Morgan witnessed

Thomas's reaction to seeing the dead bodies of black soldiers on the Nashville battlefield, and both men indicate how strongly Thomas was moved by the sight.[32]

Very few white Southern Unionists ever commanded or served with African American soldiers. Almost none of the white officers of African American regiments were from Southern backgrounds, and the enlisted men and officers in white Southern Unionist regiments had little contact with African American troops. These two factors may explain why so few white Southern Unionists had the same change of racial views as Thomas. Whatever the reason, it is a great tragedy of American history that so few white citizens, in both the North and the South, went through the same change of views as Thomas. If other whites had demonstrated Thomas's ability to overcome racial prejudice and treat blacks with fairness, the tragic racial history of our country could have been different.

While it is too late to change the past, it is not too late to change how the past is remembered. For too long, people have chosen to remember the war as a noble tragedy, a contest between two morally equivalent causes, in which whites—and only whites—on both sides fought with courage and honor. In recent years, African American soldiers have attained prominence in both academic and popular accounts of the war, but the issues of race and slavery, and the events of Reconstruction, have been given little attention in popular histories. By studying the life of George Thomas, we can place the issues of race and slavery back at the center of Civil War history, where they belong.

After many decades, Abraham Lincoln has finally become a hero both in the North and in the South. Perhaps the day will come when George Thomas will also be remembered and honored in both sections of the United States. Thomas need not replace traditional Southern heroes, such as Lee, Jackson, and Stuart, but may perhaps be added to the pantheon, as an example of a different sort of honor and courage. In the process, we will gain a new understanding of the history of the Civil War and Reconstruction—a history that is both honorable and shameful, both tragic and heroic.

Notes

Book epigraph from a letter by George H. Thomas, commander of the Department of the Tennessee, to the people of Rome, Georgia, forbidding the display of the Confederate flag. General Order No. 21, Headquarters Department of the Tennessee, Louisville, Kentucky, February 9, 1867.

CHAPTER 1, CHILDHOOD AND EARLY YEARS

1. Howard, "Thomas," 285–302.

2. Thomas family papers, Virginia Historical Society (hereafter cited as Thomas Papers, VHS).

3. Drewry, *Southampton Insurrection*, 68–69.

4. Van Horne, Thomas, 3–4.

5. Piatt and Boynton, Thomas, 50.

6. These include the Southampton County deed books, court minute books, personal property and land tax records, voting records, marriage bond records, and census books, at the Library of Virginia in Richmond, and a guide to these records in the Francis McKinney Papers, Library of Virginia.

7. George Thomas to John Thomas, May 1838, 19 October 1840, 28 April 1850, and 8 February 1851, Thomas Papers, VHS.

8. National census data and Southampton County tax records, 1830, Library of Virginia. Crofts, *Old Southampton*, 18.

9. Militia Records for John Thomas and Widow's Application for Bounty Land of Elizabeth R. Thomas, National Archives; Southampton County Records and Francis McKinney Papers, Library of Virginia. For the War of 1812 in Virginia, see Mahon, *The War of 1812*, 109–122, and Hallahan, *Craney Island*.

10. Coppee, *Thomas*, 3; Southampton County Court Minute Book, 1829, 263.

11. Thomas family account books, Thomas Papers, VHS.

12. Crofts, *Old Southampton*, 100. Jerusalem is now named Courtland.

13. Crofts, *Old Southampton*, 79; Thomas Papers, VHS.

14. George H. Thomas to Frances Thomas, 22 December 1858, Library of Virginia.

15. Van Horne, *Thomas*, 269; Society of the Army of the Cumberland, *1870 Reunion Report*; Piatt and Boynton, *Thomas*, 51, 53.

16. Crofts, *Old Southampton*, 293.

17. Crofts, *Old Southampton*, 92–93.

18. Oakes, *Ruling Race*.

19. Oates, *Fires of Jubilee*; Tragle, *Southampton Slave Revolt*.

20. Eph 6:5–8, Col 3:22–25, 1 Tim 6:1–2, Titus 2:9–10, Phlm, and 1 Pet 3:18–25.

21. Ex 21:16, Deut 24:7.

22. Drewry, *Southampton Insurrection,* 68–69; "Confessions of Nat Turner," in Andrews and Gates, *Slave Narratives*, 259; Tragle, *Southampton Slave Revolt*, 173–245.

23. A. Freehling, *Drift toward Dissolution*; W. Freehling, *Secessionists at Bay*, 178–96.

24. Van Horne, *Thomas,* 457; Southampton County Voting Records, Library of Virginia; Thomas family account books, Thomas Papers, VHS.

25. Southampton County Order Book, 1835–39, 37.

26. Van Horne, *Thomas,* 2.

27. Van Horne, *Thomas,* 2.

28. George H. Thomas to John Thomas, 23 March 1851, Thomas Papers, VHS.

CHAPTER 2, WEST POINT AND FLORIDA

1. Morrison, *West Point*, 65. Background information on the U.S. Military Academy in this chapter is taken from Morrison, *West Point,* Ambrose, *Duty, Honor, Country*; and Forman, *West Point*.

2. Coppee, *Thomas*, 322–23.

3. Marszalek, *Sherman*, 19–28.

4. Morrison, *West Point*, 65–66; *United States Military Academy Staff Records*, vol. 2, 1835–42, 30 June and 1 July 1836, USMA/West Point Archives (hereafter cited as WPA).

5. Coppee, *Thomas,* 322–23.

6. "Registers of Cadet Delinquencies, January 1838 to May 1913, WPA.

7. Marszalek, *Sherman*, 23–24.

8. Morrison, *West Point,* 47–60; Endler, *Other Leaders, Other Heroes*, 96–100.

9. Forman, *West Point*, 98; USMA *Staff Records*, vol. 2, 1835–42, WPA.

10. Garfield, "Thomas," 80.

11. R. Johnson, *Thomas*, 14.

12. George Thomas to John Thomas, 16 February 1839, VHS.

13. Thomas to Thomas, 16 February 1839, VHS.

14. Donald, *Lincoln Reconsidered*, 89–103; Engle, "Buell: Military Philosophy," 89–115; Goss, *Union High Command*, 10–12, 154–7, 168–9; A. Jones, "Jomini,"; A. Jones, *Command and Strategy*, 256–59, 274–77; Williams, "Military Leadership of North and South," in Donald, ed., *Why the North Won*; T. Williams, *Lincoln and His Generals*; and W. Wood, *Civil War Generalship.*

15. George Thomas to John Thomas, May 1838, Thomas Papers, VHS.

16. George Thomas to John Thomas, 19 October 1840, Thomas Papers, VHS.

17. George Thomas to John Thomas, 27 September 1840, Thomas Papers, VHS.

18. Thomas to Thomas, 19 October 1840.

19. Thomas to Thomas, 27 September 1840.

20. Thomas to Thomas, 19 October 1840. A corner of the letter is torn off, making it necessary to guess some words, like "supporting," from the context of the rest of the sentence.

21. Thomas to Thomas, 19 October 1840.

22. Mahon, *Second Seminole War,* 325. Where not specifically noted, the information in this chapter on the Seminoles and the Second Seminole War is taken from Mahon, *Second Seminole War;* Covington, *Seminoles of Florida;* and Peters, *Florida Wars.*

23. Keyes, *Fifty Years,* 163–65.

24. George Thomas to John Thomas, 25 January 1841, Thomas Papers, VHS.

25. Thomas to Thomas, 25 January 1841.

26. George Thomas to C. P. Kingsbury, 25 July 1841. This letter is no longer extant, but is printed in Coppee, *Thomas,* 7–9.

27. Sprague, *Florida War,* 392–94.

28. Johnson, *Thomas,* 18–20; Sprague, *Florida War,* 554–56.

29. Thomas to Nathan Towson, 14 September 1843, Letters Received, Adjutant General, Record Group (RG) 94, National Archives (NA).

30. Keyes, *Fifty Years,* 166–67.

31. Keyes, *Fifty Years,* 169.

32. Keyes, *Fifty Years,* 168–69, 166.

33. Keyes, *Fifty Years,* 176; Sherman, *Memoirs,* 1:27–35; Third Artillery Regimental Returns, RG 94, NA.

34. George H. Thomas to John Thomas, 8 November 1844, Thomas Papers, VHS.

35. French, *Two Wars,* 24.

36. Third Artillery Regimental Returns, RG 94, NA.

37. Weigley, *United States Army,* 171–72.

38. Lavender, *Buena Vista,* 226–29; Dillon, *Artillery in the Mexican War.*

39. George Thomas to John Thomas, 17 October 1844, Thomas Papers, VHS; George Thomas to John Thomas, 8 November 1844, Thomas Papers, Duke University Library (DUL).

40. Thomas to Thomas, 8 November 1844, Thomas Papers, DUL.

41. George Thomas to John Thomas, 11 January 1845, Thomas Papers, DUL.

CHAPTER 3, MEXICO

1. Eisenhower, *So Far from God,* 3–28.

2. Eisenhower, *So Far from God,* 29–48.

3. Eisenhower, *So Far from God,* 36–39; Foos, *Killing Affair,* 17–19, 98–99.

4. Eisenhower, *So Far from God,* 49–50.

5. Eisenhower, *So Far from God,* 51–68.

6. The account of the siege at Matamoros is taken from E. S. Hawkins to Taylor, and Joseph Mansfield to Taylor, filed with Taylor to the Adjutant General, 19 May 1846, RG 94, NA; Thorpe, *Our Army on the Rio Grande;* and Ripley, *War with Mexico.*

7. Hawkins to Taylor, RG 94, NA.

8. Eisenhower, *So Far from God,* 76–86.

9. Eisenhower, *So Far from God,* 98–101.

10. Eisenhower, *So Far from God,* 104–105.

11. Giddings, *Sketches,* 117; J. Smith, *War with Mexico,* 204; Third Artillery Regimental Returns, RG 94, NA.

12. Eisenhower, *So Far From God,* 106–20.

13. Taylor to Secretary of War, House Executive Document No. 4, 29th Cong., 2nd Sess.; Eisenhower, *So Far from God*, 120–51; Thorpe, *Our Army at Monterey*; Smith, *War with Mexico*, 249–59; and Wilcox, *Mexican War*, 93–110.

14. Thorpe, *Our Army at Monterey*, 53. Bragg's company had four guns, and neither Thorpe nor any other source states whether the gun involved in this fighting was Thomas's.

15. Giddings, *Sketches*, 168–69.

16. Ripley, *War with Mexico*, 214; Wilcox, *Mexican War*, 97; Thorpe, *Our Army at Monterey*, 57.

17. Smith, *War with Mexico*, 254.

18. Ripley, *War with Mexico*, 223–24.

19. Pope, *Military Memoirs*, 94.

20. Henry, *Campaign Sketches*, 207.

21. Eisenhower, *So Far from God*, 144–50.

22. Taylor to Secretary of War, House Executive Document No. 4, 29th Cong., 2nd Sess.

23. Cullum, *Biographical Register*, 600.

24. Third Artillery Regimental Returns, RG 94, NA; Thomas to "Captain" [George W. Cullum], 21 September 1859, George H. Thomas Papers, Huntington Library (HL).

25. Eisenhower, *So Far from God*, 159–61, 166–69.

26. Braxton Bragg to the commander of the Third Artillery Regiment, 22 November 1847, Braxton Bragg Papers, DUL.

27. Eisenhower, *So Far from God*, 157–59, 169–75.

28. Eisenhower, *So Far from God*, 168, 176.

29. Eisenhower, *So Far from God*, 178–82.

30. Eisenhower, *So Far From God*, 182–91; Smith, *War with Mexico*, 384–401; Wilcox, *Mexican War*, 221–36; Carleton, *Buena Vista*; and Taylor to Secretary of War, Senate Executive Committee Document No. 1, 30th Cong., 1st Sess.

31. Wilcox, *Mexican War*, 222.

32. Wilcox, *Mexican War*, 222–23.

33. Carleton, *Buena Vista*, 85; Wilcox, *Mexican War*, 226.

34. Wilcox, *Mexican War*, 230–31.

35. Wilcox, *Mexican War*, 231–33.

36. Taylor to Secretary of War, Senate Executive Committee Document No. 1, 30th Cong., 1st Sess., 142–43.

37. Taylor to Secretary of War, 138–39.

38. Taylor to Secretary of War, 150.

39. Taylor to Secretary of War, 205.

40. Gen. George Gibson to Secretary of War, 21 May 1847, Letters Received, Secretary of War, RG 107, NA.

41. Bragg to the Adjutant General, 22 November 1847; Thomas to the Adjutant General, 23 December 1847; Letters Received, Adjutant General, RG 94, NA.

42. Taylor to the Adjutant General, 9 January 1848, Letters Received, Adjutant General, RG 94, NA.

43. Van Horne, *Thomas*, 7.

44. Tidball, "First Experiences," 206.

45. George Thomas to John Thomas, 25 October 1848, Thomas Papers, VHS.

46. Thomas to Thomas, 25 October 1848, Thomas Papers, VHS.

47. George H. Thomas to James Maget, 31 March 1848, Thomas Papers, VHS.

48. Thomas to Thomas, 25 October 1848, Thomas Papers, VHS.

49. Van Horne, *Thomas*, 9.

50. Van Horne, *Thomas*, 9; Thomas Papers, VHS.

CHAPTER 4, WEST POINT, FORT YUMA, AND TEXAS

1. Van Horne, *Thomas*, 9.

2. Covington, *Seminoles of Florida*, 113–16; Missall and Missall, *Seminole Wars*, 209–13.

3. Covington, *Seminoles of Florida*, 113–16.

4. Post returns from Fort Adams, Rhode Island, and Forts Vinton, Capron, Meade, and Myers, in Florida, and Monthly returns, Third Artillery Regiment, RG 94, NA; Letters Sent and Letters Received, Department of Florida, RG 393, NA; George Thomas to John Thomas, 28 April 1850, Thomas Papers, VHS.

5. Thomas to Thomas, 28 April 1850, Thomas Papers, VHS.

6. Opdycke, *Good and Right*, 292.

7. Braxton Bragg to John Y. Mason, 17 November 1848, Bragg Papers, DUL.

8. George Thomas to John Thomas, 8 February and 3 March 1851, Thomas Papers, VHS; Post Order Book No. 3, Special Order No. 41, p. 514, RG 404, WPA.

9. Thomas to Thomas, 28 April 1850, Thomas Papers, VHS.

10. Report of the Superintendent and Board of Visitors of the U.S. Military Academy, Senate Executive Document No. 1, 33rd Cong., 1st Sess., 191.

11. Thomas to Thomas, 8 February 1851, Thomas Papers, VHS.

12. Thomas to Thomas, 8 February and 3 March 1851;, Thomas Papers, VHS.

13. Reports of the Superintendent and Board of Visitors of the U.S. Military Academy, Senate Executive Documents, 33rd Cong., 1st Sess.; 33rd Cong., 2nd Sess. Robert E. Lee to Quartermaster General Thomas Jesup, 17 March 1853, Superintendent's Letter Book, 3:10–11, RG 404, WPA.

14. Reports of the Superintendent and Board of Visitors of the U.S. Military Academy, Senate Executive Document No. 1, 32nd Cong., 2nd Sess.; 33rd Cong., 2nd Sess.

15. Meetings of the Academic Board, 29 August and 19 September 1853, USMA Staff Records, vol. 5, 1851–54, WPA.

16. Morrison, *West Point*, 99–100; Minutes of the Meeting of the Academic Board, 1 June 1853, USMA Staff Records, vol. 5, 1851–54, WPA.

17. *Official Register of the Officers and Cadets of the U.S. Military Academy*, West Point, N.Y., vol. 4, 1848–57. RG 404, WPA.

18. Morrison, *West Point*, 99.

19. E. L. Hartz to father, 10 April and 10 May 1854, E. L. Hartz Papers, Library of Congress (LOC); Ambrose, *Duty, Honor, Country*; Morrison, *West Point*, 99.

20. Morrison, *West Point*, 99–100.

21. Young, *Around the World with Grant*, 2:296.

22. Green, *Recollections and Reflections*; R. Johnson, *Thomas*, 25–27.

23. Coppee, *Thomas*, 22–23.

24. Reports of the Superintendent and Board of Visitors of the U.S. Military Academy, attached to the Report to the Secretary of War, *Senate Executive Document* No. 1, 31st Cong., 2nd Sess.; 32nd Cong., 1st Sess.; 32nd Cong., 2nd Sess.; and 33rd Cong., 1st Sess.

25. Schofield, *Forty-six Years in the Army*, 10–12, 241; McDonough, *Schofield*, 6–8.

26. West Point Post Order Book No. 3, 5 May 1851, 525–29, and 28 May 1852, 684–85, WPA.

27. Robert E. Lee to Captain S. G. French, 5 October 1853, Lee to Thomas S. Jesup, 17 March 1853, and Lee to Joseph Totten, 8 October 1853, Superintendent's Letter Book, 3:10–11, 59, WPA.

28. Report of the Superintendent and Board of Visitors of the U.S. Military Academy, Senate Executive Document No. 1, 33rd Cong., 2nd Sess., 157.

29. Pappas, *To the Point*, 301.

30. Library Circulation Book, 1848–1854, Officers, Civilians, and Soldiers, WPA; Hopkins, *The Kelloggs*, 270–71, 1288–89; M. Johnson, *That Body of Brave Men*, 505–506.

31. Johnson, *Thomas*, 27; Coppee, *Thomas*, 23; Frances K. Thomas to Alfred L. Hough, Hough Papers, University of Colorado; Meade, *Life and Letters*, 2:346.

32. Thomas Papers, VHS; Special Order No. 178, 15 November 1852, Post Order Book No. 4, p. 1, WPA.

33. Van Horne, *Thomas*, 10; R. Johnson, *Thomas*, 27; Coppee, *Thomas*, 23.

34. Frances K. Thomas to Alfred L. Hough, 21 January 1876, 18 November 1879, 27 May 1880, 10 January and 29 August 1881, 20 January and 1 May 1883, and 5 November 1884, Hough Papers, University of Colorado; George H. Thomas to Mrs. A. A. Draper, 4 March 1865, in "Cullum file" for George H. Thomas, WPA.

35. Rodenbough and Haskin, *Army of the United States*, 342–43.

36. Bee, *The Yuma*; Forbes, *Warriors of the Colorado*; and Kroeber and Fontana, *Massacre on the Gila*.

37. Bee, *The Yuma*, 52.

38. George H. Thomas to Assistant Adjutant General Lorenzo Thomas, 27 April 1854, Letters Received, RG 108, NA; Thomas to "Captain" [George W. Cullum], Thomas Papers, HL.

39. Van Horne, *Thomas*, 11; Third Artillery Regimental Returns, RG 94, NA.

40. George Thomas to John Thomas, 11 September 1854. Thomas Papers, VHS.

41. George H. Thomas to William T. Sherman, 30 November 1854 and 15 March and 29 April 1855, Sherman Papers, LOC.

42. Thomas to Townsend, Adjutant General, Department of the Pacific, 14 July 1854, Letters Received, Department of the Pacific, RG 393, NA.

43. Post Returns, Fort Yuma, RG 94, NA.

44. R. Johnson, *Thomas*, 28; and Thomas to Sherman, 29 April 1855, Sherman Papers, LOC.

45. R. Johnson, *Thomas*, 28–29.

46. Utley, *Indian Frontier*, 31–64.

47. Thomas to Townsend, 11 August 1854, Letters Received, Department of the Pacific, RG 393, NA.

48. Thomas to Townsend, 2 November 1854, Letters Received, Department of the Pacific, RG 393, NA.

49. Thomas to Townsend, 8 August 1854, Letters Received, Department of the Pacific, RG 393, NA.

50. Thomas to Townsend, 31 January 1855, Letters Received, Department of the Pacific, RG 393, NA.

51. Bee, *The Yuma*, 54.

52. Thomas to Townsend, 25 September 1854, 3 January, 12 March, and 2 and 15 May 1855, Letters Received, Department of the Pacific, RG 393, NA; Thomas to Sherman, 15 March and 29 April 1855, Sherman Papers, LOC.

53. Thomas to Townsend, 25 September 1854 and 3 January 1855, Letters Received, Department of the Pacific, RG 393, NA.

54. Thomas to Townsend, 12 February 1855, Letters Received, Department of the Pacific, RG 393, NA.

55. Thomas to Townsend, 12 March 1855, Letters Received, Department of the Pacific, RG 393, NA.

56. Thomas to Sherman, 15 March 1855, Sherman Papers, LOC.

57. Thomas to George Gibbs, 15 March 1868, Manuscript 1107 in the Smithsonian Institution National Anthropological Archives.

58. Thomas to Adjutant General Samuel Cooper, 7 July 1857, and Thomas to George Gibbs, 18 November 1867, Yale University.

59. *Smithsonian Annual Report, 1855,* 44–45; and *Smithsonian Annual Report, 1856,* 48–49; *U.S. Pacific Rail Road Report,* 8:xvi.

60. Thomas to Townsend, 24 July and 10 October 1854, Letters Received, Department of the Pacific, RG 393, NA; Thomas to Samuel Cooper, 7 July 1857, Yale University.

61. *Smithsonian Annual Report, 1855,* 44–45.

62. *Smithsonian Annual Report, 1856,* 48–49.

63. Personal communication to the author from Craig Ludwig, scientific data manager, Division of Birds and Mammals, Smithsonian Institution, 14 May 2003.

64. Goetzmann, *Army Exploration,* 313.

65. U.S. War Department, *Pacific Railroad Survey Reports,* 8:414–15, 479.

66. Morrison, *West Point,* 53.

67. *Smithsonian Annual Report, 1853,* 57.

68. *Smithsonian Annual Report, 1856,* 63–68.

69. Braxton Bragg to William T. Sherman, 3 June 1855, and Thomas to Sherman, 29 April 1855, Sherman Papers, LOC; Assistant Adjutant General Lorenzo Thomas to George H. Thomas, Letters Sent, Army Headquarters (44 T 1855), Microfilm series 1635, RG 108, NA.

70. Van Horne, *Thomas,* 13.

71. George Thomas to John Thomas, 10 October 1855, Thomas Papers, VHS.

72. Thomas to "Captain" [George W. Cullum], 21 September 1859, Thomas Papers, HL.

73. Robert E. Lee to Mary Custis Lee, 28 March 1857, Lee Papers, VHS; Thomas family account books, Thomas Papers, VHS.

74. Oakes, *Ruling Race.*

75. Van Horne, *Thomas,* 16–17.

76. Thomas to "Captain" [George W. Cullum], 21 September 1859, Thomas Papers, HL.

77. Robert E. Lee to Mary Custis Lee, 19 November 1856, Lee Papers, VHS.

78. Robert E. Lee to Mary Custis Lee, 24 October and 27 December 1856 and 26 April 1857, Lee Papers, VHS.

79. Second Cavalry, Regimental Returns, RG 94, NA.

80. Utley, *Indian Frontier,* 57; Kavanagh, *Comanches,* 356.

81. Kavanagh, *Comanches,* 356.

82. Thomas to "Captain" [George W. Cullum], 21 September 1859, Thomas Papers, HL.

83. R. Johnson, *Thomas,* 32–33.

84. George H. Thomas to Frances Thomas, 22 December 1858, Library of Virginia.

85. Thomas to Headquarters, Department of Texas, 5 May 1859; Thomas to E. Kirby Smith, 16 July 1859; Thomas to K. Horster, 21 July 1859; Letters Sent, Camp Cooper, RG 393, NA.

86. Price, *Fifth Cavalry,* 81.

87. Kavanagh, *Comanches,* 368.

88. Thomas to T. A. Washington, Acting Assistant Adjutant General for the Department of Texas, 30 July 1857, Letters Sent, Camp Cooper, RG 393, NA.

89. Kavanagh, *Comanches,* 368.

90. Thomas to T. A. Washington, 22 August 1859, Letters Sent, Camp Cooper, RG 393, NA.

91. Thomas to Assistant Adjutant General, Headquarters, Department of Texas, 2 June 1860, Letters Sent, Camp Cooper, RG 393, NA.

92. Thomas to Assistant Adjutant General, Headquarters, Department of Texas, 21 June 1860, Letters Sent, Camp Cooper, RG 393, NA.

93. Thomas to Adjutant General, 31 August 1860, RG 94, NA; R. Johnson, *Thomas,* 34.

94. Thomas to George W. Cullum, 30 December 1865, "Officers' Accounts of Civil War Service," RG 94, NA.

CHAPTER 5, DECISION

1. McPherson, *Battle Cry of Freedom*, 234–64.

2. Van Horne, *Thomas*, 19–20.

3. Van Horne, *Thomas,* 20; Thomas to Adjutant General Lorenzo Thomas, 1 January and 1 February 1860, Letters Sent, Headquarters, Department of Texas, RG 94, NA.

4. Frances Thomas to William S. Drewry, 2 November 1900, printed in Wyeth, *With Sabre and Scalpel*, 261.

5. Shanks, *Personal Recollections*, 63.

6. Van Horne, *Thomas,* 20.

7. U.S. War Department, *The War of the Rebellion: A Compilation of the Official Records of the Union and Confederate Armies*, 51:1:311 (hereafter cited as OR).

8. McPherson, *Battle Cry of Freedom*, 234–59.

9. Frances Thomas to Albert Lacey Hough, 21 January 1876, Hough Papers, University of Colorado.

10. Crofts, *Reluctant Confederates,* 130–253.

11. Crofts, *Reluctant Confederates*, 136–44.

12. Price, *Fifth Cavalry,* 95–99; Sanders, *Hands of the Enemy*, 26–31.

13. Otis, "Thomas," 1:395.

14. Thomas to S. Cooper, 1 March 1861, Letters Received, Adjutant General, RG 94, NA.

15. William Mahone to John Letcher, 8 February 1861, private manuscript collection.

16. Thomas to John Letcher, 12 March 1861, Letcher Papers, Library of Virginia, published in *Calendar of Virginia State Papers*, 11:106.

17. Thomas, "Personal Military History of Major General G. H. Thomas," and "Report on Civil War Military Service," RG 94, NA; Frances K. Thomas to Alfred L. Hough, 21 January 1876, Hough Papers, University of Colorado; Shanks, *Personal Recollections*, 62–63; Stone, "Thomas," 195; *OR*, Series 1, 32:2:421, 459, 466.

18. Thomas, "Personal Military History of Major General G. H. Thomas," and "Report on Civil War Military Service," RG 94, NA.

19. Crofts, *Reluctant Confederates*, 341.

20. Van Horne, *Thomas*, 26.

21. Van Horne, *Thomas,* 416.

22. Garfield, "Thomas," 67; Baggett, *Scalawags* 103–105; Degler, *Other South*, 175–79; Harris, "Southern Unionist Critique," 39–42; Inscoe and Kenzer, *Enemies of the Country*, 7–8; and Wakelyn, *Southern Unionist Pamphlets*, 4–5.

23. Frances K. Thomas to Alfred L. Hough, 5 November 1884, Hough Papers, University of Colorado.

24. Nevins, *War for the Union*, 1:107, 109; D. Freeman, *R. E. Lee*, 1:421, 441.

25. Emory Thomas, *Lee*, 189–90.

26. Frances K. Thomas to Hough, 21 January 1876, Hough Papers, University of Colorado.

27. Barham, "Thomas Family," 331.

28. Thomas family account books, Thomas Papers, VHS.

29. Barham, "Thomas Family," 331; Frances Thomas [sister] to John Thomas, 30 March 1850, Thomas Papers, VHS.

30. Barham, "Thomas Family," 332–33.

31. Thomas family account books, Thomas Papers, VHS.

32. Current, *Lincoln's Loyalists,* 3–28; Goodhart, *Independent Loudoun Virginia Rangers.*

33. Current, *Lincoln's Loyalists,* 27.

34. Current, *Lincoln's Loyalists,* 213–18.

35. Crabtree and Patton, *Diary of Edmondston,* 242–43.

36. Current, *Lincoln's Loyalists,* 135; Durrill, *War of Another Kind,* 229–30, 235–40.

37. Current, *Lincoln's Loyalists,* 144–45; Degler, *Other South,* 175–79; Harris, "Southern Unionist Critique," 39–42, 54–55; Inscoe and Kenzer, *Enemies of the Country,* 7–8; and Wakelyn, *Southern Unionist Pamphlets,* 4–5, 8–10.

38. Sutherland, *Guerrillas, Unionists, and Violence*; Baggett, *Scalawags,* 66–94.

39. Degler, *Other South,* 175–86.

40. Klingberg, *Southern Claims Commission*; Mills, *Southern Loyalists.*

41. Dyer, *Secret Yankees.*

42. Varon, *Southern Lady.*

43. Harris, "Southern Unionist Critique," 43; Degler, *Other South,* 175–76.

44. Crofts, *Reluctant Confederates,* 296–98.

45. Bryan, "Virginia's Yankee Generals"; Warner, *Generals in Blue.*

46. *New York Times,* 23 June 1861.

47. Crabtree and Patton, *Diary of Edmondston,* 601.

48. Gordon, "'In Time of War,'" 45–58.

49. *OR* 32:1:562; Current, *Lincoln's Loyalists,* 140.

50. J.E.B. Stuart to Flora Stuart, 18 June 1861, Stuart Papers, VHS.

51. Current, *Lincoln's Loyalists*; W. Freehling, *South v. the South,* 61.

52. Price, *Fifth Cavalry,* 94–99.

53. Price, *Fifth Cavalry,* 94–99; Thomas, "Personal Military History of Major General George H. Thomas," 25 January 1864, and "Report to the Committee on the Conduct of the War," 9 March 1866, Thomas Papers, RG 94, NA.

54. Fitz John Porter Papers, LOC.

55. Fitz John Porter Papers; Chittenden, *Lincoln,* 361–62.

56. *OR* 2:587–88, 622; Fitz John Porter Papers, LOC; Price, *Fifth Cavalry,* 97; Thomas, "Personal Military History of Major General George H. Thomas," 25 January 1864, Thomas Papers, RG 94, NA.

57. Fitz John Porter Papers.

58. Fitz John Porter Papers.

59. R. Johnson, *Thomas,* 160; Anderson, "Thomas," 38.

60. Anderson, "Thomas," 41; Van Horne, *Thomas,* 36–37.

61. Anderson, "Thomas," 41–42.

62. Fitz John Porter Papers, LOC; R. Johnson, *Thomas,* 160–61.

63. Garfield Papers, LOC; R. Johnson, *Thomas,* 161.

64. Anderson, "Thomas," 39.

65. *OR* 2:658–59; Thomas, "Personal Military History of Maj. Gen. G. H. Thomas," 25 January 1864, Thomas Papers, RG 94, NA.

66. McClure, *Lincoln,* 369–70.

67. *OR* Series 1, 2:660, 668–70, 679.

68. W. Sherman, *Memoirs,* 1:205–206; W. Sherman, *Sherman's Civil War,* 100–101.

69. J. Sherman, *Recollections*, 197.

70. *OR* 2:160, 696–703, 708.

71. J.E.B. Stuart to Flora Stuart, 18 June 1861, Stuart Papers, VHS.

72. *OR* 2:179–82, 186.

73. *OR* 2:179–82, 186.

74. *OR* 2:64.

75. Heidler and Heidler, *Encyclopedia of the Civil War*, 1462–63.

76. Anderson, "Thomas," 39–40.

77. Thomas to Anderson, 26 August 1861, in "Cullum file" for George H. Thomas, RG 404, WPA.

CHAPTER 6, MILL SPRINGS

1. McPherson, *Battle Cry of Freedom*, 293–95.

2. Daniel, *Days of Glory*, 6–7; Van Horne, *Army of the Cumberland,* 1:8–13; Kelly, "Holding Kentucky," 1:383–81.

3. McPherson, *Battle Cry of Freedom,* 296.

4. McPherson, *Battle Cry of Freedom,* 296–97.

5. Daniel, *Days of Glory,* 5–6, 40; Thomas to William T. Sherman, 19 September 1861, Sherman Papers, LOC; Perrin, Battle, and Kniffin, *Kentucky,* 370–71.

6. Tarrant, *First Kentucky Cavalry*, 34.

7. Tarrant, *First Kentucky Cavalry*, 34; Bishop, "Mill Springs Campaign," 79; McPherson, *Battle Cry of Freedom,* 477–88; Adams, *Doctors in Blue*.

8. Van Horne, *Army of the Cumberland*, 1:30–31; Thomas to the Tennessee State Senate and House of Representatives, 17 September 1861, Letters Sent, Thomas Papers, RG 94, NA.

9. *OR* Series 1, 4:268, 282–84.

10. McBride, *Thirty-third Indiana*, 19.

11. Kelly, "Holding Kentucky," 1:382.

12. Thomas to Anderson, 27 September 1861, Letters Sent, Thomas Papers, RG 94, NA; Lincoln, *Collected Works*, 4:544–45; Daniel, *Days of Glory,* 23.

13. *OR* 4:300.

14. *OR* 4:300–303.

15. Daniel, *Days of Glory*, 17; *OR* 4:275–76.

16. *OR* 4:296–97, 302–303.

17. *OR* 4:306.

18. *OR* 4:309–15; Van Horne, *Army of the Cumberland*, 51; Daniel, *Days of Glory,* 20, 39.

19. Daniel, *Days of Glory,* 24–25; *OR* 4:207, 209.

20. *OR* 4:205–206, 318, 321–22, 329–30, 338–39, 347.

21. Fisher, *War at Every Door*, 52–56; *OR* 4:350–51, 353–54, 356–58.

22. *Cincinnati Daily Commercial*, 16 and 18 November 1861; McBride, *Thirty-third Indiana,* 32; Kniffin, "Sailor on Horseback," 5; Sutherland, *Guerrillas, Unionists, and Violence*, 89–112; *OR* 4:342–43.

23. Marszalek, *Sherman*, 156–67.

24. McBride, *Thirty-third Indiana,* 26–27.

25. *OR* 7:530–31.

26. Daniel, *Days of Glory,* 49–51.

27. Shaw, *Tenth Indiana*, 137–38.

28. Keil, *Thirty-fifth Ohio*, 55–59.

29. *OR* 7:79; Prokopowicz, *All for the Regiment*, 68–82; Kelly, "Holding Kentucky," 1:373–92; Van Horne, *Army of the Cumberland*, 1:56–57; Van Horne, *Thomas*, 52–54.

30. James Scully to wife, 19 January 1862, Scully Papers, DUL.

31. Shanks, *Personal Recollections*, 66.

32. *OR* 7:80, 95; Bishop, "Mill Springs Campaign," 66.

33. *OR* 7:80, 95–96.

34. *OR* 7:80–81; Thomas, *Report to the Committee on the Conduct of the War*, 9 March 1866, Thomas Papers, RG 94, NA.

35. *OR* 7:81; Daniel, *Days of Glory*, 53; Kelly, "Holding Kentucky," 391.

36. Prokopowicz, *All for the Regiment*, 68–82; Daniel, *Days of Glory*, 52–53. For a much more critical view, see Williams, *Lincoln Finds a General*, 3:169–77, 442–48.

37. Scully to wife, 19 January 1862, Scully Papers, DUL.

38. *OR* 7:108.

39. Kelly, "Holding Kentucky," 391.

40. *Chicago Tribune*, 21 January 1862; *New York Herald*, 21 and 22 January 1862; *Boston Daily Advertiser*, 22 January 1862; *New York Tribune*, 22 January 1862.

41. *OR* 7:563–64.

CHAPTER 7, SHILOH AND PERRYVILLE

1. McPherson, *Battle Cry of Freedom*, 392–403.

2. McPherson, *Battle Cry of Freedom*, 405–14; Engle, *Don Carlos Buell*, 209–39.

3. Engle, *Don Carlos Buell*, 239.

4. Marszalek, *Sherman*, 163–83; W. Sherman, *Memoirs*, 1:278.

5. Marszalek, *Sherman*, 183–84; W. Sherman, *Memoirs*, 1:277, 283; Grant, *Memoirs*, 1:385.

6. Curry, *Four Years in the Saddle*, 59.

7. Van Horne, *Thomas*, 64.

8. McPherson, *Battle Cry of Freedom*, 404–405, 415–27.

9. McDonough, *War in Kentucky*, 30–38.

10. Engle, *Don Carlos Buell*, 257–77; Daniel, *Days of Glory*, 91–106; Prokopowicz, *All for the Regiment*, 113–35; and McDonough, *War in Kentucky*, 39–60.

11. McDonough, *War in Kentucky*, 39–60.

12. Grebner, *Ninth Ohio*, 104–105; Keil, *Thirty-fifth Ohio*, 78.

13. Thomas to Andrew Johnson, 16 August 1862, Thomas Papers, HL.

14. McDonough, *War in Kentucky*, 88, 104–105.

15. McDonough, *War in Kentucky*, 104–108; Noe, *Perryville*, 50–51.

16. *OR* 16:2:392, 399, 445–46; McDonough, *War in Kentucky*, 104–10, Noe, *Perryville*, 51–53.

17. *OR* 16:1:182–83; 16:2:451, 471; McDonough, *War in Kentucky*, 110, 112; Noe, *Perryville*, 59–60; Daniel, *Days of Glory*, 112–13.

18. McDonough, *War in Kentucky*, 158–200; Noe, *Perryville*, 63–79.

19. McDonough, *War in Kentucky*, 117–54, 199–200; McPherson, *Battle Cry of Freedom*, 529–32.

20. McDonough, *War in Kentucky*, 158–87; Noe, *Perryville*, 68–71, 75.

21. McPherson, *Battle Cry of Freedom*, 535–45.

22. Daniel, *Days of Glory*, 128–31; *OR* 16:2:538; Ambrose, *Halleck*, 89–90; Chase, *Papers*, 1:398.

23. A "private, unpublished note" by Buell, printed in Matthews, "Thomas." Further evidence that Buell did not blame Thomas for his removal comes from a letter Buell wrote

on 30 October 1862, ten days after being relieved by Rosecrans, in which Buell encouraged Thomas to ask whether he could do anything "privately" to help Thomas's career. There is no record of whether Thomas responded. *OR* 16:2:654.

24. *OR* 16:2:555.

25. *OR* 16:2:549, 554–55.

26. Van Horne, *Thomas,* 75–76.

27. Daniel, *Days of Glory,* 135.

28. Noe, *Perryville,* 95–97; Daniel, *Days of Glory,* 132–34; Jenkins, "Shooting at the Galt House," 101–18.

29. Daniel, *Days of Glory,* 137; Warner, *Generals in Blue,* 173–74; *OR* 16:1:375–77.

30. Noe, *Perryville,* 97–98; Daniel, *Days of Glory,* 137–38; Shaw, *Tenth Indiana,* 169–70.

31. McDonough, *War in Kentucky,* 199–200, 204–207, Noe, *Perryville,* 107–33.

32. McDonough, *War in Kentucky,* 209–23; Noe, *Perryville,* 121–22; Daniel, *Days of Glory,* 141–47; Van Horne, *Army of the Cumberland,* 1:186.

33. *OR* 16:2:580–81, 587; Van Horne, *Army of the Cumberland,* 1:186.

34. This explanation follows Noe, *Perryville,* 166–69. Other interpretations of Thomas's actions include Van Horne, *Army of the Cumberland,* 1:186; Van Horne, *Thomas,* 78–79; K. Williams, *Lincoln Finds a General,* 4:129; McDonough, *War in Kentucky,* 226; and Daniel, *Days of Glory,* 148, 155.

35. *OR* 16:1:124–25, 134–36, 221–22.

36. This account of the Battle of Perryville is based on Noe, *Perryville,* 144–326; Engle, *Don Carlos Buell,* 306–11; McDonough, *War in Kentucky,* 233–96, and Daniel, *Days of Glory,* 148–56.

37. Tarrant, *First Kentucky Cavalry,* 119.

38. *OR* 16:1:187; Noe, *Perryville,* 235–37; Van Horne, *Thomas,* 82; *OR* 16:2:588.

39. McDonough, *War in Kentucky,* 304–10; Noe, *Perryville,* 327–29.

40. Noe, *Perryville,* 327–43; McDonough, *War in Kentucky,* 305–14.

41. Shanks, *Personal Recollections,* 65–66.

42. Stone, "Thomas," 10:196–97.

43. McDonough, *War in Kentucky,* 289; and Noe, *Perryville,* 344.

CHAPTER 8, STONES RIVER

1. Cozzens, *Stones River,* 22. I relied heavily on Cozzens's book, the best study of the Battle of Stones River, in writing this chapter. I also consulted McDonough, *Stones River,* but Cozzens's book is much more extensively researched.

2. Lamers, *Edge of Glory;* Cozzens, *Stones River,* 16.

3. *OR* 16:2:657.

4. Society of the Army of the Cumberland, *1869 Reunion Report,* 74–75.

5. Van Horne, *Thomas,* 87–88.

6. Bickham, *Rosecrans' Campaign,* 31–32, 135.

7. Cozzens, *Stones River,* 12–28; Lamers, *Edge of Glory,* 184–95.

8. Lamers, *Edge of Glory,* 187; Cozzens, *Stones River,* 20–21, 25–26; Daniel, *Days of Glory,* 187–90.

9. Shiman, "Engineering and Command," 84–117, and Shiman,

10. Gordon, "Hospital Trains," 150.

11. McElfresh, *Maps and Mapmakers,* 67–71, 147, 244.

12. Cozzens, *Stones River,* 48–72; Daniel, *Days of Glory,* 201–206.

13. The proper spelling was originally "Stone's River," but the spelling "Stones River" has been used in so many accounts that either spelling is now acceptable. McDonough, *Stones River*, 10.

14. Cozzens, *Stones River*, 77.

15. Cozzens, *Stones River*, 70–71, 74–75, 221–24; *OR* 21:1:177–79, 372.

16. Cozzens, *Stones River*, 78–129; John Parkhurst to "My Dear Sister," 2 January 1863, Parkhurst Papers, University of Michigan.

17. Cozzens, *Stones River*, 130–31; *OR* 20:1:193, 652–53; Parkhurst to "My Dear Sister," 2 January 1863, Parkhurst Papers.

18. Cozzens, *Stones River*, 129–30.

19. Curry, *Four Years in the Saddle*, 303.

20. Bisbee, *Four American Wars*, 125; Curry, *Four Years in the Saddle,* 302; Dornblaser, *Pennsylvania Dragoons*, 100; Parkhurst, "Stone's River," 10; Scribner, *How Soldiers Were Made*, 78–79; and Stevenson, *Stone's River*, 78.

21. *OR* 20:1:441–42.

22. *OR* 20:1:349, 373, 407–408; Cozzens, *Stones River*, 128–43; Bickham, *Rosecrans' Campaign,* 251; Van Horne, *Army of the Cumberland*, 1:238.

23. Kniffin, "Stone's River," 3:627; *New York Times*, 8 April 1870.

24. Cozzens, *Stones River*, 144–66.

25. Cozzens, *Stones River*, 78–79, 83–85.

26. The accounts of this meeting conflict: Van Horne, *Thomas*, 97; Yaryan, "Stone River," 1:170; Lamers, *Edge of Glory*, 235–37; Scribner, *How Soldiers Were Made,* 81; Bickham, *Rosecrans' Campaign,* 270; Sheridan, *Memoirs*, 1:236–37. Crittenden, "Stone's River," 3:632–34; Stanley, *Memoirs*, 127–28. The account in the book follows the interpretation of Cozzens, *Stones River*, 173, and McDonough, *Stones River*, 161–62; the officer quoted is Scribner, *How Soldiers Were Made,* 81.

27. Cozzens, *Stones River*, 174–75.

28. Bisbee, *Four American Wars*, 126; Curry, *Four Years in the Saddle*, 301–302.

29. Cozzens, *Stones River*, 175–76; *OR* 20:1:379; Crittenden, "Stone's River," 644.

30. Cozzens, *Stones River*, 177–83.

31. Cozzens, *Stones River*, 183–98; Daniel, *Days of Glory,* 222; *OR* 20:1:374.

32. *OR* 20:1:374.

33. Cozzens, *Stones River*, 199–203.

34. McDonough, *Stones River*, 230–31.

35. *OR* 20:1:652–53.

CHAPTER 9, FROM STONES RIVER TO CHICKAMAUGA CREEK

1. Cozzens, *Chickamauga*, 14–17; Daniel, *Days of Glory*, 225–64; *OR* 23:1:8, 23:2:414–415.

2. Cozzens, *Chickamauga,* 14–15; Daniel, *Days of Glory*, 232–38.

3. Scribner, *How Soldiers Were Made*, 116–17; Shanks, *Personal Recollections*, 75–76.

4. Scribner, *How Soldiers Were Made*, 114–16.

5. Scribner, *How Soldiers Were Made*, 117–18; Shanks, *Personal Recollections,* 71–72.

6. Porter, *Campaigning with Grant*, 295.

7. Shanks, *Personal Recollections,* 76.

8. Collection of the museum of the U.S. Military Academy at West Point.

9. Beatty, *The Citizen Soldier*, 278.

10. Cozzens, *Chickamauga,* 17–18; Daniel, *Days of Glory,* 265–69.

11. Cozzens, *Chickamauga,* 17–18; Daniel, *Days of Glory,* 265–69.

12. Cozzens, *Chickamauga,* 17–18; Daniel, *Days of Glory,* 265–69; Baumgartner, *Blue Lightning,* 49.

13. Cozzens, *Chickamauga,* 19–20; Daniel, *Days of Glory,* 270–76.

14. Daniel, *Days of Glory,* 276–82.

15. Cozzens, *Chickamauga,* 21–27, Daniel, *Days of Glory,* 276–82.

16. Cozzens, *Chickamauga,* 29–37; Daniel, *Days of Glory,* 285–92.

17. Cozzens, *Chickamauga,* 39–60; Daniel, *Days of Glory,* 293–300; OR 30:1:245–47.

18. Cozzens, *Chickamauga,* 62–63; OR 30:1:53; 30:3:482, 488, 493.

19. Cozzens, *Chickamauga,* 67–69; Daniel, *Days of Glory,* 301–3; OR 30:1:326; 30:3:510–11, 534–35, 564.

20. OR 30:3:534–35.

21. Puntenney, *Thirty-seventh Indiana,* 51–52; Calkins, *One Hundred and Fourth Illinois,* 118.

22. OR 30:1:247, 327–28; Cozzens, *Chickamauga,* 68–69, Daniel, *Days of Glory,* 302–303.

23. OR 30:3:564–65; Cozzens, *Chickamauga,* 70–75; Daniel, *Days of Glory,* 303.

24. Cozzens, *Chickamauga,* 80–95; OR 30:3:568.

25. Cozzens, *Chickamauga,* 95–100.

26. Cozzens, *Chickamauga,* 59–60, 78, 95–100.

27. Cozzens, *Chickamauga,* 101–18.

28. OR 30:1:55–56, 248–49, 336–37; Cozzens, *Chickamauga,* 118.

29. Cozzens, *Chickamauga,* 122; OR 30:1:56, 123–24, 249, 871; Scribner, *How Soldiers Were Made,* 143.

30. Cozzens, *Chickamauga,* 123–28; OR 30:1:247; "Journal of the Fourteenth Army Corps," 92–93, Thomas Papers, RG 94, NA.

31. Cozzens, *Chickamauga,* 128–29.

32. Duffield, "Chickamauga," 5.

33. Cozzens, *Chickamauga,* 133; OR 30:1:249–50; "Journal of the Fourteenth Army Corps," 96, Thomas Papers, RG 94, NA.

34. OR 30:1:124.

35. OR 30:1:73.

36. Cozzens, *Chickamauga,* 134–38.

37. Cozzens, *Chickamauga,* 139–51.

38. R. Johnson, *Soldier's Reminiscences,* 230; Cozzens, *Chickamauga,* 152–66; OR 30:1:250, 535, 713.

39. Cozzens, *Chickamauga,* 178; OR 30:1:440.

40. Cozzens, *Chickamauga,* 167–262; OR 30:1:250.

41. DeVelling, *Seventeenth Regiment,* 101–102.

42. Cozzens, *Chickamauga,* 263–79.

43. Cozzens, *Chickamauga,* 294.

44. OR 30:1:134–35, 251; Cozzens, *Chickamauga,* 294, 298; *New York Herald,* 27 September 1863.

45. Dana, *Recollections,* 113; Van Horne, *Thomas,* 121–22; Van Horne, *Army of the Cumberland,* 1:342.

46. Dana, *Recollections,* 114.

47. OR 30:1:251; *New York Herald,* 27 September 1863; Fitch, *Echoes of the Civil War,* 136.

48. Cozzens, *Chickamauga,* 293–97; OR 30:1:69.

CHAPTER 10, THE ROCK OF CHICKAMAUGA

1. Livermore, "Thomas," 10:209–44; Dana, *Recollections*, 114; *New York Herald*, 27 September 1863; Shanks, *Personal Recollections*, 66–67.

2. *OR* 30:1:137–38.

3. Cozzens, *Chickamauga*, 311–13, 317.

4. Cozzens, *Chickamauga,* 317–18; *OR* 30:1:277, 367–68.

5. Cozzens, *Chickamauga*, 319–56.

6. Cozzens, *Chickamauga,* 319–56.

7. Shanks, *Personal Recollections,* 69–70.

8. Cozzens, *Chickamauga*, 326–29, 359–61; *OR* 30:1:251, 330, 338.

9. *OR* 30:1:379; Van Horne, *Army of the Cumberland*, 1:351.

10. *OR* 30:1:252; Cozzens, *Chickamauga,* 406.

11. This brigade, commanded by Col. Sidney M. Barnes, was actually in the division of Horatio Van Cleve but was taking orders from Wood at that time. Cozzens, *Chickamauga,* 367, 406, 542–43.

12. *OR* 30:1:635; Cozzens, *Chickamauga,* 406–407, 413.

13. *OR* 30:1:252, 694.

14. Clarke, *Opdycke Tigers,* 107–108; Van Horne, *Army of the Cumberland*, 1:351; Cozzens, *Chickamauga,* 407–16.

15. Cozzens, *Chickamauga*, 380–81.

16. Cozzens, *Chickamauga,* 417–23; *OR* 30:1:252.

17. Cozzens, *Chickamauga,* 423; Calkins, *One Hundred and Fourth Illinois*, 143; Walker, "Chickamauga."

18. Horace C. Long to wife, 19 November 1863, Chickamauga/Chattanooga National Military Park Archives.

19. Opdycke, "Chickamauga," 671.

20. Cozzens, *Chickamauga,* 424–31.

21. Cozzens, *Chickamauga,* 431.

22. *New York Herald*, 27 September 1863; Shanks, *Personal Recollections,* 68–69; Fullerton, "Chickamauga," 3:667; Calkins, *One Hundred and Fourth Illinois*, 144.

23. Fullerton, "Chickamauga," 665–67; Shanks, *Personal Recollections,* 64.

24. Cozzens, *Chickamauga,* 443–44; *OR* 30:1:402, 860; Royse, *115th Illinois*, 164.

25. Cozzens, *Chickamauga,* 452–53; *OR* 30:1:430; Bishop, *Second Minnesota*, 108.

26. Thruston, "Chickamauga," 3:665.

27. Walker, "Chickamauga."

28. Calkins, *One Hundred and Fourth Illinois*, 145.

29. *OR* 30:1:140, 948, 978.

30. Garfield to Rosecrans, 14 December 1870, in T. Smith, *Life and Letters of Garfield,* 1:345; Cozzens, *Chickamauga,* 477.

31. Cozzens, *Chickamauga,* 479–80; *OR* 30:1:253.

32. *OR* 30:1:253, 442; Fullerton, "Chickamauga," 667; High, *Sixty-eighth Indiana*.

33. *OR* 30:1:254.

34. Cozzens, *Chickamauga,* 494–501.

35. *OR* 30:1:501, 581; Cozzens, *Chickamauga,* 501–502; Sheridan, *Memoirs,* 2:286–87.

36. Cozzens, *Chickamauga,* 502.

37. Cozzens, *Chickamauga,* 503–509.

38. Sheridan, *Memoirs*, 1:287.

39. Scribner, *How Soldiers Were Made*, 161–62; Shanks, *Personal Recollections*, 70.

40. Keil, *Thirty-fifth Ohio*, 149.

41. King, *Ninety-second Illinois*, 129–30.

42. Beatty, *Citizen Soldier*, 345.

43. Hough, *Soldier in the West*, 150.

44. *OR* 30:1:254–55.

45. High, *Sixty-eighth Indiana*, 120; *OR* 30:1:635; Cozzens, *Chickamauga*, 359–67.

46. Cozzens, *Chickamauga*, 368–75.

47. Cozzens, *Chickamauga*, 376–405.

48. Cozzens, *Chickamauga*, 423–24; *OR* 30:1:331.

49. Cozzens, *Chickamauga*, 534. For a more critical view of Thomas's performance, see Daniel, *Days of Glory*, 332.

50. Hough, *Soldier in the West*, 150–51.

51. *Chicago Tribune*, 22–25 September 1863; *Louisville Journal*, 21–29 September 1863; *New York Times*, 23 September 1863; *New York Herald*, 27 September 1863; *Cincinnati Commercial*, quoted in the *Chicago Tribune*, 25 September 1863.

52. Letter from Dana to Rosecrans, 21 March 1882, Rosecrans Papers, University of California at Los Angeles; cited in Cozzens, *Chickamauga*, 523.

53. Bates, *Lincoln in the Telegraph Office*, 169–71.

54. Hay, *Civil War Diary*, 1:104–105.

55. Cozzens, *Chickamauga*, 524–27; Lamers, *Edge of Glory*, 380; Sword, *Mountains Touched with Fire*, 50–51.

CHAPTER 11, CHATTANOOGA

1. Cozzens, *Shipwreck of Their Hopes*, 14–22; McDonough, *Chattanooga*, 46–48; Wiley Sword, *Chattanooga*, 42–45.

2. Scribner, *How Soldiers Were Made*, 173–74.

3. Cozzens, *Shipwreck of Their Hopes*, 21–22; McDonough, *Chattanooga*, 58–60.

4. Cozzens, *Shipwreck of Their Hopes*, 18; Sword, *Chattanooga*, 40–41.

5. Hay, *Civil War Diary*, 99; Welles, *Diary*, 1:447.

6. *OR* 30:4:404.

7. Dana, *Recollections*, 125–26; and *OR* 30:1:211; Society of the Army of the Cumberland, *1869 Reunion Report*, 76; Cozzens, *Chickamauga*, 528; Lamers, *Edge of Glory*, 391–92.

8. Society of the Army of the Cumberland, *1869 Reunion Report*, 77; Lamers, *Edge of Glory*, 391–92.

9. *OR* 30:4:478.

10. *OR* 30:4:211.

11. *New York Herald*, 29 October 1863; Aldritch, *Quest for a Star*, 76; Calkins, *One Hundred and Fourth Illinois*, 157; Gibson, *Seventy-eighth Pennsylvania*, 126; Hannaford, *Sixth Ohio*, 486; Lamers, *Edge of Glory*, 392–96; Newlin, *Seventy-third Illinois*, 256; G. Palmer, *Conscientious Turncoat*, 121; E. Wilson, *Memoirs*, 237–38.

12. Tourgee, *One Hundred Fifth Ohio*, 259.

13. *OR* 30:1:221, 30:4:479.

14. Sword, *Chattanooga*, 58–59; *OR* 31:1:43, 69, 739; W. Smith, "Historical Sketch," 8:169–70; Grant, *Memoirs*, 2:31, 35.

15. W. Smith, "Historical Sketch," 169–71, and W. Smith, "Comments on Grant's 'Chattanooga,'" 3:714–18.

16. J. Wilson, *Under the Old Flag*, 1:269–76; Porter, *Campaigning with Grant*, 4; James H. Wilson to Adam Badeau, 26 January 1865, Wilson Papers, Library of Congress; James P. Jones, "Wilson's Letters," 230–45.

17. Porter, *Campaigning with Grant*, 4–5; Cozzens, *Shipwreck of Their Hopes*, 46–47; Sword, *Chattanooga*, 112–15.

18. OR 31:1:43–54; Van Horne, *Army of the Cumberland*, 1:396; Cozzens, *Shipwreck of Their Hopes*, 48–100; McDonough, *Chattanooga*, 76–94; and Sword, *Chattanooga*, 115–44; Hebert, *Hooker*, 258; Howard, *Autobiography*, 1:459.

19. McDonough, *Chattanooga*, 92–93; Curry, *Four Years in the Saddle*, 321.

20. Cozzens, *Shipwreck of Their Hopes*, 107–108; Sword, *Chattanooga*, 145–47.

21. Cozzens, *Shipwreck of Their Hopes*, 101–105; McDonough, *Chattanooga*, 95–104.

22. OR 30:4:59; J. Wilson, *Under the Old Flag*, 1:275.

23. Palmer, *Conscientious Turncoat*, 118–26.

24. Thomas, "Personal Military History of Major General George H. Thomas," Thomas Papers, RG 94, NA.

25. OR 31:3:3–230.

26. Grant, *Memoirs and Selected Letters*, 1037–38; J. Wilson, *Under the Old Flag*, 1:280–81.

27. Catton, *Grant Takes Command*, 40.

28. J. Wilson, *Under the Old Flag*, 1:273–74.

29. Cozzens, *Shipwreck of Their Hopes*, 105–108; McDonough, *Chattanooga*, 106–108; Sword, *Chattanooga*, 148–51.

30. OR 31:3:73.

31. OR 31:3:73.

32. Smith, "Historical Sketch," 193–94.

33. OR 31:2:57–59.

34. Cozzens, *Shipwreck of Their Hopes*, 108–10; Sword, *Chattanooga*, 153–57.

35. Cozzens, *Shipwreck of Their Hopes*, 111–16; McDonough, *Chattanooga*, 108–109; Sword, *Chattanooga*, 158–63.

36. Thomas to Rosecrans, 19 November 1863, Rosecrans Papers, UCLA.

37. OR 31:2:65–66; Sword, *Chattanooga*, 158–60; Cozzens, *Shipwreck of Their Hopes*, 120–24.

38. OR 31:2:64.

39. OR 31:3:216.

40. OR 31:2:32, 41; Cozzens, *Shipwreck of Their Hopes*, 127; Sword, *Chattanooga*, 176.

41. Buell, *Warrior Generals*, 286.

42. Sword, *Chattanooga*, 178; Buell, *Warrior Generals*, 286.

43. OR 31:2:65–66, 94–95, 128–30; Cozzens, *Shipwreck of Their Hopes*, 126–42; McDonough, *Chattanooga*, 106–16; Sword, *Chattanooga*, 175–85.

44. Fullerton, "Chattanooga," 3:721.

45. Cozzens, *Shipwreck of Their Hopes*, 128.

46. Howard, "Chattanooga," 203–19; and Howard, "Grant at Chattanooga," 1:244–57.

47. Kimberly, *Forty-first Ohio*, 59; OR 31:2:24; Cozzens, *Shipwreck of Their Hopes*, 135.

48. OR 31:2:66; Sword, *Chattanooga*, 184.

49. OR 31:2:42, 130; Sword, *Chattanooga*, 200–201.

50. Cozzens, *Shipwreck of Their Hopes*, 143–44; Van Horne, *Army of the Cumberland*, 1:412; OR 31:2:106.

51. Cozzens, *Shipwreck of Their Hopes*, 159–98.

52. Cozzens, *Shipwreck of Their Hopes*, 159–98; McDonough, *Chattanooga*, 129–42.

53. Cozzens, *Shipwreck of Their Hopes*, 199–204.

54. W. W. Smith, "Holocaust Holiday," 36.

55. Dana, *Recollections*, 149.

56. *OR* 31:2:44; Cozzens, *Shipwreck of Their Hopes*, 245–46; Sword, *Chattanooga*, 262.

57. This conversation and sequence of events was reconstructed by Cozzens using primary sources, particularly the postwar writings of Wood. Cozzens, *Shipwreck of Their Hopes*, 247–48, 452n, 453n. The eyewitness accounts of others present on Orchard Knob that day confirm that something like this series of events occurred. Cadwallader, *Three Years with Grant*, 153–54, and J. Wilson, *Under the Old Flag*, 1:297.

58. Sword, *Chattanooga*, 271.

59. Cozzens, *Shipwreck of Their Hopes*, 257–72; Sword, *Chattanooga*, 269–75.

60. Cozzens, *Shipwreck of Their Hopes*, 272–81; McDonough, *Chattanooga*, 165–67; Sword, *Chattanooga*, 275–79; Tourgee, *One Hundred Fifth Ohio*, 286.

61. Fullerton, "Chattanooga," 3:725.

62. Cozzens, *Shipwreck of Their Hopes*, 283–84.

63. Cozzens, *Shipwreck of Their Hopes*, 284–88; McDonough, *Chattanooga*, 167–80; Sword, *Chattanooga*, 282–95.

64. Cozzens, *Shipwreck of Their Hopes*, 282–337; McDonough, *Chattanooga*, 189–205; and Sword, *Chattanooga*, 282–95. Dana's telegram is at *OR* 32:2:68.

65. Cozzens, *Shipwreck of Their Hopes*, 204–43; McDonough, *Chattanooga*, 143–59; Sword, *Chattanooga*, 237–58.

66. R. Johnson, *Thomas*, 242.

67. Cozzens, *Shipwreck of Their Hopes*, 250–53; McDonough, *Chattanooga*, 185–89; Sword, *Chattanooga*, 271–74.

68. Cozzens, *Shipwreck of Their Hopes*, 362–69; Sword, *Chattanooga*, 326–46.

69. Cozzens, *Shipwreck of Their Hopes*, 370–86; McDonough, *Chattanooga*, 220–25.

70. *OR* 31:2:35, 49; Cozzens, *Shipwreck of Their Hopes*, 386–88; Sword, *Chattanooga*, 348–49.

71. *OR* 31:2:51; J. Wilson, *Under the Old Flag*, 1:301.

CHAPTER 12, THE ARMY OF THE CUMBERLAND

1. R. Gordon, "Hospital Trains," 147–56.

2. McElfresh, *Maps and Mapmakers*, 11, 161.

3. Thomas to Miss M. S. Worth, 15 January 1864, New York State Archives, Albany; Haynie, *Nineteenth Illinois*, 308–10.

4. *OR* 31:3:487; Steere, "National Cemetery System."

5. Van Horne, *Thomas*, 212–13.

6. Castel, *Decision in the West*, 9–12.

7. Castel, *Tom Taylor's Civil War*, 101–102.

8. Shanks, *Personal Recollections*, 72–73; Scribner, *How Soldiers Were Made*, 116; Kimberly, *Forty-first Ohio*, 59; and Piatt, *Memories*, 215–16.

9. Coppee, *Thomas*, 323–24. Coppee mistakenly takes this story as evidence that Thomas lacked a sense of humor.

10. Pavelka, "Where Were You Johnny Shiloh?" 35–41; Richard W. Johnson to Harry Johnson, 27 January 1864, Manuscript Collection, LOC.

11. Jonathan Clem to Sanford Kellogg, 16 September 1864, Service Records of Jonathan Lincoln Clem, RG 94, NA. Clem originally spelled his last name "Klem," and his name is spelled "Klem" in many of his service records.

12. Edson, "Life of Thomas."

13. Edson, "Life of Thomas."

14. Maslowski, *Treason Must Be Made Odious*, 20–22, 37–40, 44–49, 62–66.

15. Maslowski, *Treason Must Be Made Odious*, 89–90.

16. *OR* 32:2:38–39; Van Horne, *Thomas*, 214–16; Grimsley, *Hard Hand of War*, 111–19.

17. O'Brien, *Mountain Partisans*, 101–10.

18. Cimprich, *Slavery's End in Tennessee*, 37–39.

19. Cimprich, *Slavery's End in Tennessee*, 38–39; Maslowski, *Treason Must Be Made Odious*, 92; Thomas to Maj. Gen. Lovell H. Rousseau, 4 February 1865, Letters Sent, Department of the Cumberland, RG 393, NA; Berlin, *Freedom*, 429–33; *OR* 16:2:291–92.

20. Cimprich, *Slavery's End in Tennessee*, 39; Berlin, *Freedom*, 440; Official Records, Series 3, 4:770–71.

21. Thomas to Capt. Samuel J. Curtis, 4 February 1864, and Thomas to Col. Thomas J. Morgan, 8 February 1864, Letters Sent, Department of the Cumberland, RG 393, NA; Ash, *When the Yankees Came*, 152.

22. Berlin, *Freedom*, 2:408–10.

23. De Peyster, "Thomas," 18.

24. George H. Thomas to Lorenzo Thomas, 4 January 1864, Thomas to Van Horne, 5 February 1864, and Thomas to Captain Chenoweth, 3 January 1864, Letters Sent, Army of the Cumberland, RG 393, NA; R. D. Mussey to Lorenzo Thomas, 14 March and 2 May 1864, Letters Received by the Adjutant General Relating to Colored Troops, RG 94, NA (hereafter cited as Letters Relating to Colored Troops). The mayor is identified as "Mayor Andrews" of "Columbia," which is probably Columbia, Tennessee. Thomas also arrested the associates of the mayor who had participated in the flogging. Maj. George Stearns to George H. Thomas, 6 March 1864 (a copy of a letter that Stearns had sent to James A. Garfield, who at that time had left the army and was serving as a congressman in Washington), Letters Received, Army of the Cumberland, RG 393, NA.

25. Durham, *Reluctant Partners*, 57; G. Williams, *History of the Negro Troops*, 122; Col. R. D. Mussey to Adjutant General Lorenzo Thomas, 6 June 1864, Letters Relating to Colored Troops, RG 94, NA.

26. Mussey to Capt. George B. Halstead, Assistant Adjutant General's Staff, Louisville, Kentucky, 25 June 1864; George H. Thomas to Lorenzo Thomas, 28 June 1864; Mussey to Lorenzo Thomas, 28 and 29 February 1864, and 23 January and 6 March 1865; Adjutant General's Office, Letters Relating to Colored Troops, RG 94, NA; George H. Thomas to Adjutant General Lorenzo Thomas, 9 August and 16 September 1864, Letters Sent, Department of the Cumberland, RG 393, NA.

27. Thomas to Morgan, 29 July 1864, Letters Sent, Department of the Cumberland, RG 393, NA.

28. Morgan, *Reminiscences*, 22.

29. Current, *Lincoln's Loyalists*; Degler, *Other South*.

30. Eicher, *Longest Night*, 617–19; Chase, *Papers*, 4:214; Opdycke, *Good and Right*, 147.

31. Thomas to Garfield, 17 December 1863, Garfield Papers, LOC.

32. *OR* 32:2:429, 464, 480–82; Van Horne, *Thomas*, 206–209; Van Horne, *Army of the Cumberland*, 2:18–19.

33. *OR* 32:1:164–390; Castel, *Decision in the West*, 43–53.

34. *OR* 32:1:417–83; Castel, *Decision in the West*, 51–55.

35. Thomas to Grant, 27 February 1864, quoted in "Report of Major General Thomas to the Committee on the Conduct of the War," *Report of the Committee on the Conduct of the War*, vol. 1, suppl. 1, Senate Report [not numbered], 39th Cong., 1st Sess.

36. Castel, *Decision in the West,* 62–68.

37. *OR* 32:2:142–43.

38. *OR* 32:2:264.

39. Squires, *Days of Yester-Year,* 195; Balfour, *Franklin and Southampton County,* 74; Parramore, *Southampton County,* 157–77.

40. Castel, *Decision in the West,* 68.

41. Shiman, "Sherman's Pioneers," 251–69; Shiman, "Engineering Sherman's March"; Van Horne, *Army of the Cumberland,* 2:439–58.

42. Shanks, *Personal Recollections,* 58.

CHAPTER 13, THE ATLANTA CAMPAIGN

1. *OR* 38:1:62–63.

2. Thomas, "Report to the Committee on the Conduct of the War," Senate Report, 39th Cong., 1st Sess., 201–202; *OR* 38:1:63.

3. *OR* 38:1:139–41; Daniel, *Days of Glory,* 397; Castel, *Decision in the West,* 121–85; McMurry, *Atlanta 1864,* 56–74.

4. *OR* 38:1:141, 189–92; 38:2:27–28; Castel, *Decision in the West,* 163–66.

5. *OR* 38:1:141, 189–91.

6. Eicher, *Longest Night,* 679.

7. W. Sherman, *Memoirs,* 2:34; McDonough and Jones, *"War So Terrible,"* 105–106; McMurry, *Atlanta 1864,* 73–74; Castel, *Decision in the West,* 181–82.

8. Castel, *Decision in the West,* 181–82.

9. Castel, *Decision in the West,* 186–209; McMurry, *Atlanta 1864,* 75–84.

10. Castel, *Decision in the West,* 209–54; McMurry, *Atlanta 1864,* 85–99.

11. Castel, *Decision in the West,* 221–89; McMurry, *Atlanta 1864,* 88–89.

12. Stone, "Thomas," 10:195–96.

13. Strayer and Baumgartner, *Echoes of Battle,* 65.

14. Van Horne, *Thomas,* 237.

15. Castel, *Decision in the West,* 290–95.

16. *OR* 38:4:507–508.

17. W. Sherman, *Memoirs,* 2:22; Daniel, *Days of Glory,* 392.

18. De Peyster, "Thomas," 19; Van Horne, *Thomas,* 230; Shanks, *Personal Recollections,* 77; Morse, *Letters and Diaries,* 149.

19. *OR* 38:4:559–60, 569; Castel, *Decision in the West,* 297; Daniel, *Days of Glory,* 392.

20. Castel, *Decision in the West,* 303–24; McMurry, *Atlanta 1864,* 100–112; Royster, *Destructive War,* 296–320; *OR* 38:1:151.

21. Castel, *Decision in the West,* 304–305; *OR* 38:4:602–603.

22. Castel, *Decision in the West,* 316–20; *OR* 38:4:607–609.

23. *OR* 38:4:609–10.

24. *OR* 38:4:611–12.

25. Castel, *Decision in the West,* 330–49; McMurry, *Atlanta 1864,* 111; McPherson, *Battle Cry of Freedom,* 741–43.

26. *OR* 38:4:629; Castel, *Decision in the West,* 322, 358–59.

27. Castel, *Decision in the West,* 365–83; McMurry, *Atlanta 1864,* 146–52; *OR* 38:1:156–57, 195–207.

28. Castel, *Decision in the West,* 372.

29. Van Horne, *Army of the Cumberland,* 2:115; Van Horne, *Thomas,* 244.

30. Castel, *Decision in the West,* 377–78.

31. Castel, *Decision in the West,* 418–22.

32. Castel, *Decision in the West,* 425–507; McMurry, *Atlanta 1864,* 156–57.

33. Castel, *Decision in the West,* 480–507; McMurry, *Atlanta 1864,* 169–76.

34. *OR* 38:5:718–19; Castel, *Decision in the West,* 530–36; McMurry, *Atlanta 1864,* 174–76.

35. Castel, *Decision in the West,* 8, 478–79; Castel, *Winning and Losing,* 15–32; Daniel, "Rebuttal," 44–51; McMurry, *Atlanta 1864,* 203–208.

CHAPTER 14, NASHVILLE

1. Bailey, *Chessboard of War,* 13–26; Sword, *Embrace an Angry Wind,* 42–50, 58–60; McDonough, *Nashville.*

2. *OR* 39:3:162.

3. *OR* 39:3:3, 25–26, 63–64, 202, 334; W. Sherman, *Memoirs,* 2:156–57.

4. *OR* 39:3:202, 222, 594; Bailey, *Chessboard of War,* 13–16; Sword, *Embrace an Angry Wind,* 58–62.

5. Bailey, *Chessboard of War,* 26–47; Sword, *Embrace an Angry Wind,* 58–74.

6. *OR* 39:1:583–84, 590–91, 750–51; 39:3:514–15, 528, 535, 576–77, 580, 594–95, 599.

7. *OR* 45:1:52.

8. *OR* 39:3:756.

9. *OR* 39:1:581, 584–90; 39:3; Coppee, *Thomas,* ix, 309; Quaife, *From the Cannon's Mouth,* 290–91.

10. *OR* 45:1:32, 943–44; Sword, *Embrace an Angry Wind,* 79–86.

11. *OR* 45:1:944.

12. *OR* 45:1:33, 341, 955–58, 972–73, 983–84, 994–98, 1016–18, 1036; Sword, *Embrace an Angry Wind,* 87–109.

13. Sword, *Embrace an Angry Wind,* 110–55; Bailey, *Chessboard of War,* 88–94; McDonough and Connelly, *Five Tragic Hours*; Horn, "Spring Hill Legend," 20–32; and McDonough, *Schofield,* 110–13.

14. Sword, *Embrace an Angry Wind,* 159–62; Bailey, *Chessboard of War,* 94–95; *OR* 45:1:1107–1108; Schofield, *Forty-six Years in the Army,* 219–21.

15. McDonough and Connelly, *Five Tragic Hours*; Sword, *Embrace an Angry Wind,* 156–271; Bailey, *Chessboard of War,* 91–111.

16. *OR* 45:1:1168–71, 45:2:3; Rusling, *Civil War Days,* 87.

17. Schofield, *Forty-six Years in the Army,* 189–225.

18. *OR* 39:3:666, 685.

19. *OR* 45:1:1169–70; 45:2:3, 17.

20. Sword, *Embrace an Angry Wind,* 276–77; *OR* 45:1:52–58.

21. *OR* 45:1:34, 503, 1050, 1100, 1126, 1159–60, 1190; 45:2:3.

22. *OR* 45:1:54; J. Wilson, *Under the Old Flag,* 2:33–34.

23. Sword, *Embrace an Angry Wind,* 274–76; *OR* 45:1:152, 1015, 1167–68; 45:2:3.

24. Thomas to Dennis Hart Mahan, 15 April 1867, Thomas Papers, HL.

25. *OR* 45:2:3, 15–18.

26. *OR* 45:1:36; 45:2:18, 55, 70–71, 84–85, 101–102, 149, 153–54.

27. Sword, *Embrace an Angry Wind,* 293–99; *OR* 45:1:654.

28. Sword, *Embrace an Angry Wind,* 293–99; *OR* 45:1:612–15.

29. *OR* 45:2:96–97, 114–16.

30. *OR* 45:2:114–16; Bates, *Lincoln in the Telegraph Office,* 313; Chittenden, *Lincoln,* 364.

31. Stone, "Repelling Hood's Invasion," 4:455.

32. *OR* 45:2:118, 120, 130, 143, 147–49, 155.

33. J. Wilson, *Under the Old Flag*, 100–102; Schofield, *Forty-six Years in the Army*, 237–38; Steedman, "Robbing the Dead," *New York Times*, 22 June 1881.

34. Frances Thomas to Alfred L. Hough, 29 August 1881, Hough Papers, University of Colorado.

35. *OR* 45:2:114–16; Schofield, *Forty-six Years in the Army*, 239–41; McDonough, *Schofield*, 130–35; McDonough, *Schofield*, 148–55. Steedman accused Schofield of sending secret telegrams to Grant in a letter to the *Toledo Northern Ohio Democrat*, reprinted in the 22 June 1881, *New York Times*, under the headline "Robbing the Dead: Gen. Schofield's Attempt to Seize the Laurels of General Thomas." Grant's letter defending Schofield appeared in the 4 August 1881, *New York Times*, to which Steedman responded in another letter in the *Toledo Northern Ohio Democrat*, reprinted in the 15 August *Times*.

36. J. Wilson, *Under the Old Flag*, 2:102–106.

37. *OR* 45:2:155.

38. *OR* 45:2:171, 195; Porter, *Campaigning with Grant*, 348–49; Sword, *Embrace an Angry Wind*, 319; Bates, *Lincoln in the Telegraph Office*, 315–19.

39. *OR* 45:2:180; Simpson, *Grant*, 395–99; Catton, *Grant Takes Command*, 394–401; J. E. Smith, *Grant*, 389; W. Wood, *Civil War Generalship*, 228–29.

40. Sauers, *Meade*, 75–76, 89; Rafuse, *Meade*, 115, 130–31.

41. *OR* 45:2:168, 172, 180, 183–84.

42. *OR* 45:3:183–84.

43. Schofield, *Forty-six Years in the Army*, 242–44; *OR* 35:1:38.

44. Thatcher, *Second Michigan Cavalry*, 222.

45. Van Horne, *Thomas*, 323; *OR* 45:1:562.

46. Sword, *Embrace an Angry Wind*, 328–29; *OR* 45:1:128–29.

47. Sword, *Embrace an Angry Wind*, 329; *OR* 45:1:128–29, 155, 289, 294, 304.

48. Sword, *Embrace an Angry Wind*, 331–34; *OR* 45:1:38, 200–201, 345, 438, 472, 551, 562, 589.

49. Sword, *Embrace an Angry Wind*, 322–26; *OR* 45:1:38, 504, 507, 527, 536, 539, 739; 45:2:199.

50. Sword, *Embrace an Angry Wind*, 330; *OR* 45:1:722.

51. Sword, *Embrace an Angry Wind*, 331–43; *OR* 45:1:38–39, 128–30, 433–34.

52. Sword, *Embrace an Angry Wind*, 343; *OR* 45:1:155, 392, 406, 417; 45:2:201.

53. *OR* 45:2:202.

54. R. Johnson, *Thomas*, 196–97.

55. *OR* 45:1:194–95.

56. Bates, *Lincoln in the Telegraph Office*, 316–18.

57. *OR* 45:1:194–95, 210.

58. Rusling, *Civil War Days*, 96; Schofield, *Forty-six Years in the Army*, 244–45; Sanford Kellogg to Emerson Opdycke, 15 December 1881, Opdycke Papers, Ohio Historical Society; Van Horne, *Army of the Cumberland*, 2:236; *OR* 45:1:130, 156.

59. Sword, *Embrace an Angry Wind*, 347–51.

60. *OR* 45:1:39, 346, 434.

61. Sword, *Embrace an Angry Wind*, 351–55; *OR* 45:1:130–31, 346, 434–35, 505, 564, 591; 45:2:215–16; Van Horne, *Thomas*, 330.

62. C. Walton, *Private Smith's Journal*, 194.

63. *OR* 45:1:131–33, 156, 505.

64. Sword, *Embrace an Angry Wind*, 357–63; *OR* 45:1:705.

65. *OR* 45:1:435; 45:2:215, 217.

66. Sword, *Embrace an Angry Wind*, 365–67; *OR* 45:1:435, 438–39.

67. *OR* 45:1:435; Stibbs, "MacArthur's Division at Nashville," 4:498–99; J. Wilson, *Under the Old Flag,* 116; Van Horne, *Thomas,* 331–32.

68. LeDuc, *Autobiography,* 135–36; Stibbs, "MacArthur's Division at Nashville," 500–501.

69. Sword, *Embrace an Angry Wind,* 369–86; *OR* 45:1:40, 346, 435–36, 552.

70. *OR* 45:1:218, 436, 552.

71. J. Wilson, *Under the Old Flag,* 126.

CHAPTER 15, VICTORY AND FRUSTRATION

1. *OR* 45:1:40, 45:2:210–11; Eicher, *Longest Night,* 780.

2. *New York Herald,* 19 December 1864; *New York Times,* 16 and 24 December 1864; *Chicago Tribune,* 18 and 20 December 1864; *Louisville Journal,* 20 and 21 December 1864.

3. The sword is described in the *Gallipolis [Ohio] Journal,* 15 October 1863, in Chickamauga/Chattanooga National Military Park Archives; the spurs are referred to in Thomas to Bvt. Brig. Gen. William Landrum, 14 November 1867, "General's Box," NA; the other gifts are described in Van Horne, *Thomas,* 423–24.

4. *OR* 45:2:228–30, 248.

5. *OR* 45:2:342, 561; Coppee, *Thomas,* 286; Van Horne, *Thomas,* 313.

6. Sherman to Thomas, 25 December 1864; Thomas Papers, HL.

7. *OR* 45:2:218–219, 237.

8. *OR* 45:1:161–2, 45:2:214; Van Horne, *Army of the Cumberland,* 2:243.

9. *OR* 45:1:41.

10. *OR* 45:1:40–41; Sword, *Embrace an Angry Wind,* 387–410.

11. Sword, *Embrace an Angry Wind,* 411–13; *OR* 45:1:41–42, 135–36, 162, 360–61, 553–54; 45:2:272, 287–90, 293–300.

12. *OR* 45:2:295–96, 307.

13. Sword, *Embrace an Angry Wind,* 401–402, 416–20; *OR* 45:1:43, 566–67; 45:2:260–61, 384–85, 388–89, 394, 397, 402, 403.

14. Grant, *Memoirs,* 2:385–6, 524–5; see also Young, *Grant,* 2:295–6.

15. Thomas to Rosecrans, 9 January 1865, Rosecrans Papers, UCLA; Thomas to Garfield, 10 January 1865, Garfield Papers, LOC.

16. Van Horne, *Thomas,* 344–5.

17. Sword, *Embrace an Angry Wind,* 414, 425–28.

18. Sword, *Embrace an Angry Wind,* 426; *OR* 45:2:756, 805.

19. Morgan, *Reminiscences,* 22.

20. Morgan, *Reminiscences,* 48; Van Horne, *Thomas,* 347.

21. Cornish, *Sable Arm,* 263–4, 272–8; Trudeau, *Black Like Men of War;* Wood, *Black Scare,* 40–50.

22. Baggett, *Scalawags,* 130–41.

23. *OR* 49:1:725.

24. *OR* 45:2:377–78, 441–42; 47:2:4, 101–102; McDonough, *Schofield,* 150.

25. *OR* 47:2:59, 101–104.

26. *OR* 45:2:474; 47:1:909; 47:2:101–102; 49:1:584, 605–606, 616–17, 623–24, 636–37.

27. *OR* 49:1:653–54.

28. *OR* 49:1:708–709, 716–17.

29. *OR* 49:1:342–43, 777–78, 875, 916–17; 49:2:17–18, 28; 47:2:859–60.

30. James H. Wilson to Adam Badeau, 26 January 1865, Wilson Papers, LOC; Jones, "Wilson's Letters to Badeau," 230–45.

31. *OR* 49:1:708–709; J. Wilson, *Under the Old Flag,* 180–81.

32. *OR* 49:1:783, 850–51, 854; 49:2:53.

33. *OR* 49:1:350–70; J. Jones, *Yankee Blitzkrieg*; Keenan, *Wilson's Cavalry Corps.*

34. *OR* 49:1:91–100, 323–25, 344–46; Eicher, *Longest Night,* 836–40.

35. *OR* 49:2:376, 378–79, 395–97, 418–19, 456–57, 471–72, 484–89, 498–99, 507–508, 518, 550, 552–53, 582–83, 613–14, 621–22, 648–49, 678, 732–33, 760–62, 774–75, 849; Van Horne, *Army of the Cumberland,* 2:363–64.

36. *OR* 49:2:342–43, 506–507, 874; Thomas to the citizens of Morgan, Marshall, and Lawrence Counties, Alabama, 2 April 1865, Thomas Papers, HL.

37. See chap. 10, above, and *OR* 4:342–43.

38. Trefousse, *Johnson.*

CHAPTER 16, OCCUPATION

1. *OR* 49:2:564, 613.

2. *OR* 49:2:582, 680.

3. *OR* 49:2:850–51, 919, 923, 945, 949–50, 968, 1002.

4. Thomas to Sherman, 26 May 1865, Sherman Papers, LOC.

5. Snetsinger, *Kiss Clara for Me,* 160.

6. *OR* 49:2:827, 847; *New York Herald,* 31 May 1865.

7. Sefton, *Army and Reconstruction,* 35; *OR* 49:2:859.

8. Johnson to Brownlow, 16 July 1865, Johnson, *Papers of Johnson,* 8:413; *OR* 49:2:1083, 1086.

9. Sefton, *U.S. Army and Reconstruction,* 26.

10. Brownlow to Johnson, 8 June 1865, Johnson, *Papers of Johnson,* 8:199–200; Van Horne, *Thomas,* 414–17.

11. *OR* 49:2:1016–17, 1039–41, 1057; Grant to Thomas, 17 July, 21 August, and 4 November 1865, Grant, *Papers of Grant,* 15:268–69, 307–309, 390–92.

12. *OR* 49:2:465, 737; Carter, *When the War Was Over,* 6–23; Rable, *But There Was No Peace,* 13.

13. General Order No. 29, Military Division of the Tennessee, 21 September 1865, in Thomas, Annual Report, 12 November 1866, Letters Sent, Department of the Cumberland, RG 393, NA. While the Department of the Cumberland changed names a number of times during Reconstruction, at times being called the Department of the Tennessee, all documents are filed at the National Archives under the name "Department of the Cumberland" and are cited as such here.

14. Grant, General Order No. 3, 12 January 1866, Grant, *Papers of Grant,* 16:7–8; Sefton, *Army and Reconstruction,* 66.

15. Otis, "Thomas," 1:122–47.

16. Cimprich, *Slavery's End in Tennessee,* 119.

17. Sefton, *Army and Reconstruction,* 30; *OR* 49:2:1092.

18. Van Horne, *Thomas,* 347.

19. Thomas to Bvt. Maj. Gen. John E. Smith, 3 July 1865, Letters Sent, Department of the Cumberland, RG 393, NA.

20. Thomas to Smith, 3 July 1865, Letters Sent, Department of the Cumberland, RG 393, NA.

21. Cimprich, "Thomas," 175–76; Bvt. Brig. Gen. W.W. Barrett et al. to George H. Thomas, 21 August 1865, Letters Received, Department of the Cumberland, RG 393, NA.

22. Johnson, *Papers of Johnson,* 8:585; *OR* 49:2:1100–1101.

23. Johnson, *Papers of Johnson,* 9:26–27; *OR* 49:2:1108–1109.

24. Thomas to Bvt. Maj. Gen. John S. Smith, commanding at Memphis, 26 December 1865; Rable, *But There Was No Peace*, 23–28; C. Williams, "Symbols of Freedom and Defeat," 210–30.

25. Johnson, *Papers of Johnson*, 9:26–27, 41, 48–49, 57–58; *OR* 49:2:1111–12.

26. Grant, *Papers of Grant*, 16:139–41.

27. Cimprich, "Thomas," 176–77; Johnson, *Papers of Johnson*, 9:48–49.

28. Thomas to Captain Coleman, 31 August 1865, and Thomas to Judge S. D. Shackleford, August 1865, Letters Sent, Department of the Cumberland, RG 393, NA.

29. Thomas to Lt. John H. Carter, 4 and 5 September 1865, Letters Sent, Department of the Cumberland, RG 393, NA.

30. Johnson, *Papers of Johnson*, 9:150–51; Stowell, "Religious Meaning of Confederate Defeat."

31. Van Horne, *Thomas*, 409–10.

32. Johnson, *Papers of Johnson*, 9:280–81; Van Horne, *Thomas*, 411–13. Stowell, "Religious Meaning of Confederate Defeat."

33. Grant, *Papers of Grant*, 15:309; *OR* 49:2:1112; Opdycke, *Good and Right*, 290–91.

34. Van Horne, *Thomas*, 16–17.

35. Foner, *Reconstruction*, 187–88, 193–204.

36. Maslowski, *Treason Must Be Made Odious*, 148–49.

37. Foner, *Reconstruction*, 199–209; Johnson, *Papers of Johnson*, 9:400; Van Horne, *Thomas*, 401–402.

38. Sefton, *Army and Reconstruction*, 60; House Report No. 30, 39th Cong., 2nd Sess., Pt. 1, pp. 108–11.

39. Garfield, "Thomas," 89.

40. House Report No. 30; Rable, *But There Was No Peace*, 1–15.

41. Sefton, *Army and Reconstruction*, 60.

42. Grant, *Papers of Grant*, 16:69–70, 114–15.

43. Grant, *Papers of Grant*, 16:54.

44. Sefton, *Army and Reconstruction*, 65.

45. Thomas to Rosecrans, 16 January 1866, Rosecrans Papers, UCLA.

46. Foner, *Reconstruction*, 243–51; McPherson, *Ordeal By Fire*, 508, 513–15.

CHAPTER 17, RECONSTRUCTION

1. Simpson, *Let Us Have Peace*, 135–36.

2. Thomas, Annual Report, 12 November 1866, Letters Sent, Department of the Cumberland, RG 393, NA.

3. Thomas to S. J. Martin and W. N. R. Jones, 12 April 1866; Thomas to Mrs. John A. Jackson, 14 April 1866; Thomas to John Williams, 28 April 1866; Thomas to Maj. Gen. Thomas J. Wood, 5 June 1866; Thomas to Wood, 10 September 1866; Letters Sent, Department of the Cumberland, RG 393, NA.

4. Thomas to Mrs. John A. Jackson, 14 April 1866, Letters Sent, Department of the Cumberland, RG 393, NA.

5. Foner, *Reconstruction*, 261–62; Sefton, *Army and Reconstruction*, 82–84; Hardwick, "Black Soldiers and the Memphis Race Riot," 109–29; Lovett, "Memphis Riots," 9–33; Ryan, "Memphis Riot," 243–57; House Report No. 101, 39th Cong., 1st Sess.

6. Thomas to Stoneman, 3–4 May 1866, Telegrams Sent, Department of the Cumberland, RG 393, NA; Stoneman to Thomas, 3–5 May 1866, Telegrams Received, Department of the Cumberland, RG 393, NA.

7. Sefton, *Army and Reconstruction*, 73; Simpson, *Let Us Have Peace*, 138; Grant, *Papers of Grant*, 16:228.

8. Thomas, Annual Report, 12 November 1866; and Thomas to Grant, 28 November 1866; Letters Sent, Department of the Cumberland, RG 393, NA; Grant, *Papers of Grant*, 16:392–93.

9. Thomas to C. R. Comstock, 5 October 1866, Letters Sent, Department of the Cumberland, RG 393, NA; Cimprich, "Thomas," 179–80.

10. *Opinions of the Attorneys General,* 11: 531–32; Grant, *Papers of Grant*, 16:231–34.

11. Sefton, *Army and Reconstruction,* 101; Grant, *Papers of Grant,* 16:243.

12. Foner, *Reconstruction,* 262–64; Sefton, *Army and Reconstruction,* 84–89.

13. Foner, *Reconstruction,* 265–68.

14. Simpson, *Let Us Have Peace,* 162–63.

15. Cimprich, "Thomas," 178; Thomas, Annual Report, 12 November 1866, Letters Sent, Department of the Cumberland, RG 393, NA.

16. Thomas, Annual Report, 30 September 1867; Thomas to Smiley, 18 and 24 October 1866; and Thomas to E. A. Cheatham, 20 October 1866; Letters Sent, Department of the Cumberland, RG 393, NA.

17. Van Horne, *Thomas,* 415–18.

18. Van Horne, *Thomas,* 416–17.

19. Thomas, Annual Report, 12 November 1866, Letters Sent, Department of the Cumberland, RG 393, NA.

20. Thomas to Grant, 26 November 1866, and attachments, Letters Received, by the Headquarters of the Army, RG 108, M1635, Roll 96, NA.

21. Thomas to Charles H. Smith, mayor of Rome, Georgia; James Pencherton, member of the city council; and others, 9 February 1867, Letters Sent, Department of the Cumberland, RG 393, NA.

22. Rable, *But There Was No Peace.*

23. Grant, *Papers of Grant*, 17:9–10.

24. Simpson, *Let Us Have Peace,* 171; Hayes, *Diary and Letters*, 3:41.

25. Thomas to 1st Lt. Fred Rosencrantz, 6 May 1867, Letters Sent, Department of the Cumberland, RG 393, NA.

26. Thomas to Lt. Col. E. J. Townsend, 8 August 1867; Thomas to Bvt. Brig. Gen. Sidney Burbank, 28 August 1867; Letters Sent, Department of the Cumberland, RG 393, NA; Thomas to Grant, 21 July 1867, Telegrams Received, Headquarters of the Army, RG 108, NA.

27. Grant, *Papers of Grant*, 17:238–39.

28. Thomas to U.S. Attorney Marlan Perkins, 21 September 1867, Letters Sent, Department of the Cumberland, RG 393, NA.

29. "Milliken, a Returned Rebel," House Executive Document No. 75, 40th Cong., 2nd Sess.

30. "Milliken, a Returned Rebel"; Thomas to Bvt. Brig. Gen. Sidney Burbank, 21 July 1867, Letters Sent, Department of the Cumberland, RG 393, NA; *Memphis Post*, 3 August and 12 October 1867; Grant, *Papers of Grant*, 18:396; Thomas, Annual Report, 1 October 1868, Letters Sent, Department of the Cumberland, RG 393, NA.

31. "Milliken, a Returned Rebel."

32. Stone, "Thomas," 10:198–99.

33. Grant, *Papers of Grant*, 17:80–84.

34. Grant, *Papers of Grant*, 17:281–82.

35. Johnson, *Papers of Johnson,* 12:489–91, 493–96, 511; Grant, *Papers of Grant,* 17:277–84, 301–305; House Executive Document No. 57, 40th Cong., 2nd Sess., 3–6; Coppee, *Thomas,* 296–97.

36. R. Johnson, *Thomas,* 255; Welsh, *Medical Histories.*

37. Grant, *Papers of Grant,* 17:236–38, 606–607; Thomas, Annual Report, 30 September 1867, Letters Sent, Department of the Cumberland, RG 393, NA.

38. Thomas, Annual Report, 30 September 1867, Letters Sent, Department of the Cumberland, RG 393, NA.; Johnson, *Papers of Johnson,* 13:115–16; *Papers of. Grant,* 17:360–62.

39. Thomas, Annual Report, 30 September 1867, Letters Sent, Department of the Cumberland, RG 393, NA.

40. Thomas, Annual Report, 30 September 1867, Letters Sent, Department of the Cumberland, RG 393, NA.

41. Trelease, *White Terror.*

42. Trelease, *White Terror.*

43. Thomas to Carlin, 11 April 1868; Thomas, Annual Report, 1 October 1868; Letters Sent, Department of the Cumberland, RG 393, NA; Grant, *Papers of Grant,* 18:196–97.

44. Grant, *Papers of Grant,* 18:214.

45. Thomas to Col. Thomas J. Harrison, 9 March 1868; Thomas to Bvt. Maj. Gen. William P. Carlin, 21 March 1868; Thomas to Bvt. Maj. T. H. Torbett, 30 April 1868; Thomas to Carlin, 10 July 1868; Thomas to Bvt. Brig. Gen. Sidney Burbank, 10 July 1868; Thomas, Annual Report, 1 October 1868; Letters Sent, Department of the Cumberland, RG 393, NA.

46. Thomas, Annual Report, 1 October 1868, Letters Sent, Department of the Cumberland, RG 393, NA; Trelease, *White Terror,* 3–48.

47. Marszalek, *Halleck,* 246–47.

48. Thomas to Adjutant General E. D. Townsend, 11 September 1868, Letters Sent, Department of the Cumberland, RG 393, NA; Cimprich, "Thomas," 183.

49. Grant, *Papers of Grant,* 18:567.

50. Thomas, Annual Report, 1 October 1868, Letters Sent, Department of the Cumberland, RG 393, NA.

51. Thomas, Annual Report, 1 October 1868, Letters Sent, Department of the Cumberland, RG 393, NA.

52. Attachments to Thomas, Annual Report, 1 October 1868, Letters Sent, Department of the Cumberland, RG 393, NA; Thomas to Burbank, 10 July 1868; Thomas to Carlin, 10 July 1868; Letters Sent, Department of the Cumberland, RG 393, NA.

53. Thomas, Annual Report, 1 October 1868, Letters Sent, Department of the Cumberland, RG 393, NA.

CHAPTER 18, LATE CAREER AND DEATH

Epigraph. These are Thomas's last written words. The manuscript trails off here, when Thomas suffered a stroke while writing. He died later that day. This document is reprinted in full in Van Horne, *Thomas,* 450–55.

1. Johnson, *Papers of Johnson,* 13:586–87.

2. *New York Times,* 7 April 1870.

3. Thomas to Henry Cist, 11 March 1867, Thomas Papers, HL. Thomas authorized Cist to publish this letter, but I did not find any record of Cist having done so. Other letters on the subject are Thomas to Cist, 8 April 1867; Thomas to General Joshua H. Bates, 6 April 1867;

and Thomas to John Tyler, Jr., 5 December 1867, all in Thomas Papers, HL; and Thomas to Gen. J. Watts De Peyster, 20 April 1867, quoted in Van Horne, *Thomas*, 422.

4. Resolution of the Tennessee Republican Convention, printed in the *Memphis Post*, 27 January 1868; Johnson, *Papers of Johnson*, 13:263–64, 318–19; Coleman, *Election of 1868*, 111; Dearing, *Veterans in Politics*, 24, 159; Simpson, *Let Us Have Peace*, 207–12, 244–45, 248–51.

5. Thomas to William R. Plum, 11 August 1868, Thomas Papers, HL.

6. Thomas to Thomas Duncan, 29 July 1867; Thomas to Gordon Granger, 25 October 1868; Thomas to Brownlow, 27 October 1868; Thomas to Brownlow and Thomas to Granger, 30 October 1868; Letters Sent, Department of the Cumberland, RG 393, NA.

7. Thomas, Annual Report, 15 May 1869, Letters Sent, Department of the Cumberland, RG 393, NA.

8. Thomas to Lucien Anderson, 13 January 1869, Letters Sent, Department of the Cumberland, RG 393, NA.

9. Thomas, Annual Report, 15 May 1869, Letters Sent, Department of the Cumberland, RG 393, NA.

10. Van Horne, *Thomas*, 432–33.

11. Thomas to Alfred L. Hough, 16 March 1869, Hough Papers, University of Colorado; Van Horne, *Thomas*, 433–36; Thomas to Col. R. H. Ramsey, 22 March 1869, Thomas Papers, HL.

12. Scribner, *How Soldiers Were Made*, 299–300.

13. Thomas to Hough, 1 and 10 February and 2 March 1869; Hough Papers, University of Colorado; Sefton, *Army and Reconstruction,* 207–208; Holzmann, *Stormy Ben Butler*, 191–95; West, *Lincoln's Scapegoat General,* 337–39.

14. Society of the Army of the Cumberland, *1869 Reunion Report*; Scribner, *How Soldiers Were Made*, 208–209.

15. Thomas to Hough, 5 April 1869, Hough Papers, University of Colorado.

16. Warner, *Generals in Blue*, 135–36; Grant, *Papers of Grant,* 19:187.

17. Trelease, *White Terror,* 175–89, 278–84.

18. Trelease, *White Terror,* 383–418; Baggett, *Scalawags*, 125–41; McKinney, "Southern Mountain Republicans," 199–202; Current, *Lincoln's Loyalists*, 206–207.

19. Van Horne, *Thomas,* 437–39; quoted in Matthews, "Thomas," 30; W. O. N. Perkins to Thomas, 8 December 1869, G. P. Thruston to Thomas, 25 and 31 December 1869, General George Thomas Letters, University of Tennessee.

20. Where not otherwise noted, information about Thomas's trip to Alaska is taken from his Annual Report, 27 September 1869, attached to the Report of the Secretary of War, House Executive Document No. 1, 41st Cong., 2nd Sess.

21. Hinckley, *The Americanization of Alaska*; Haycox, *Alaska: An American Colony*.

22. Thomas to Fitz John Porter, 18 October 1869, Thomas Papers, WPA.

23. Thomas to Baird, 25 September 1869, Smithsonian Institution Archives; Thomas to General Rucker, Autumn 1869; Van Horne, *Thomas*, 437.

24. *New York Tribune*, 12 March 1870; Van Horne, *Thomas,* 439–42; McDonough, *Schofield*, 136–37.

25. Van Horne, *Thomas,* 440.

26. Van Horne, *Thomas,* 442–43; *New York Tribune*, 6 April 1870; R. Johnson, *Thomas*, 255.

27. *New York Times*, 31 March and 2 April 1870; Frances Thomas to William T. Sherman, 2 April 1870, Sherman Papers, LOC; Sherman, General Order No. 37, 3 April 1870; printed in the *New York Times*, 4 April 1870.

28. *New York Times*, 4 and 5 April 1870; *New York Tribune*, 6 April 1870.

29. *New York Times*, April 7, 1870, *[Washington, D.C.] National Intelligencer*, 7 April 1870.

30. *New York Times*, 9 April 1870.

31. *New York Tribune*, 6 April 1870; Frances Thomas to William T. Sherman, no date; and Sherman to Frances Thomas, 31 April 1870; Sherman Papers, LOC.

32. *New Orleans Picayune*, 30 March 1870; and *Richmond Dispatch*, 18 April 1870; cited in Francis McDonnell, "Confederate Spin," 260–61.

33. Frances K. Thomas to Alfred L. Hough, 29 April 1870, Hough Papers, University of Colorado; Sanford Kellogg to Emerson Opdycke, 26 September and 28 October 1882; Thomas Van Horne to Emerson Opdycke, 29 March 1883; Opdycke Papers, Ohio Historical Society.

34. Frances K. Thomas to Hough, 27 May 1880, Hough Papers, University of Colorado.

35. Pension file of Frances K. Thomas, RG 15, NA; Otis, "Thomas," 1:397.

36. The wills of Judith and Frances Thomas are in the Southampton County records, on microfilm, at the Library of Virginia. Judith Thomas's will, dated 14 September 1901, is in Will Book No. 22, p. 50; Frances Thomas's will, dated 18 March 1903, is on p. 76. There are no extant records of deaths between 1896 and 1914 in Virginia, so it is not clear exactly when Judith and Frances died, but it seems that they died within a few years after writing their wills. Land tax records and personal property tax records, Southampton County, Library of Virginia; Frances Thomas to Mattie Rochelle Tyler, 23 October 1900, Thomas Papers, VHS; "Sisters of General Thomas Living in Southampton,"; *Richmond Times*, 31 March 1901; Rodeffer, "Yankee Hero 'Deserted' Virginia," *Norfolk-Portsmouth Virginian-Pilot*, 4 November 1962.

37. "Sisters of General.".

38. Barham, "Thomas Family," 328–34.

39. William Barham to W. G. Stanard, 15 June 1915, VHS.

CHAPTER 19, THOMAS IN HISTORICAL MEMORY

Epigraph. Society of the Army of the Cumberland, *1879 Reunion Report*. A slightly different version of Sherman's remarks is given in the 20 November 1879, *National Republican*.

1. Brockett, *Our Great Captains*; Shanks, *Personal Recollections*.

2. Van Horne, *Thomas*, 424; Society of the Army of the Cumberland, *Reunion Reports* [annual], 1870–1907.

3. R. Johnson, *Thomas*; Coppee, *Thomas*; Van Horne, *Thomas*; Piatt and Boynton, *Thomas*.

4. Society of the Army of the Cumberland, *1879 Reunion Report*; Garfield, *Diary*, 4:325; *National Republican*, 20 November 1879.

5. Grant, *Memoirs*, 2:524–25; *OR* 38:4:611–12; Sherman, *Memoirs*, 2:60–61.

6. Castel, "Prevaricating through Georgia," 48–71; Marszalek, "Sherman Called It the Way He Saw It," 72–78.

7. Sherman, "Grant, Thomas, Lee," 438–50.

8. Schofield, *Forty-Six Years*, 189–226, 255–298.

9. Early criticisms of Sherman's and Grant's memoirs, and defenses of Thomas, include Boynton, *Was General Thomas Slow at Nashville?*; Sherratt, "Corrections of Grant's Memoirs," 500–514; and Van Horne, *Thomas*.

10. Foster, *Ghosts of the Confederacy*; Davis, *Cause Lost*, 175–90; Horwitz, *Confederates in the Attic*.

11. Gallagher and Nolan, *Myth of the Lost Cause*, 11–34; see C. Wilson, *Baptized in Blood*; and Connelly and Bellows, *God and General Longstreet*.

12. McDonnell, "Confederate Spin," 255–66.

13. "The Virginia State Guard and the Yankee Gen. Thomas," from the *Richmond Examiner*, reprinted in the *New York Times*, 14 November 1863; Ruffin, *Diary*, 3:531.

14. Thomas to Capt. S. A. Letcher, 11 August 1868, Thomas Papers, HL.

15. McDonnell, "Confederate Spin," 263.

16. Thomas to John Letcher, 12 March 1861, *Calendar of Virginia State Papers*, 11:106.

17. *New York Tribune*, 4 May 1870; *New York Times*, 17 May 1870.

18. *New York Herald*, 31 December 1875; Frances K. Thomas to the editors of the *New York Herald*, attached to Frances K. Thomas to Alfred L. Hough, 21 January 1876, Hough Papers, University of Colorado; Francis Smith to Frances Thomas, 8 February 1876, Fitzhugh Lee Papers, University of Virginia.

19. Southern Historical Society, *Papers*, 12:568–70; *New York Times*, 12 January 1883.

20. Frances K. Thomas to Alfred L. Hough, 20 January 1883, no date [1883], and 1 May 1883, Hough Papers, University of Colorado.

21. Southern Historical Society, *Papers*, 1:425–26; Chandler, *Building of the Nation*, 12:449–50; "Sisters of General Thomas," Oglesby, "South's Contribution," 117–18; Squires, *Days of Yester-Year*, 184–97.

22. William Barham to W. G. Stanard, corresponding secretary of the Virginia Historical Society, 15 June 1915, Thomas Papers, VHS; Parramore, *Southampton County*, 152–53, 156, 171–73, 193; Balfour, "Thomas," 12–22; Shands, "Thomas," 14–16; Friddell, "Southerner Finally Honored," *Richmond News Leader*, 15 July 1985.

23. Bryan, "Civil War Split," *Richmond Times-Dispatch*, 11 April 2004.

24. The nine biographies of Thomas are those by R. Johnson (1881), Van Horne (1882), Piatt and Boynton (1893), Coppee (1898), Cleaves (1948), O'Connor (1948), Wilbur Thomas (1964), McKinney (1961), and Palumbo (1983).

25. Blight, *Beyond the Battlefield*; Blight, *Race and Reunion*; Blight and Simpson, *Union and Emancipation*; Cullen, *Civil War in Popular Culture*, 8–28; Silber, *Romance of Reunion*; Urwin, *Black Flag Over Dixie*, 1–5.

26. Blight, *Beyond the Battlefield*, 211–22.

27. Advocates of Thomas include Henry Boynton, Francis McKinney, and Thomas Buell, while the pro-Grant or pro-Sherman, and anti-Thomas, camp includes Bruce Catton, John Marszalek, and Kenneth P. Williams. A more balanced view is taken by military historians such as Albert Castel, Herman Hattaway and Archer Jones, W. J. Wood, and Richard McMurry, who give all three generals credit for their accomplishments while making critical distinctions among them.

28. Braxton Bragg to William T. Sherman, 3 June 1855, Sherman Papers, LOC; Sherman, *Sherman's Civil War*, 100–101; Catton, *Grant Takes Command*, 40.

29. Accurate and balanced accounts of Thomas's generalship at Nashville include Sword, *Embrace an Angry Wind*, and Wood, *Civil War Generalship*, 228–31.

30. Hattaway and Jones, *How the North Won*, 654; Woodworth et al., "Top Ten Generals?" 12–22; Castel, "Why the North Won," 56–60; Daniel, *Days of Glory*, 362.

31. W. Freehling, *South v. the South*.

32. Glathaar, *Forged in Battle*, 16–18.

Bibliography

MANUSCRIPT SOURCES

Chickamauga/Chattanooga National Military Park Archives
Long, Capt. Horace C., Company F., 87th Indiana Volunteer Infantry. Letter to wife, November 19, 1863.

Duke University Library (DUL)
Bragg, Braxton. Papers.
Scully, James. Papers.
Thomas, George H. Papers.

Huntington Library (HL)
Thomas, George H. Papers.

Library of Congress (LOC)
Garfield, James A. Papers.
Hartz, E. L. Papers.
Johnson, Richard W. Letter to Harry Johnson, January 27, 1864.
Porter, Fitz John. Papers.
Sherman, William T. Papers.
Wilson, James H. Papers.

Library of Virginia
McKinney, Francis. Papers.
Southampton County courthouse records.
Shands, Betty. Notes on the Thomas family.
Thomas, George H. Letter to Frances Thomas (copy), December 22, 1858.

National Archives (NA)
Record Group 94, Adjutant General's Office.
Record Group 107, Records of the Office of the Secretary of War.
Record Group 108, Headquarters of the Army.
Record Group 393, Records of U.S. Army Continental Commands, 1821–1920.

New York State Archives, Albany
Thomas, George H. Letter to Miss M. S. Worth, January 15, 1864.

Ohio Historical Society
Opdycke, Emerson. Papers.

Smithsonian Institution Archives
Thomas, George H. Letter to Spencer F. Baird, September 25, 1869.
Thomas, George H. Letter to George Gibbs, March 5, 1868, and a list of Yuma Indian words.

University of Colorado, Boulder
Hough, Alfred L. Papers.

University of Michigan
Parkhurst, John G. Papers.

University of Tennessee
General George Thomas Letters, 1869.

United States Military Academy (USMA)
Record Group 404, U.S. Military Academy / West Point Archives

University of Virginia
Lee, Fitzhugh. Papers.

Virginia Historical Society (VHS)
Barham, William Blount. Letter to W. G. Stanard, corresponding secretary of the VHS, June 15, 1915.
Bryan, Charles. "Virginia's Yankee Generals."
Lee, Robert E. Papers.
Stuart, James Ewell Brown. Papers.
Thomas family. Papers.

Yale University
Thomas, George H. Letter to Adjutant General Samuel Cooper, July 7, 1857; and letter to George Gibbs, November 18, 1867.

PRINTED GOVERNMENT DOCUMENTS

Calendar of Virginia State Papers and Other Manuscripts Stored in the Virginia State Capitol at Richmond. Arranged and edited by William P. Palmer. Richmond: Virginia State Library, 1875–93.

Official Opinions of the Attorneys General of the United States, vol. 11. Edited by J. Hubley Ashton. Washington, D.C.: Published by Authority of Congress, 1869.

U.S. Congress. House. Executive Document No. 4, 29th Cong., 2nd Sess., Report of Zachary Taylor to the Secretary of War, and attached documents.

U.S. Congress. Senate. Executive Document No. 1, 30th Cong., 1st Sess., Report of Zachary Taylor to the Secretary of War, and attached documents.

U.S. Congress. Senate. Executive Document No. 1, 32nd Cong., 2nd Sess., Report of the Superintendent and Board of Visitors of the U.S. Military Academy.

U.S. Congress. Senate. Executive Document No. 1, 33rd Cong., 1st Sess. Report of the Superintendent and Board of Visitors of the U.S. Military Academy.

U.S. Congress. Senate. Executive Document No. 1, 33rd Cong., 2nd Sess. Report of the Superintendent and Board of Visitors of the U.S. Military Academy.

U.S. Congress. House. Report No. 101, 39th Cong., 1st Sess., "Memphis Riots and Massacres: The Reports of the Committees of the House of Representatives."

U.S. Congress. Senate. Reports, 39th Cong., 1st Sess., Report of the Committee on the Conduct of the War [no report number].

U.S. Congress. House. Executive Document No. 1, 40th Cong., 2nd Sess. "Annual Report of the Secretary of War, 1867," 186–94.

U.S. Congress. House. Executive Document No. 57, 40th Cong., 2nd Sess.

U.S. Congress. House. Executive Document No. 75, 40th Cong., 2nd Sess., "Milliken, a Returned Rebel."

U.S. Congress. House. Executive Document No. 1, 40th Congress, 3rd Session. "Annual Report of the Secretary of War, 1868," 142–202.

U.S. Congress. House. Executive Document No. 1, 41st Congress, 2nd Session. "Annual Report of the Secretary of War, 1869," 113–21.

U.S. Military Academy at West Point, New York. *Official Register of the Officers and Cadets of the U.S. Military Academy.*

U.S. War Department. *Reports of Explorations and Surveys, to Ascertain the Most Practicable and Economical Route for a Railroad from the Mississippi River to the Pacific Ocean [Pacific Railroad Survey Reports].* Washington, D.C.: A. O. P. Nicholson, 1855–60.

U.S. War Department. *The War of the Rebellion: A Compilation of the Official Records of the Union and Confederate Armies.* 128 vols. Washington, D.C.: Government Printing Office, 1880–1901.

NEWSPAPERS

Boston Daily Advertiser, January 22, 1862.

Chicago Tribune, 1862–64

Cincinnati Daily Commercial, November 16 and 18, 1861.

Gallipolis (Ohio) Journal, October 15, 1863.

Louisville Journal, 1863–64

Memphis Post, August 3 and October 12, 1867; January 27, 1868.

National Intelligencer, April 7, 1870.

National Republican, November 20, 1879.

New York Herald, January 21 and 22, 1862; September 27 and October 29, 1863; December 19, 1864; May 31, 1865; and December 31, 1875.

New York Times, June 23, 1861; September 23 and November 14, 1863; December 16 and 24, 1864; March 30–April 9 and May 17, 1870; June 6, 13, 14, and 22 August 4 and 15, and October 4, 1881; September 10, 1882; and January 12, 1883.

New York Tribune, January 21 and 22, 1862; March 12, April 6, and May 4, 1870.
Richmond News Leader, July 15, 1985.
Richmond Times, March 31, 1901.
Richmond Times-Dispatch, April 11, 2004.

PUBLISHED PRIMARY SOURCES

Aldritch, C. Knight. *Quest for a Star: The Civil War Letters and Diaries of Colonel Francis T. Sherman of the 88th Illinois.* Knoxville: University of Tennessee Press, 1999.

Anderson, Thomas M. "General George H. Thomas." *Military Service Institution Journal* 56 (January–February 1915): 37–42.

Andrews, William L., and Henry Louis Gates, Jr., eds. *Slave Narratives.* New York: Library of America, 2000. Contains "The Confessions of Nat Turner," 243–66.

The Army Reunion: With Reports of the Meetings of the Societies of the Army of the Cumberland, the Army of the Tennessee, the Army of the Ohio, and the Army of Georgia. Chicago: S. C. Griggs and Co., 1869.

Barham, William B. "Recollections of the Thomas Family of Southampton County." *Virginia Magazine of History and Biography* 40 (1932): 328–34.

Bates, David Homer. *Lincoln in the Telegraph Office.* New York: Century Company, 1907.

Beatty, John. *The Citizen Soldier.* Cincinnati: Wilstach, Baldwin, 1879.

Bickham, William D. *Rosecrans' Campaign with the Fourteenth Army Corps, or the Army of the Cumberland: A Narrative of Personal Observations, with Official Reports of the Battle of Stone River.* Cincinnati: Moore, Wilstach, Keys, and Co., 1863.

Bisbee, William Henry. *Through Four American Wars.* Boston: Meador Publishing Company, 1931.

Bishop, J. W. "The Mill Springs Campaign." In Military Order of the Loyal Legion of the United States, Minnesota Commandery, *Glimpses of the Nation's Struggle: Papers Read before the Minnesota Commandery of the Military Order of the Loyal Legion of the United States,* 2nd ser., 52–79. St. Paul: n.p., 1889.

Bishop, J. W. *The Story of a Regiment: Being a Narrative of the Service of the Second Regiment, Minnesota Volunteer Infantry, in the Civil War of 1861–1865.* St. Paul: n.p., 1890.

Buell, Clarence, and Robert Johnson, eds. *Battles and Leaders of the Civil War.* New York: Century Company, 1887.

Cadwallader, Sylvanus. *Three Years with Grant.* New York: Alfred A. Knopf, 1956.

Calkins, William W. *The History of the One Hundred and Fourth Regiment of Illinois Volunteer Infantry, War of the Great Rebellion, 1862–1865.* Chicago: Donohue and Henneberry, 1895.

Castel, Albert, ed. *Tom Taylor's Civil War.* Lawrence: University Press of Kansas, 2000.

Chase, Salmon P. *The Salmon P. Chase Papers.* Edited by John Niven. Kent, Ohio: Kent State University Press, 1993.

Chittenden, Lucius E. *Recollections of President Lincoln and His Administration.* New York: Harper and Brothers, 1891.

Clarke, Charles T. *Opdycke Tigers, 125th O.V.I., a History of the Regiment and of the Campaigns and Battles of the Army of the Cumberland.* Columbus, Ohio: Spahr and Glenn, 1895.

Cohen, Myer M. *Notices of Florida and the Campaigns.* Charleston, 1836. Reprint, Gainesville: University Press of Florida, 1964.

Crabtree, Beth G., and James W. Patton, eds. *"Journal of a Secesh Lady": The Diary of Catherine Ann Devereux Edmondston, 1860–1866.* Raleigh: North Carolina Division of Archives and History, 1979.

Crittenden, Thomas L. "The Union Left at Stone's River." In Buell and Johnson, *Battles and Leaders of the Civil War*, 3:632–34.

Cullum, George W. *Biographical Register of Officers and Cadets of the U.S. Military Academy at West Point, New York*. Boston: Houghton, Mifflin, 1891.

Curry, William L. *Four Years in the Saddle: History of the First Regiment, Ohio Volunteer Cavalry, War of the Rebellion, 1861–1865*. Columbus, Ohio: Champlin Printing Co., 1898.

Dana, Charles A. *Recollections of the Civil War: With the Leaders at Washington and in the Field in the Sixties*. New York: D. Appleton and Co., 1898.

De Peyster, John Watts. "Major General George H. Thomas." Annual address delivered before the New York Historical Society, 1875.

De Velling, Charles T. *History of the Seventeenth Regiment, First Brigade, Third Division, Fourteenth Corps, Army of the Cumberland, War of the Rebellion*. Zanesville, Ohio: E. R. Sullivan, 1889.

Dornblaser, Thomas Franklin. *Sabre Strokes of the Pennsylvania Dragoons, in the War of 1861–1865*. Philadelphia: Lutheran Publication Society, 1884.

Drewry, William Sidney. *The Southampton Insurrection*. Washington, D.C.: Neal Company, 1900.

Duffield, Henry M. "Chickamauga." *Papers Read before the Michigan Commandery of the Military Order of the Loyal Legion of the United States*, vol. 1, no. 4. Detroit: Ostler Printing Company, 1888.

Edson, Hanford A. "The Life of Gen. George H. Thomas: Its Lessons for Young Men." Pamphlet based on a sermon preached at the Second Presbyterian Church, Indianapolis, Indiana, April 3, 1870. The only extant pamphlet that I am aware of is contained in the Garfield Papers at the Library of Congress.

Fitch, Michael. *Echoes of the Civil War as I Heard Them*. New York: R. F. Fenno, 1905.

French, Samuel G. *Two Wars: An Autobiography of General Samuel G. French*. Nashville: Confederate Veteran Press, 1901.

Fullerton, Joseph S. "The Army of the Cumberland at Chattanooga." In Buell and Johnson, *Battles and Leaders of the Civil War*, 3:719–26.

———. "Reinforcing Thomas at Chickamauga." In Buell and Johnson, *Battles and Leaders of the Civil War*, 3:665–67.

Garfield, James A. *The Diary of James A. Garfield*. Edited by Harry James Brown and Frederick Williams. 4 vols. East Lansing: Michigan State University, 1967.

———. "Oration on the Life and Character of General George H. Thomas." In Society of the Army of the Cumberland, *1870 Reunion Report*. Cincinnati: n.p.

Gibson, Joseph. *History of the Seventy-eighth Pennsylvania Volunteer Infantry*. Pittsburgh: Pittsburgh Print Co., 1905.

Giddings, Luther. *Sketches of the Campaign in Northern Mexico in Eighteen Hundred Forty-six and Seven*. New York: George P. Putnam and Co., 1853.

Goodhart, Briscoe. *History of the Independent Loudoun Virginia Rangers, U.S. Volunteer Cavalry (Scouts), 1862–1865*. Washington, D.C.: Press of McGill and Wallace, 1896.

Grant, Ulysses S. *The Papers of Ulysses S. Grant*. Edited by John Y. Simon. Carbondale: Southern Illinois University Press, 1967.

———. *Personal Memoirs and Selected Letters, 1839–65*. New York: Library of America, 1990.

———. *Personal Memoirs of U. S. Grant*. 2 vols. New York: Charles L. Webster, 1885–86.

Grebner, Constantin. *"We Were the Ninth": A History of the Ninth Regiment, Ohio Volunteer Infantry, April 17, 1861 to June 7, 1864*. Translated and edited by Frederic Trautmann. Kent, Ohio: Kent State University Press, 1987.

Green, Wharton J. *Recollections and Reflections: An Auto of Half A Century and More*. Raleigh: Edwards and Broughton, 1906.

Hay, John. *Inside Lincoln's White House: The Complete Civil War Diary of John Hay*. Edited by Michael Burlingame and John R. Turner Ettlinger. Carbondale: Southern Illinois University Press, 1997.

Hayes, Rutherford B. *Diary and Letters of Rutherford Birchard Hayes*. 5 vols. Columbus: Ohio State Archaeological and Historical Society, 1922–26.

Haynie, James Henry. *The Nineteenth Illinois: A Memoir of a Regiment of Volunteer Infantry Famous in the Civil War Fifty Years Ago for Its Drill, Bravery, and Distinguished Services*. Chicago: M. A. Donohue, 1912.

High, Edwin W. *History of the Sixty-eighth Indiana Volunteer Infantry, 1862–1865, with a Sketch of E. A. King's Brigade, Reynold's Division, Thomas' Corps, in the Battle of Chickamauga*. Metamora, Ind.: Sixty-eighth Indiana Infantry Association, 1902.

Hough, Alfred L. *Soldier in the West: The Civil War Letters of Alfred Lacey Hough*. Philadelphia: University of Pennsylvania Press, 1957.

Howard, Oliver O. *Autobiography of Oliver Otis Howard*. New York: Baker and Taylor, 1908.

———. "Chattanooga." *Atlantic Monthly* 38 (1876): 203–19.

———. "Grant at Chattanooga." In *Personal Recollections of the War of the Rebellion: Addresses Delivered before the New York Commandery of the Loyal Legion of the United States, 1883–1891*, 1:244–57. New York: Published by the Commandery, 1891.

———. "Sketch of General George H. Thomas." In Military Order of the Loyal Legion of the United States, New York Commandery, *Personal Recollections of the War of the Rebellion: Addresses Delivered before the New York Commandery*, 1:285–302. New York: Published by the Commandery, 1890.

Johnson, Andrew. *The Papers of Andrew Johnson*. Edited by LeRoy P. Graf and Ralph W. Haskins. 16 vols. Knoxville: University of Tennessee Press, 1967–69.

Johnson, Richard W. *A Soldier's Reminiscences in Peace and War*. Philadelphia: J. B. Lippincott, 1886.

Keil, F. W. *Thirty-fifth Ohio: A Narrative of Service from August 1861 to 1864*. Fort Wayne, Ind.: Archer, Housh, and Company, 1894.

Kelly, R. M. "Holding Kentucky for the Union." In Buell and Johnson, *Battles and Leaders of the Civil War*, 1:373–92.

Keyes, Erasmus D. *Fifty Years Observation of Men and Events, Civil and Military*. New York: Charles Scribner's Sons, 1885.

Kimberly, Robert. *The Forty-first Ohio Veteran Volunteer Infantry in the War of the Rebellion, 1861–1865*. Cleveland: R. H. Smellie, 1897.

King, John M. *Three Years with the Ninety-second Illinois: The Civil War Diary of John M. King*. Edited by Claire E. Swedberg. Mechanicsburg, Pa.: Stackpole Books, 1999.

Kniffin, Gilbert C. "The Battle of Stone's River." In Buell and Johnson, *Battles and Leaders of the Civil War*, 3:613–32.

———. "A Sailor on Horseback." In Military Order of the Loyal Legion of the United States, D.C. Commandery, *War Papers*, no. 19. Washington, D.C.: Published by the Commandery, 1887–1916.

LeDuc, William G. *Recollections of a Civil War Quartermaster: The Autobiography of William G. LeDuc*. St. Paul: North Central Publishing Company, 1963.

Lincoln, Abraham. *The Collected Works of Abraham Lincoln*. Edited by Roy P. Basler. 11 vols. New Brunswick, N.J.: Rutgers University Press, 1953–55, 1990.

Livermore, Thomas L. "Patterson's Shenandoah Campaign." In *Papers of the Military Historical Society of Massachusetts*, 1:1–58. Boston: Military Historical Society of Massachusetts, 1881.

Matthews, Stanley. *Unveiling of Ward's Equestrian Statue of Major General George H. Thomas, Washington, November 19, 1879*. Cincinnati: Robert Clarke and Co., 1879.

McClure, Alexander K. *Lincoln and Men of War Times*. Philadelphia: Times Publishing Company, 1892.

Mills, Gary B., ed. *Southern Loyalists in the Civil War: The Southern Claims Commission*. Baltimore: Genealogical Publishing Company, 1994.

Morgan, Thomas J. *Reminiscences of Service with Colored Troops in the Army of the Cumberland, 1863–65*. Providence: Soldiers and Sailors Historical Society of Rhode Island, 1885.

Morse, Bliss. *Civil War Letters and Diaries of Bliss Morse*. Edited by Loren J. Morse. Wagoner, Okla.: Loren J. Morse, 1985.

Newlin, W. H. *A History of the Seventy-third Regiment Illinois Volunteers*. Springfield, Ill.: n.p., 1890.

Opdycke, Emerson. "Notes on the Chickamauga Campaign." In Buell and Johnson, *Battles and Leaders of the Civil War*, 3:668–71.

Opdycke, Emerson. *To Battle for What Is Good and Right*. Urbana: University of Illinois Press, 2002.

Otis, Ephraim. "General George H. Thomas." In Military Order of the Loyal Legion of the United States, Illinois Commandery, *Military Essays and Recollections*, 1:122–47. Chicago: Cozzens and Beaton, 1891.

Parkhurst, John G. "Recollections of Stone's River." In Military Order of the Loyal Legion of the United States, Michigan Commandery, *War Papers*. Detroit: Ostler Printing Company, 1888–98.

Pope, John. *The Military Memoirs of General John Pope*. Edited by Peter Cozzens and Robert I. Girardi. Chapel Hill: University of North Carolina Press, 1998.

Porter, Horace. *Campaigning with Grant*. New York: Century Company, 1906.

Price, George. *Across the Continent with the Fifth Cavalry*. New York: D. Von Nostrand, 1883.

Puntenney, George H. *History of the Thirty-seventh Regiment of Indiana Infantry Volunteers*. Rushville, Ind.: Jacksonian Book and Job Department, 1896.

Quaife, Milo M., ed. *From the Cannon's Mouth: The Civil War Letters of General Alpheus S. Williams*. Detroit: Wayne State University Press and the Detroit Historical Society, 1959.

Royse, Isaac Henry Clay. *History of the 115th Regiment, Illinois Volunteer Infantry*. Terre Haute, Ind.: n.p., 1900.

Ruffin, Edmund. *The Diary of Edmund Ruffin*. Edited by William Kauffman Scarborough. Baton Rouge: Louisiana State University Press, 1989.

Rusling, James F. "Major General George H. Thomas and the Battle of Nashville." In Military Order of the Loyal Legion of the United States, Pennsylvania Commandery, *Military Essays and Recollections*, 1:351–70. Wilmington, N.C.: Broadfoot, 1995.

———. *Men and Things I Saw in Civil War Days*. New York: Eaton and Mains, 1899.

Schofield, John. *Forty-six Years in the Army*. New York: Century Company, 1897.

Scribner, Benjamin Franklin. *How Soldiers Were Made; or, the War as I Saw It under Buell, Rosecrans, Thomas, Grant, and Sherman*. Chicago: Donohue and Henneberry, 1887.

Shanks, William. *Personal Recollections of Distinguished Generals*. New York: Harper's, 1866.

———. "Recollections of Thomas." *Harper's Magazine* 30 (1864–65): 754–59.

Shaw, James Birney. *History of the Tenth Regiment Indiana Volunteer Infantry, Three Months and Three Years Organization*. Lafayette, Ind.: Burt-Haywood, 1912.

Sheridan, Philip H. *Personal Memoirs of P. H. Sheridan*. New York: D. Appleton and Co., 1888.

Sherman, John. *Recollections of Forty Years in the House, Senate, and Cabinet: An Autobiography*. Chicago: Werner, 1896.

Sherman, William T. *Memoirs of General W. T. Sherman: Written by Himself*. 2 vols. New York: D. Appleton and Co., 1875, 1886.

————. *Sherman's Civil War: Selected Correspondence of William T. Sherman, 1860–1865.* Edited by Brooks D. Simpson and Jean V. Berlin. Chapel Hill: University of North Carolina Press, 1999.

————. "An Historical Sketch of the Military Operations around Chattanooga, Tennessee, September 22 to November 27, 1863." In *Papers of the Military Historical Society of Massachusetts,* 8:193–94. Boston: Military Historical Society of Massachusetts, 1910.

Smith, William F. "Comments on General Grant's 'Chattanooga.'" In Buell and Johnson, *Battles and Leaders of the Civil War,* 3:714–18.

Smith, William Wrenshall. "Holocaust Holiday: The Journal of a Strange Vacation to the War-Torn South and a Visit with U. S. Grant." *Civil War Times Illustrated* 18 (October 1979): 28–40.

Smithsonian Institution, Board of Regents. *Annual Report of the Board of Regents of the Smithsonian Institution.* Washington: Smithsonian Institution, 1855 and 1856.

Snetsinger, Robert J., ed. *Kiss Clara for Me: The Story of Joseph Whitney and His Family, Early Days in the Midwest, and Soldiering in the American Civil War.* State College, Pa.: Carnation Press, 1969.

Society of the Army of the Cumberland. *Reunion Reports.* Annual. Cincinnati: n.p., 1867–1907.

Southern Historical Society. *Southern Historical Society Papers.* 52 vols. Richmond: Southern Historical Society, 1876–1959.

Stanley, David S. *Personal Memoirs of Major-General David Sloane Stanley, U.S.A.* Cambridge: Harvard University Press, 1917.

Stibbs, John H. "MacArthur's Division at Nashville as Seen by a Regimental Commander." In Military Order of the Loyal Legion of the United States, Illinois Commandery, *Military Essays and Recollections,* 4:498–99. Chicago: Published by the Commandery, 1907.

Stone, Henry. "Major-General George Henry Thomas." In *Papers of the Military Historical Society of Massachusetts,* 10:162–208. Boston: Military Historical Society of Massachusetts, 1910.

————. "Repelling Hood's Invasion of Tennessee." In Buell and Johnson, *Battles and Leaders of the Civil War,* 4:440–64.

Strother, David Hunter. *A Virginia Yankee in the Civil War: The Diaries of David Hunter Strother.* Edited by Cecil D. Eby. Chapel Hill: University of North Carolina Press, 1961.

Tarrant, Eastham. *The Wild Riders of the First Kentucky Cavalry.* Louisville: R. H. Carrothers, 1894.

Thatcher, Marshall P. *A Hundred Battles in the West—St. Louis to Atlanta, 1861–1865—the Second Michigan Cavalry.* Detroit: Thatcher, 1884.

Thruston, Gates P. "The Crisis at Chickamauga." In Buell and Johnson, *Battles and Leaders of the Civil War,* 3:663–65.

Tidball, Eugene C. "A Subaltern's First Experiences in the Old Army." *Civil War History* 45, no. 3 (September 1999): 197–222.

Tourgee, Albion. *The Story of a Thousand, Being a History of the Service of the One Hundred Fifth Ohio Volunteer Infantry in the War for the Union from August 21, 1862, to June 6, 1865.* Buffalo: S. McGerald and Son, 1896.

Tragle, Henry Irving, ed. *The Southampton Slave Revolt of 1831: A Compilation of Source Material.* Amherst: University of Massachusetts Press, 1971.

Van Horne, Thomas B. *History of the Army of the Cumberland: Its Organization, Campaigns, and Battles, Written at the Request of Major-General George H. Thomas Chiefly from His Private Military Journal and Official and Other Documents Furnished by Him.* Cincinnati: Robert Clarke and Co., 1875.

Walker, Israel B. "Chickamauga: Going into Action with Hands Full of Bacon and Coffee." *National Tribune*, July 2, 1891.

Walton, Clyde C., ed. *Private Smith's Journal: Recollections of the Late War.* Chicago: Lakeside Press, 1963.

Welles, Gideon. *Diary of Gideon Welles.* Edited by Howard K. Beale. 3 vols. New York: W. W. Norton, 1960.

Wilson, Ephraim A. *Memoirs of the War.* Cleveland: W. M. Bayne Printing Co., 1893.

Wilson, James Harrison. *Under the Old Flag: Recollections of Military Operations in the War for the Union, the Spanish War, the Boxer Rebellion, etc.* New York: D. Appleton and Co., 1912.

Wyeth, John Allen. *With Sabre and Scalpel.* New York: Harper Brothers, 1914.

Yaryan, John Lee. "Stone River." In Military Order of the Loyal Legion of the United States, Indiana Commandery, *War Papers*, 1:157–77. Indianapolis: Published by the Commandery, 1898.

Young, John Russell. *Around the World with General Grant.* 2 vols. New York: American News Company, 1879.

PUBLISHED SECONDARY SOURCES

Adams, George W. *Doctors in Blue: The Medical History of the Union Army in the Civil War.* New York: Collier, 1961.

Ambrose, Stephen E. *Duty, Honor, Country: A History of West Point.* Baltimore: Johns Hopkins University Press, 1999.

———. *Halleck: Lincoln's Chief of Staff.* Baton Rouge: Louisiana State University Press, 1962.

Ash, Stephen V. *When the Yankees Came: Conflict and Chaos in the Occupied South, 1861–1865.* Chapel Hill: University of North Carolina Press, 1995.

Baggett, James A. *The Scalawags: Southern Dissenters in the Civil War and Reconstruction.* Baton Rouge: Louisiana State University Press, 2003.

Bailey, Anne J. *The Chessboard of War: Sherman and Hood in the Autumn Campaigns of 1864.* Lincoln: University of Nebraska Press, 2000.

Balfour, Daniel T. *Franklin and Southampton County in the Civil War.* Appomattox, Va.: H. E. Howard Inc., 2002.

———. "A Sketch of the Life of General George H. Thomas." *Southampton County Historical Society Bulletin*, March 1983, 12–22.

Baumgartner, Richard A. *Blue Lightning: Wilder's Mounted Infantry Brigade in the Battle of Chickamauga.* Huntington, W. V.: Blue Acorn Press, 1997.

Bee, Robert L. *The Yuma.* New York: Chelsea House, 1989.

Berlin, Ira, ed. *Freedom: A Documentary History of Emancipation, 1861–1867.* 1st ser., vol. 2, *The Wartime Genesis of Free Labor: The Upper South.* Cambridge: Cambridge University Press, 1993.

Blight, David W. *Beyond the Battlefield: Race, Memory, and the American Civil War.* Amherst: University of Massachusetts Press, 2002.

———. *Race and Reunion: The Civil War in American Memory.* Cambridge: Belknap Press of Harvard University Press, 2001.

Blight, David W., and Brooks D. Simpson, eds. *Union and Emancipation: Essays on Politics and Race in the Civil War Era.* Kent, Ohio: Kent State University Press, 1997.

Boynton, Henry V. *Was General Thomas Slow at Nashville? With a Description of the Greatest Cavalry Movement of the War and General James H. Wilson's Cavalry Operations in Tennessee, Alabama, and Georgia.* New York: Harper's, 1896.

Brockett, Linus Pierpoint. *Our Great Captains: Grant, Sherman, Thomas, Sheridan, and Farragut.* New York: C. B. Richardson, 1865.

Buell, Thomas. *The Warrior Generals: Combat Leadership in the Civil War.* New York: Crown, 1997.

Calos, Katherine. "No Plaques Around to These War Leaders." *Richmond News Leader,* January 11, 1990.

Carleton, James H. *The Battle of Buena Vista.* New York: Harper and Brothers, 1848.

Carter, Dan T. *When the War Was Over: The Failure of Self-Reconstruction in the South, 1865–1867.* Baton Rouge: Louisiana State University Press, 1985.

Castel, Albert. *Decision in the West: The Atlanta Campaign of 1864.* Lawrence: University Press of Kansas, 1992.

———. "Prevaricating through Georgia: Sherman's Memoirs as a Source on the Atlanta Campaign." *Civil War History* 40 (March 1994): 48–71.

———. "Why the North Won and the South Lost." *Civil War Times Illustrated* 39 (May 2000): 56–60.

———. *Winning and Losing in the Civil War: Essays and Stories.* Columbia: University of South Carolina Press, 1996.

———. *Grant Takes Command.* Boston: Little, Brown, and Co., 1968.

Chandler, J. A. C., ed. *The South in the Building of the Nation.* Richmond: Southern Historical Publication Society, 1909–13.

Cimprich, John. "A Critical Moment and Its Aftermath for George H. Thomas." In Randall M. Miller and John R. McKivigan, eds., *The Moment of Decision: Biographical Essays on American Character and Regional Identity.* Westport, Conn.: Greenwood Press, 1994.

———. *Slavery's End in Tennessee, 1861–1865.* Tuscaloosa: University of Alabama Press, 1985.

Cleaves, Freeman. *Rock of Chickamauga: The Life of General George H. Thomas.* Norman: University of Oklahoma Press, 1948.

Coleman, Charles H. *The Election of 1868: The Democratic Effort to Regain Control.* New York: Columbia University Press, 1933.

Connelly, Thomas L., and Barbara L. Bellows. *God and General Longstreet: The Lost Cause and the Southern Mind.* Baton Rouge: Louisiana State University Press, 1982.

Coppee, Henry. *General Thomas.* New York: D. Appleton and Co., 1898.

Cornish, Dudley T. *The Sable Arm: Negro Troops in the Union Army, 1861–1865.* New York: W. W. Norton, 1966 [1956].

Covington, James W. *The Seminoles of Florida.* Gainesville: University of Florida Press, 1993.

Cozzens, Peter. *No Better Place to Die: The Battle of Stones River.* Urbana: University of Illinois Press, 1990.

———. *The Shipwreck of Their Hopes: The Battles for Chattanooga.* Urbana: University of Illinois Press, 1994.

———. *This Terrible Sound: The Battle of Chickamauga.* Urbana: University of Illinois Press, 1992.

Crofts, Daniel. *Cobb's Ordeal: The Diaries of a Virginia Farmer, 1842–1872.* Athens: University of Georgia Press, 1997.

———. *Old Southampton: Politics and Society in a Virginia County, 1834–1869.* Charlottesville: University of Virginia Press, 1992.

———. *Reluctant Confederates: Upper South Unionists in the Secession Crisis.* Chapel Hill: University of North Carolina Press, 1989.

Cullen, Jim. *The Civil War in Popular Culture: A Reusable Past.* Washington, D.C.: Smithsonian Institution Press, 1995.

Current, Richard Nelson. *Lincoln's Loyalists: Union Soldiers from the Confederacy.* Boston: Northeastern University Press, 1992.

Daniel, Larry J. *Days of Glory: The Army of the Cumberland, 1861–1865*. Baton Rouge: Louisiana State University Press, 2004.

———. "The South Almost Won by Not Losing: A Rebuttal." *North and South* 1, no. 3 (February 1998): 44–61.

Davis, William C. *The Cause Lost: Myths and Realities of the Confederacy*. Lawrence: University Press of Kansas, 1996.

Dearing, Mary R. *Veterans in Politics: The Story of the G.A.R. [Grand Army of the Republic]*. Baton Rouge: Louisiana State University Press, 1952.

Degler, Carl. *The Other South: Southern Dissenters in the Nineteenth Century*. New York: Harper and Row, 1974.

Dillon, Lester R., Jr. *Artillery in the Mexican War, 1846–1847*. Austin, Tex.: Presidial Press, 1975.

Donald, David Herbert, ed. *Why the North Won the Civil War*. Baton Rouge: Louisiana State University Press, 1960.

Donald, David Herbert. *Lincoln Reconsidered: Essays on the Civil War Era*. 3rd ed. Revised and Updated. New York: Vintage, 2001.

Durham, Walter T. *Reluctant Partners: Nashville and the Union, July 1, 1863, to June 30, 1865*. Nashville: Tennessee Historical Society, 1987.

Durrill, Wayne K. *War of Another Kind: A Southern Community in the Great Rebellion*. New York: Oxford University Press, 1990.

Dyer, Thomas G. *Secret Yankees: The Union Circle in Confederate Atlanta*. Baltimore: Johns Hopkins University Press, 1999.

Eicher, David J. *The Longest Night: A Military History of the Civil War*. New York: Simon and Schuster, 2001.

Eisenhower, John S. D. *So Far From God: The U.S. War with Mexico 1846–1848*. New York: Random House, 1989.

Endler, James R. *Other Leaders, Other Heroes: West Point's Legacy to America beyond the Field of Battle*. Westport, Conn.: Praeger, 1998.

Engle, Stephen D. "Don Carlos Buell: Military Philosophy and Command Problems in the West." *Civil War History* 41, no. 2 (June 1995): 89–115.

———. *Don Carlos Buell: Most Promising of All*. Chapel Hill: University of North Carolina Press, 1999.

Fisher, Noel C. *War at Every Door: Partisan Politics and Guerrilla Violence in East Tennessee, 1860–1869*. Chapel Hill: University of North Carolina Press, 1997.

Foner, Eric. *Reconstruction: America's Unfinished Revolution, 1863–1877*. New York: Harper and Row, 1988.

Foos, Paul. *A Short, Offhand, Killing Affair: Soldiers and Social Conflict during the Mexican-American War*. Chapel Hill: University of North Carolina Press, 2002.

Forbes, Jack D. *Warriors of the Colorado: The Yumas of the Quechan Nation and Their Neighbors*. Norman: University of Oklahoma Press, 1965.

Forman, Sidney. *West Point: A History of the United States Military Academy*. New York: Columbia University Press, 1950.

Foster, Gaines. *Ghosts of the Confederacy: Defeat, the Lost Cause, and the Emergence of the New South*. New York: Oxford University Press, 1987.

Freehling, Alison Goodyear. *Drift toward Dissolution: The Virginia Slavery Debate of 1831–1832*. Baton Rouge: Louisiana State University Press, 1982.

Freehling, William W. *The Road to Disunion*, vol. 1: *Secessionists at Bay, 1776–1854*. New York: Oxford University Press, 1990.

———. *The South v. the South: How Anti-Confederate Southerners Shaped the Course of the Civil War*. New York: Oxford University Press, 2001.

Freeman, Douglas Southall. *R. E. Lee: A Biography*. 4 vols. New York: Charles Scribner's Sons, 1934–35.

Gallagher, Gary W., and Alan T. Nolan, eds. *The Myth of the Lost Cause and Civil War History*. Bloomington and Indianapolis: Indiana University Press, 2000.

Glathaar, Joseph T. *Forged in Battle: The Civil War Alliance of Black Soldiers and White Officers*. New York: Free Press, 1990.

Goetzmann, William H. *Army Exploration in the American West, 1803–1863*. Lincoln: University of Nebraska Press, 1979.

———. *Exploration and Empire: The Explorer and the Scientist in the Winning of the West*. New York: W. W. Norton, 1978.

Gordon, Lesley J. "'In Time of War': Unionists Hanged in Kinston, North Carolina, February 1864." In Sutherland, *Guerrillas, Unionists, and Violence*, 45–58.

Gordon, Ralph C. "Hospital Trains of the Army of the Cumberland," *Tennessee Historical Quarterly* 51, no. 3 (Fall 1992): 150.

Goss, Thomas J. *The War within the Union High Command: Politics and Generalship during the Civil War*. Lawrence: University Press of Kansas, 2003.

Grimsley, Mark. *The Hard Hand of War: Union Military Policy toward Southern Civilians, 1861–1865*. Cambridge: Cambridge University Press, 1995.

Grow, Matthew J. "The Shadow of the Civil War: A Historiography of Civil War Memory." *American Nineteenth-Century History* 4, no. 2 (summer 2003): 77–103.

Hallahan, John M. *The Battle of Craney Island: A Matter of Credit*. Portsmouth, Va.: Saint Michael's Press, 1986.

Hannaford, Ebenezer. *The Story of a Regiment: A History of the Campaigns, and Associations in the Field, of the Sixth Regiment Ohio Volunteer Infantry*. Cincinnati: Self-published, 1868.

Hardwick, Kevin R. "'Your Old Father Abe Lincoln Is Dead and Damned': Black Soldiers and the Memphis Race Riot of 1866." *Journal of Social History* 27, no. 1 (Fall 1993): 109–29.

Harris, William C. "The Southern Unionist Critique of the Civil War." *Civil War History* 31 (March 1985): 39–42.

Hattaway, Herman, and Archer Jones. *How the North Won: A Military History of the Civil War*. Urbana: University of Illinois Press, 1983.

Haycox, Stephen. *Alaska: An American Colony*. London: Hurst and Co., 2002.

Hebert, Walter H. *Fighting Joe Hooker*. Indianapolis: Bobbs-Merrill, 1944.

Heidler, David S., and Jeanne T. Heidler, eds. *Encyclopedia of the American Civil War*. Santa Barbara, Calif.: ABC-CLIO, 2000.

Henry, William S. *Campaign Sketches of the War with Mexico*. New York: Harper Brothers, 1847.

Hinckley, Ted C. *The Americanization of Alaska, 1867–1897*. Palo Alto, Calif.: Pacific Books, 1972.

Holzmann, Robert S. *Stormy Ben Butler*. New York: Macmillan, 1954.

Hopkins, Timothy. *The Kelloggs in the Old World and the New*. San Francisco: Sunset Press and Photo Engraving Company, 1903.

———. "The Spring Hill Legend." *Civil War Times Illustrated* 8 (April 1969): 20–32.

Horwitz, Tony. *Confederates in the Attic*. New York: Pantheon, 1998.

Inscoe, John C., and Robert C. Kenzer, eds. *Enemies of the Country: New Perspectives on Unionists in the Civil War South*. Athens: University of Georgia Press, 2001.

Jenkins, Kirk C. "A Shooting at the Galt House: The Death of General William Nelson." *Civil War History* 43 (June 1997): 101–18.

Johnson, Mark W. *That Body of Brave Men: The U.S. Regular Infantry and the Civil War in the West*. New York: Da Capo Press, 2003.

Johnson, Richard W. *Memoir of Maj.-Gen. George H. Thomas*. Philadelphia: J. B. Lippincott, 1881.

Jones, Archer. "Jomini and the Strategy of the American Civil War: A Reinterpretation." *Military Affairs* 24 (Summer 1960): 68–77.

———. *Civil War Command and Strategy: The Process of Victory and Defeat*. New York: Free Press, 1992.

Jones, James Pickett. *Yankee Blitzkrieg: Wilson's Raid through Alabama and Georgia*. Lexington: University Press of Kentucky, 2000.

———. "'Your Left Arm': James H. Wilson's Letters to Adam Badeau." *Civil War History* 12 (September 1966): 230–45.

Kavanagh, Thomas W. *The Comanches: A History, 1706–1875*. Lincoln: University of Nebraska Press, 1996.

Keenan, Jerry. *Wilson's Cavalry Corps: Union Campaigns in the Western Theatre, October 1864 through Spring 1865*. Jefferson, N.C.: McFarland and Company, 1998.

Klingberg, Frank W. *The Southern Claims Commission*. Berkeley: University of California Press, 1955.

Kroeber, Clifton B., and Bernard L. Fontana. *Massacre on the Gila*. Tucson: University of Arizona Press, 1986.

Lamers, William M. *The Edge of Glory: A Biography of General William S. Rosecrans*. New York: Harcourt, Brace, and World, 1961. Reprint, Baton Rouge: Louisiana State University Press, 1999.

Lavender, David S. *Climax at Buena Vista: The American Campaigns in Northeastern Mexico, 1846–47*. Philadelphia: J. B. Lippincott, 1966.

Lovett, Bobby L. "Memphis Riots: White Reaction to Blacks in Memphis, May 1865–July 1866." *Tennessee Historical Quarterly* 38 (Spring 1979): 9–33.

Mahon, John K. *History of the Second Seminole War, 1835–1842*. Gainesville: University of Florida Press, 1967.

———. *The War of 1812*. Gainesville: University of Florida Press, 1972.

Marszalek, John F. *Commander of All Lincoln's Armies: A Life of General Henry W. Halleck*. Cambridge: Belknap Press of Harvard University Press, 2004.

———. *Sherman: A Soldier's Passion for Order*. New York: Free Press, 1993.

———. "Sherman Called It the Way He Saw It." *Civil War History* 40 (March 1994): 72–78.

Maslowski, Peter. *Treason Must Be Made Odious: Military Occupation and Wartime Reconstruction in Nashville, Tennessee, 1862–65*. Millwood, N.Y.: KTO Press, 1978.

MacDonnell, Francis. "The Confederate Spin on Winfield Scott and George Thomas." *Civil War History* 44, no. 4 (December 1998): 255–66.

McDonough, James L. *Chattanooga: A Death Grip on the Confederacy*. Knoxville: University of Tennessee Press, 1984.

———. *Nashville: The Western Confederacy's Final Gamble*. Knoxville: University of Tennessee Press, 2004.

———. *Schofield: Union General in the Civil War and Reconstruction*. Tallahassee: Florida State University Press, 1972.

———. *Stones River: Bloody Winter in Tennessee*. Knoxville: University of Tennessee Press, 1980.

———. *War in Kentucky: From Shiloh to Perryville*. Knoxville: University of Tennessee Press, 1994.

McDonough, James L., and Thomas L. Connelly. *Five Tragic Hours: The Battle of Franklin*. Knoxville: University of Tennessee Press, 1983.

McDonough, James L., and James Pickett Jones. *"War So Terrible": Sherman and Atlanta*. New York: W. W. Norton, 1987.

McElfresh, Earl B. *Maps and Mapmakers of the Civil War*. New York: Harry N. Abrams, 1999.

McKinney, Francis F. *Education in Violence: The Life of George H. Thomas and the History of the Army of the Cumberland*. Detroit: Wayne State University Press, 1961.

McKinney, Gordon B. "Southern Mountain Republicans and the Negro, 1865–1900." In John C. Inscoe, ed., *Appalachians and Race: The Mountain South from Slavery to Segregation*. Lexington: University Press of Kentucky, 2001.

McMurry, Richard M. *Atlanta 1864: Last Chance for the Confederacy*. Lincoln: University of Nebraska Press, 2000.

———. *The Fourth Battle of Winchester: Toward a New Civil War Paradigm*. Kent, Ohio: Kent State University Press, 2002.

McPherson, James M. *Battle Cry of Freedom: The Civil War Era*. New York: Oxford University Press, 1988.

———. *Ordeal by Fire: The Civil War and Reconstruction*. New York: McGraw-Hill, 2000.

Meade, George. *The Life and Letters of George Gordon Meade, Major-General, U.S. Army*. New York: Charles Scribner's Sons, 1913.

Missall, John, and Mary Lou Missall. *The Seminole Wars: America's Longest Indian Conflict*. Gainesville: University Press of Florida, 2004.

Morrison, James L., Jr. *"The Best School in the World": West Point, the Pre–Civil War Years, 1833–1866*. Kent, Ohio: Kent State University Press, 1986.

Nevins, Allan. *The War for the Union*. 4 vols. New York: Scribner, 1959–1971.

Noe, Kenneth W. *Perryville: This Grand Havoc of Battle*. Lexington: University Press of Kentucky, 2001.

Oakes, James. *The Ruling Race: A History of American Slaveholders*. New York: Alfred A. Knopf, 1982.

Oates, Stephen B. *The Fires of Jubilee: Nat Turner's Fierce Rebellion*. New York: Harper and Row, 1975.

O'Brien, Sean Michael. *Mountain Partisans: Guerrilla Warfare in the Southern Appalachians, 1861–1865*. Westport, Conn.: Praeger, 1999.

O'Connor, Richard. *Thomas, Rock of Chickamauga*. New York: Prentice-Hall, 1948.

Oglesby, T. K. "The South's Contribution to History." *William and Mary Quarterly Historical Magazine* 16, no. 2 (October 1907): 111–19.

Palmer, George Thomas. *A Conscientious Turncoat: The Story of John M. Palmer, 1817–1900*. New Haven: Yale University Press, 1941.

Palumbo, Frank A. *George Henry Thomas, Major General, U.S.A.: The Dependable General, Supreme in Tactics of Strategy and Command*. Dayton, Ohio: Morningside, 1983.

Pappas, George S. *To the Point: The United States Military Academy, 1802–1902*. Westport, Conn.: Praeger, 1993.

Paquette, William. *United States Colored Troops from Lower Tidewater in the Civil War*. Portsmouth, Va.: Portsmouth Public Library, 1982.

Parramore, Thomas C. *Southampton County, Virginia*. Charlottesville: University of Virginia Press for the Southampton Historical Society, 1978.

Pavelka, Greg. "Where Were You Johnny Shiloh?" *Civil War Times Illustrated* 27 (January 1989): 34–41.

Perrin, W. H., J. H. Battle, and G. C. Kniffin. *Kentucky: A History of the State*. Louisville: F. A. Battey and Company, 1888.

Peters, Virginia Bergman. *The Florida Wars*. Hamden, Conn.: Archon Books, 1979.

Piatt, Don, and Henry V. Boynton. *General George H. Thomas: A Critical Biography*. Cincinnati: Robert Clarke and Co., 1893.

Prokopowicz, Gerald J. *All for the Regiment: The Army of the Ohio, 1861–1862*. Chapel Hill: University of North Carolina Press, 2001.

Rable, George C. *But There Was No Peace: The Role of Violence in the Politics of Reconstruction.* Athens: University of Georgia Press, 1984.

Rafuse, Ethan S. 2003. *George Gordon Meade and the War in the East.* Abilene, Tex.: McWhiney Foundation Press.

Ripley, R. S. *The War with Mexico.* New York: Harper and Brothers, 1849.

Rodeffer, Charles. "Yankee Hero 'Deserted' Virginia." *Norfolk-Portsmouth Virginian-Pilot,* November 4, 1962.

Rodenbough, Theophilus F., and William L. Haskin. *The Army of the United States: Historical Sketches of Staff and Line with Portraits of Generals-in-Chief.* New York: Maynard, Merrill, and Co., 1896.

Royster, Charles. *The Destructive War: William Tecumseh Sherman, Stonewall Jackson, and the Americans.* New York: Alfred A. Knopf, 1991.

Ryan, James G. "The Memphis Riot of 1866: Terror in a Black Community during Reconstruction." *Journal of Negro History* 62 (July 1977): 243–57.

Sanders, Charles W., Jr. *While in the Hands of the Enemy: Military Prisons of the Civil War.* Baton Rouge: Louisiana State University Press, 2005.

Sauers, Richard A. 2003. *Meade: Victor of Gettysburg.* Washington, D.C.: Brassey's.

Sefton, James E. *The United States Army and Reconstruction, 1865–1877.* Baton Rouge: Louisiana State University Press, 1967.

Shands, Bessie Thomas. "General George Henry Thomas." *Bulletin of the Southampton County Historical Society,* Courtland, Va., Summer 1980, 14–16.

Sherman, William T. "Grant, Thomas, Lee." *North American Review* 144 (May 1887): 438–50.

Sherratt, John H. "Some Corrections of Grant's Memoirs as Regards General George H. Thomas." In Military Order of the Loyal Legion of the United States, *Military Essays and Recollections: Papers Read before the Commandery of the State of Illinois,* 1:500–514. Chicago: Cozzens and Beaton, 1907.

Shiman, Philip. "Engineering and Command: The Case of William S. Rosecrans, 1862–1863." In Steven E. Woodworth, ed., *The Art of Command in the Civil War,* 84–117. Lincoln: University of Nebraska Press, 1998.

———. "Engineering Sherman's March: Army Engineers and the Management of Modern War, 1862–1865." Ph.D. diss., Duke University, 1991.

———. "Sherman's Pioneers in the Campaign to Atlanta." In Theodore P. Savas and David A. Woodbury, eds., *The Campaign for Atlanta and Sherman's March to the Sea: Essays on the American Civil War in Georgia, 1864,* 251–69. Campbell, Calif.: Savas Woodbury Publishers, 1994.

Silber, Nina. *The Romance of Reunion: Northerners and the South, 1865–1900.* Chapel Hill: University of North Carolina Press, 1993.

Simpson, Brooks D. *Let Us Have Peace: Ulysses S. Grant and the Politics of War and Reconstruction, 1861–1868.* Chapel Hill: University of North Carolina Press, 1991.

———. *Ulysses S. Grant: Triumph over Adversity, 1822–1865.* Boston: Houghton Mifflin, 2000.

Smith, Jean Edward. *Grant.* New York: Simon and Schuster, 2001.

Smith, Justin H. *The War with Mexico.* New York: Macmillan, 1919.

Smith, Theodore C. *The Life and Letters of James Abram Garfield.* New Haven: Yale University Press, 1925.

Sprague, John T. *The Origin, Progress, and Conclusion of the Florida War.* Gainesville: University of Florida Press, 1964.

Squires, W. H. T. *The Days of Yester-Year in Colony and Commonwealth: A Sketch Book of Virginia.* Portsmouth, Va.: Printcraft Press, 1928.

Steere, Edward. "Early Growth of the National Cemetery System." *Quartermaster Review,* March–April 1953.

Stevenson, A. F. *The Battle of Stone's River near Murfreesboro, Tennessee.* Boston: J. R. Osgood and Company, 1884.

Stowell, Daniel W. "'We Have Sinned, and God Has Smitten Us!'": John H. Caldwell and the Religious Meaning of Confederate Defeat." *Georgia Historical Quarterly* 78, no. 1 (Spring 1994): 1–38.

Strayer, Larry M., and Richard A. Baumgartner. *Echoes of Battle: The Atlanta Campaign.* Huntington, W.V.: Blue Acorn Press, 1991.

Sutherland, Daniel E., ed. *Guerrillas, Unionists, and Violence on the Confederate Home Front.* Fayetteville: University of Arkansas Press, 1999.

Sword, Wiley. *Embrace an Angry Wind: The Confederacy's Last Hurrah—Spring Hill, Franklin, and Nashville.* New York: HarperCollins, 1992.

———. *Mountains Touched with Fire: Chattanooga Besieged, 1863.* New York: St. Martin's Press, 1995.

Thomas, Wilbur D. *General George H. Thomas, the Indomitable Warrior, Supreme in Defense and in Counterattack: A Biography.* New York: Exposition Press, 1964.

Thorpe, Thomas B. *Our Army at Monterey.* Philadelphia: Carey and Hart, 1847.

———. *Our Army on the Rio Grande.* Philadelphia: Carey and Hart, 1846.

Trefousse, Hans Louis. *Andrew Johnson: A Biography.* New York: W. W. Norton, 1989.

Trelease, Allen W. *White Terror: The Ku Klux Klan Conspiracy and Southern Reconstruction.* New York: Harper and Row, 1971.

Trudeau, Noah Andre. *Like Men of War: Black Troops in the Civil War, 1862–1865.* Boston: Little, Brown, and Co., 1998.

Tucker, Glenn. *Chickamauga: Bloody Battle in the West.* Indianapolis: Bobbs-Merrill, 1961.

Urwin, Gregory J., ed. *Black Flag over Dixie: Racial Atrocities and Reprisals in the Civil War.* Carbondale: Southern Illinois University Press, 2004.

Utley, Robert M. *Frontiersmen in Blue: The United States Army and the Indian, 1848–1865.* New York: Macmillan, 1967.

———. *History of the Indian Wars.* New York: Simon and Schuster, 1977.

———. *The Indian Frontier of the American West.* Albuquerque: University of New Mexico Press, 1984.

Van Horne, Thomas Budd. *The Life of Major-General George H. Thomas.* New York: Charles Scribner's Sons, 1882.

Varon, Elizabeth R. *Southern Lady, Yankee Spy: The True Story of Elizabeth Van Lew, a Union Agent in the Heart of the Confederacy.* New York: Oxford University Press, 2003.

Wakelyn, Jon L. *Southern Unionist Pamphlets and the Civil War.* Columbia: University of Missouri Press, 1999.

Warner, Ezra J. *Generals in Blue: Lives of the Union Commanders.* Baton Rouge: Louisiana State University Press, 1964.

Weigley, Russell F. *History of the United States Army.* New York: Macmillan, 1967.

Welsh, Jack D. *Medical Histories of Union Generals.* Kent, Ohio: Kent State University Press, 1996.

West, Richard S. *Lincoln's Scapegoat General: A Life of Benjamin F. Butler, 1818–1893.* Boston: Houghton Mifflin, 1965.

Wilcox, Cadmus M. *History of the Mexican War.* Washington, D.C.: Church News Publishing, 1892.

Williams, Chad L. "Symbols of Freedom and Defeat: African American Soldiers, White Southerners, and the Christmas Insurrection Scare of 1865." In Urwin, *Black Flag over Dixie,* 210–30.

Williams, George W. *A History of the Negro Troops in the War of the Rebellion.* New York: Harper and Brothers, 1888.

Williams, Kenneth P. *Lincoln Finds a General: A Military Study of the Civil War.* 5 vols. New York: Macmillan, 1949–59.

Williams, T. Harry. *Lincoln and His Generals.* New York: Alfred A. Knopf, 1952.

Wilson, Charles R. *Baptized in Blood: The Religion of the Lost Cause.* Athens: University of Georgia Press, 1980.

Wood, Forrest G. *Black Scare: The Racist Response to Emancipation and Reconstruction.* Berkeley: University of California Press, 1968.

Wood, William J. *Civil War Generalship: The Art of Command.* Westport, Conn.: Praeger, 1997.

Woodworth, Steven E. *Six Armies in Tennessee: The Chickamauga and Chattanooga Campaigns.* Lincoln: University of Nebraska Press, 1998.

Woodworth, Steven E., Reid Mitchell, Gordon C. Rhea, John Y. Simon, Steven H. Newton, and Keith Poulter. "Who Were the Top Ten Generals?" *North and South* 6, no. 4 (March 2003): 12–22.

Zipf, Catherine W. "Marking Union Victory in the South: The Construction of the National Cemetery System." In Cynthia Mills and Pamela H. Simpson, eds., *Monuments to the Lost Cause: Women, Art, and the Landscapes of Southern Memory,* 27–45. Knoxville: University of Tennessee Press, 2003.

Index

Ampudia, Pedro de, 44, 47–48

Anderson, Robert., 101–102, 105, 109–10, 350

Anderson, Thomas M., 96, 101

Army of Tennessee (Confederate), 7, 62, 239, 256, 281, 287

Army of the Cumberland, 7, 8, 17, 120, 186, 197–206, 210–11, 218, 220–25, 235, 241, 267, 282, 299, 341, 345, 352–54

Army of the Potomac, 114, 144, 199, 202, 222, 233–35, 268

Army of the Tennessee (Union), 241–42, 254, 258

Army of the Ohio, 111, 241, 243, 245, 254

Artise (boyhood companion of Thomas), 12–13

Atlanta, Georgia, 90–91, 259; Union's abandonment of, 256–58, 261; campaign, 227, 237–55, 342, 351–52; capture of, 254–55; significance of, 249, 254.

Bailey, Jacob, 28, 71

Banks, Nathaniel P., 101

Beatty, John, 171, 184

Beatty, Wilk, 115–16

Belknap, William Worth, 331, 336

Beauregard, Pierre Gustave Toutant, 101

Bragg, Braxton, 52, 54–55, 234, 351, 360n14; commands the Confederate Army of Tennessee, 129–38, 144–45, 149, 152–53, 157–71, 177, 181, 184, 186, 188, 198–99, 201, 204–213, 218–19; commands Thomas, 37, 46–49; helps Thomas's career, 60, 72

Brannan, John Milton, 162–65, 185

Brewerton, Henry, 64

Brockett, Linus P., 340

Brown, John, 245

Brown, William Matt, 320–21

Brownlow, William, 297, 299, 312–13, 320, 322

Browne, L. R., 64

Bryan, Charles, 348

Buell, Don Carlos, 101, 152, 215, 220, 352, 354, 367–8n23; commands Thomas, 115, 122–140, 142–43; compared to Thomas, 7, 8, 114, 130–32, 138, 228, 352; Thomas refuses to replace, 124, 132–33, 140, 200–201

Buell, Thomas, 353–54

Buena Vista, Battle of, 49–55, 57

Bull Run, First Battle of, 7, 101, 122, 190

Bull Run, Second Battle of, 131, 250

Bureau of Refugees, Freedmen, and Abandoned Lands. *See* Freedmen's Bureau

Burnside, Ambrose E., 127, 144, 208, 219

Butler, Benjamin F., 97, 331

Cadwallader, Sylvanus, 98

Caldwell, John H., 304–305

Calhoun, John C., 345

Cameron, Simon, 94, 111, 113, 347

Camp Dick Robinson, 105–111, 122

Canby, Edward R. S., 290–92

Carter, Samuel P., 112

Castel, Albert, 342

Chase, Salmon P., 140, 336

Chattanooga, Tennessee, 99, 115, 128–30, 144, 157–61, 163, 166, 168, 172, 179–80, 184–88, 222–25, 231, 232, 237–38, 262, 314; battle of, 210–19, 342; campaign of, 197–210, 220, 222, 342

Chickamauga, Battle of, 7, 162–88, 197, 200–202, 211, 218, 226, 234, 250, 282, 354

Chia-chee (Seminole Indian), 33–34

Chittenden, Lucius, 94

Church, Albert E., 27

Cist, Henry M., 327, 383n3

Civil War: effect on Thomas, 10, 88; historical interpretations of, 10–11, 340, 343–44, 349; Thomas's views of, 85, 98–99, 315–16, 324–25

Clay, Henry, 91

Clem, Jonathan Lincoln, 226–28, 347n11

Cocopa Indians, 58, 67, 69

Cold Harbor, Battle of, 352

Colfax, Schuyler, 306

Comanche Indians, 58–59, 74–78, 250

Conservative Party, 299, 305, 319, 320, 322, 329

Cooke, Philip St. George, 91–92

Coppee, Henry, 63, 65, 341

Corrick's Ford, Battle of, 100

Cozzens, Peter, 142

Crater, Battle of (Petersburg, Virginia), 288

Crittenden, George B., 116, 119

Crittenden, Thomas L., 133, 135–37, 145–46, 150, 161, 180, 185, 187, 206

Croxton, John T., 162–63, 165

Current, Richard, 93

Dana, Charles, 187, 200, 202, 210, 213–14, 217

Daniel, Larry, 120

Davis, Jefferson (Confederate President), 52, 64, 72–73, 234, 249, 287, 290, 292

Davis, Jefferson C. (Union General), 133, 179, 182, 185, 244, 247

Delafield, Richard, 28

Democratic Party, 21, 140, 187, 288, 299, 326, 328

Doubleday, Abner, 98

Drewry, William Sidney, 13

Dyer, Alexander B., 91, 329, 332–33

East Tennessee, 89, 92–93, 103, 105–115, 122–23, 125, 129, 207–208, 219, 292, 299

Edmonston, Catherine, 89, 92

Ellen (Thomas's slave), 74, 81, 87, 305

Elliot, Washington L., 241

Emancipation Proclamation, 5, 9, 90, 229, 233

Federalist Party, 21

Fishing Creek, Battle of. *See* Mill Springs

Forrest, Nathan Bedford, 92; raids behind Union lines, 128, 184, 258; in the Nashville campaign, 261–62, 265, 273, 284–85; defends against Wilson's raids, 290, 292

Fort Henry and Fort Donelson, Battle of, 120, 125–26, 352

Fort Pillow, Battle of, 92–93

Fort Sumter, 84, 91, 94, 101, 345

Fort Wagner, Battle of, 288

Foster, Senator L. F. S., 286

Frederick the Great, 65
Freedmen's Bureau, 6, 12, 300, 302, 307–309, 313, 324
Freehling, William W., 93, 354
French, Samuel G., 50–52
Fry, Speed S., 118, 120.

Garfield, James A., 179–80, 200, 227, 233, 285, 336, 341, 375n24
Garland, John, 45–46
Gilbert, Charles C., 133–36.
Gilham, William, 81, 83
Granger, Gordon, 161–62, 177–80, 183–84, 187, 206, 213–17, 219–20, 336
Grant, Ulysses S., 105, 120, 124–27, 133, 140, 154, 158, 194, 326, 349, 353; Civil War general in chief, 237, 239, 241, 242, 245, 249, 261, 262–68, 274, 280, 281, 285, 289–92; commands at Chattanooga, 7, 197, 200, 202–220; compared to Thomas, 125, 154, 340, 350–52; Reconstruction general in chief, 298, 299, 307–322; friendship with Sherman, 127, 210, 220–21, 235; opinion of Thomas, 207, 209, 210, 219–21, 234–36, 245–46, 267–68, 274, 281, 290–91, 341–43; President, 329–30, 332, 336; Thomas's opinion of, 207, 330, 334
Gurley, Frank, 229

Halleck, Henry W., 154, 210, 212, 235, 245, 249, 257, 263, 292, 308, 323, 330, 334; commands Thomas in the field, 124, 126–28; commands Thomas as general in chief, 132–33, 142–43, 263, 265, 267–68, 280, 285, 290–91; compared to Thomas, 352; opinion of Thomas, 290–91
Hancock, Winfield Scott, 319, 336
Hanson, Roger W., 315
Hardee, William J., 73–76, 93, 254
Harker, Charles G., 173–74, 176, 248
Hartsuff, George L., 85
Hawes, Lieutenant, 62

Hayes, Rutherford B., 316
Hazen, William B., 149, 180–81, 336
Heintzelman, Samuel P., 67–68
Henderson, J. Pinkney, 48
Holtzclaw, James T., 277–78
Hood, John Bell, 62, 245, 249–87, 290–92, 294, 326, 351–53
Hooker, Joseph B., 199, 208–209, 211, 213–15, 336; commanded by Thomas, 202–204, 219–20, 241–42, 245, 250–53
Hough, Alfred Lacey, 80, 330–31, 335, 338, 346
Howard, Oliver Otis, 12–13, 62, 64, 241–42, 247–48, 251, 253–54

Jackson, Thomas Jonathan "Stonewall", 98, 340, 356
Jerusalem (now Courtland), Virginia, 3–4, 13, 16, 20, 357n12
Johnson, Andrew, 193–94, 201, 262; and Thomas, 9, 112–13, 129, 133, 194, 228, 229, 265–66, 293, 296–97, 301–305, 309, 310–11, 318–19, 322, 326–27; Governor of Tennessee, 129, 228; loyalist Senator, 108, 112, 293; President, 293–94; Reconstruction policy, 9, 193, 294, 295, 296–97, 299, 301–313, 317–19, 322, 329
Johnson, Richard W., 65, 76, 83, 95, 97, 164–5, 341
Johnston, Albert Sidney, 73, 75, 93, 97, 114, 125–26
Johnston, Joseph E., 234–35, 237, 239–50, 255
Jomini, Henri, 29

Keim, William H., 98
Kellogg, Frances Lucretia. See Thomas, Frances Lucretia Kellogg
Kellogg, Lyman M., 65
Kellogg, Sanford C., 172–73, 227, 258, 337
Kelly, R. M., 108
Kennesaw Mountain, Battle of, 246–49, 342, 352

Keyes, Erasmus D., 34–35

Kimball, Nathan, 248

Kiowa Indians, 58–59, 74, 77

Ku Klux Klan, 6, 10, 309, 311, 322–23, 329, 332

Landrum, William, 282

Lee, Fitzhugh, 62, 346

Lee, Robert Edward, 75, 76, 93, 96–97, 131, 158, 161, 233, 236–37, 239, 242, 249–50, 290, 292, 343, 346, 348, 356; compared with Thomas, 86, 340, 348, 356; commands Thomas at West Point, 64–65, commands Thomas in Texas, 73–74; friendship with Thomas, 74

Lee, Stephen D., 254

Lee, Samuel P., 285

Letcher, John, 83, 345–46

Lewis, Barbour, 317

Lincoln, Abraham, 80, 83–84, 91, 103, 105, 108–109, 111, 132–33, 140–41, 143, 197, 199, 219, 228, 233–35, 255, 257, 282, 293, 295, 297, 305, 347, 356; and Thomas, 200, 263; opinion of Thomas, 154, 169, 187–88, 274; questions Thomas's loyalty, 94, 350–51

Logan's Creek, Battle of. See Mill Springs

Longstreet, James, 161, 185, 208–209, 250

Louisville, Kentucky, 105, 112, 114, 131–34, 136, 140, 282, 315

Lyon, Nathaniel, 100, 114

MacDonnell, Francis, 346

Mackay, Andrew J., 336

Mahan, Dennis Hart, 28–29, 62, 65, 263, 286

Mahone, William, 83

Manassas, First Battle of. See Bull Run, First Battle of

Manassas, Second Battle of. See Bull Run, Second Battle of

Mansfield, Joseph K., 45–46

Manson, Mahlon, 116

Maricopa Indians, 69

Marszalek, John, 342–43

Mason, John Y., 22–23, 60

Maury, Dabney H., 347

Maxwell, Robert A., 187

Maynard, Horace, 112

McArthur, John, 278–79

McClellan, George B., 100, 114, 128, 131, 236, 250, 263, 352

McClernand, John, 126

McClure, Alexander, 98

McCook, Alexander, 62, 133, 135–36, 145–49, 153, 161, 163–64, 179–80, 184–87, 206

McCook, Daniel, 162, 248

McCook, Robert L., 119, 229

McPherson, James, 62, 241–43, 247–53

Meade, George Gordon, 158, 233, 235, 268, 307–308, 336

Merrill, William, 144

Mexican-American War, 6, 12–13, 38–59, 61, 73, 76, 79, 87, 91, 114, 189, 348

Mill Springs, Battle of, 17, 103, 108, 115–122, 124–25, 163, 178, 282, 330–31

Milliken, William A., 317–318

Milliken's Bend, Battle of, 288

Missionary Ridge, Battle of, 214–20, 247, 278, 352

Mitchel, Ormsby M., 101, 109–111, 123, 351

Monterrey, Battle of, 44–48, 57

Morgan, John Hunt, 128

Morgan, Thomas J., 230, 232–33, 287, 355–56

Murfreesboro, Battle of. See Stones River

Mussey, Robert D., 231–32

Napoleon Bonaparte, 29, 36

Nashville, Tenn., 99, 105, 109, 114, 125, 129–31, 133, 137, 143–45, 155, 199, 230, 231, 237, 257–63, 265–67, 295, 297, 299, 302, 305, 307, 320–21, 329, 332; battle of, 4–6, 155, 268–83, 285–90, 291, 313–14, 326–27, 334–35, 351–54, 356; campaign of, 62, 257–89, 326–27, 334–35

Nast, Thomas, 193
Negley, James S., 145–46, 148–49, 151, 159–60, 163, 172, 185–86, 327
Nelson, William "Bull," 105–106, 133
Newton, John, 91, 250–53, 336

O'Brien, John P., 51–54

Palmer, John M., 163–65, 206, 241, 247, 250, 252–53
Palo Alto, Battle of, 43
Patterson, Robert, 98–101, 190
Pea Ridge, Battle of, 127
Peachtree Creek, Battle of, 250–53
Perryville, Battle of, 136–38
Pheiffer, Nicolas, 223
Piatt, Don, 341
Pierce, Franklin, 64
Polk, James, 39–43, 49
Polk, Leonidas K., 105, 166
Pope, John, 126, 127, 318
Port Hudson, Battle of, 288
Porter, Fitz John, 95, 98, 156, 347

Rawlins, John A., 215
Republican Party, 91, 200, 288, 299, 308, 310, 313, 316, 319, 322, 326, 328, 331
Resaca, Battle of, 342
Resaca de la Palma, Battle of, 43
Reynolds, Joseph J., 163–65, 173, 181, 185, 207, 352
Richmond, Virginia, 17, 60, 92, 99, 109, 114, 125, 131, 236, 255, 282, 291, 345; Grant's campaign against, 242, 249, 250, 267, 290, 291–92
Rich Mountain, Battle of, 100
Ringgold, Samuel, 36–37, 43
Robinson, Richard M., 105
Rochelle, John, 15–16, 22
Rosecrans, William Starke, 7–8, 26, 100, 120, 133, 197–202, 205, 207, 209, 215, 220, 222, 226–30, 237, 263, 285, 308, 336, 341, 351, 353–54, 367–68n23; and Thomas, 124, 146, 149–50, 154, 158–59, 167–68;
Chickamauga, 162–88; military leadership assessed, 166–68, 180, 186–88; opinion of Thomas, 142, 143, 152, 160; Stones River, 145–55; trains and equips Army of the Cumberland, 143–44, 154–55
Rousseau, Lovell H., 145, 147–49, 152, 264–65
Ruffin, Edmund, 345

Santa Anna, 49–54
Schoepf, Albin, 111, 113, 115–16
Schofield, John M., 62, 64, 241–80, 283, 290, 330, 343, 351, 353; postwar writings on Thomas, 326, 334–35, 378n35
Scott, Winfield, 49, 55, 81, 83–84, 86, 91, 94, 99, 101, 348, 350
Scribner, Benjamin Franklin, 155–56, 182–3, 330, 331
Second Cavalry Regiment, 72–79, 82–84, 93–102
Second Seminole War. See Seminole Indians
Seminole Indians, 6, 24, 30–34, 59–60
Shands, William, 339
Shanks, William B., 137–38, 155, 157, 168–69, 171, 177, 186, 220, 237, 340–41
Sheridan, Philip H., 62, 147–49, 172, 179, 182–83, 185, 196, 216, 308, 318–19, 330, 336, 340
Sherman, John, 98–99, 351
Sherman, Thomas W., 49–54
Sherman, William Tecumseh, 7, 105–106, 108–109, 120, 125, 154, 261–2, 287, 289–91, 307, 326–27, 336–37, 349–54; and Thomas, 283, 289–91, 308, 334–36, 351; Atlanta Campaign, 236–56; at Chattanooga, 199, 213, 214, 219, 219–21; commanded by Thomas, 126; commands Thomas, 110–14, 124, 126, 237–38, 239, 257–58; compared to Thomas, 239, 242, 254–55, 386n27; friendship with Grant, 127, 220–21, 235; friendship with Thomas, 24–25, 36, 67–68, 70, 72, 98–99, 102, 296; generalship evaluated, 241–42, 255, 258; March through Georgia and

Sherman, William Tecumseh *(continued)*
  the Carolinas, 256–69, 267, 283; opinion
  of Thomas, 98–99, 245–46, 341–43
Shiloh, Battle of, 120, 125–27, 152
Shy, William M., 278
Smith, Edmund Kirby, 73, 129, 131, 134,
  137
Smith, Andrew Jackson, 258–62, 268–73,
  276–79, 291, 353
Smith, Francis H., 81, 346
Smith, William F. "Baldy," 62, 203–204,
  208–209, 217
Smithsonian Institution, 28, 70–72, 334
Southampton County, Virginia, 11–22, 28,
  36, 55, 56, 59, 60, 65, 73, 79, 80–83, 87–
  88, 102, 156, 189, 236, 339, 348–49
Southampton County Historical Society,
  348
Southern Unionists, 9–10, 82, 84–85, 88–
  93, 103, 112–13, 228, 233, 288, 289,
  293–94, 298–99, 313, 340, 343–44, 348–
  50, 354–56
Squires, William, 348
Stanley, David S., 62, 257, 259
Stanton, Edwin McMasters, 132, 199, 206,
  210, 217, 257, 262, 268, 274, 295, 310–
  11, 319; opinion of Thomas, 140, 154,
  187, 200, 233, 263–64, 280, 282, 285, 350
Stearns, George, 231
Steedman, James B., 177, 262, 266, 268–72,
  276–79, 285, 287, 289, 353, 378n35
Stevenson, John D., 91
Stone, Henry, 138, 243
Stoneman, George, 73, 291–92, 295, 298,
  312
Stones River, Battle of, 120, 145–55, 166,
  264, 369n13
Stuart, James Ewell Brown, 62, 93, 99–101,
  340, 356
Sutherland, Donald, 90

Taylor, Richard, 287
Taylor, Thomas, 224–25
Taylor, Zachary, 41–57

Terrill, William R., 91
Thomas, Benjamin (brother), 14–16, 28,
  55–56, 87, 305, 332, 339
Thomas, Elizabeth (sister), 14
Thomas, Elizabeth Rochelle (mother), 3,
  15–16, 20
Thomas, Emory, 96
Thomas, Frances "Fannie" (sister), 12, 14–
  15, 81, 87–88, 338–39, 348, 385n36
Thomas, Frances Lucretia Kellogg (wife),
  14, 17, 65–66, 72–74, 79–88, 102, 156,
  189, 258, 266, 274, 305, 335–38, 343–48.
Thomas, George Henry, ancestry, 15;
  approach to discipline, 63, 95–97;
  attitude toward African-Americans and
  slavery, 4–13, 18–21, 58–59, 74, 222,
  229–31, 238, 273–74, 287–89, 295, 299–
  301, 305–307, 354–56; attitude toward
  African-American soldiers, 4–6, 8–10,
  222, 224, 229–33, 238, 262, 273–74, 281,
  287–89, 354–56; attitude toward
  American Indians, 34, 58–59, 68–71, 74–
  79, 334–35; attitude toward secessionists,
  9–10, 228, 304, 306–307, 310, 314–16,
  321–25; back injury, 80–81, 83–84, 244,
  246, 346; brevet promotions, 6, 24, 34–
  36, 38, 48, 55, 79; childhood, 11–23;
  choice of military career, 22, 59–60, 308;
  considered potential 1868 candidate,
  326–29; death, 327, 335; deputy county
  clerk, 22; described as slow, 7, 63, 99, 107,
  202, 207, 210, 220, 235–36, 245, 281,
  290–91, 334, 341–42, 350–52; desire for
  marriage, 31, 38, 56; education, 17;
  establishes National Cemetery in
  Chattanooga, 223; fear of public
  speaking, 108, 306, 314; fights guerrillas,
  228–29, 298, 303–304, 314; fights the Ku
  Klux Klan, 309, 311, 322–24, 329, 322;
  friendship with Scribner, 156, 330;
  funeral services, 335–37; honored by
  Tennessee legislature, 298, 313–14; illness,
  319, 327, 335; love of children, 156, 226–
  28; maintains order during elections, 299,

320–21, 329; marriage, 65–66; military education, 6–7, 24–30, 35–38, 57–58, 79; military leadership assessed, 6–7, 79, 95–96, 106–109, 120–23, 124, 135, 137–39, 152–53, 157, 162–63, 166–67, 169–70, 180, 186–88, 239, 260–61, 270, 273, 281–82, 283–84, 286–87, 291, 350–54; monument in Washington, D.C., 337–8, 341; moral values, 8, 10, 11, 60, 354; nicknames, 26, 63, 107, 143; ownership of slaves, 74, 80–81, 87, 305; political views, 8, 21–32, 85, 133, 138, 319, 327–29, 331; posthumous reputation, 340–56; privacy about personal life, 14, 155–56, 348–49; promotions: to cadet sergeant, 29; to cadet lieutenant, 29; to second lieutenant, 30; to first lieutenant, 36; to brevet captain, 55; to major, 72; to lieutenant colonel, 97; to colonel, 97; to brigadier general of volunteers, 101; to major general of volunteers, 141; to commander of the Army of the Cumberland, 200–201; to brigadier general in the regular army, 206; to major general in the regular army, 284, 308; protects African-Americans during Reconstruction, 300–304, 309, 311–13, 317–18, 321–24, 379n24; refuses promotion, 7–8, 124, 127, 132–33, 138–39, 140, 194, 200–201, 233–34, 337; relationship with siblings, 12, 14–15, 23, 55–57, 60–81, 81, 87–88, 156, 305, 338–39; religious beliefs, 17–18; scientific interests, 28, 33, 70–72, 334; sense of humor, 29, 35, 38, 156–57, 183, 205, 332, 334, 374n9; soldiers' opinion of, 63–64, 106–108, 134, 151, 155, 160, 175–76, 183, 202, 217–18, 225–26, 244, 297, 331, 336–38, 341; Southerners' opinion of, 85, 92, 99, 337, 339, 340, 343–48; trains and equips the Army of the Cumberland, 205–206, 222–24; trains soldiers, 95–96, 102–103, 105–107, 153; Turner's Rebellion, 3–4, 19–20; Unionism, 4–5,

10, 12, 81–88, 93–94, 97–99, 101–102, 341–42, 354; wounded, 78–79

Thomas, George Henry, and other military commanders: and Bragg, 55; commanded by, 37, 46–49; helped by, 60, 72; and Buell, 220, 367–68n23; commanded by, 115, 122–40, 142–43; compared to, 7, 8, 114, 130–32, 138, 228, 352; opinion of, 132, 135–36, 138, 140, 200; refuses to replace, 124, 132–33, 140, 200–201; and Johnny Clem, 226–28; and Garfield, 285–86, 336; and Grant, 197, 203–204, 206–210, 213–15, 219, 234–36, 262–68, 280, 281–83, 285, 289–92, 308, 319, 322, 326, 327, 330, 336; commanded by, 124, 197, 200, 202–220; compared to, 340, 350, 352–54, 386n27; Grant's opinion of Thomas, 207, 209, 210, 219–21, 234–36, 245–46, 267–68, 274, 281, 290–91, 341–43; Thomas's opinion of Grant, 207, 330, 334; and Halleck, 334–35; commands Thomas in the field, 124, 126–28; commands Thomas as general in chief, 132–33, 142–43, 263, 265, 267–68, 280, 285, 290–91; compared to, 352; opinion of Thomas, 290–91; and Johnson, 9, 112–13, 129, 133, 194, 228, 229, 265–66, 293, 296–97, 301–305, 309, 310–11, 318–19, 322, 326–27; and Lee: compared with, 86, 340, 348, 356; commanded by at West Point, 64–65, commanded by in Texas, 73–74; friendship, 74; and Lincoln, 200, 263, 274; opinion of Thomas, 154, 169, 187–88, 274; questions Thomas's loyalty, 94, 350–51; and Rosecrans, 124, 141, 146, 149–50, 153, 154, 158–60, 167–68, 202, 220, 285, 308; commanded by, 124, 141–97; Thomas's opinion of Rosecrans, 142–43, 152, 200–201; Rosecrans's opinion of Thomas, 142, 143, 152, 160; and Sherman, 283, 289–91, 308, 334–36, 351; commanded by Sherman, 110–14, 124, 126, 237–38, 239, 257–58; commands Sherman, 126; compared to

Thomas, George Henry *(continued)*
    Sherman, 239, 242, 254–55, 386n27;
    friendship with Sherman, 24–25, 36, 67–
    68, 70, 72, 98–99, 102, 296; Sherman's
    opinion of, 98–99, 245–46, 341–43; and
    Stanton, Stanton's opinion of, 140, 154,
    187, 200, 233, 263–64, 280, 282, 285,
    350; and Schofield, 64, 260–61, 266, 270,
    278–79; postwar writings on Thomas,
    326, 334–35, 378n35
Thomas, George Henry, military service:
    after the Nashville campaign, 7, 289–94;
    Alaska, 333–34; Atlanta campaign, 239–
    55; artillery officer, 6, 24, 30, 36–43,
    46–48, 50–57, 59–60, 79; Brown's Ferry
    (Chattanooga), 202–205; Camp Dick
    Robinson, Kentucky, 105–108; cavalry
    officer, 6, 73–79; Chattanooga, Battle of,
    210–19, 342; Chattanooga campaign,
    197–222, 342; Chickamauga, Battle of, 7,
    162–88, 282; Chickamauga campaign,
    157–88; commands Army of the
    Cumberland, 200–255; Division of the
    Pacific, 326–33; Falling Waters, Virginia,
    Battle of, 99–100; First Bull Run
    (Manassas) campaign, 97–101; Florida, 6,
    24, 30–34, 59–60, 79; Fort Belknap, 75;
    Fort Brown, 42–43, 57, 74; Fort
    Columbus, 30; Fort Lauderdale, 24, 32–
    33; Fort Mason, 73–75; Fort McHenry,
    36; Fort Moultrie, 36, 38; Fort Yuma, 6,
    58, 66–72, 79; Horseshoe Ridge. *See*
    Snodrass Ridge; Maryland and
    Pennsylvania (1861), 94–95; Mexican
    War, 6, 39–57, 79, 360n14; Mill Springs,
    Battle of, 7, 116–22; Mill Springs
    campaign, 103, 106–123; Missionary
    Ridge (Chattanooga), 214–18; Nashville,
    Battle of, 4–6, 155, 268–83, 285–90, 291,
    313–14, 326–27, 334–35, 351–54, 356;
    Nashville campaign, 257–84; Orchard
    Knob (Chattanooga), 211–12; Peachtree
    Creek, Battle of, 250–53; Perryville,
    Battle of, 135–37; Perryville campaign, 7,

128–39; proposed invasion of East
    Tennessee, 108–109, 111–15, 122–23;
    pursuit after Nashville, 281, 283–87,
    352–53; Resaca, Battle of, 235, 241–42;
    Reconstruction, 295–325; Second
    Seminole War, 24, 30–34; Shiloh and
    Corinth campaigns, 125–27; Snodgrass
    Ridge, 174–82; Stones River, Battle of,
    145–55; Stones River campaign, 140–53;
    Texas, 6, 73–79; West Point cadet, 6, 22–
    31, 79; West Point instructor, 58–65, 67,
    79
Thomas, John (father), 15–16
Thomas, John William (brother), 11, 14–16,
    21, 23, 28, 31, 38, 55–56, 59–61, 87
Thomas, Judith Elvira (sister), 12, 14–16, 81,
    87, 338–39, 348, 385n36
Thomas, Juliette (sister), 14
Thomas, Lorenzo, 111, 230–31
Thruston, Gates P., 318
Tidball, John C., 55
Turner, Nat, 3–4, 19–20
Twiggs, David E., 48, 75–76, 81–83, 93
Tyler, John, Sr., 15
Tyler, John, Jr., 334
Tyler, Mattie Rochelle, 338

U.S. Military Academy at West Point. *See*
    West Point, U.S. Military Academy

Vallandigham, Clement L., 187–88
Van Derveer, Ferdinand, 162, 178
Van Dorn, Earl, 73, 76
Van Horne, Thomas Budd, 13, 17, 65, 73–
    74, 79, 81, 83, 85, 127, 132, 224, 244,
    270, 282, 305, 330, 337, 341, 347, 353,
    355–56
Van Vliet, Stewart, 24–25, 36, 71, 341
Vicksburg campaign, 140, 154, 158, 199
Virginia Historical Society, 339, 348
Virginia Military Institute, 81–82, 346

Wade, Richard D. A., 33–35
Walker, Moses B., 146–48, 153

Walker, William, 252–53

War of 1812, 25, 36, 91

Washington, D.C., 12, 55, 59, 72, 81, 82, 99, 101, 109, 124, 143, 158, 206, 231, 235–36, 270, 274, 285, 295, 322, 328, 336, 337; Thomas sends troops to, 94–95, 98; Thomas visits, 23, 286, 296–97, 306–308, 316, 326, 329–32; Thomas monument, 337–38, 340–41

Washington, George, 16, 26, 97, 143

West Point, U.S. Military Academy, 36, 38, 41, 55, 71, 74–76, 81, 92, 107, 114, 141, 184, 207, 226, 250, 263, 314, 335, 341; Thomas attends, 6, 8, 11, 14, 17, 22–31, 79; Thomas teaches at, 58–65, 67, 79

Whig Party, 21, 91

Whipple, William D., 62, 205, 225, 252, 313

Wilmer, Richard H., 304

Wilson, James H., 203, 205, 207, 220, 291–92; 333, 353; Nashville campaign, 256, 261–64, 266–80, 284–85

Wilson's Creek, Battle of, 114

Wood, Thomas J., 173–74, 185, 213–16, 262, 268, 271, 273, 276–79, 284, 353, 371n11, 357n57

Woodcock, Captain, 183

Woodford, Stewart L., 337

Wool, John E., 53–54

Worth, William J., 34, 44–45, 47

Yuma (Quechan) Indians, 58–59, 66–71

Zollicoffer, Felix, 107, 109, 115–16, 119–20, 122